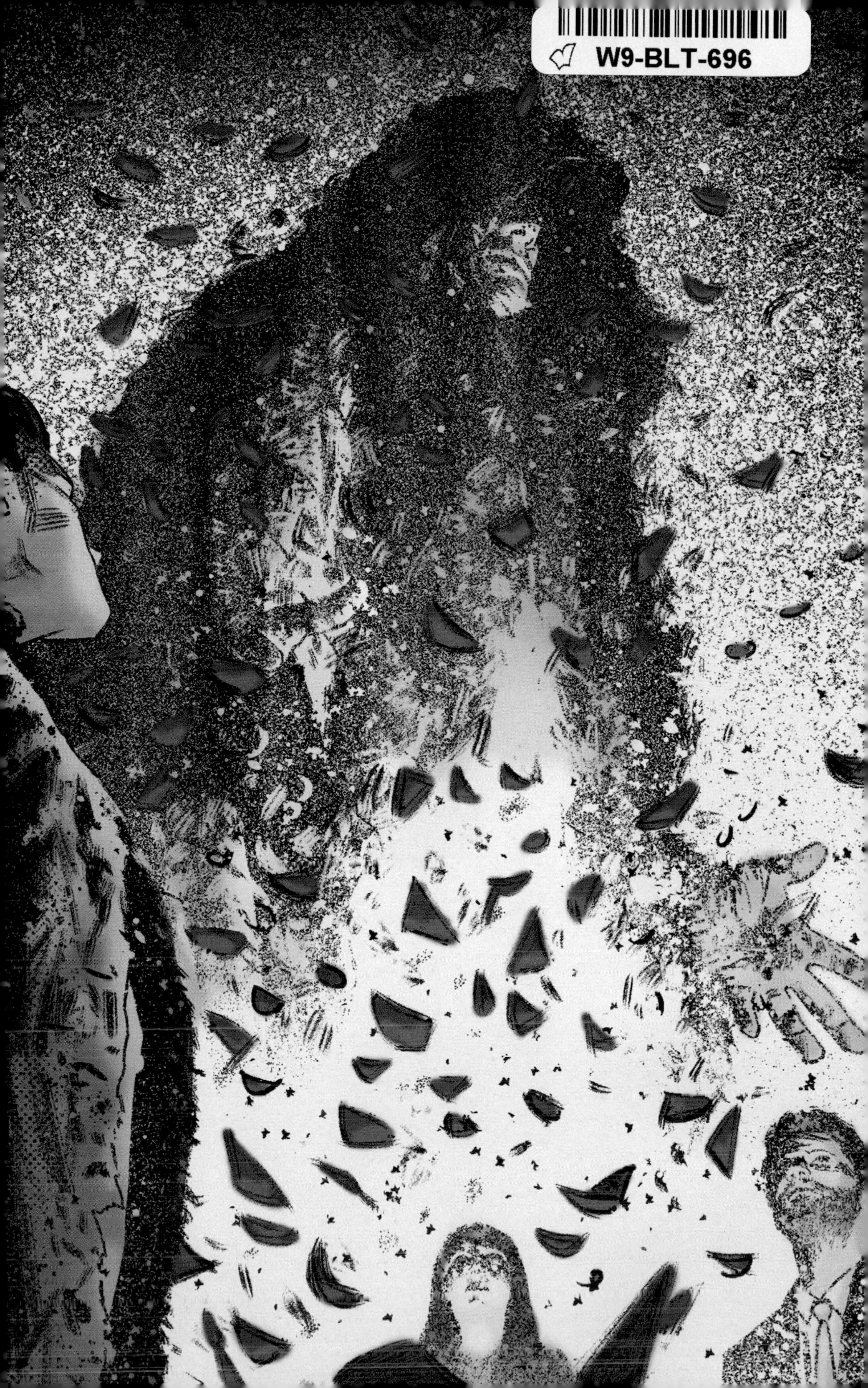

FROM THE PAGES OF PROJECT SUPERPOWERS®

BLACKCROSS

WRITER
WARREN ELLIS

ARTIST
COLTON WORLEY

COLORIST
MORGAN HICKMAN

LETTERER
SIMON BOWLAND

COVER BY
TULA LOTAY

COLLECTION DESIGN BY
GEOFF HARKINS

Nick Barrucci, CEO / Publisher
Juan Collado, President / COO

Joe Rybandt, Senior Editor
Rachel Pinnelas, Associate Editor
Kevin Ketner, Editorial Assistant

Jason Ullmeyer, Design Director
Geoff Harkins, Graphic Designer
Alexis Persson, Production Artist

Chris Caniano, Digital Associate
Rachel Kilbury, Digital Assistant

Brandon Dante Primavera, Dir. of IT/Operations
Rich Young, Dir. of Business Development

Keith Davidsen, Marketing Manager
Pat O'Connell, Sales Manager

Online at www.DYNAMITE.com
On Facebook /Dynamitecomics
Instagram /Dynamitecomics
On Tumblr dynamitecomics.tumblr.com
On Twitter @Dynamitecomics
On YouTube /Dynamitecomics

First Printing
ISBN-10: 1-60690-849-9
ISBN-13: 978-1-60690-849-5
10 9 8 7 6 5 4 3 2 1

PEFC Certi
Printed on pape
sustainably man
forests and con
sources
PEFC/01-31-106   www.pefc.o

PROJECT SUPERPOWERS ® : BLACKCROSS, VOLUME ONE. First printing. Contains materials originally published in PRO
SUPERPOWERS: BLACKCROSS #1-6 Published by Dynamite Entertainment. 113 Gaither Dr., STE 205, Mt. Laurel, NJ 0
Project Superpowers, Black Terror, The Scarab, The Flame, and Greem Lama are ® & © 2016 Dynamite Characters, I
Rights Reserved. Lady Satan and The American Spirit are ™ & © 2016 Dynamtie Characters, llc. DYNAMITE, DYNA
ENTERTAINMENT and its logo are ® & © 2016 Dynamite. All rights reserved. All names, characters, events, and locales i
publication are entirely fictional. Any resemblance to actual persons (living or dead), events or places, without satiric inte
coincidental. No portion of this book may be reproduced by any means (digital or print) without the written permissi
Dynamite Entertainment except for review purposes. The scanning, uploading and distribution of this book via the Inter
via any other means without the permission of the publisher is illegal and punishable by law. Please purchase only autho
electronic editions, and do not participate in or encourage electronic piracy of copyrighted materials. Printed in Canada.

For media rights, foreign rights, promotions, licensing, and advertising: marketing@dynamite.com

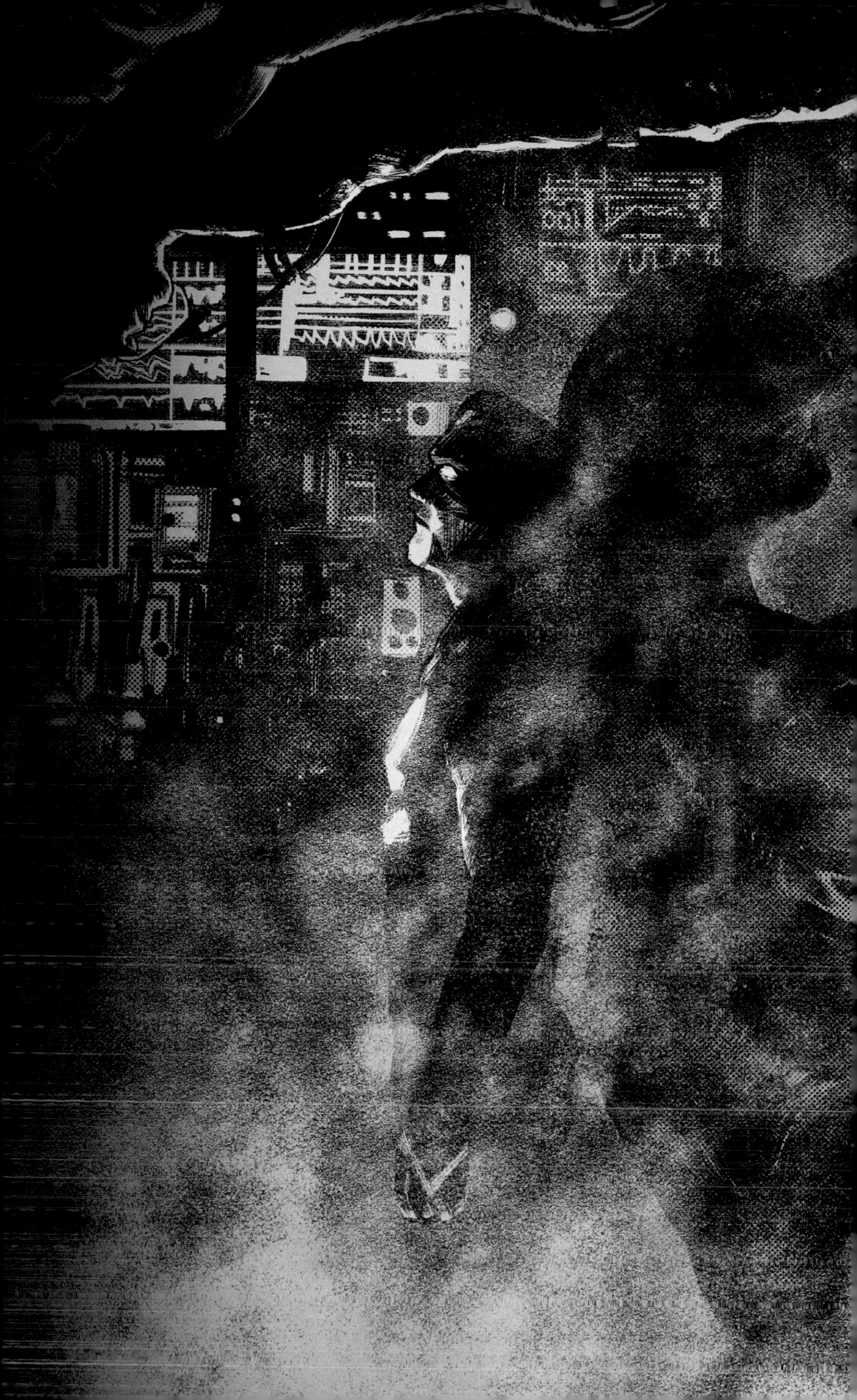

I've never written a fan letter. Well, I've never written a fan letter before today, to be more precise. It's not that I haven't gushed and expressed my deep, innermost feelings to creators of various stripes over the years - but any gushing has been over the course of my "professional" career.

The closest I'd come to a true fan letter would have been something I wrote to Warren Ellis while reading his Stormwatch run as it unfolded in the late '90s. I was working in the periphery of the industry at the time, but was so impressed with the work he was doing on that title that I took a moment and sent him an email. I introduced myself, praised his work and made myself known should he ever need anything. I doubt he remembers that letter now, or possibly even then, but that's not the point of this little tale.

I'd been familiar with Warren's writing, as well as his pioneering forum – aptly named the Warren Ellis Forum - of which I was a member. (Aside from all the ideas and talent, the amount of music that place introduced to me was staggering in and of itself.) His work of that period laid a lot of groundwork. Stormwatch led to The Authority, which led to Planetary and Transmetropolitan and so many other classic bits of comic book storytelling. From the start, Warren was a force and the work he touched always changed, becoming his.

Flash forward to the near-now, and Dynamite was working on a relaunch/reboot/re-whatever for the Superpowers characters and Nick [Barrucci] wrangled Warren into talking about projects. One was a re-casting of the Superpowers universe. Superpowers had been sitting to the side of our publishing schedule, waiting for a new spark. Funny that Warren started his work with fire or, more specifically, with a man on fire.

Paired here with the artwork of Colton Worley – who expertly exposes the darkness and horror unfolding throughout Blackcross, and backed up by colorist Morgan Hickman and unsung hero Simon Bowland on letters – Blackcross stands as a true re-imagining…a true divergence from its super-hero origins and the tropes of that genre, becoming a genre all its own…

Welcome to Blackcross.

Joe Rybandt
Mt. Laurel, NJ
January, 2016

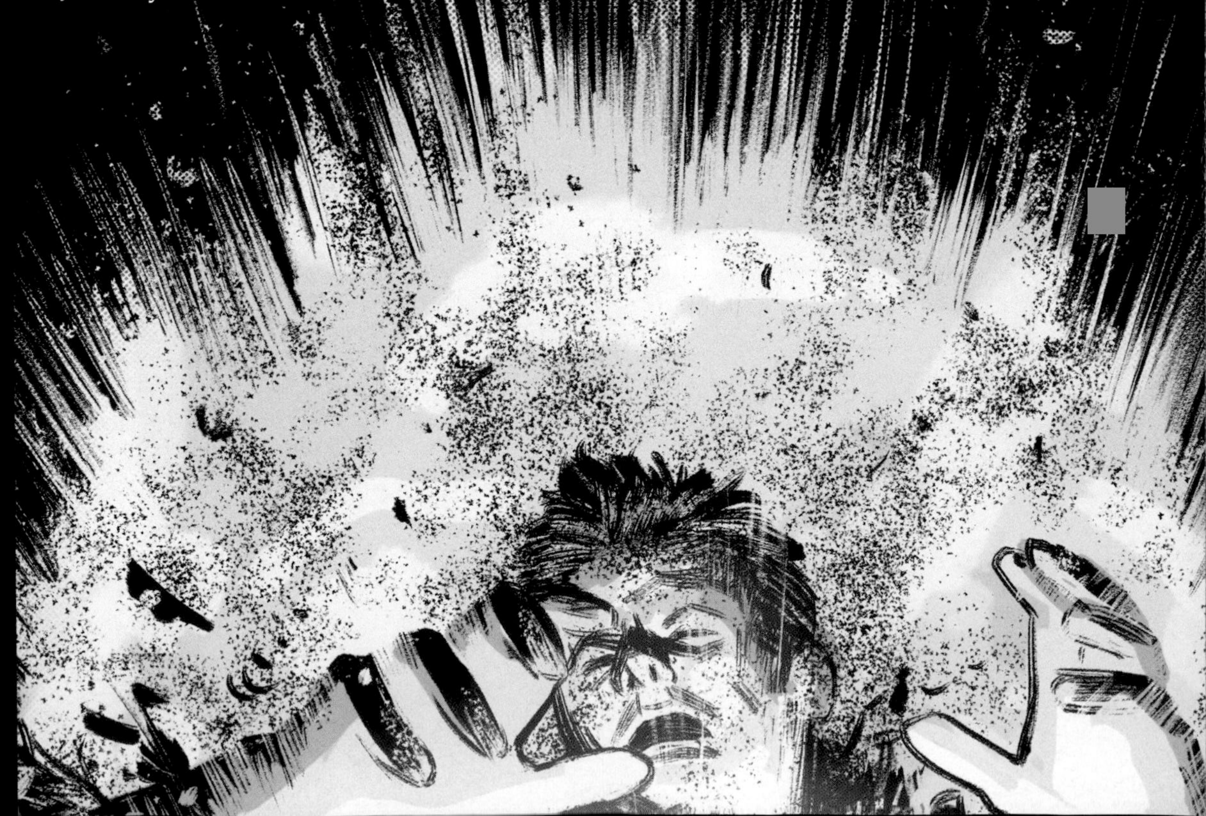

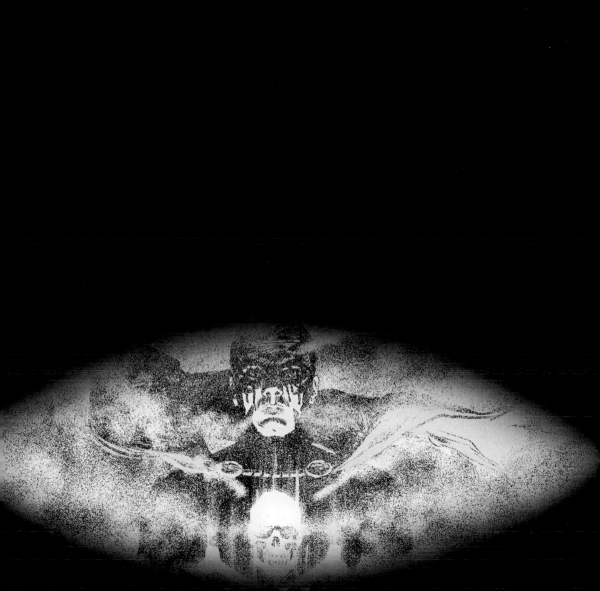

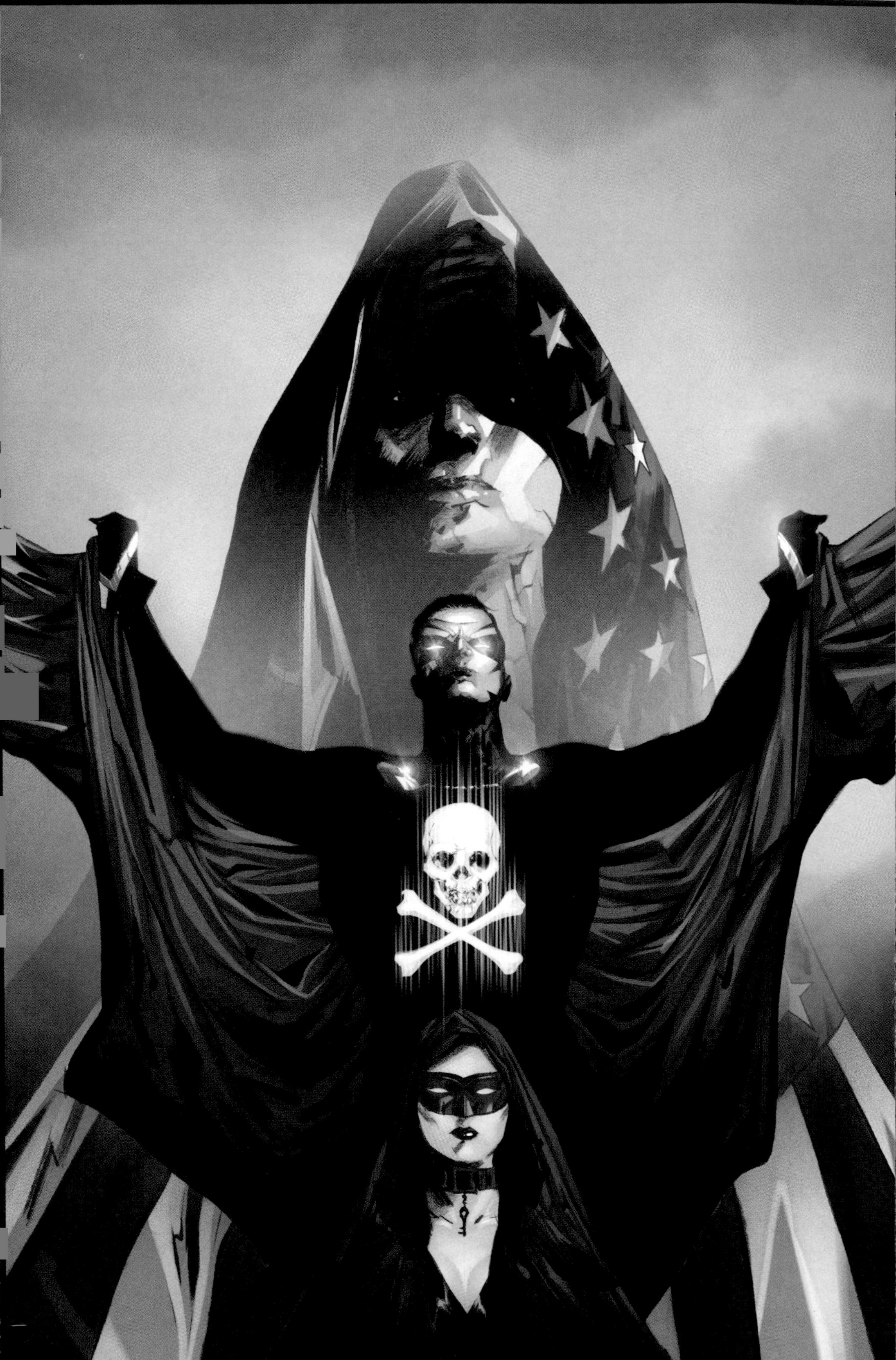

ISSUE #1 COVER BY JAE LEE COLORS BY IVAN NUNES

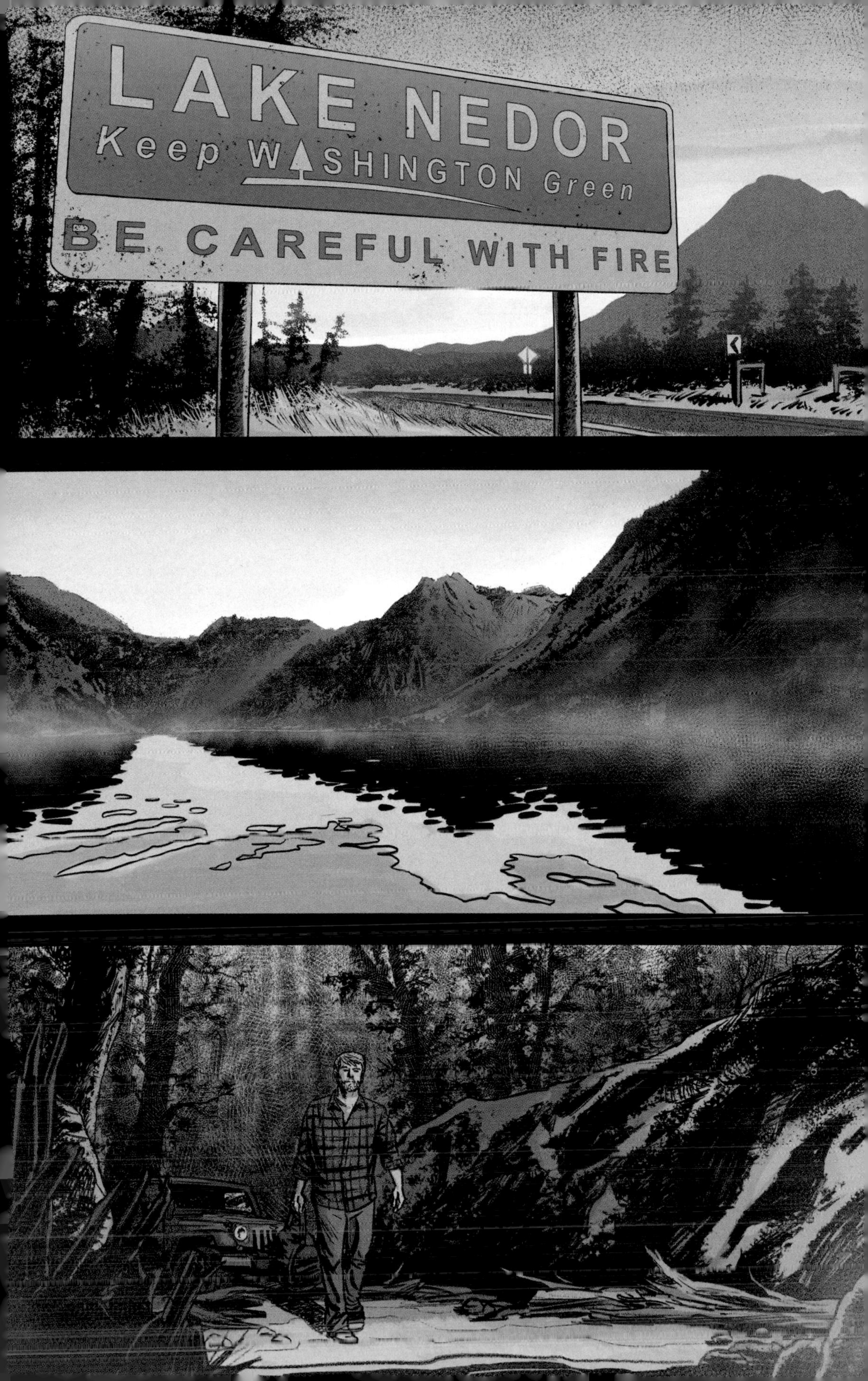
LAKE NEDOR
Keep WASHINGTON Green
BE CAREFUL WITH FIRE

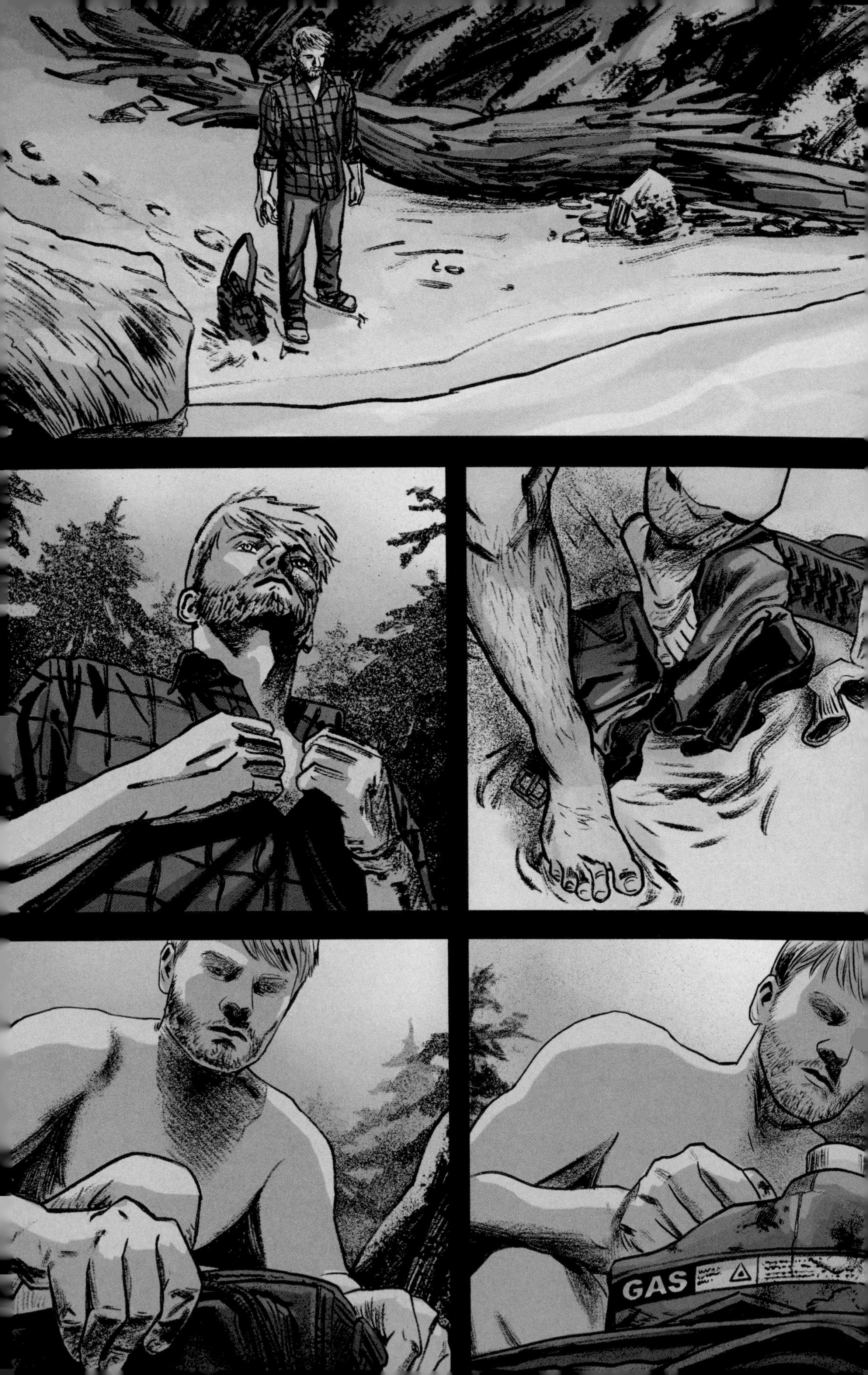
GAS

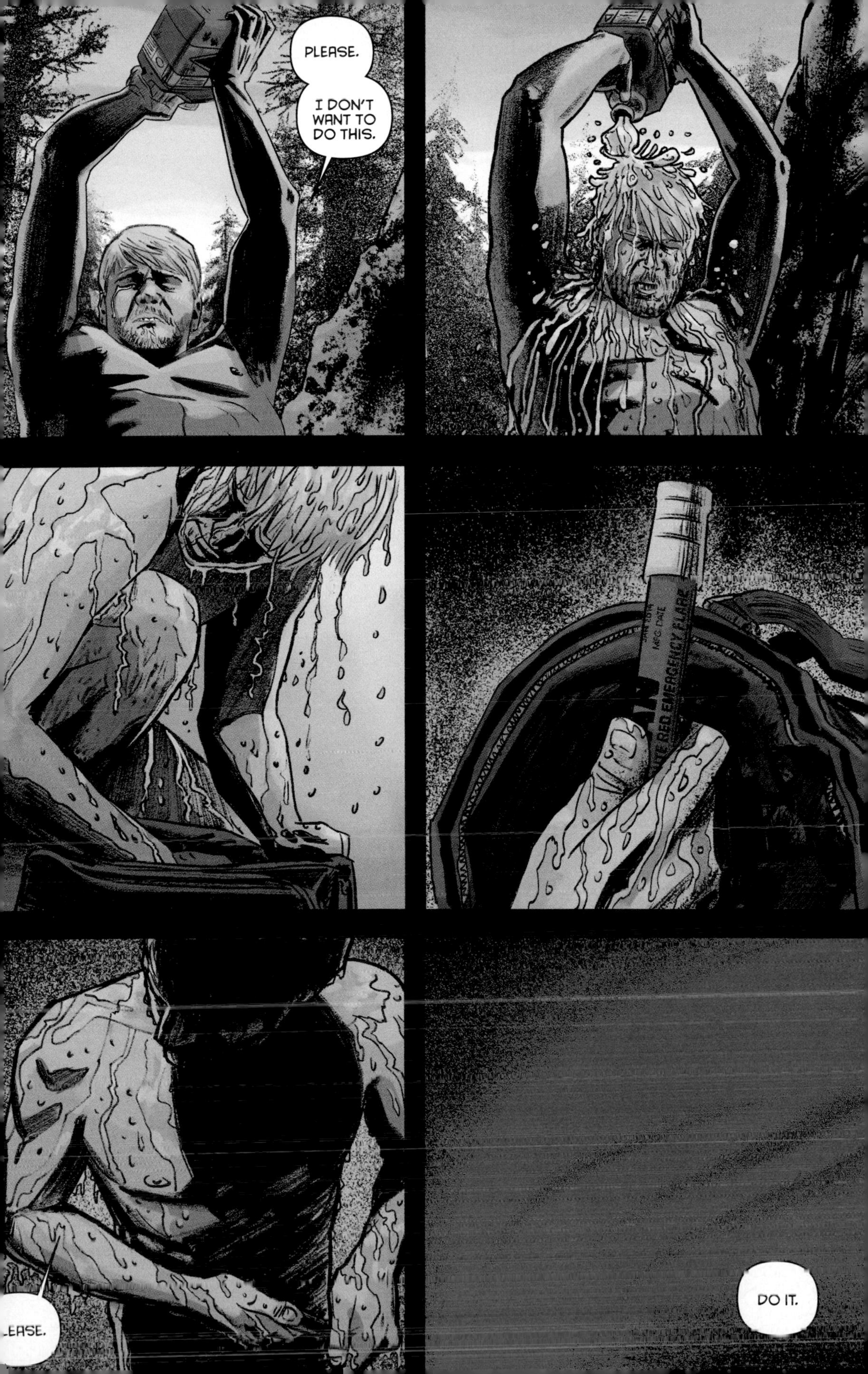
PLEASE.
I DON'T WANT TO DO THIS.
LEASE.
DO IT.

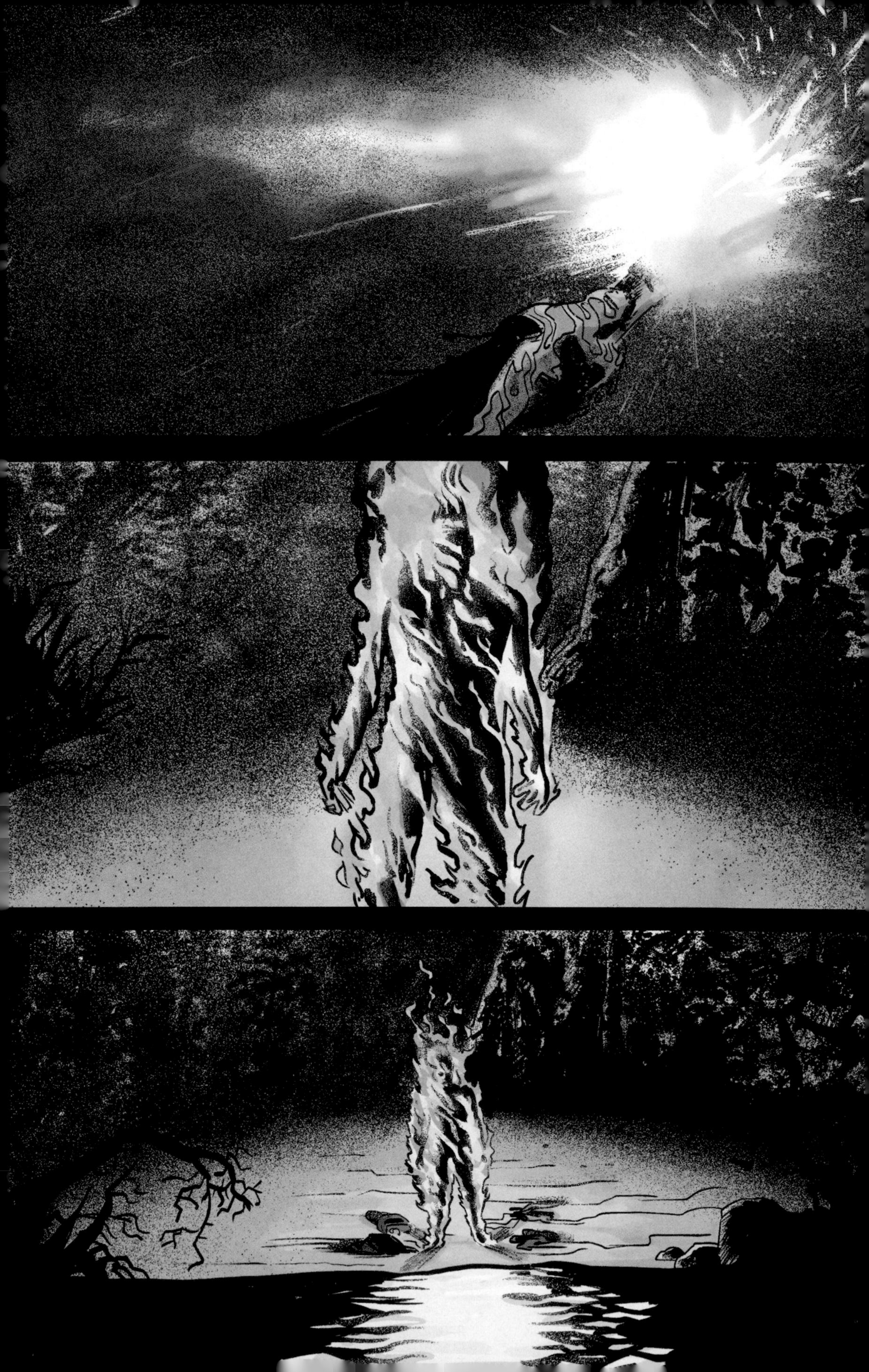

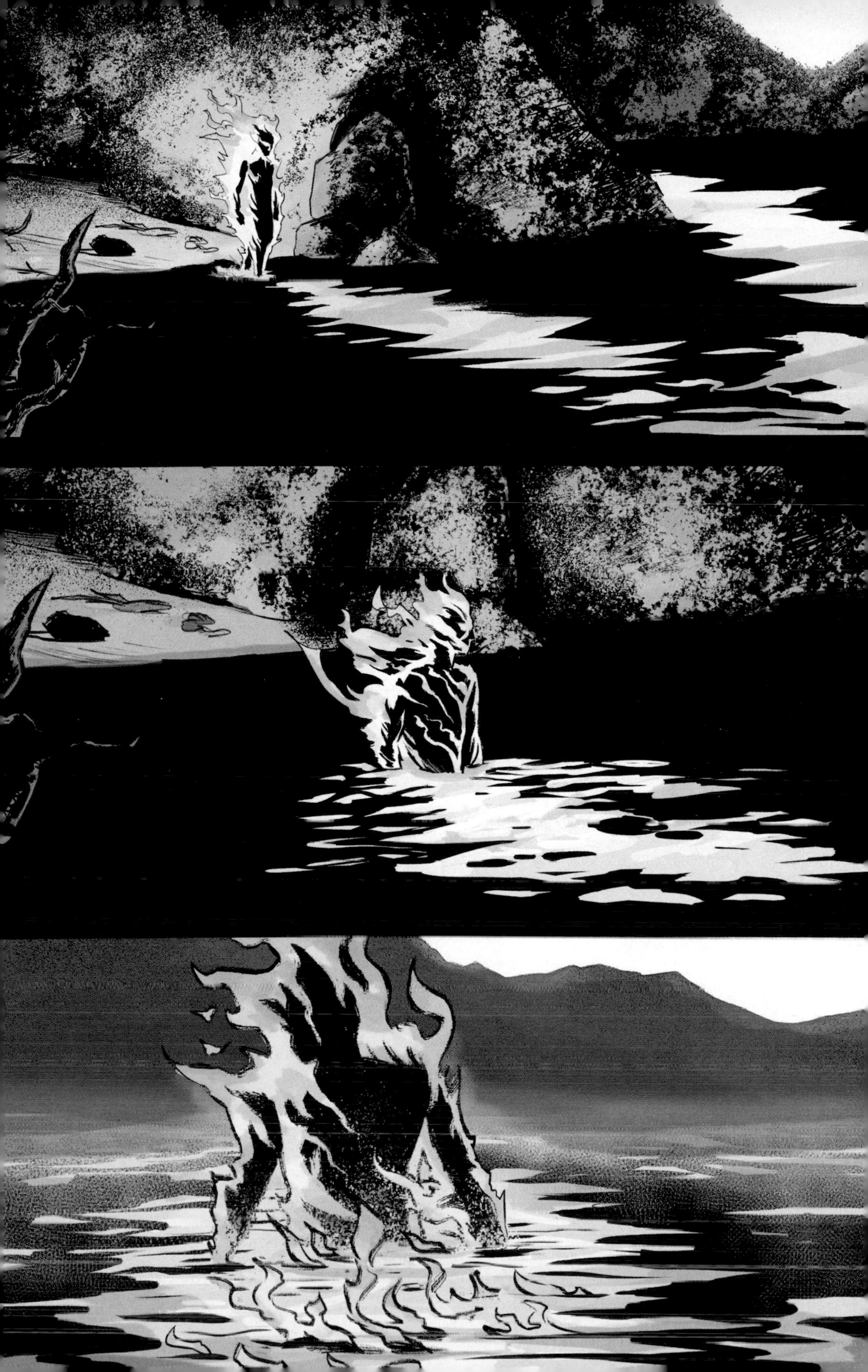

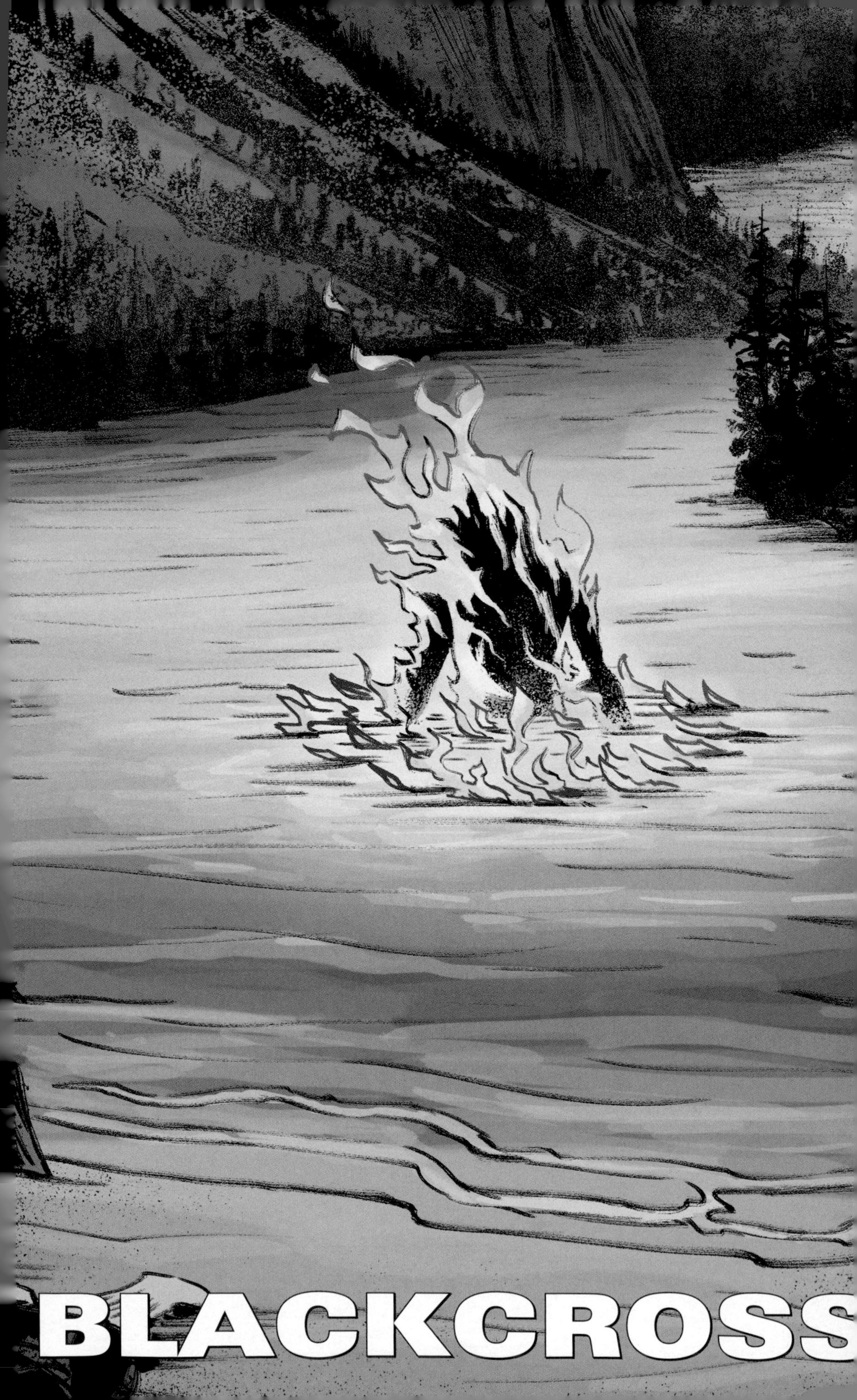
BLACKCROSS

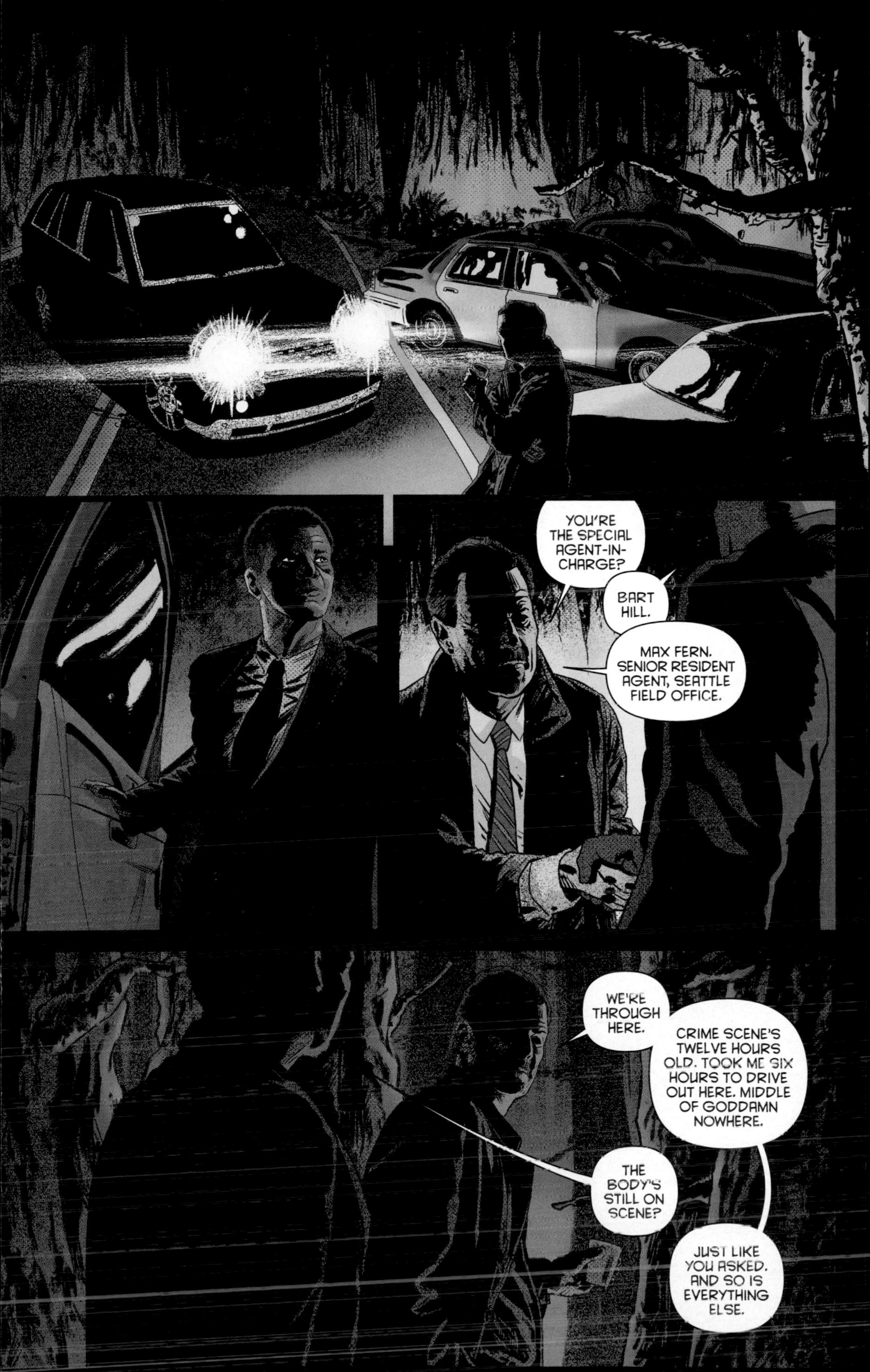
YOU'RE THE SPECIAL AGENT-IN-CHARGE?
BART HILL.
MAX FERN. SENIOR RESIDENT AGENT, SEATTLE FIELD OFFICE.
WE'RE THROUGH HERE.
CRIME SCENE'S TWELVE HOURS OLD. TOOK ME SIX HOURS TO DRIVE OUT HERE. MIDDLE OF GODDAMN NOWHERE.
THE BODY'S STILL ON SCENE?
JUST LIKE YOU ASKED. AND SO IS EVERYTHING ELSE.

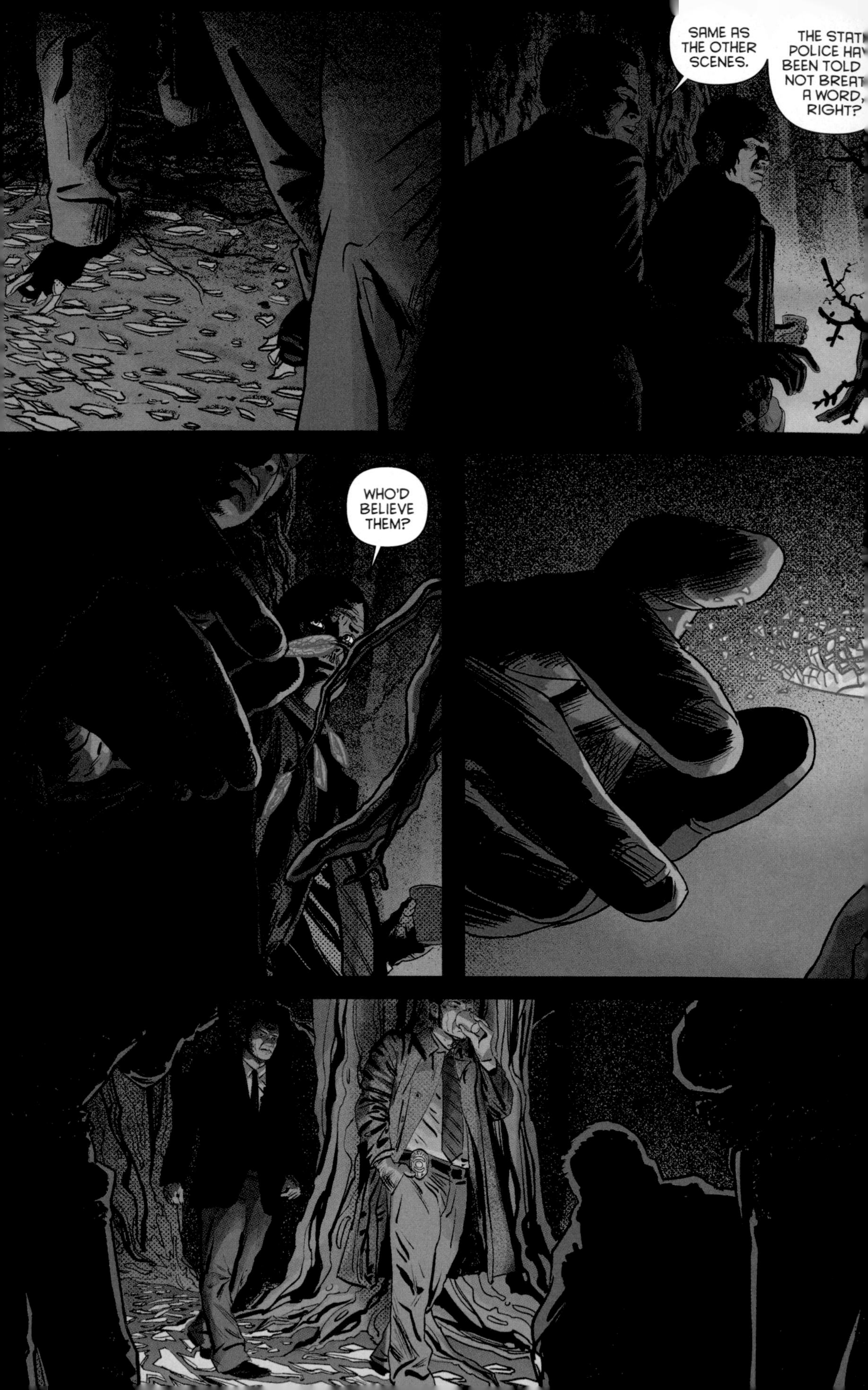
SAME AS THE OTHER SCENES.
THE STAT POLICE HA BEEN TOLD NOT BREAT A WORD, RIGHT?
WHO'D BELIEVE THEM?

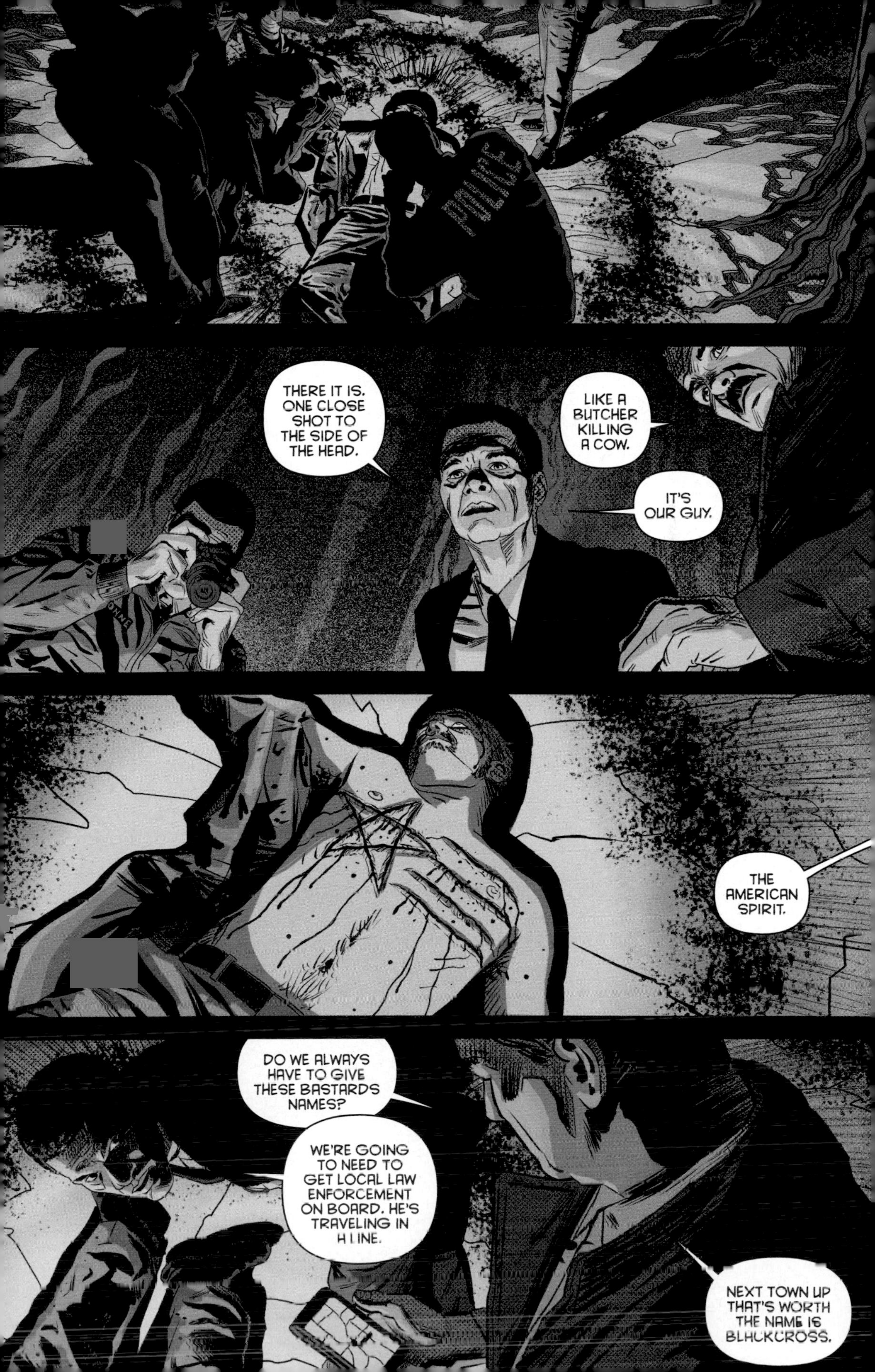

THERE IT IS. ONE CLOSE SHOT TO THE SIDE OF THE HEAD.
LIKE A BUTCHER KILLING A COW.
IT'S OUR GUY.
THE AMERICAN SPIRIT.
DO WE ALWAYS HAVE TO GIVE THESE BASTARDS NAMES?
WE'RE GOING TO NEED TO GET LOCAL LAW ENFORCEMENT ON BOARD. HE'S TRAVELING IN A LINE.
NEXT TOWN UP THAT'S WORTH THE NAME IS BLACKCROSS.

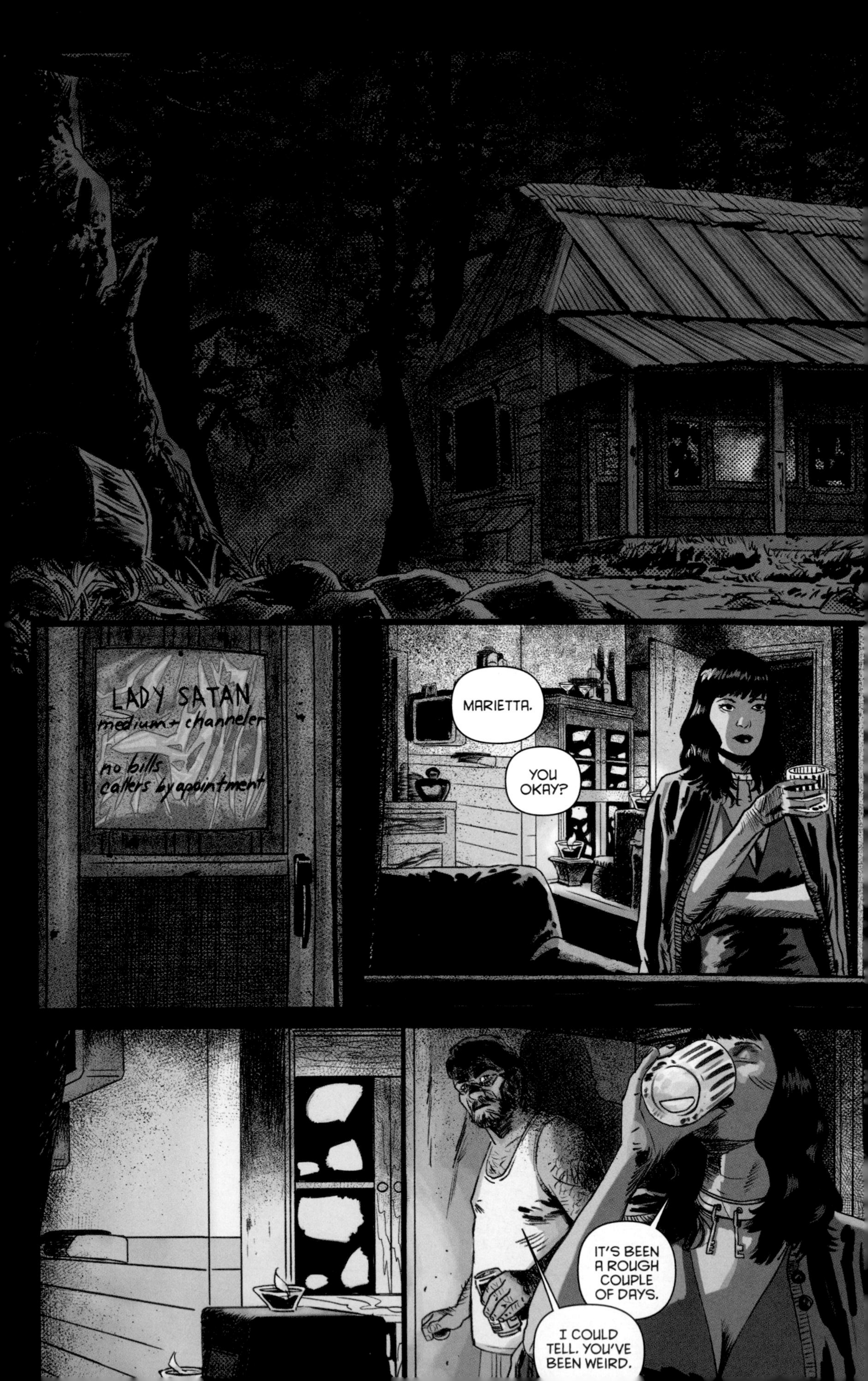
LADY SATAN
medium + channeler
no bills
callers by appointment
MARIETTA.
YOU OKAY?
IT'S BEEN A ROUGH COUPLE OF DAYS.
I COULD TELL. YOU'VE BEEN WEIRD.

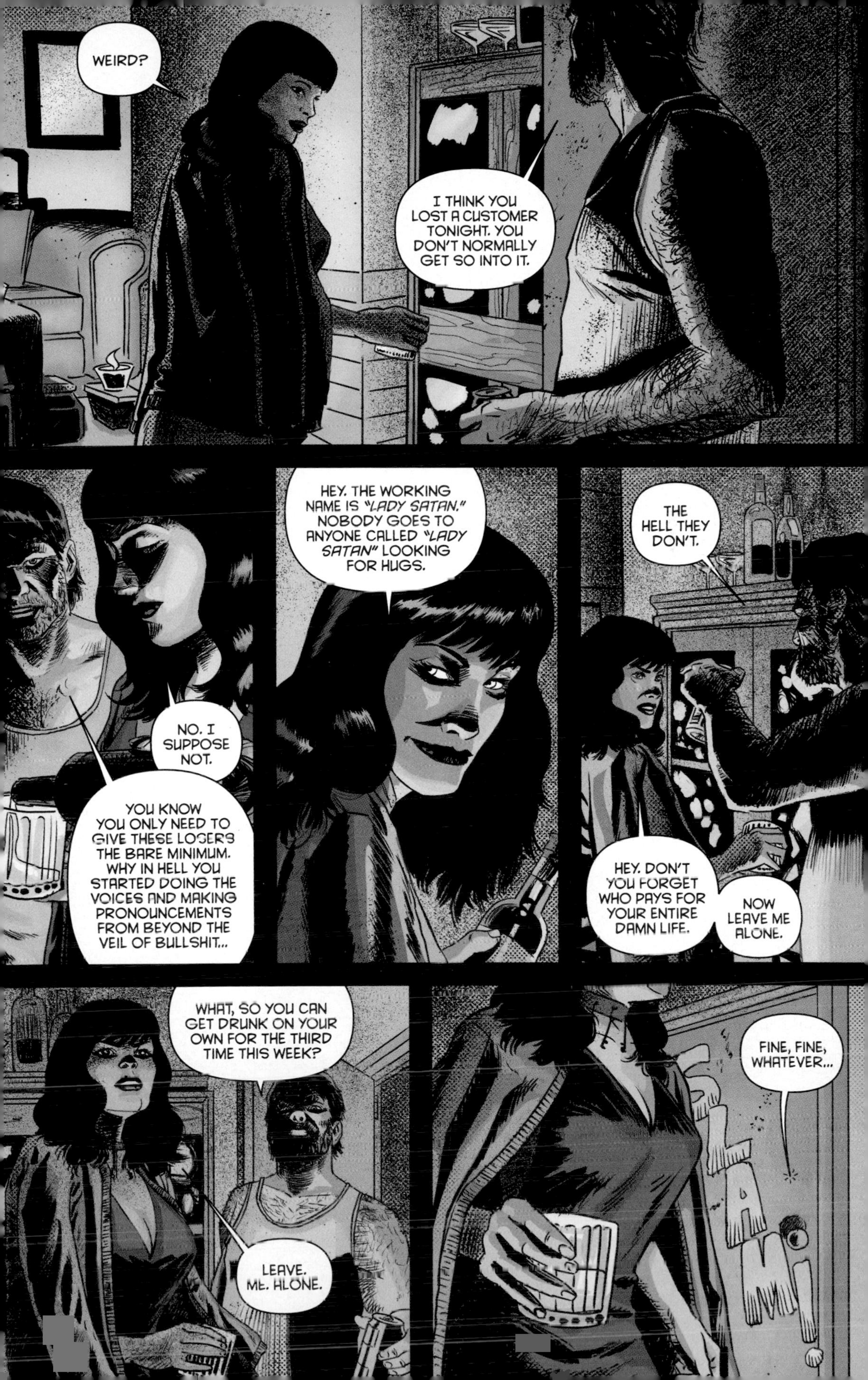

WEIRD?
I THINK YOU LOST A CUSTOMER TONIGHT. YOU DON'T NORMALLY GET SO INTO IT.
NO. I SUPPOSE NOT.
YOU KNOW YOU ONLY NEED TO GIVE THESE LOSERS THE BARE MINIMUM. WHY IN HELL YOU STARTED DOING THE VOICES AND MAKING PRONOUNCEMENTS FROM BEYOND THE VEIL OF BULLSHIT...
HEY. THE WORKING NAME IS "LADY SATAN." NOBODY GOES TO ANYONE CALLED "LADY SATAN" LOOKING FOR HUGS.
THE HELL THEY DON'T.
HEY. DON'T YOU FORGET WHO PAYS FOR YOUR ENTIRE DAMN LIFE.
NOW LEAVE ME ALONE.
WHAT, SO YOU CAN GET DRUNK ON YOUR OWN FOR THE THIRD TIME THIS WEEK?
LEAVE. ME. ALONE.
FINE, FINE, WHATEVER...
SLAM!

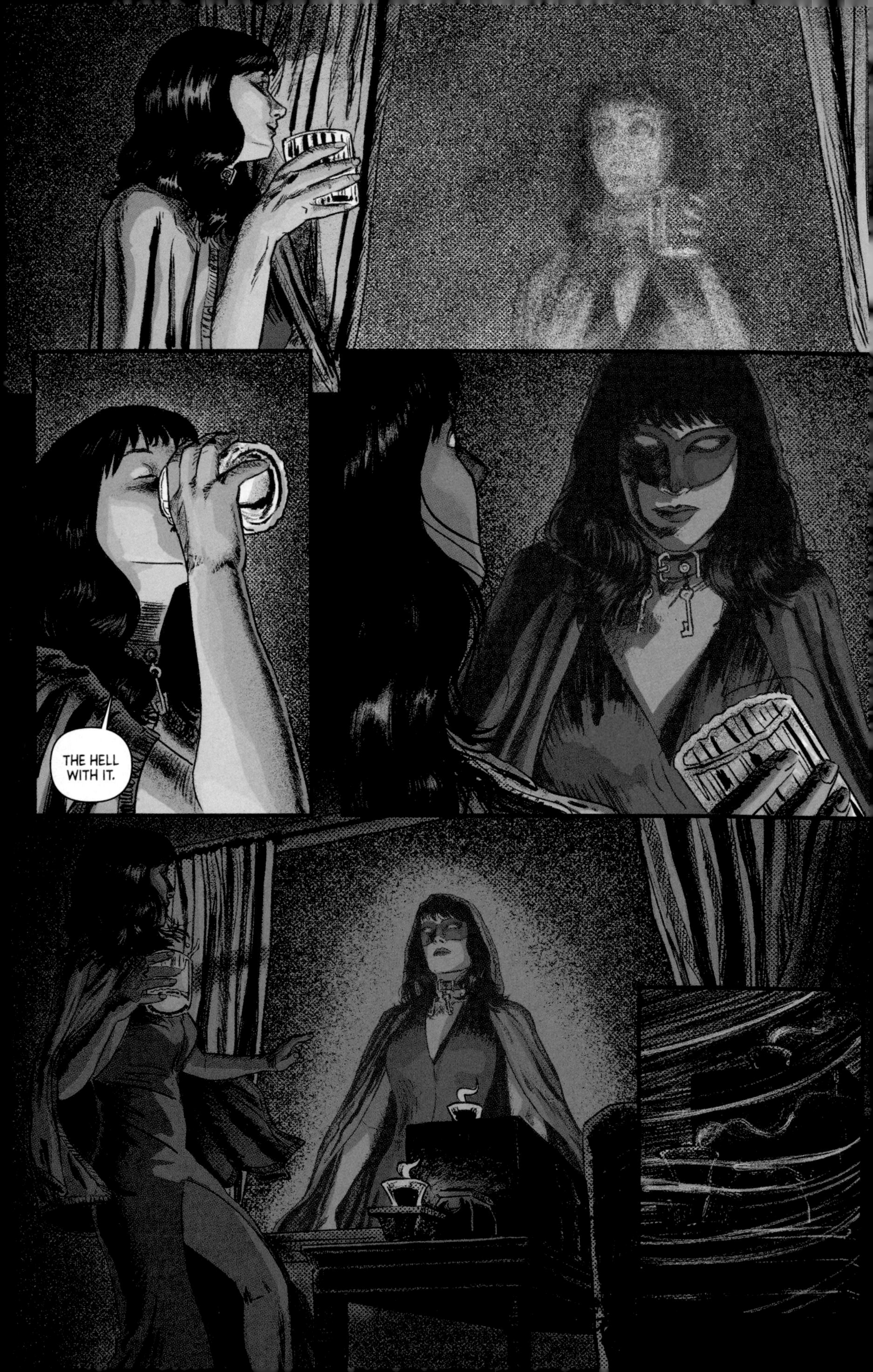
THE HELL WITH IT.

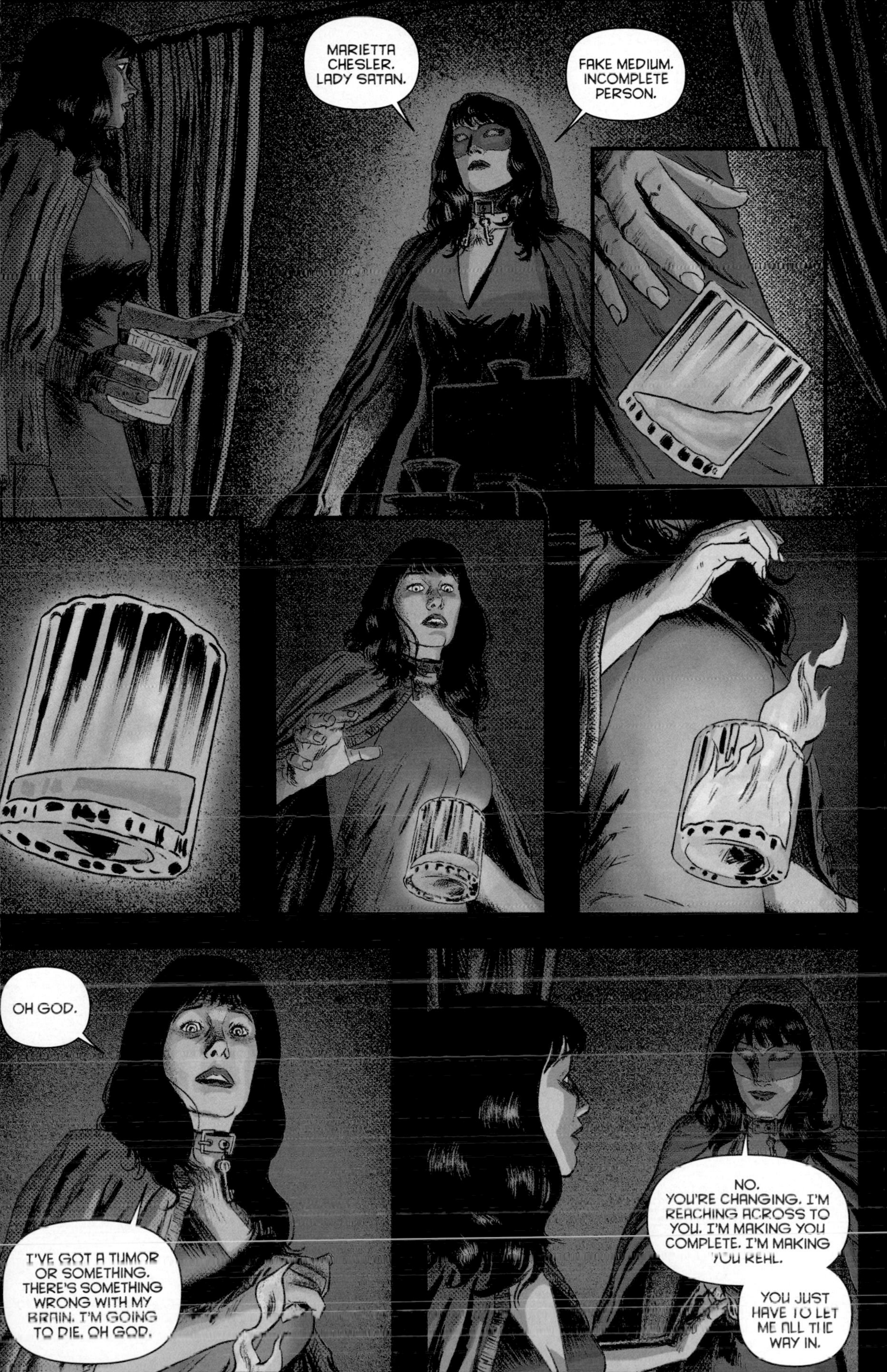
MARIETTA CHESLER. LADY SATAN.
FAKE MEDIUM. INCOMPLETE PERSON.
OH GOD.
I'VE GOT A TUMOR OR SOMETHING. THERE'S SOMETHING WRONG WITH MY BRAIN. I'M GOING TO DIE. OH GOD.
NO. YOU'RE CHANGING. I'M REACHING ACROSS TO YOU. I'M MAKING YOU COMPLETE. I'M MAKING YOU REAL.
YOU JUST HAVE TO LET ME ALL THE WAY IN.

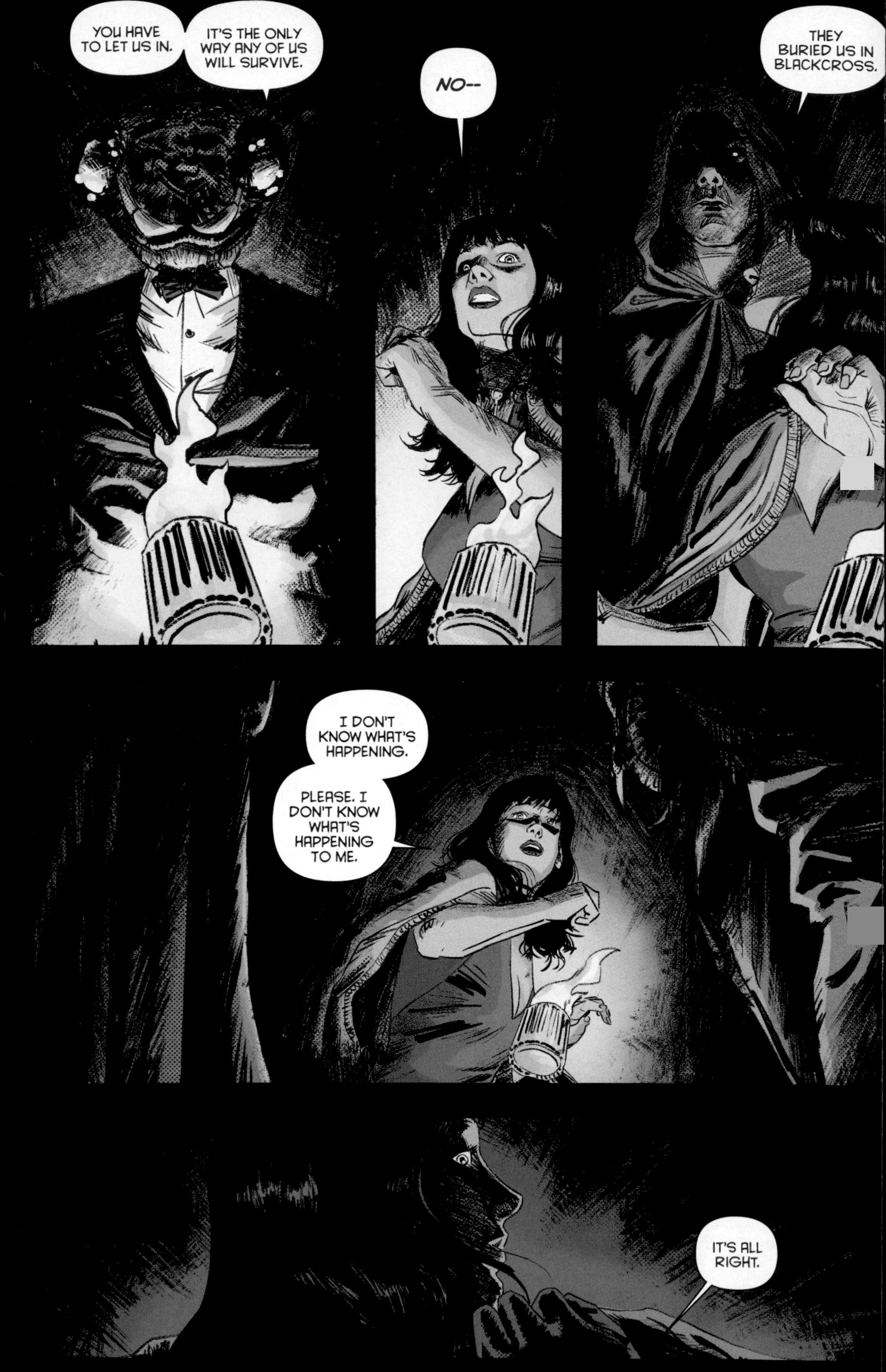
YOU HAVE TO LET US IN.
IT'S THE ONLY WAY ANY OF US WILL SURVIVE.
NO--
THEY BURIED US IN BLACKCROSS.
I DON'T KNOW WHAT'S HAPPENING.
PLEASE. I DON'T KNOW WHAT'S HAPPENING TO ME.
IT'S ALL RIGHT.

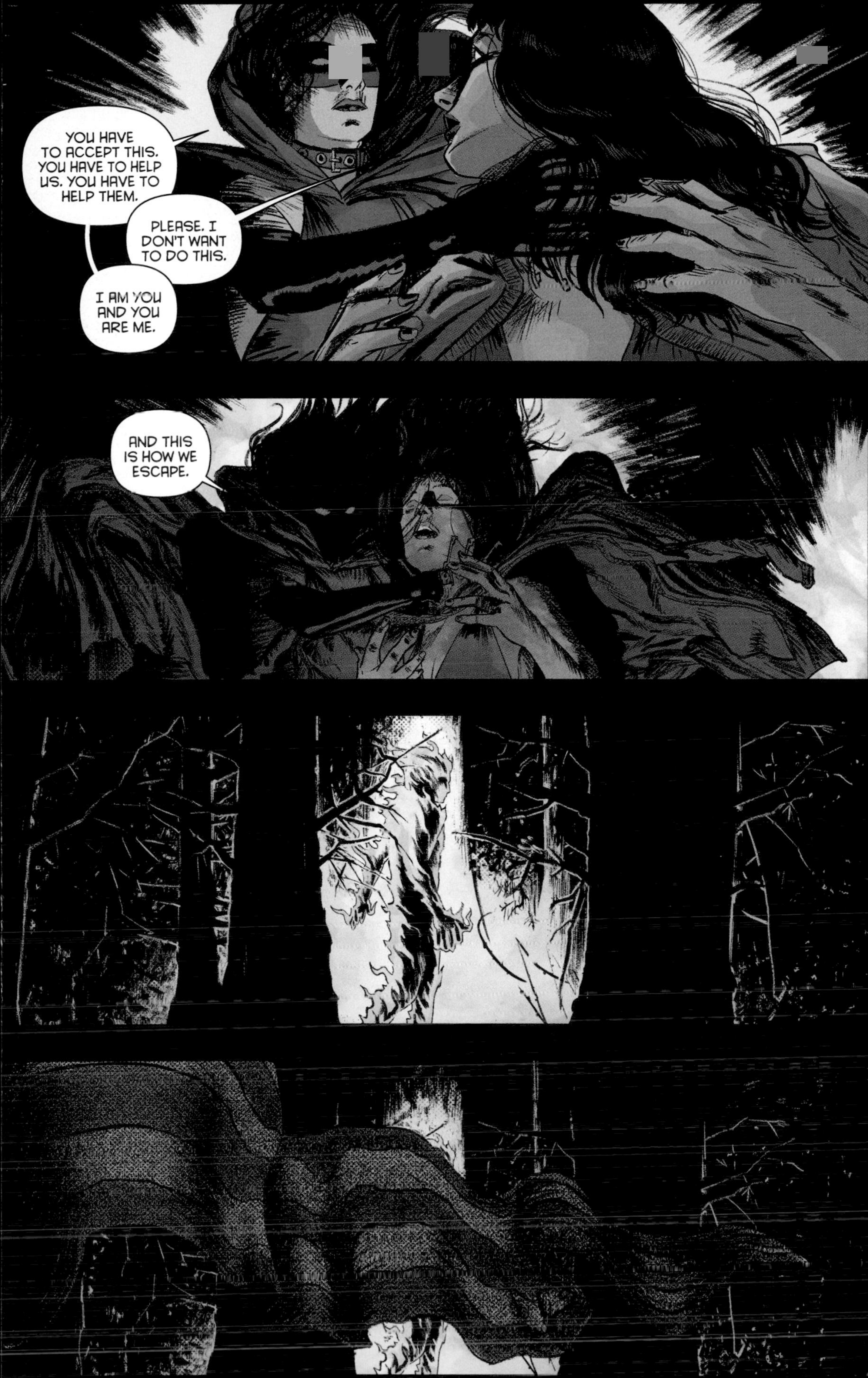
YOU HAVE TO ACCEPT THIS. YOU HAVE TO HELP US. YOU HAVE TO HELP THEM.
PLEASE. I DON'T WANT TO DO THIS.
I AM YOU AND YOU ARE ME.
AND THIS IS HOW WE ESCAPE.

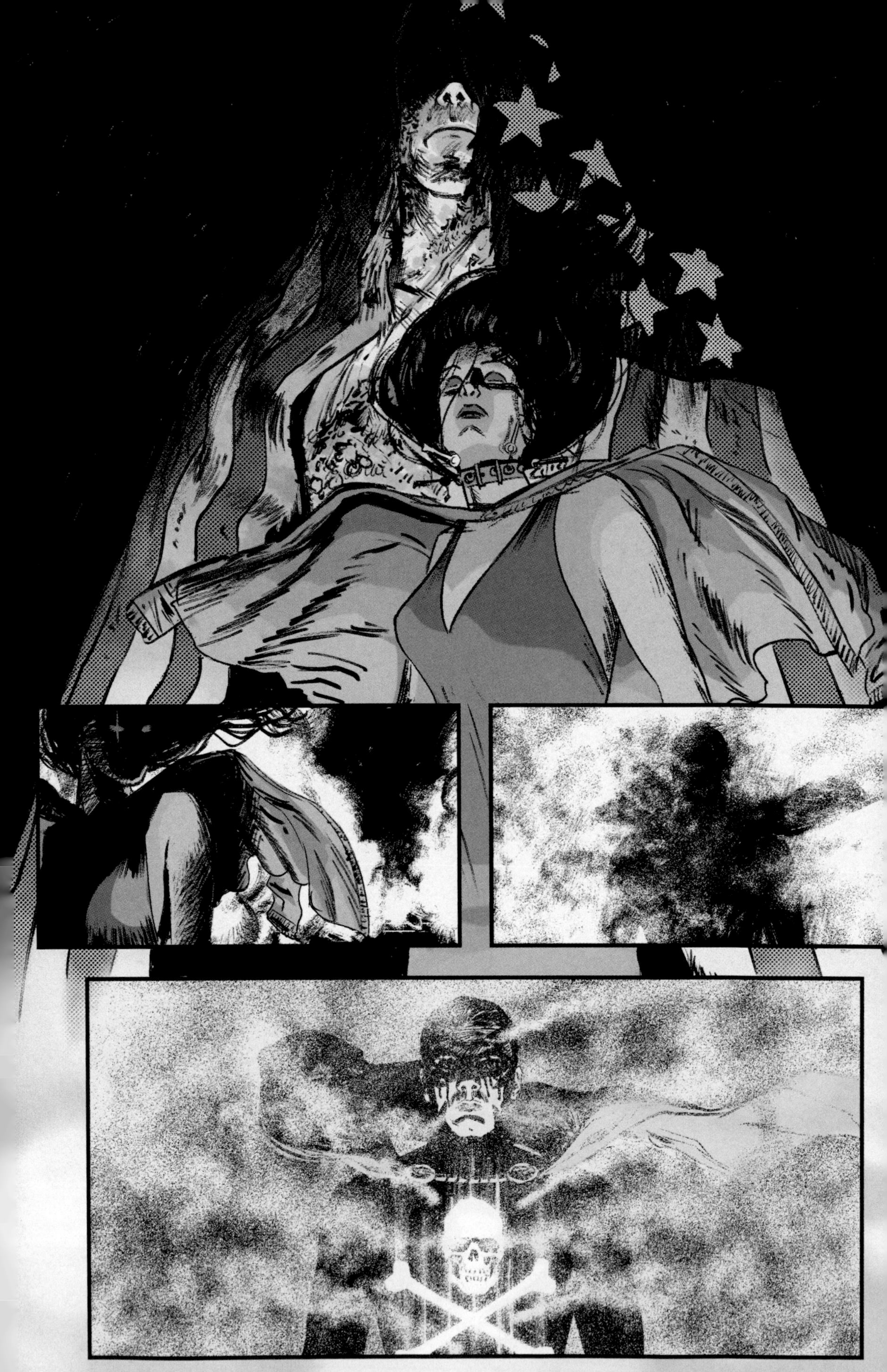

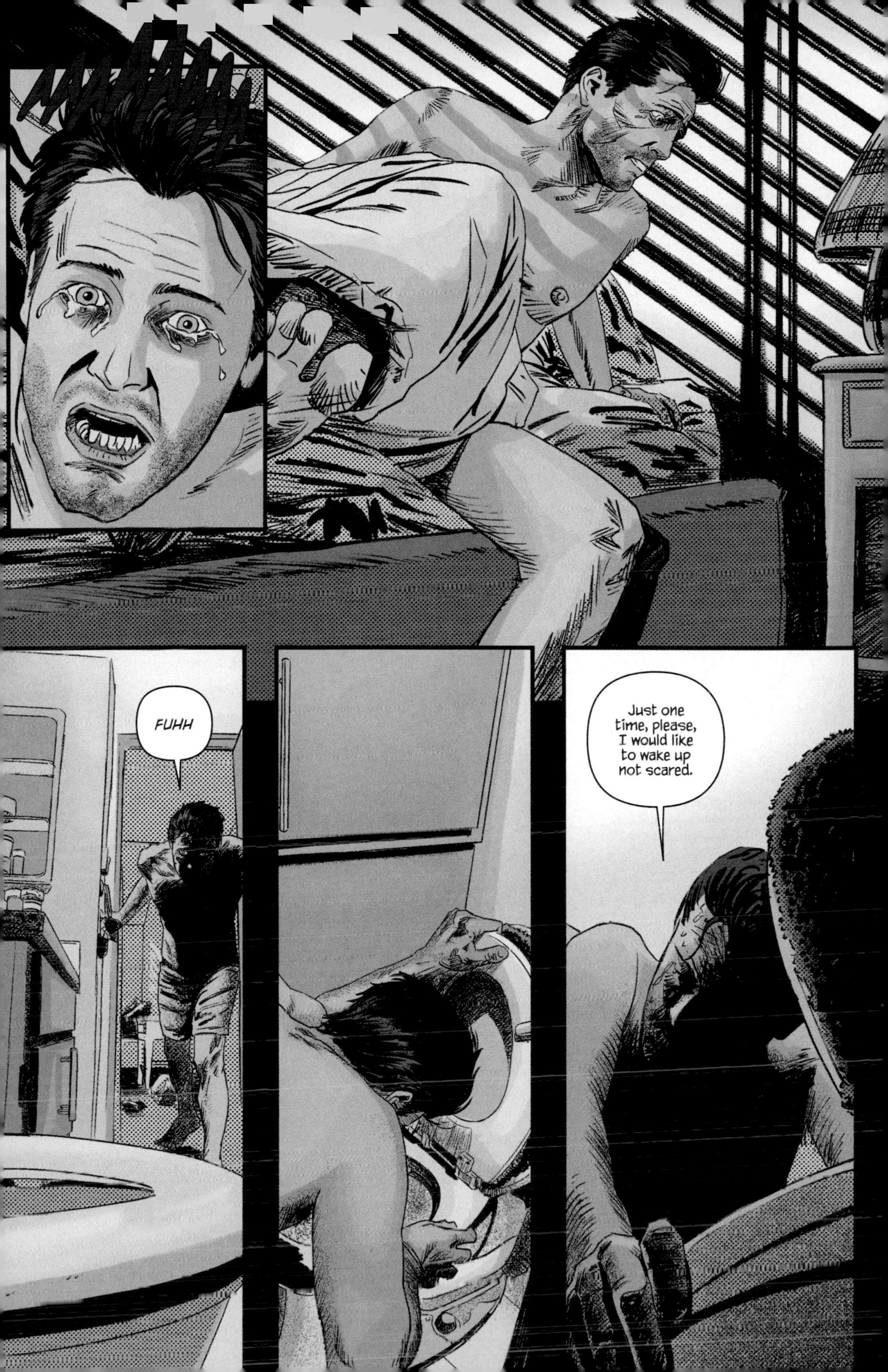
FUHH
Just one time, please, I would like to wake up not scared.

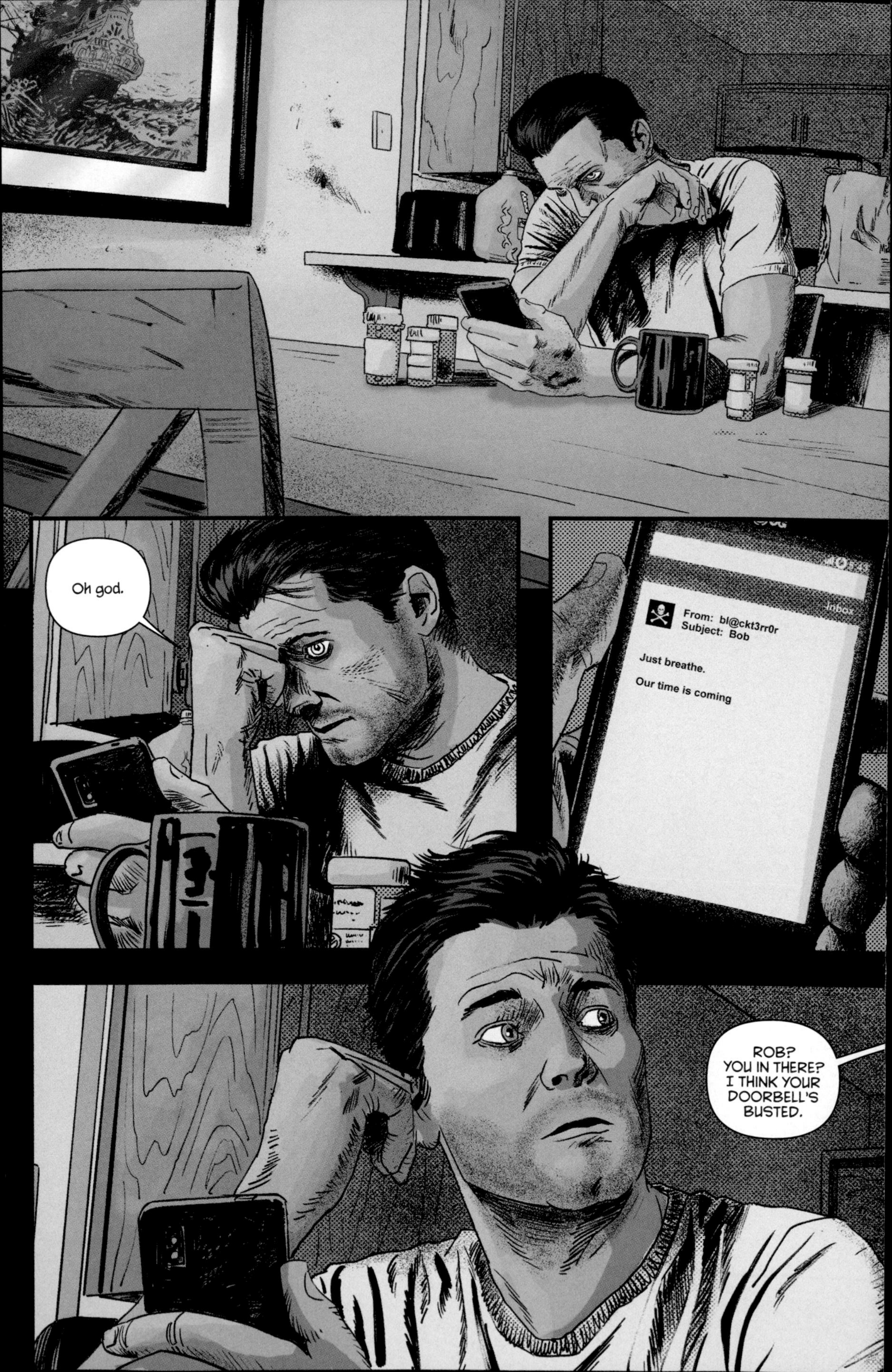
Oh god.
From: bl@ckt3rr0r
Subject: Bob
Just breathe.
Our time is coming
ROB? YOU IN THERE? I THINK YOUR DOORBELL'S BUSTED.

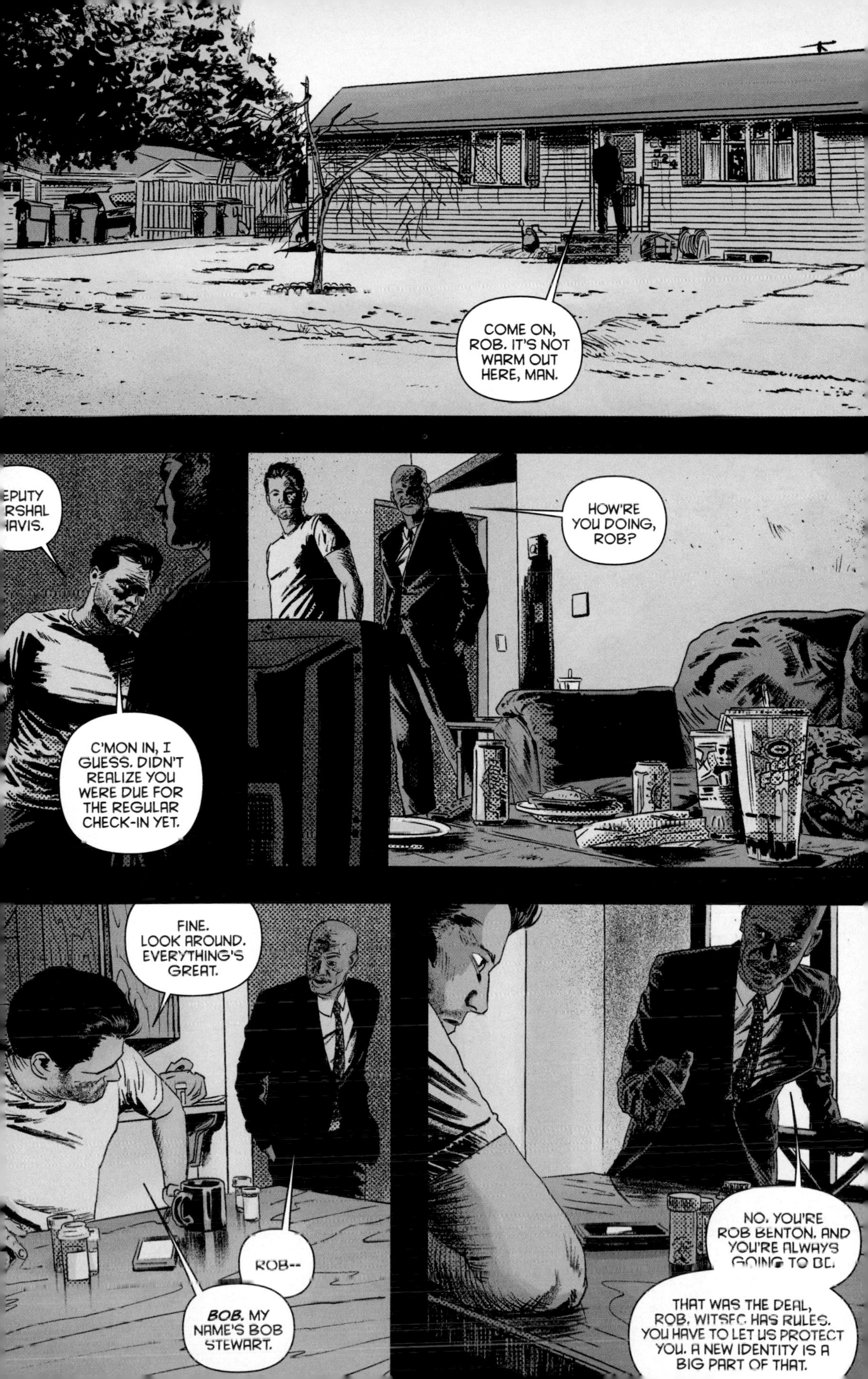

COME ON, ROB. IT'S NOT WARM OUT HERE, MAN.
EPUTY RSHAL HAVIS.
C'MON IN, I GUESS. DIDN'T REALIZE YOU WERE DUE FOR THE REGULAR CHECK-IN YET.
HOW'RE YOU DOING, ROB?
FINE. LOOK AROUND. EVERYTHING'S GREAT.
ROB--
BOB. MY NAME'S BOB STEWART.
NO. YOU'RE ROB BENTON. AND YOU'RE ALWAYS GOING TO BE.
THAT WAS THE DEAL, ROB. WITSEC HAS RULES. YOU HAVE TO LET US PROTECT YOU. A NEW IDENTITY IS A BIG PART OF THAT.

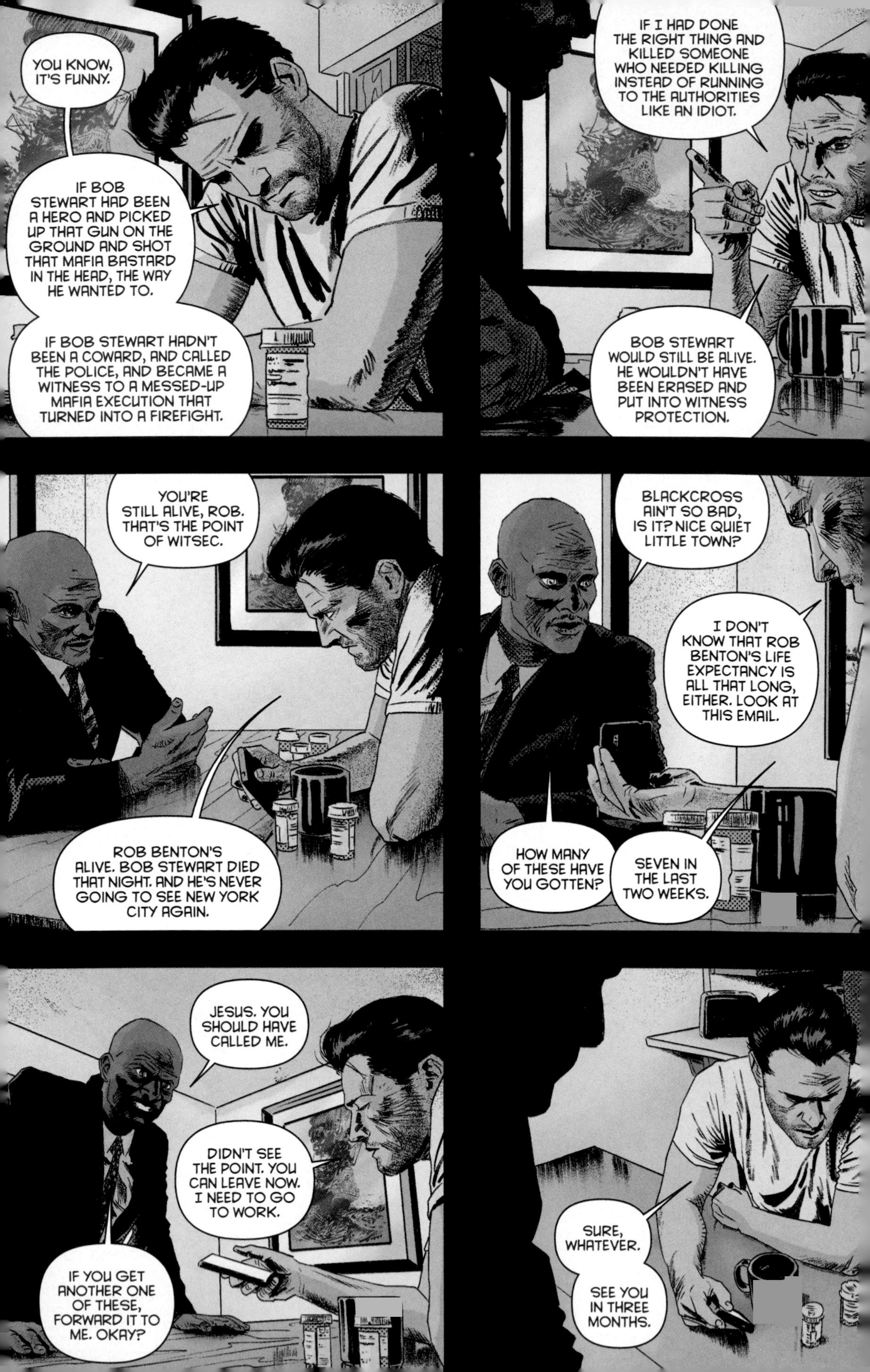
YOU KNOW, IT'S FUNNY.
IF BOB STEWART HAD BEEN A HERO AND PICKED UP THAT GUN ON THE GROUND AND SHOT THAT MAFIA BASTARD IN THE HEAD, THE WAY HE WANTED TO.
IF BOB STEWART HADN'T BEEN A COWARD, AND CALLED THE POLICE, AND BECAME A WITNESS TO A MESSED-UP MAFIA EXECUTION THAT TURNED INTO A FIREFIGHT.
IF I HAD DONE THE RIGHT THING AND KILLED SOMEONE WHO NEEDED KILLING INSTEAD OF RUNNING TO THE AUTHORITIES LIKE AN IDIOT.
BOB STEWART WOULD STILL BE ALIVE. HE WOULDN'T HAVE BEEN ERASED AND PUT INTO WITNESS PROTECTION.
YOU'RE STILL ALIVE, ROB. THAT'S THE POINT OF WITSEC.
ROB BENTON'S ALIVE. BOB STEWART DIED THAT NIGHT. AND HE'S NEVER GOING TO SEE NEW YORK CITY AGAIN.
BLACKCROSS AIN'T SO BAD, IS IT? NICE QUIET LITTLE TOWN?
I DON'T KNOW THAT ROB BENTON'S LIFE EXPECTANCY IS ALL THAT LONG, EITHER. LOOK AT THIS EMAIL.
HOW MANY OF THESE HAVE YOU GOTTEN?
SEVEN IN THE LAST TWO WEEKS.
JESUS. YOU SHOULD HAVE CALLED ME.
DIDN'T SEE THE POINT. YOU CAN LEAVE NOW. I NEED TO GO TO WORK.
IF YOU GET ANOTHER ONE OF THESE, FORWARD IT TO ME. OKAY?
SURE, WHATEVER.
SEE YOU IN THREE MONTHS.

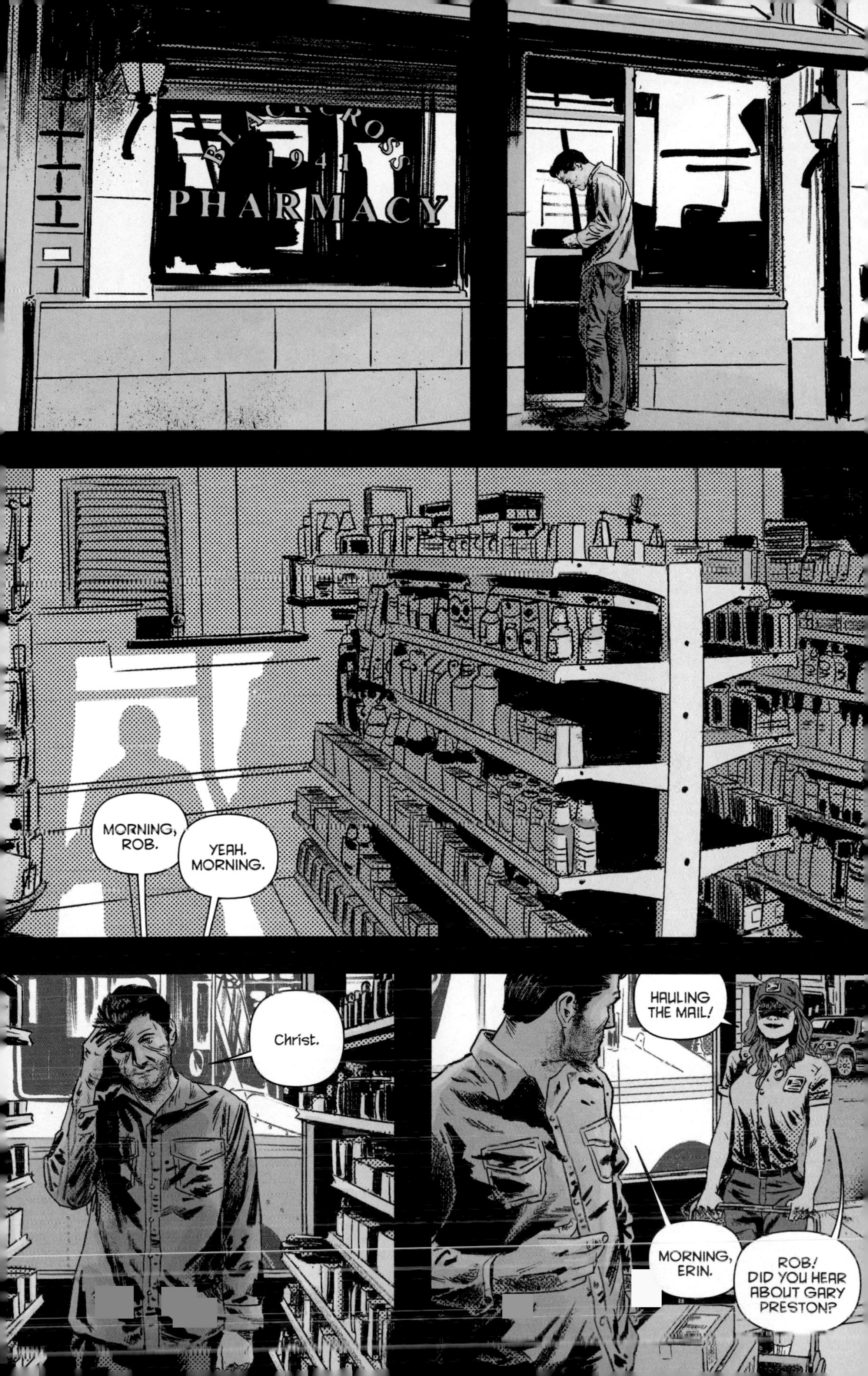
BLACKCROSS
1941
PHARMACY
MORNING, ROB.
YEAH. MORNING.
Christ.
HAULING THE MAIL!
MORNING, ERIN.
ROB! DID YOU HEAR ABOUT GARY PRESTON?

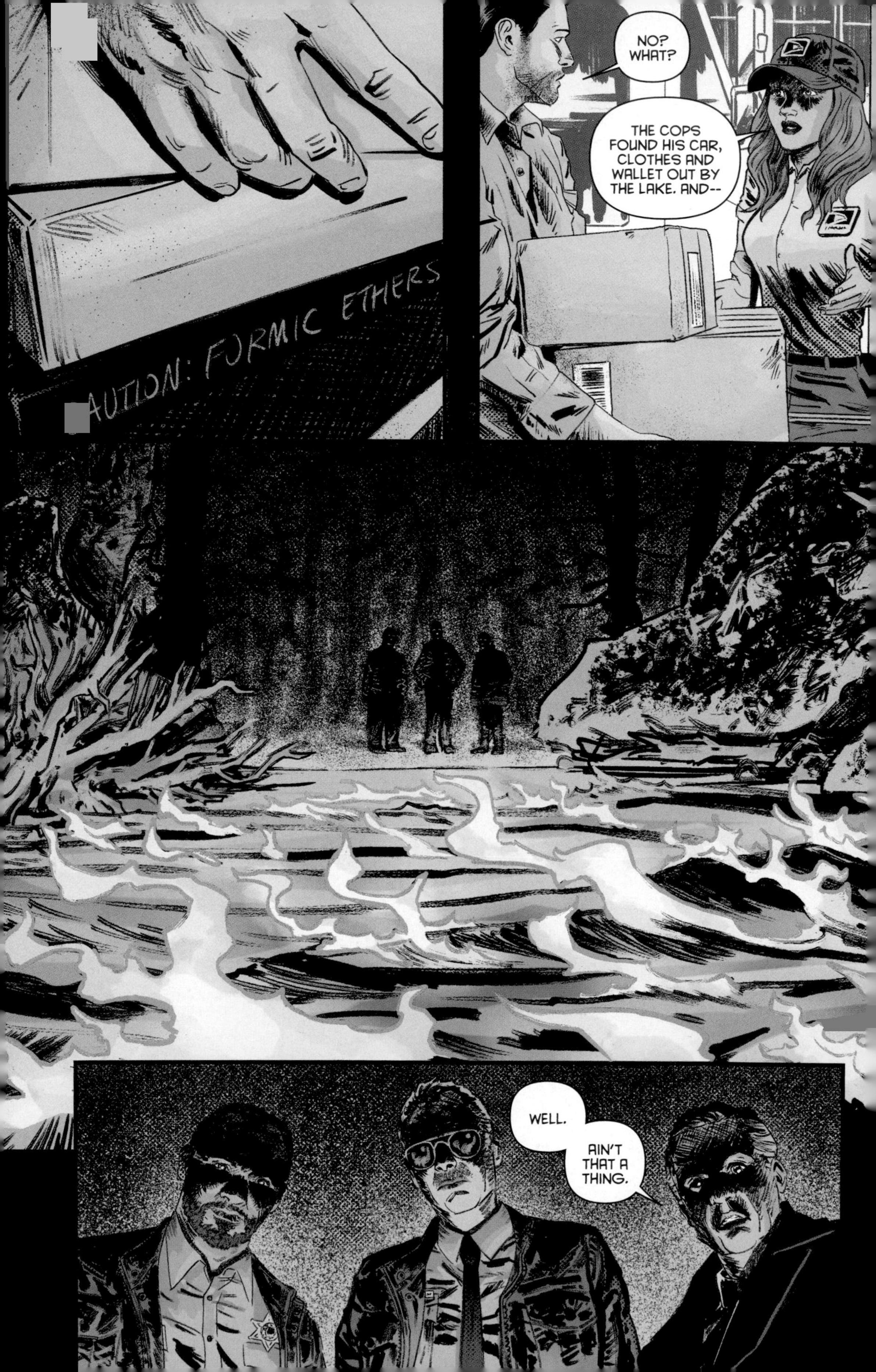

CAUTION: FORMIC ETHERS
NO? WHAT?
THE COPS FOUND HIS CAR, CLOTHES AND WALLET OUT BY THE LAKE. AND--
WELL.
AIN'T THAT A THING.

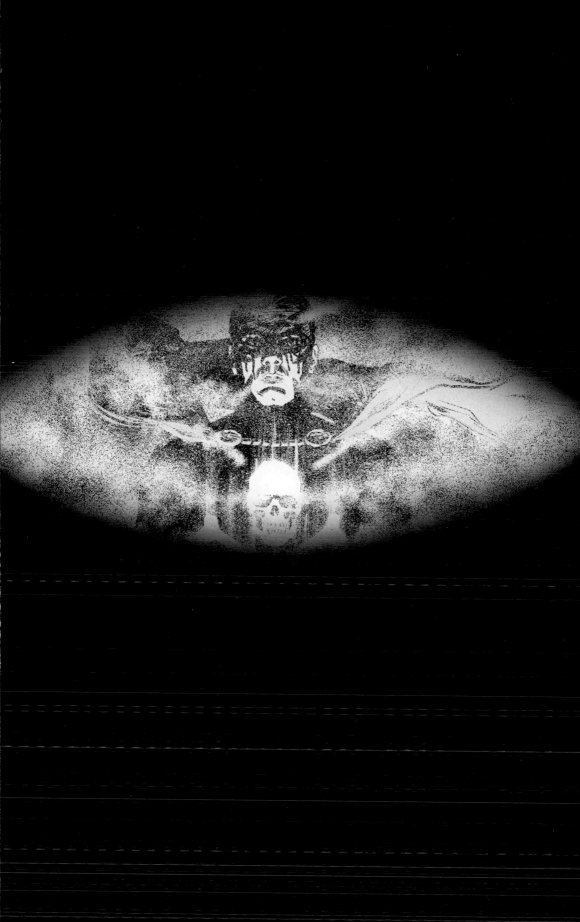

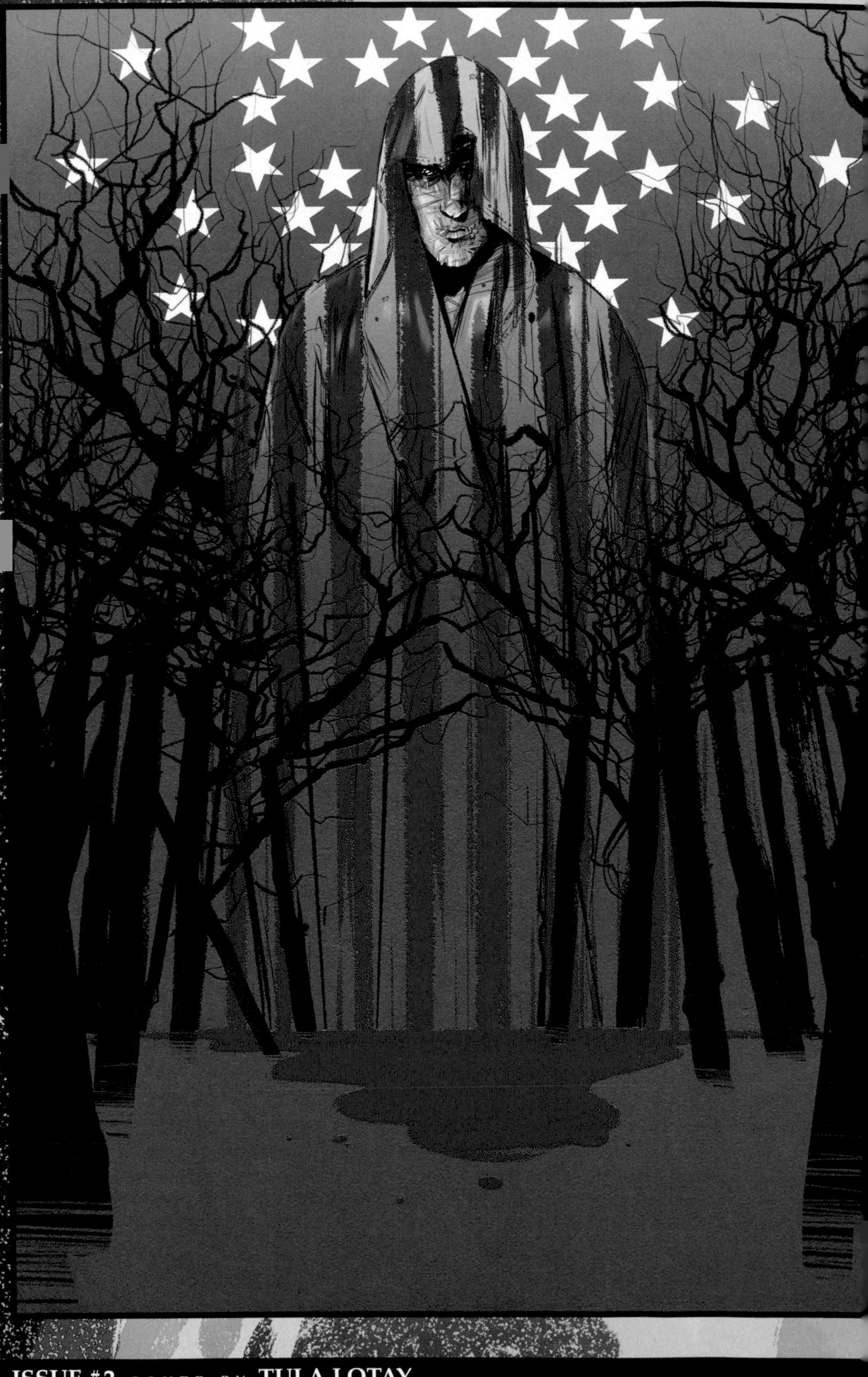

ISSUE #2 COVER BY TULA LOTAY

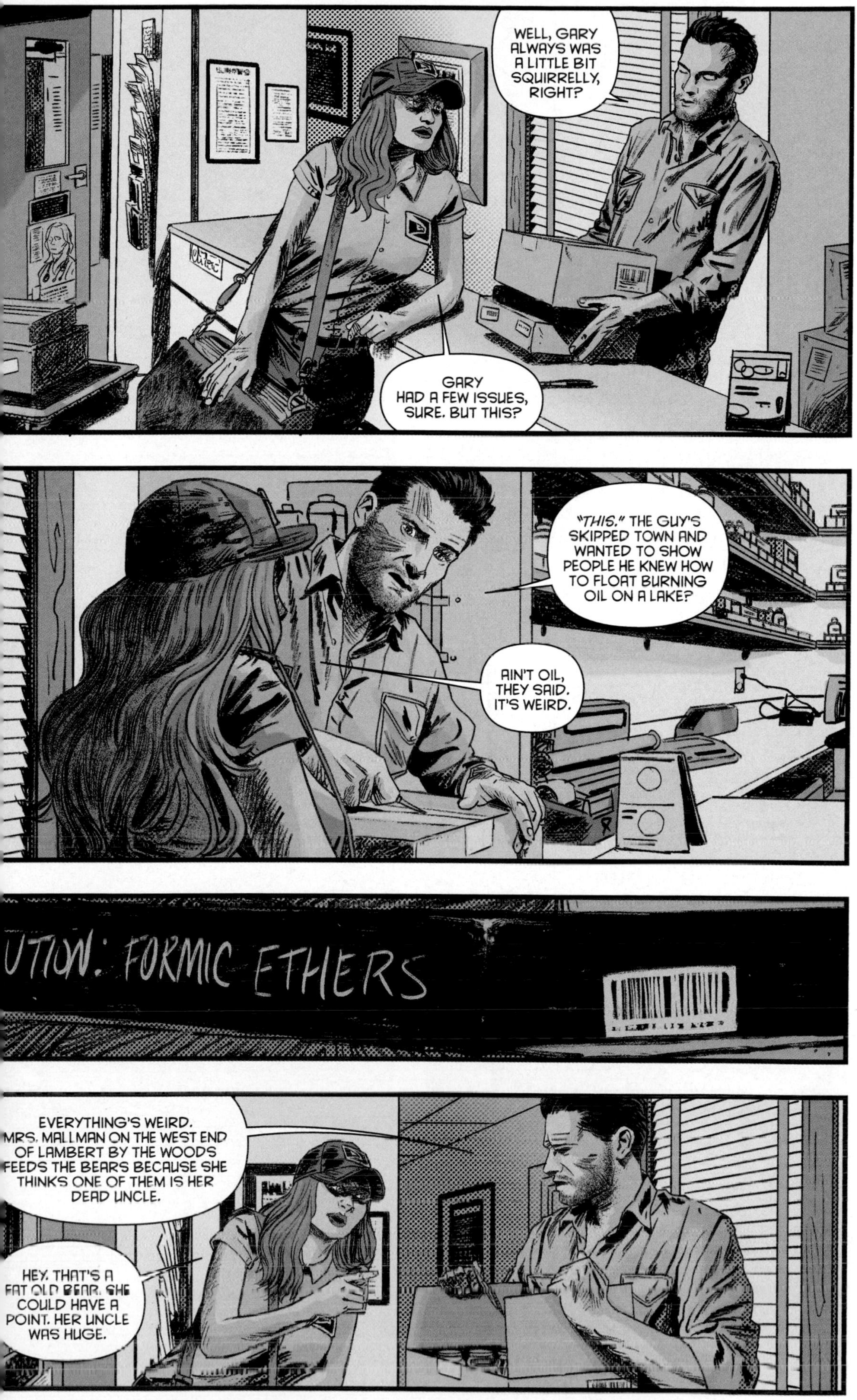
WELL, GARY ALWAYS WAS A LITTLE BIT SQUIRRELLY, RIGHT?
GARY HAD A FEW ISSUES, SURE. BUT THIS?
"THIS." THE GUY'S SKIPPED TOWN AND WANTED TO SHOW PEOPLE HE KNEW HOW TO FLOAT BURNING OIL ON A LAKE?
AIN'T OIL, THEY SAID. IT'S WEIRD.
UTION: FORMIC ETHERS
EVERYTHING'S WEIRD. MRS. MALLMAN ON THE WEST END OF LAMBERT BY THE WOODS FEEDS THE BEARS BECAUSE SHE THINKS ONE OF THEM IS HER DEAD UNCLE.
HEY. THAT'S A FAT OLD BEAR. SHE COULD HAVE A POINT. HER UNCLE WAS HUGE.

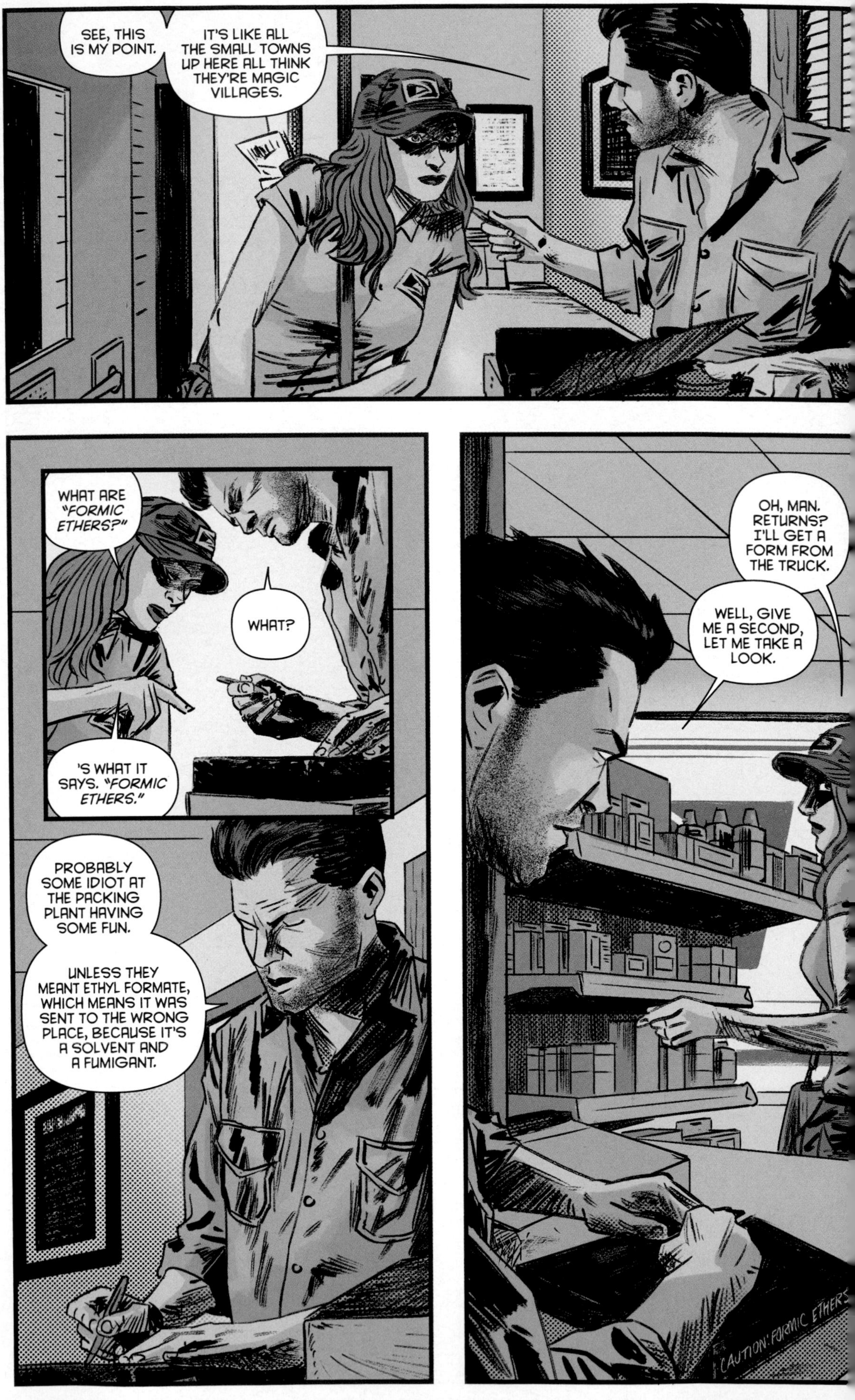
SEE, THIS IS MY POINT.
IT'S LIKE ALL THE SMALL TOWNS UP HERE ALL THINK THEY'RE MAGIC VILLAGES.
WHAT ARE "FORMIC ETHERS?"
WHAT?
'S WHAT IT SAYS. "FORMIC ETHERS."
PROBABLY SOME IDIOT AT THE PACKING PLANT HAVING SOME FUN.
UNLESS THEY MEANT ETHYL FORMATE, WHICH MEANS IT WAS SENT TO THE WRONG PLACE, BECAUSE IT'S A SOLVENT AND A FUMIGANT.
OH, MAN. RETURNS? I'LL GET A FORM FROM THE TRUCK.
WELL, GIVE ME A SECOND, LET ME TAKE A LOOK.
CAUTION: FORMIC ETHERS

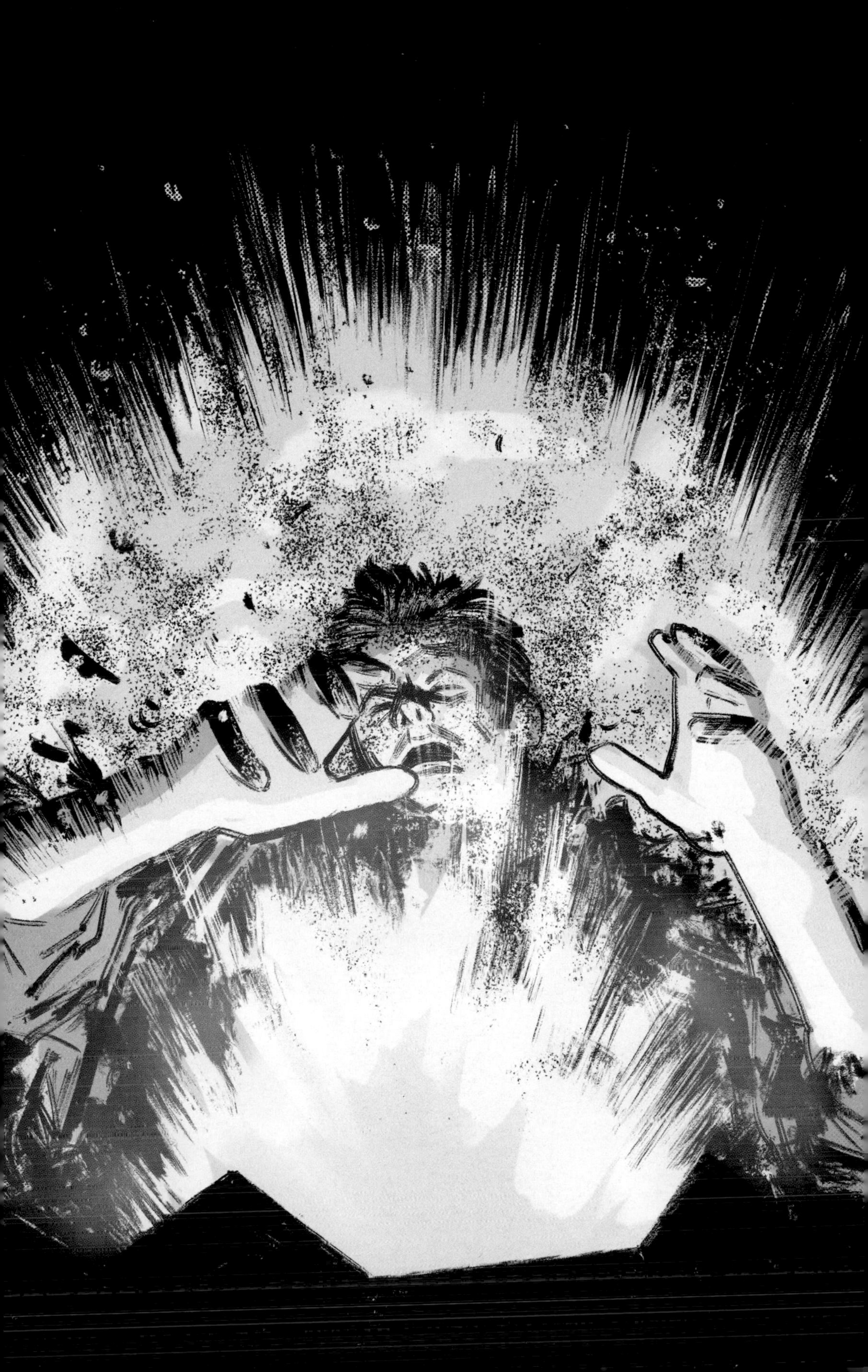

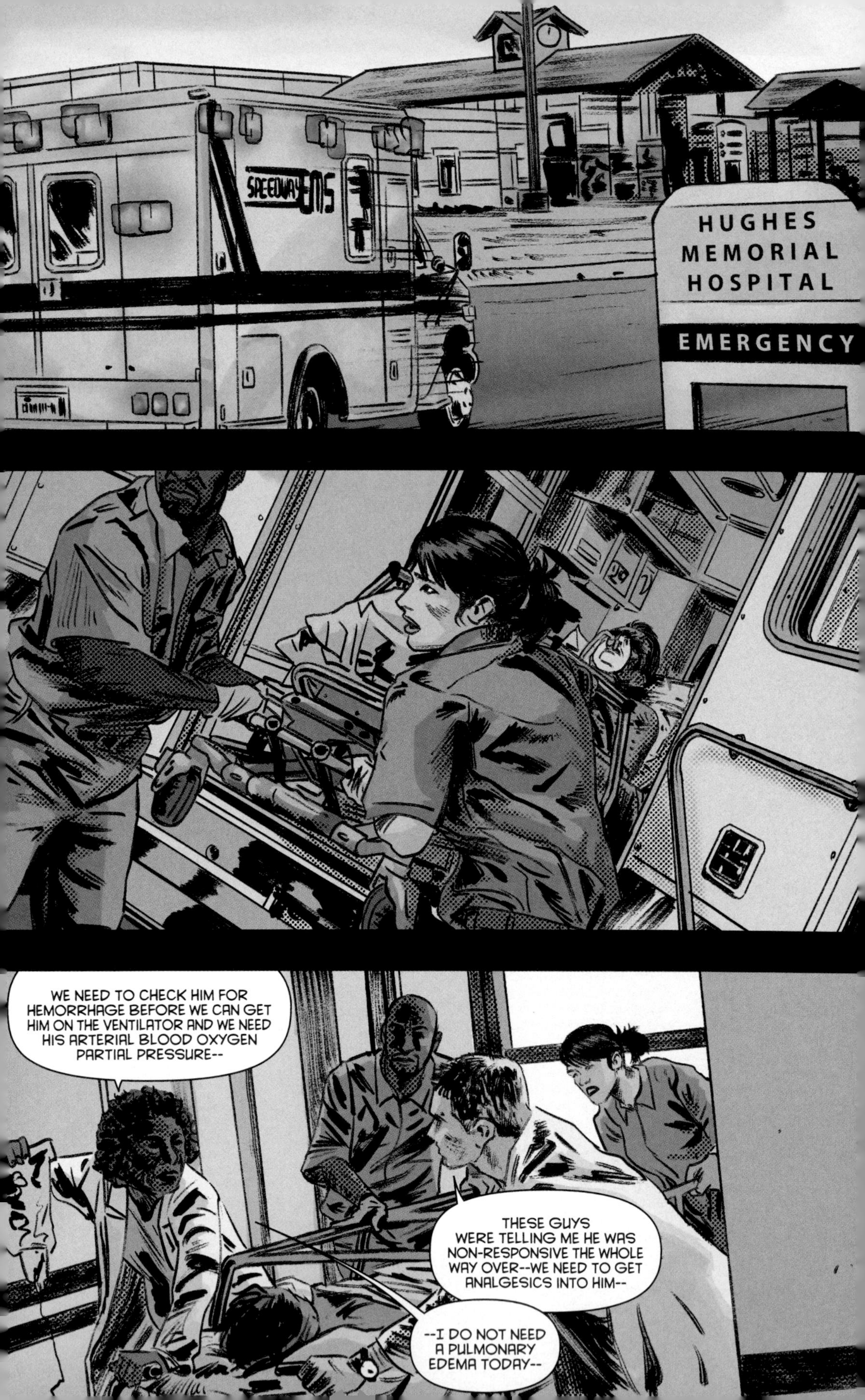
SPEEDWAY EMS
HUGHES MEMORIAL HOSPITAL
EMERGENCY
WE NEED TO CHECK HIM FOR HEMORRHAGE BEFORE WE CAN GET HIM ON THE VENTILATOR AND WE NEED HIS ARTERIAL BLOOD OXYGEN PARTIAL PRESSURE--
THESE GUYS WERE TELLING ME HE WAS NON-RESPONSIVE THE WHOLE WAY OVER--WE NEED TO GET ANALGESICS INTO HIM--
--I DO NOT NEED A PULMONARY EDEMA TODAY--

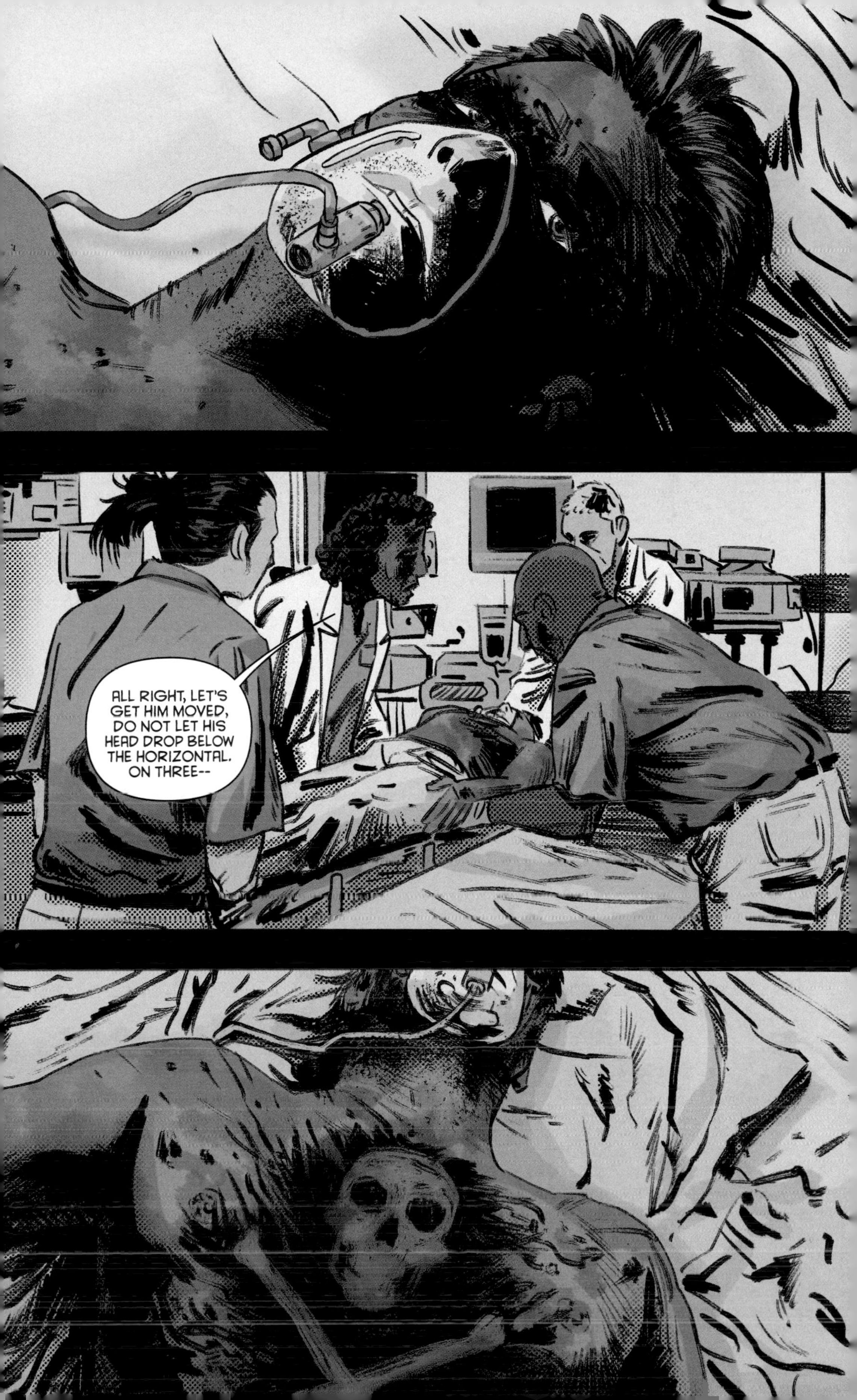
ALL RIGHT, LET'S GET HIM MOVED, DO NOT LET HIS HEAD DROP BELOW THE HORIZONTAL. ON THREE--

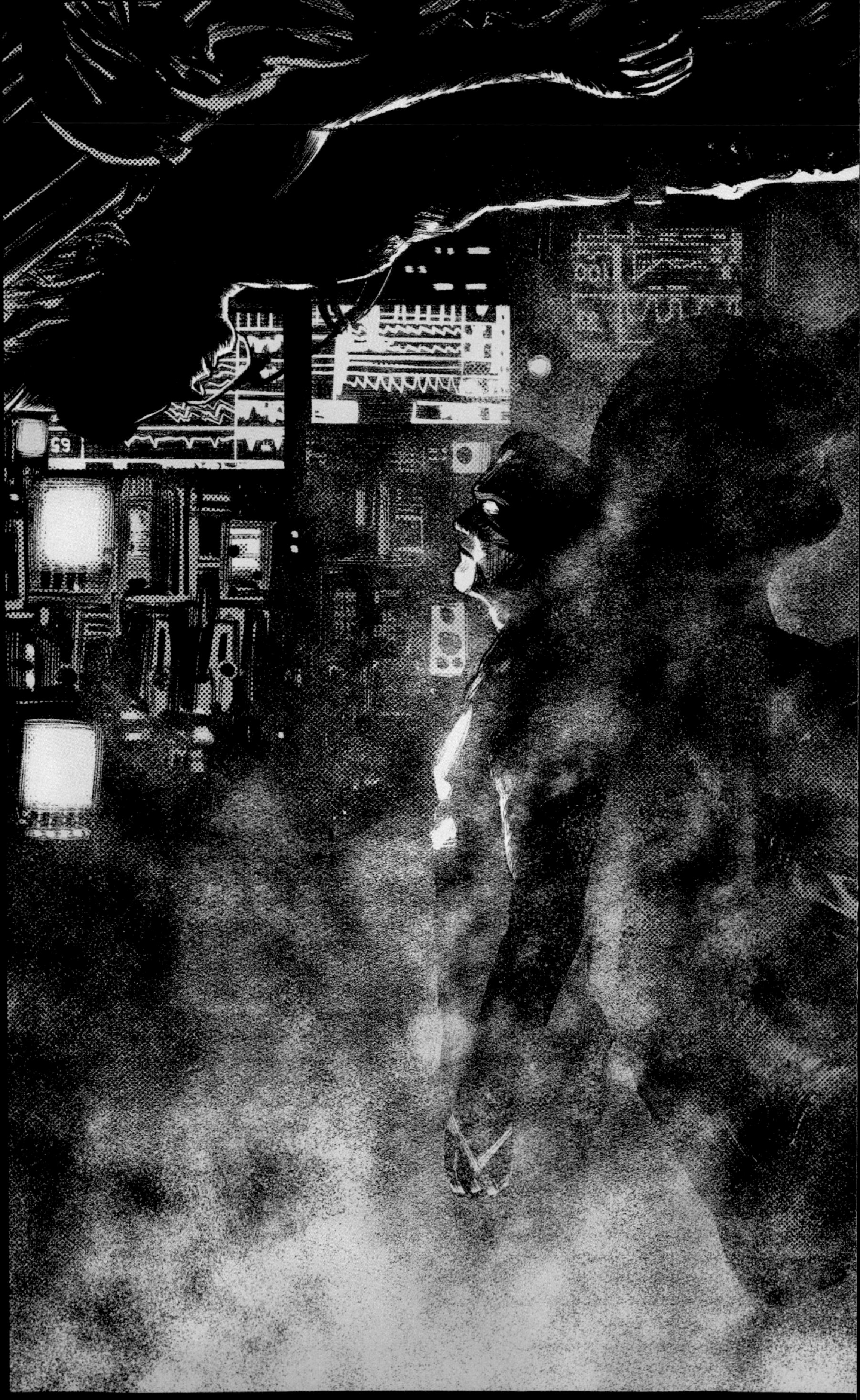

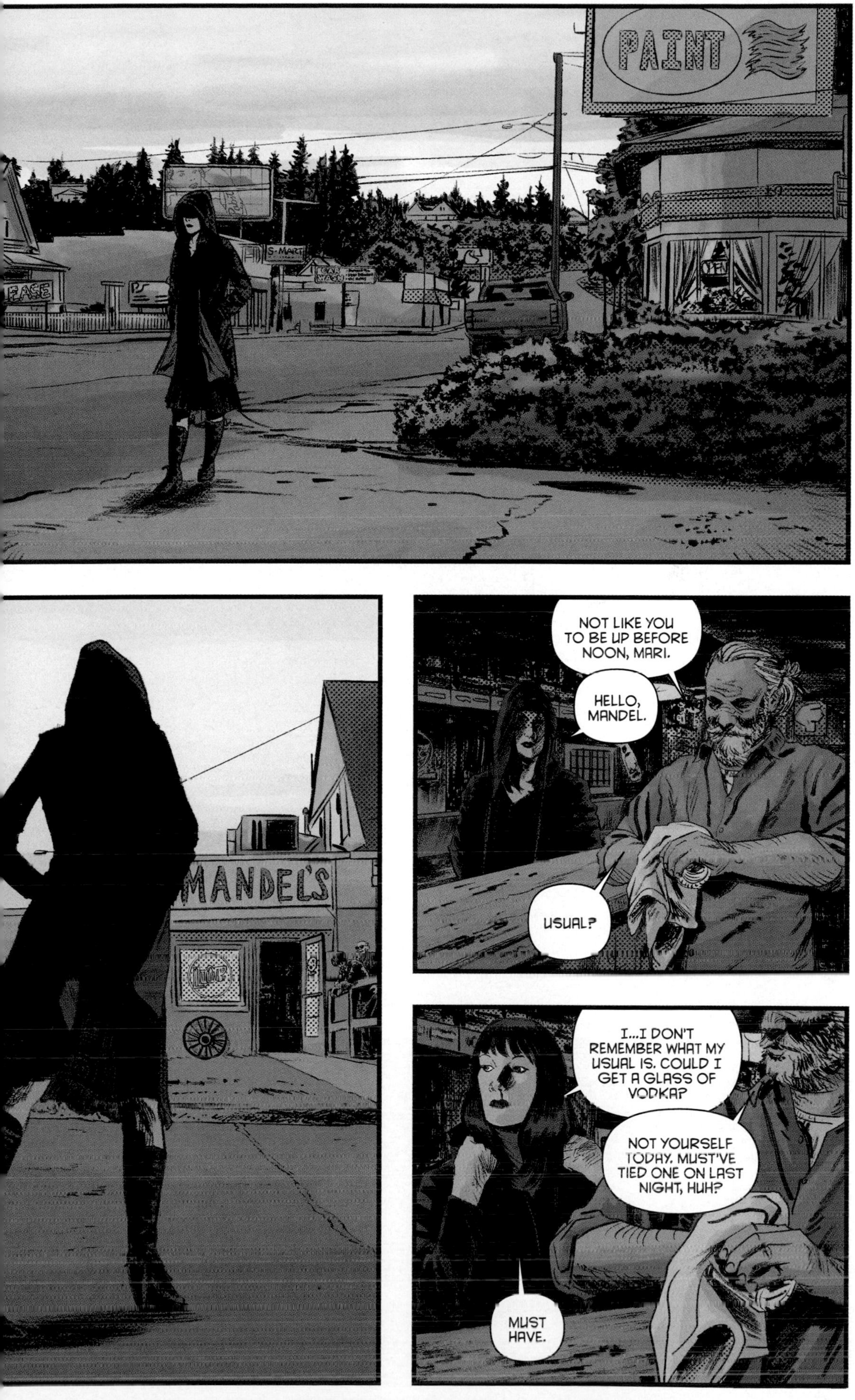
PAINT
S-MART
MANDEL'S
NOT LIKE YOU TO BE UP BEFORE NOON, MARI.
HELLO, MANDEL.
USUAL?
I...I DON'T REMEMBER WHAT MY USUAL IS. COULD I GET A GLASS OF VODKA?
NOT YOURSELF TODAY. MUST'VE TIED ONE ON LAST NIGHT, HUH?
MUST HAVE.

YOU HEAR ABOUT THAT MISERABLE BASTARD BENTON?

BENTON?

BENTON. THE PHARMACIST. ALWAYS LOOKS AT EVERYONE LIKE HE'S BETTER THAN THEM.

RIGHT. I KNOW THAT GUY. WHAT HAPPENED?

SOMEONE BOMBED THE ASSHOLE. ERIN WAS THERE. HE OPENED A BOX AND A GAS BOMB WENT OFF IN HIS FACE.

SHE'S FINE, BY THE WAY. IT WAS LIKE A JET OR SOMETHING. HUGE GODDAMN CLOUD OF GREEN GAS ALL OVER HIM.

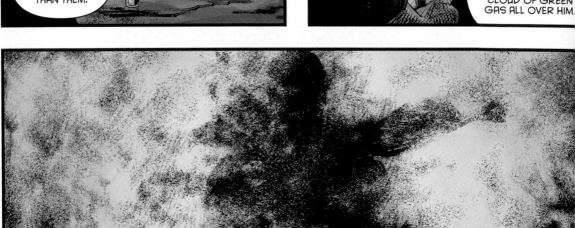

I'D SAY THAT IT MAKES YOU WONDER WHO HE PISSED OFF, BUT HE PISSED OFF PRETTY MUCH EVERYBODY.

ERIN SAID THE BOX WAS MARKED "FORMIC ETHERS" AND "BLACK TERROR", ONLY WITH LIKE NUMBERS AND AN "AT" SYMBOL? BUT THE BOX BURNED UP.

HELL OF A DAY. WHAT WITH THAT AND GARY PRESTON OFFING HIMSELF. DUNNO WHAT THIS TOWN IS COMING TO.

HOW BAD HAS IT GOT TO GET FOR ONE ASSHOLE TO GET BOMBED AND ONE GOOD GUY TO SET HIMSELF ON FIRE?

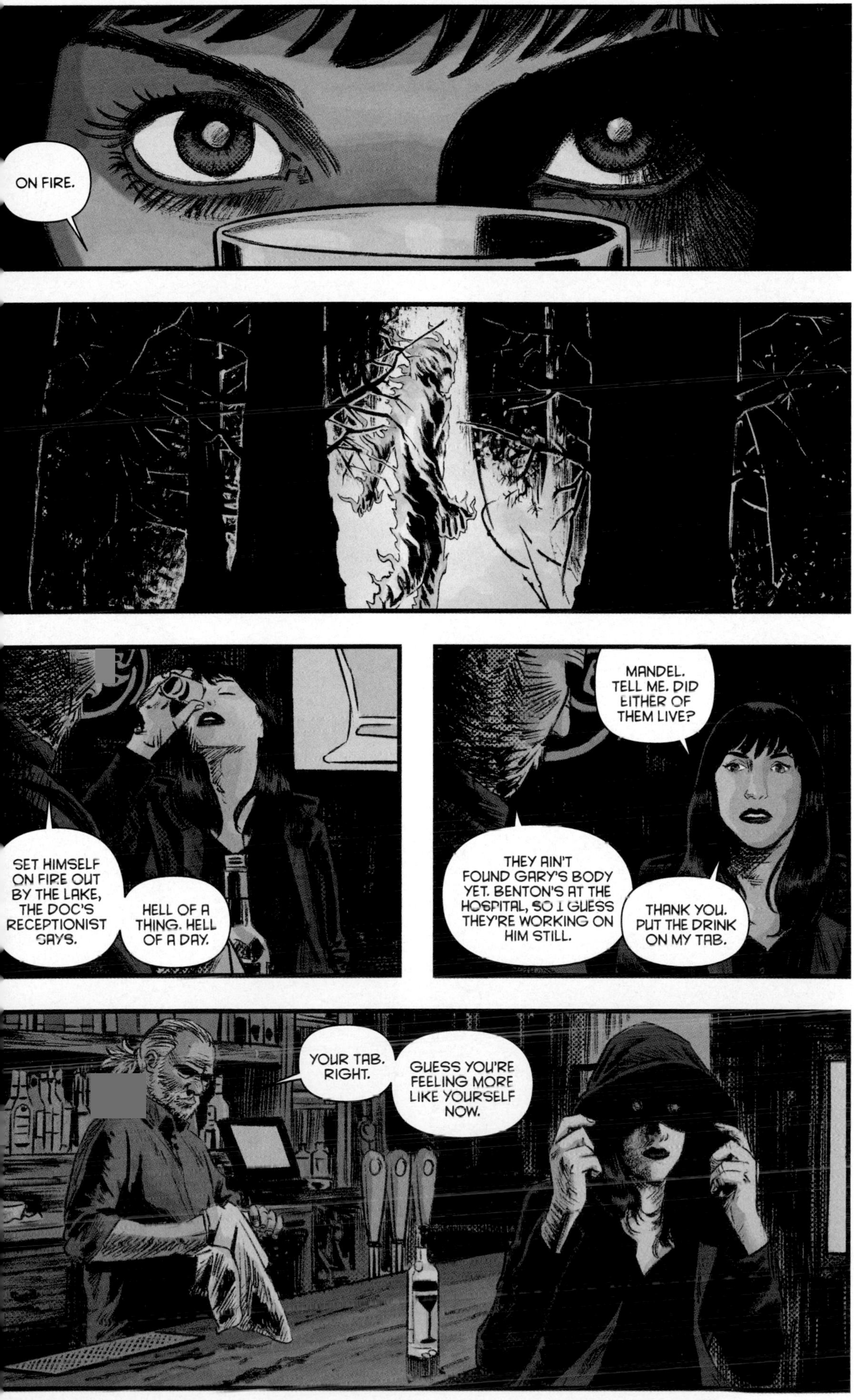
ON FIRE.
SET HIMSELF ON FIRE OUT BY THE LAKE, THE DOC'S RECEPTIONIST SAYS.
HELL OF A THING. HELL OF A DAY.
MANDEL. TELL ME. DID EITHER OF THEM LIVE?
THEY AIN'T FOUND GARY'S BODY YET. BENTON'S AT THE HOSPITAL, SO I GUESS THEY'RE WORKING ON HIM STILL.
THANK YOU. PUT THE DRINK ON MY TAB.
YOUR TAB. RIGHT.
GUESS YOU'RE FEELING MORE LIKE YOURSELF NOW.

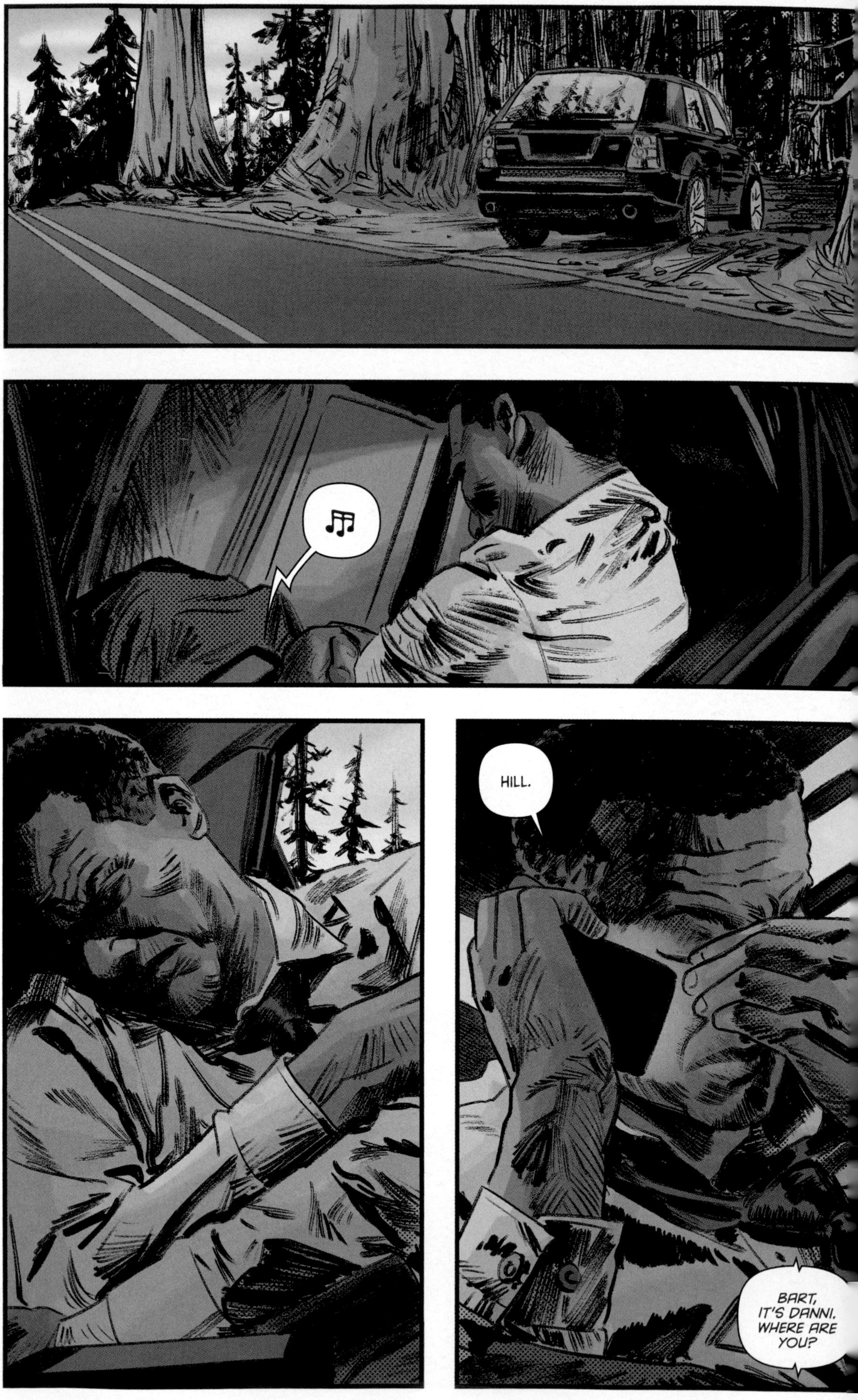
♬
HILL.
BART, IT'S DANNI. WHERE ARE YOU?

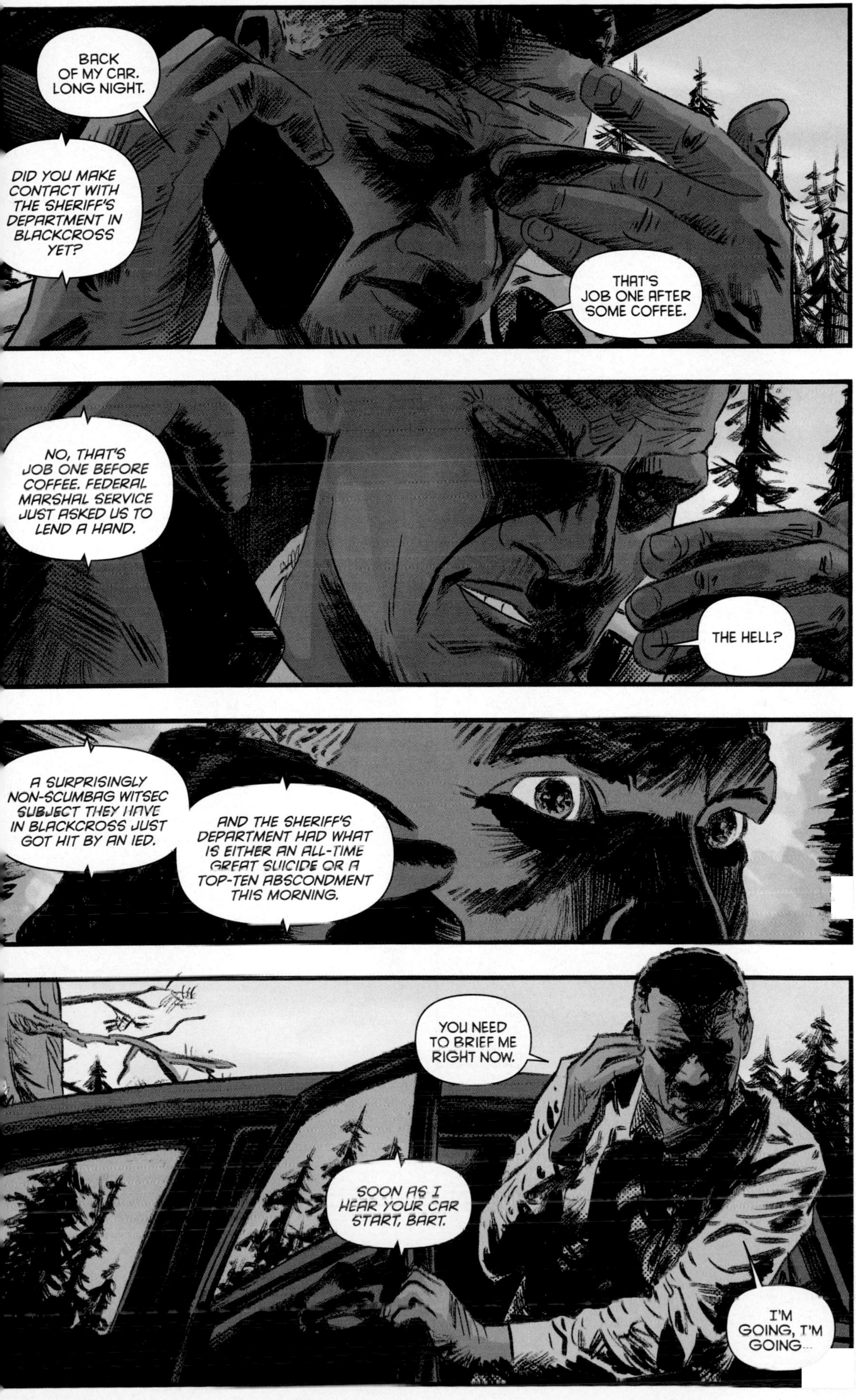
BACK OF MY CAR. LONG NIGHT.
DID YOU MAKE CONTACT WITH THE SHERIFF'S DEPARTMENT IN BLACKCROSS YET?
THAT'S JOB ONE AFTER SOME COFFEE.
NO, THAT'S JOB ONE BEFORE COFFEE. FEDERAL MARSHAL SERVICE JUST ASKED US TO LEND A HAND.
THE HELL?
A SURPRISINGLY NON-SCUMBAG WITSEC SUBJECT THEY HAVE IN BLACKCROSS JUST GOT HIT BY AN IED.
AND THE SHERIFF'S DEPARTMENT HAD WHAT IS EITHER AN ALL-TIME GREAT SUICIDE OR A TOP-TEN ABSCONDMENT THIS MORNING.
YOU NEED TO BRIEF ME RIGHT NOW.
SOON AS I HEAR YOUR CAR START, BART.
I'M GOING, I'M GOING...

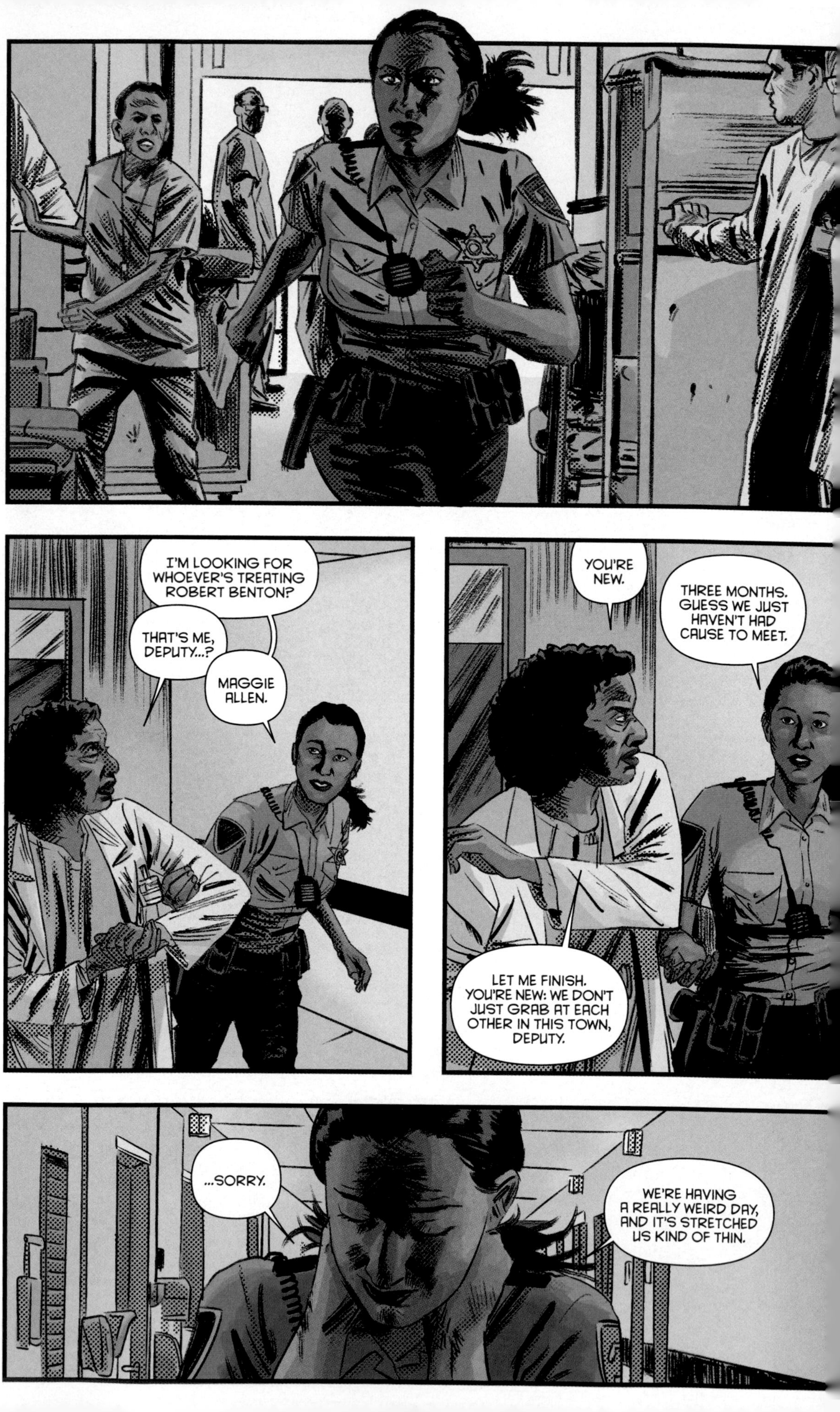
I'M LOOKING FOR WHOEVER'S TREATING ROBERT BENTON?
THAT'S ME, DEPUTY...?
MAGGIE ALLEN.
YOU'RE NEW.
THREE MONTHS. GUESS WE JUST HAVEN'T HAD CAUSE TO MEET.
LET ME FINISH. YOU'RE NEW: WE DON'T JUST GRAB AT EACH OTHER IN THIS TOWN, DEPUTY.
...SORRY.
WE'RE HAVING A REALLY WEIRD DAY, AND IT'S STRETCHED US KIND OF THIN.

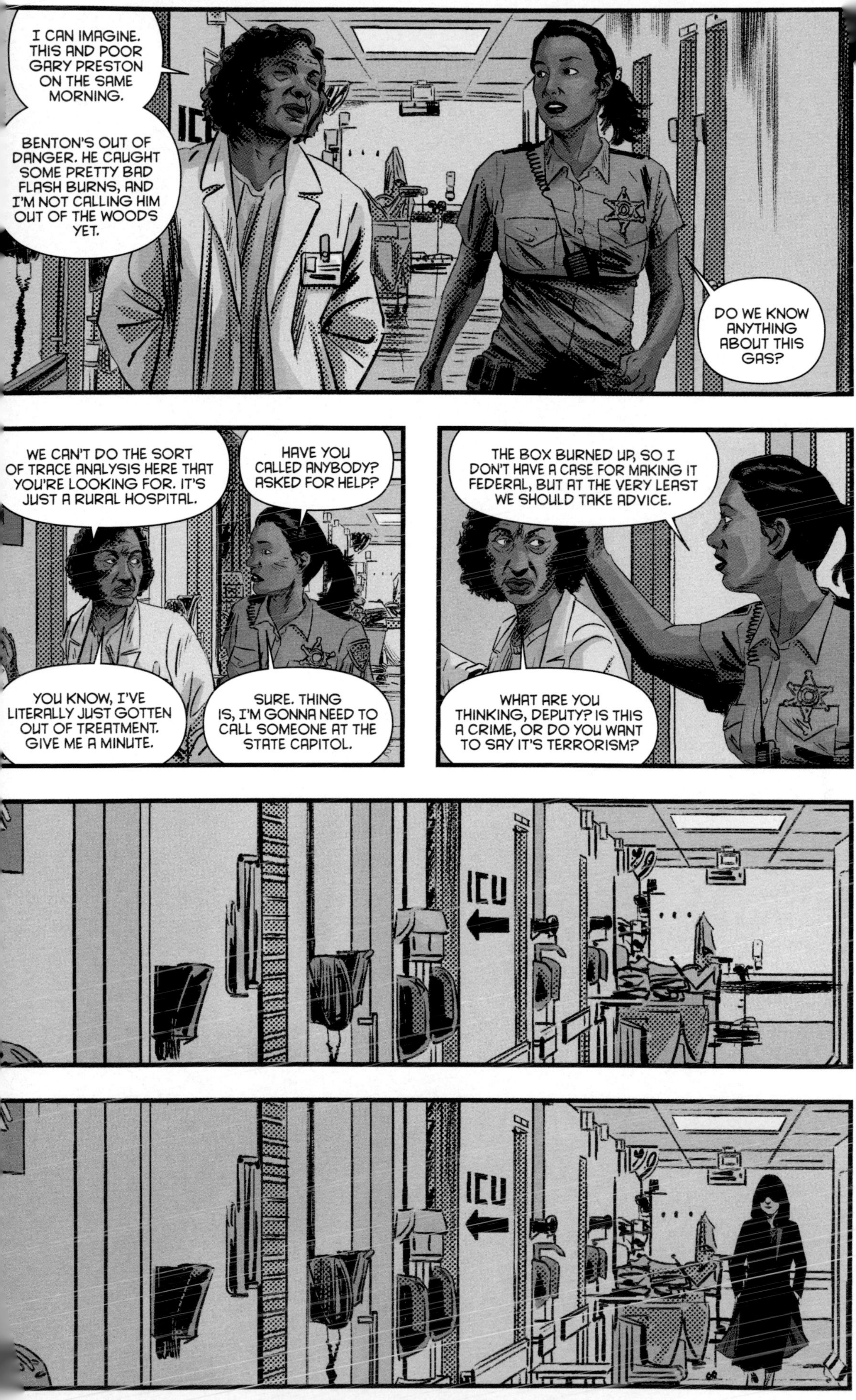
I CAN IMAGINE. THIS AND POOR GARY PRESTON ON THE SAME MORNING.
BENTON'S OUT OF DANGER. HE CAUGHT SOME PRETTY BAD FLASH BURNS, AND I'M NOT CALLING HIM OUT OF THE WOODS YET.
ICU
DO WE KNOW ANYTHING ABOUT THIS GAS?
WE CAN'T DO THE SORT OF TRACE ANALYSIS HERE THAT YOU'RE LOOKING FOR. IT'S JUST A RURAL HOSPITAL.
HAVE YOU CALLED ANYBODY? ASKED FOR HELP?
YOU KNOW, I'VE LITERALLY JUST GOTTEN OUT OF TREATMENT. GIVE ME A MINUTE.
SURE. THING IS, I'M GONNA NEED TO CALL SOMEONE AT THE STATE CAPITOL.
THE BOX BURNED UP, SO I DON'T HAVE A CASE FOR MAKING IT FEDERAL, BUT AT THE VERY LEAST WE SHOULD TAKE ADVICE.
WHAT ARE YOU THINKING, DEPUTY? IS THIS A CRIME, OR DO YOU WANT TO SAY IT'S TERRORISM?
ICU
ICU

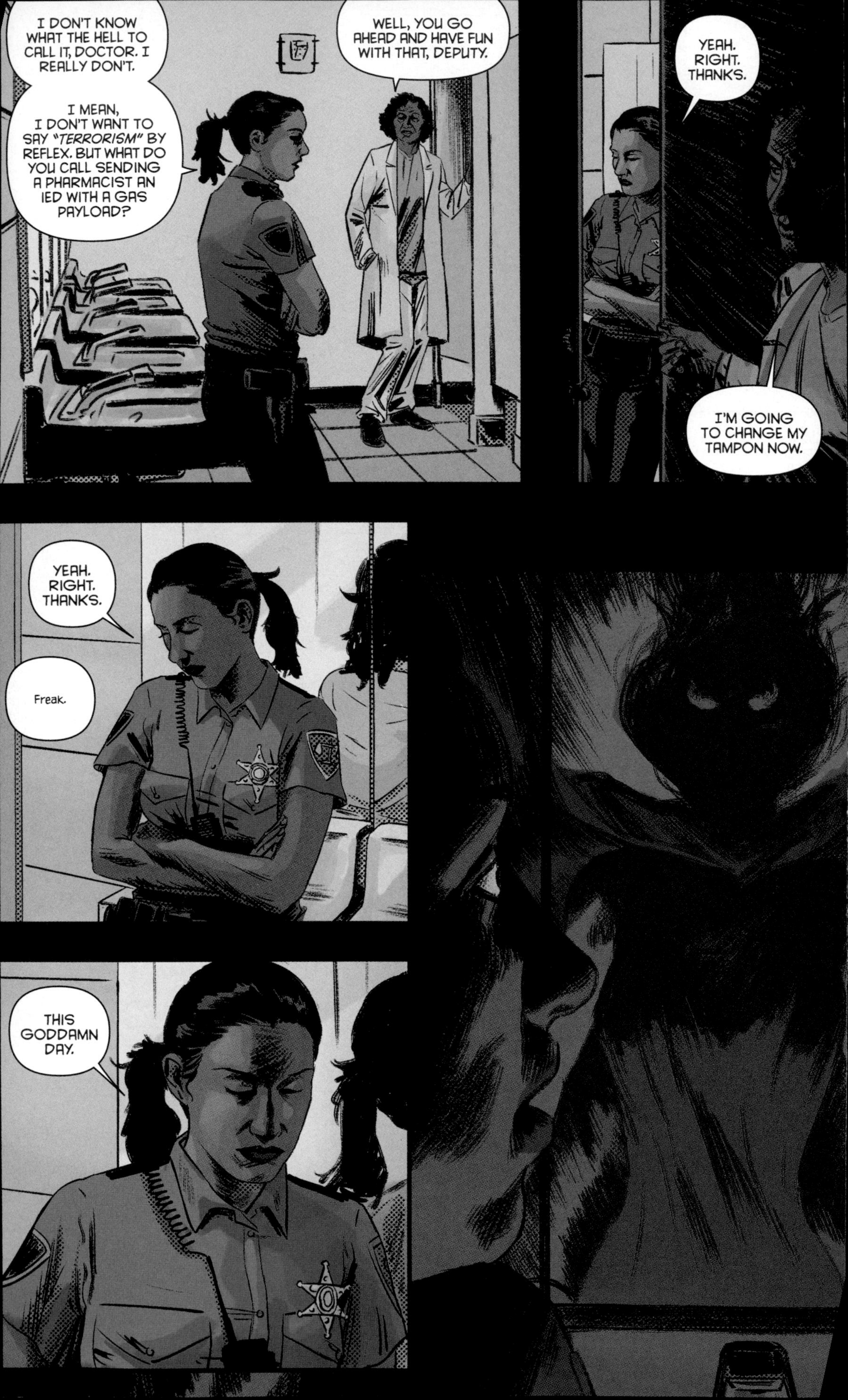
I DON'T KNOW WHAT THE HELL TO CALL IT, DOCTOR. I REALLY DON'T.
I MEAN, I DON'T WANT TO SAY "TERRORISM" BY REFLEX. BUT WHAT DO YOU CALL SENDING A PHARMACIST AN IED WITH A GAS PAYLOAD?
WELL, YOU GO AHEAD AND HAVE FUN WITH THAT, DEPUTY.
YEAH. RIGHT. THANKS.
I'M GOING TO CHANGE MY TAMPON NOW.
YEAH. RIGHT. THANKS.
Freak.
THIS GODDAMN DAY.

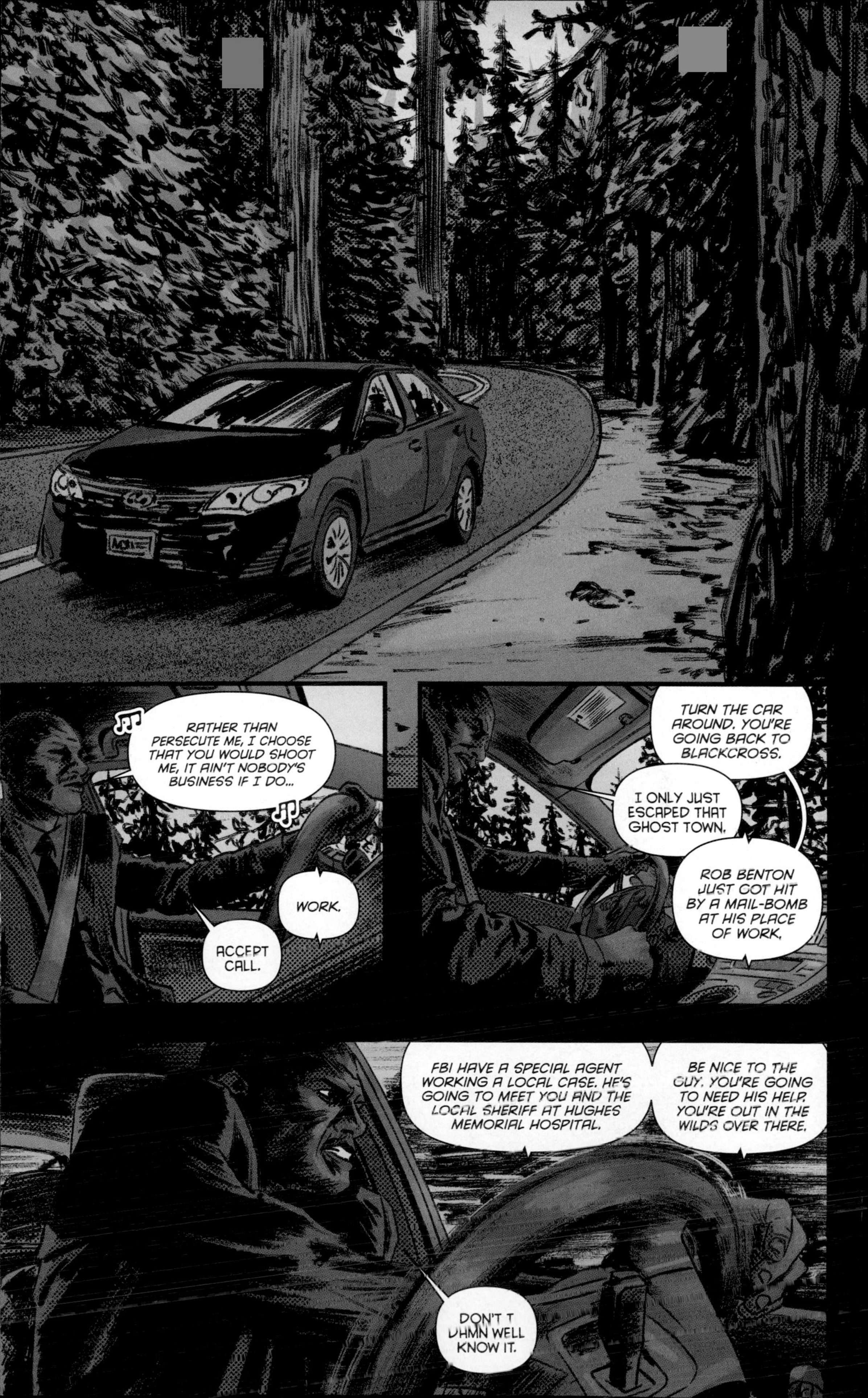
RATHER THAN PERSECUTE ME, I CHOOSE THAT YOU WOULD SHOOT ME, IT AIN'T NOBODY'S BUSINESS IF I DO...
WORK.
ACCEPT CALL.
TURN THE CAR AROUND. YOU'RE GOING BACK TO BLACKCROSS.
I ONLY JUST ESCAPED THAT GHOST TOWN.
ROB BENTON JUST GOT HIT BY A MAIL-BOMB AT HIS PLACE OF WORK.
FBI HAVE A SPECIAL AGENT WORKING A LOCAL CASE. HE'S GOING TO MEET YOU AND THE LOCAL SHERIFF AT HUGHES MEMORIAL HOSPITAL.
BE NICE TO THE GUY. YOU'RE GOING TO NEED HIS HELP. YOU'RE OUT IN THE WILDS OVER THERE.
DON'T I DAMN WELL KNOW IT.

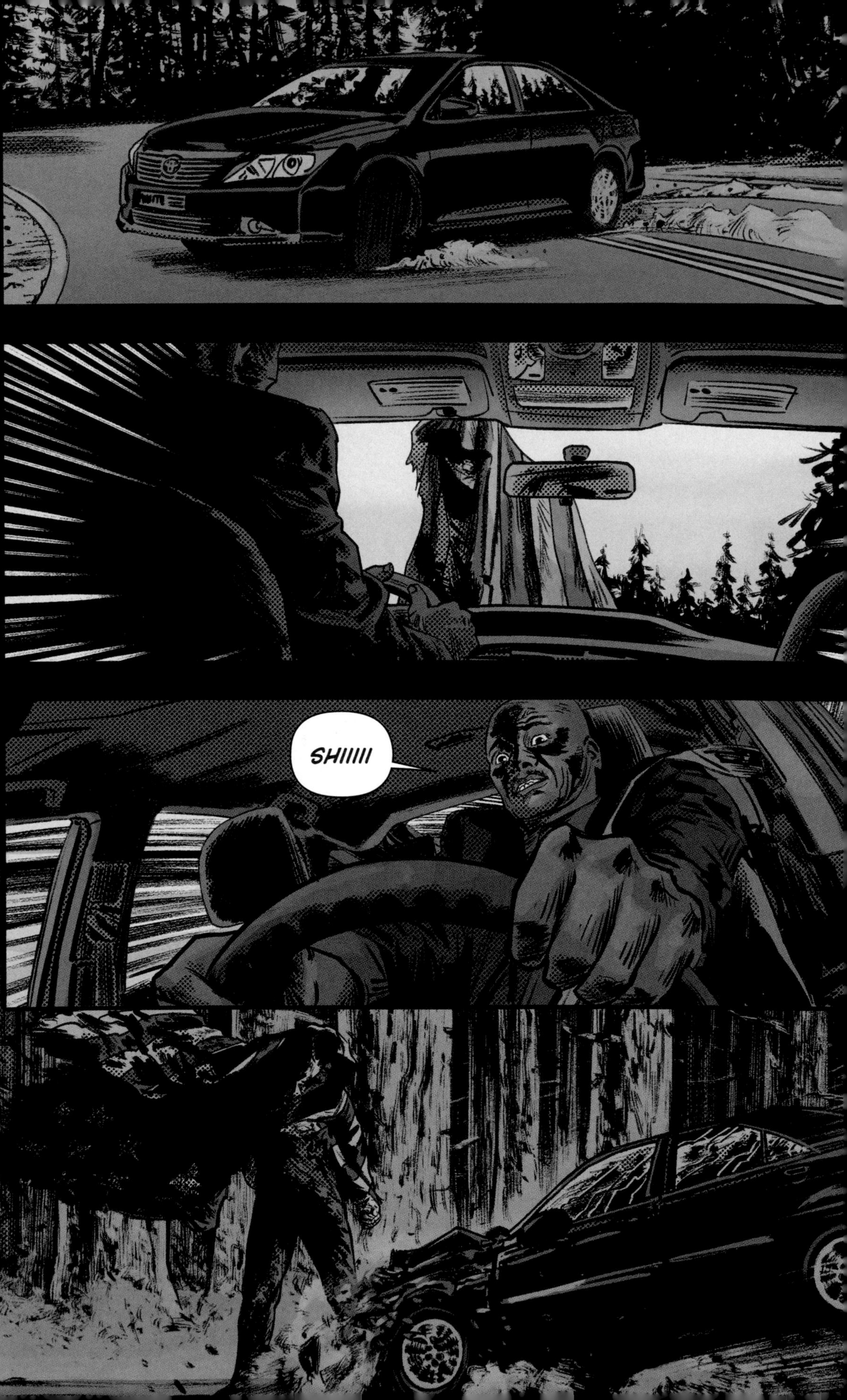
SHIIIII

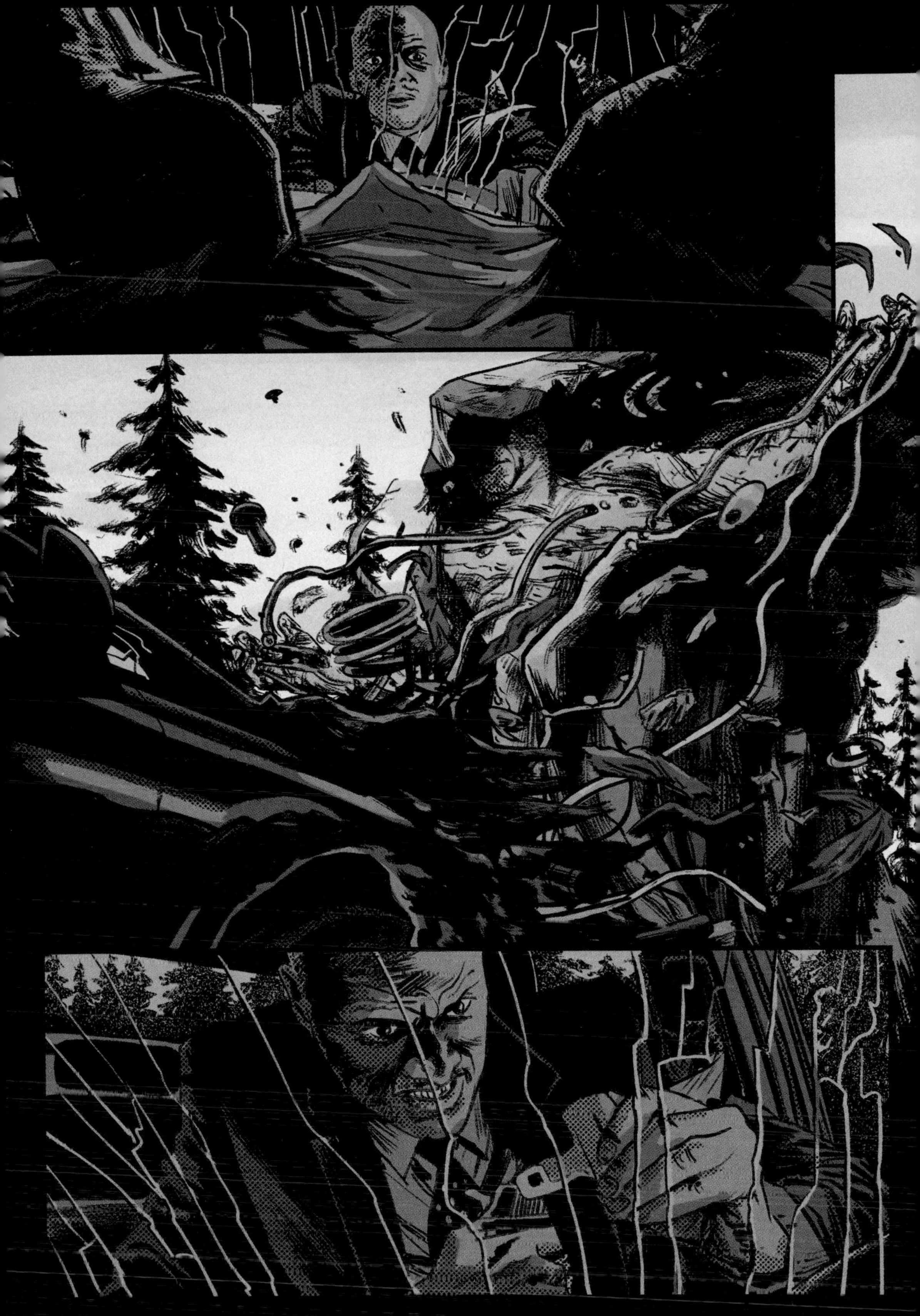

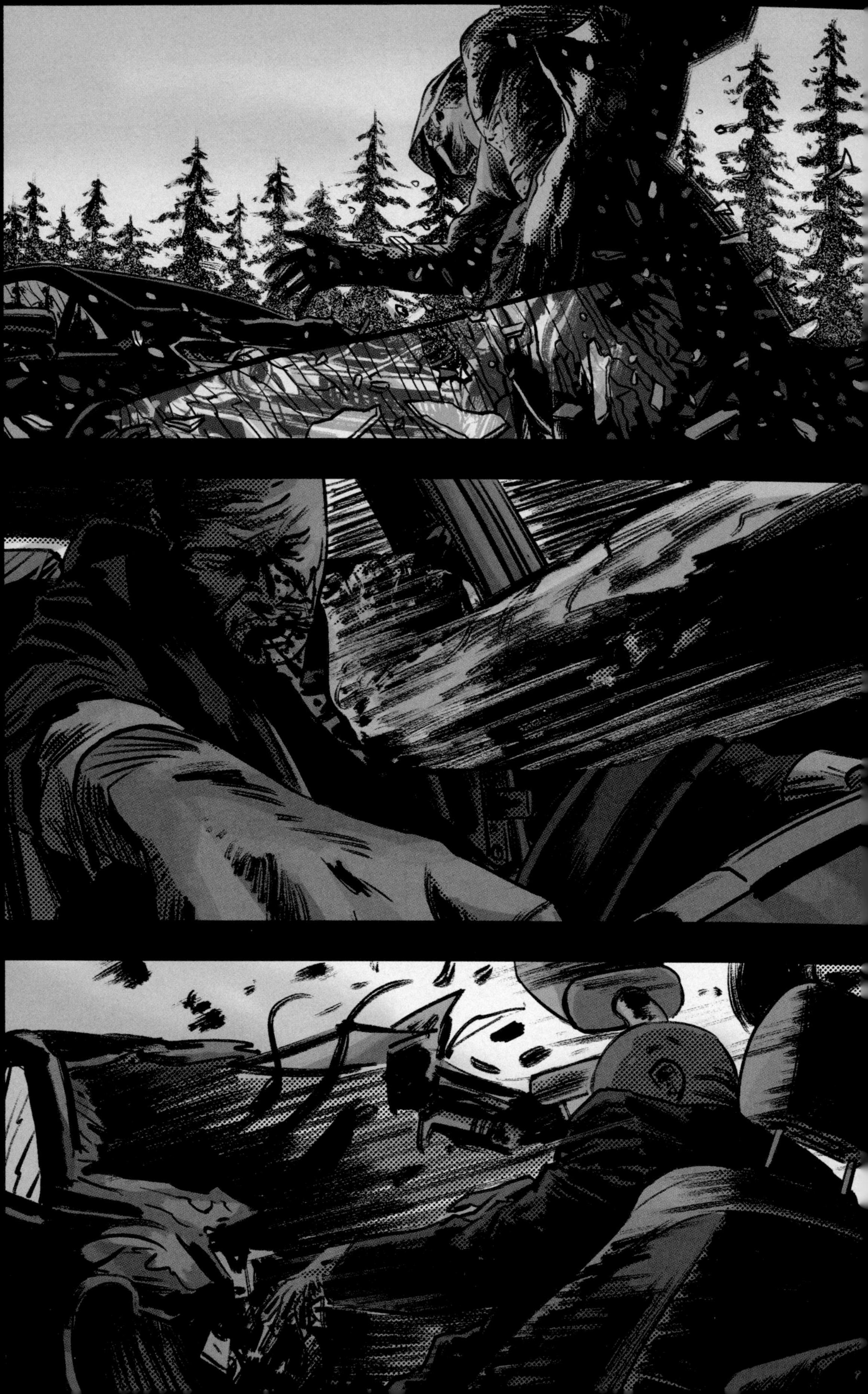

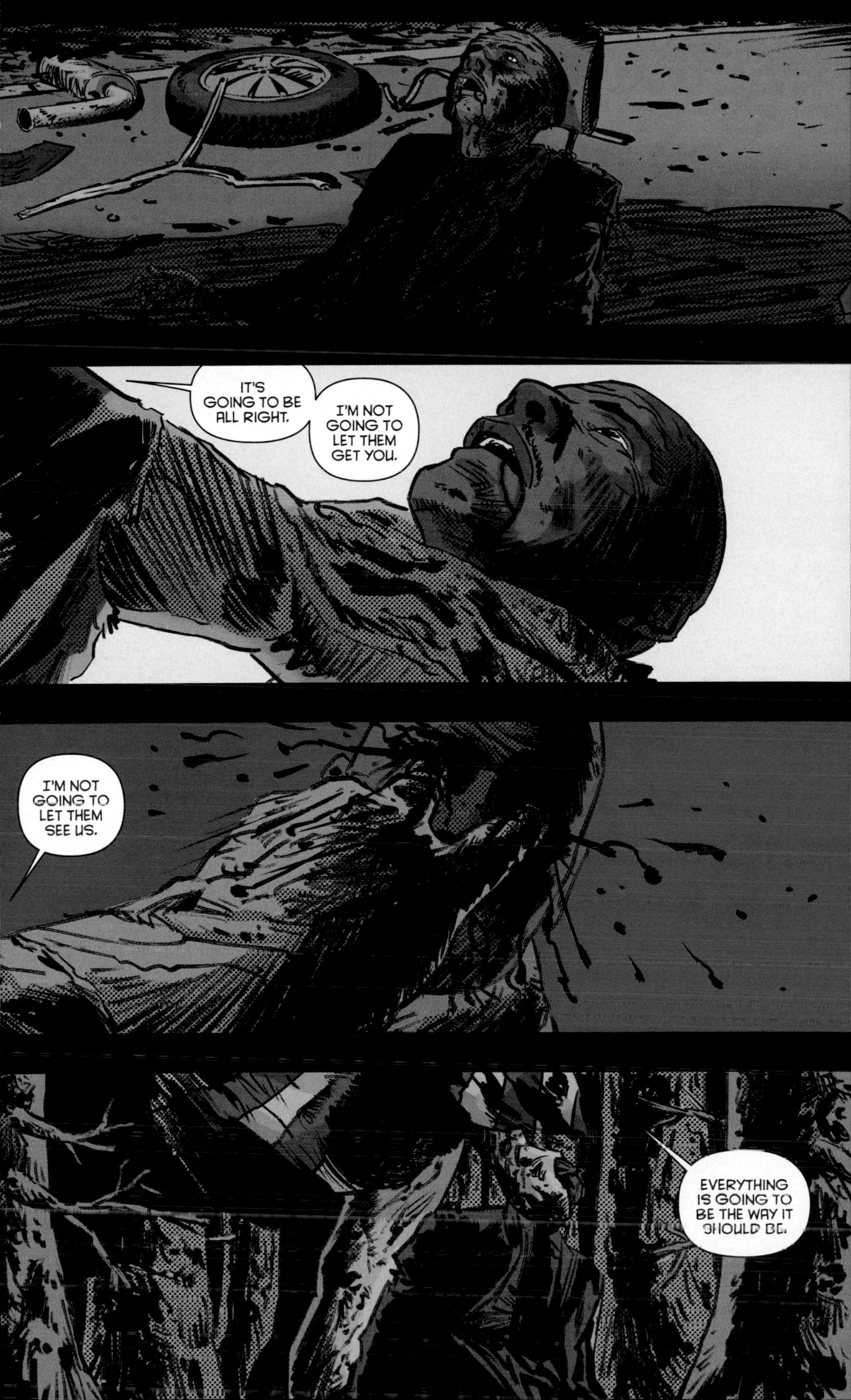
IT'S GOING TO BE ALL RIGHT.
I'M NOT GOING TO LET THEM GET YOU.
I'M NOT GOING TO LET THEM SEE US.
EVERYTHING IS GOING TO BE THE WAY IT SHOULD BE.

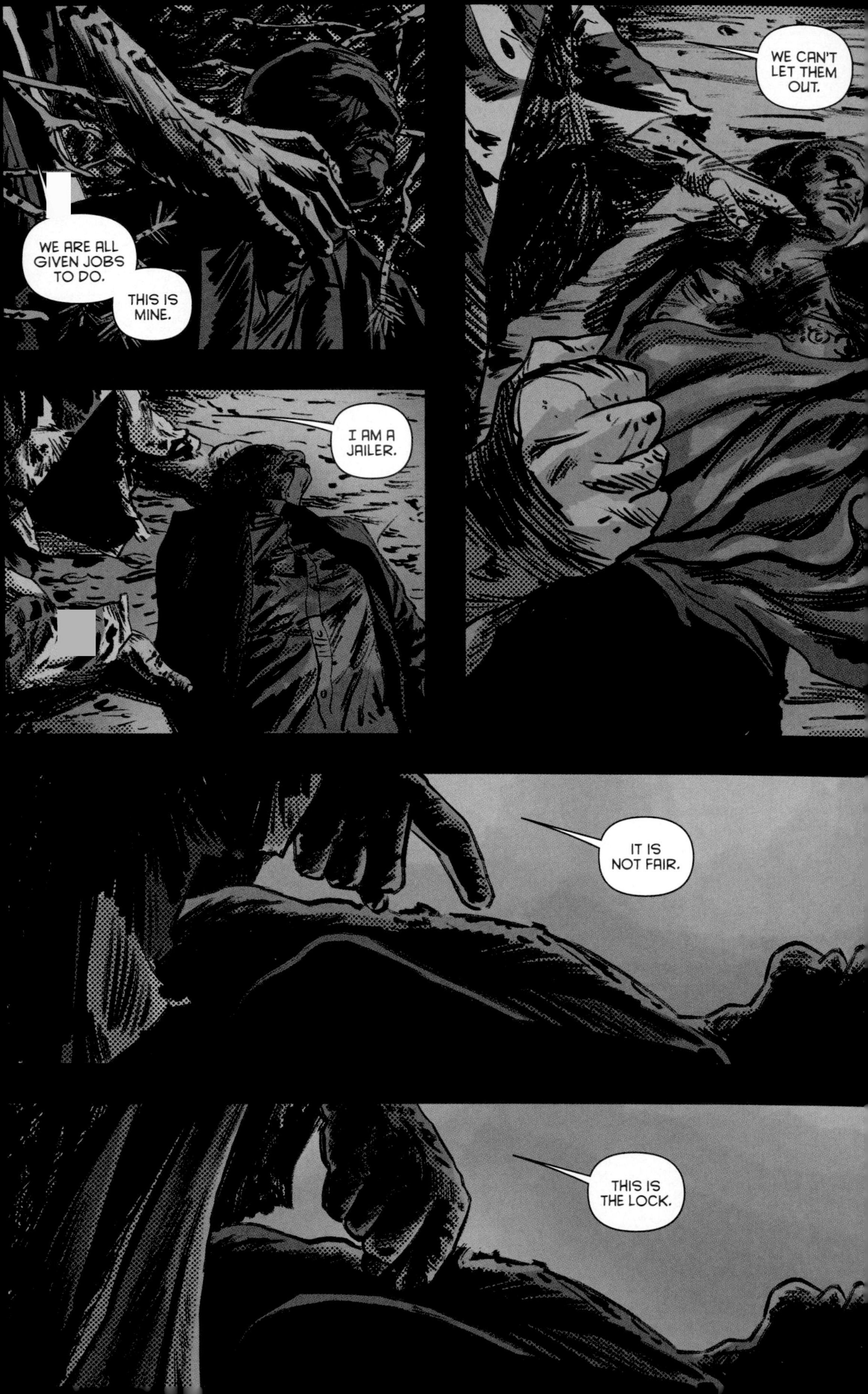
WE ARE ALL GIVEN JOBS TO DO.
THIS IS MINE.
I AM A JAILER.
WE CAN'T LET THEM OUT.
IT IS NOT FAIR.
THIS IS THE LOCK.

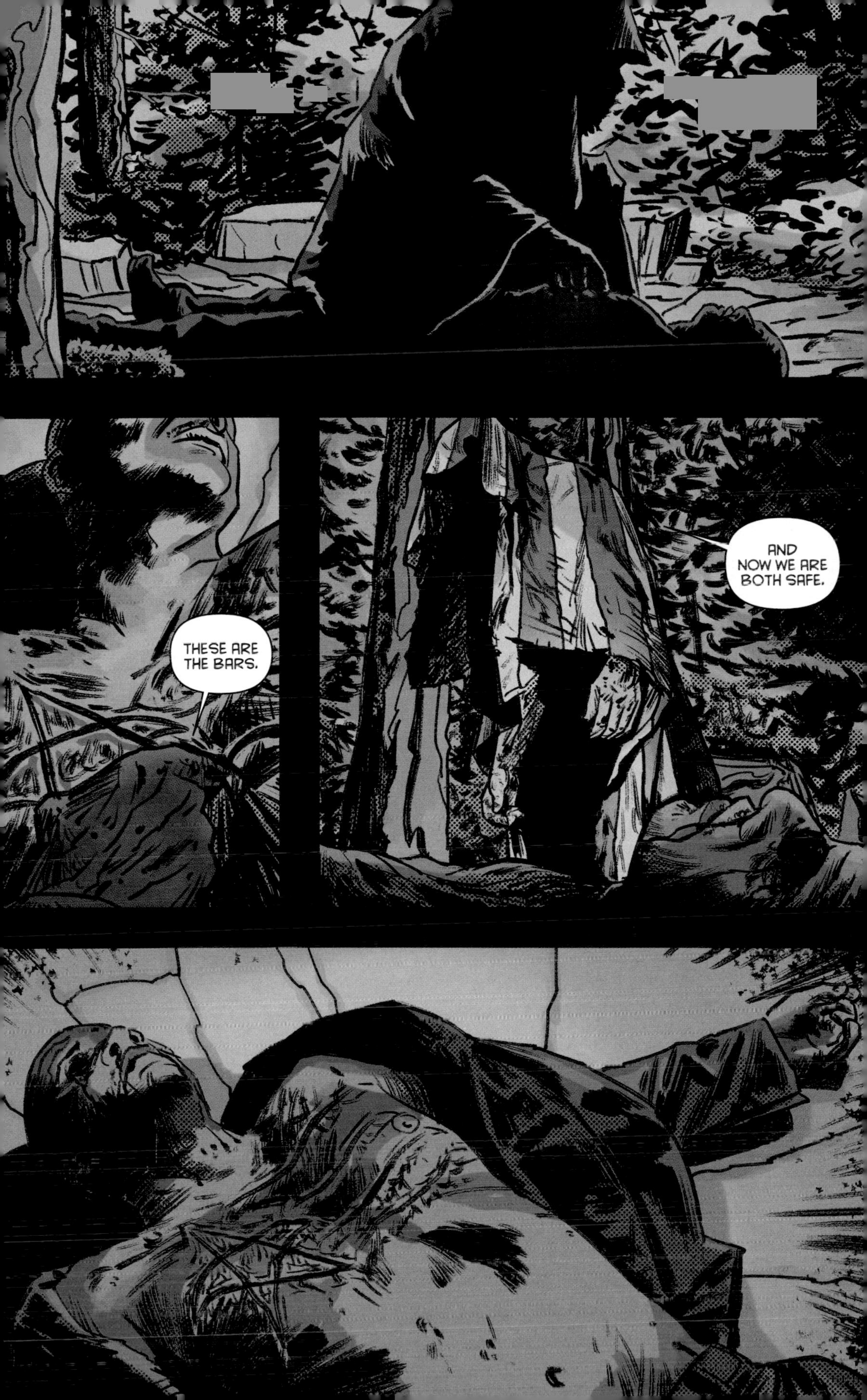
THESE ARE THE BARS.
AND NOW WE ARE BOTH SAFE.

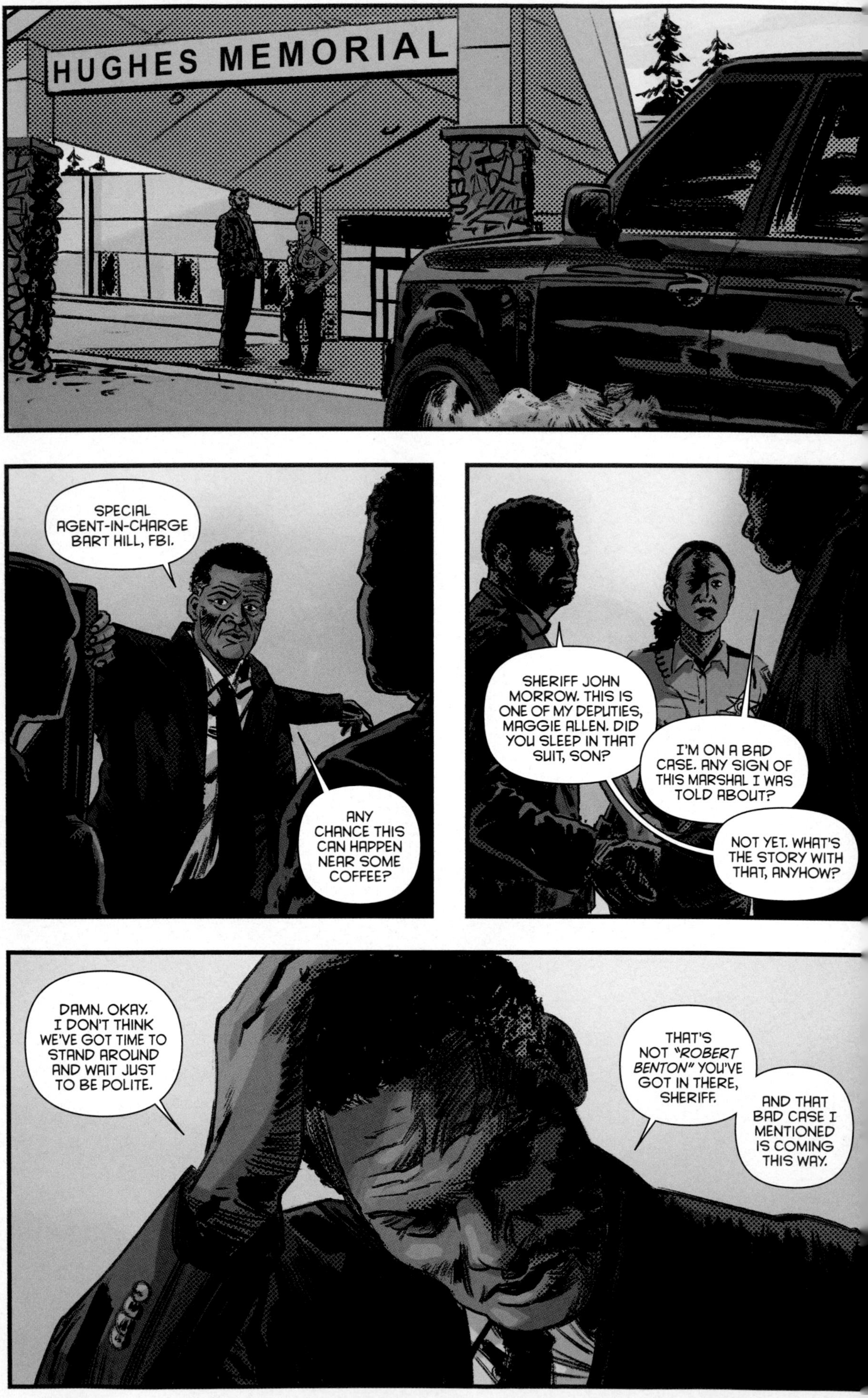
HUGHES MEMORIAL
SPECIAL AGENT-IN-CHARGE BART HILL, FBI.
ANY CHANCE THIS CAN HAPPEN NEAR SOME COFFEE?
SHERIFF JOHN MORROW. THIS IS ONE OF MY DEPUTIES, MAGGIE ALLEN. DID YOU SLEEP IN THAT SUIT, SON?
I'M ON A BAD CASE. ANY SIGN OF THIS MARSHAL I WAS TOLD ABOUT?
NOT YET. WHAT'S THE STORY WITH THAT, ANYHOW?
DAMN. OKAY. I DON'T THINK WE'VE GOT TIME TO STAND AROUND AND WAIT JUST TO BE POLITE.
THAT'S NOT *"ROBERT BENTON"* YOU'VE GOT IN THERE, SHERIFF.
AND THAT BAD CASE I MENTIONED IS COMING THIS WAY.

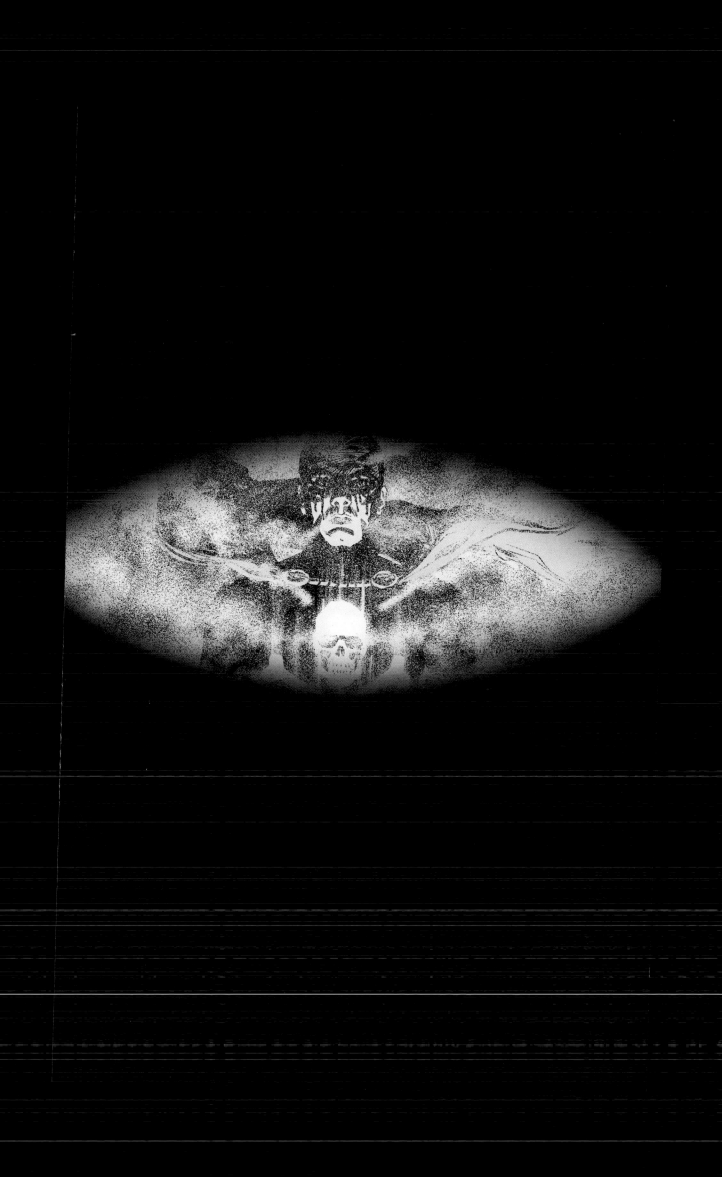

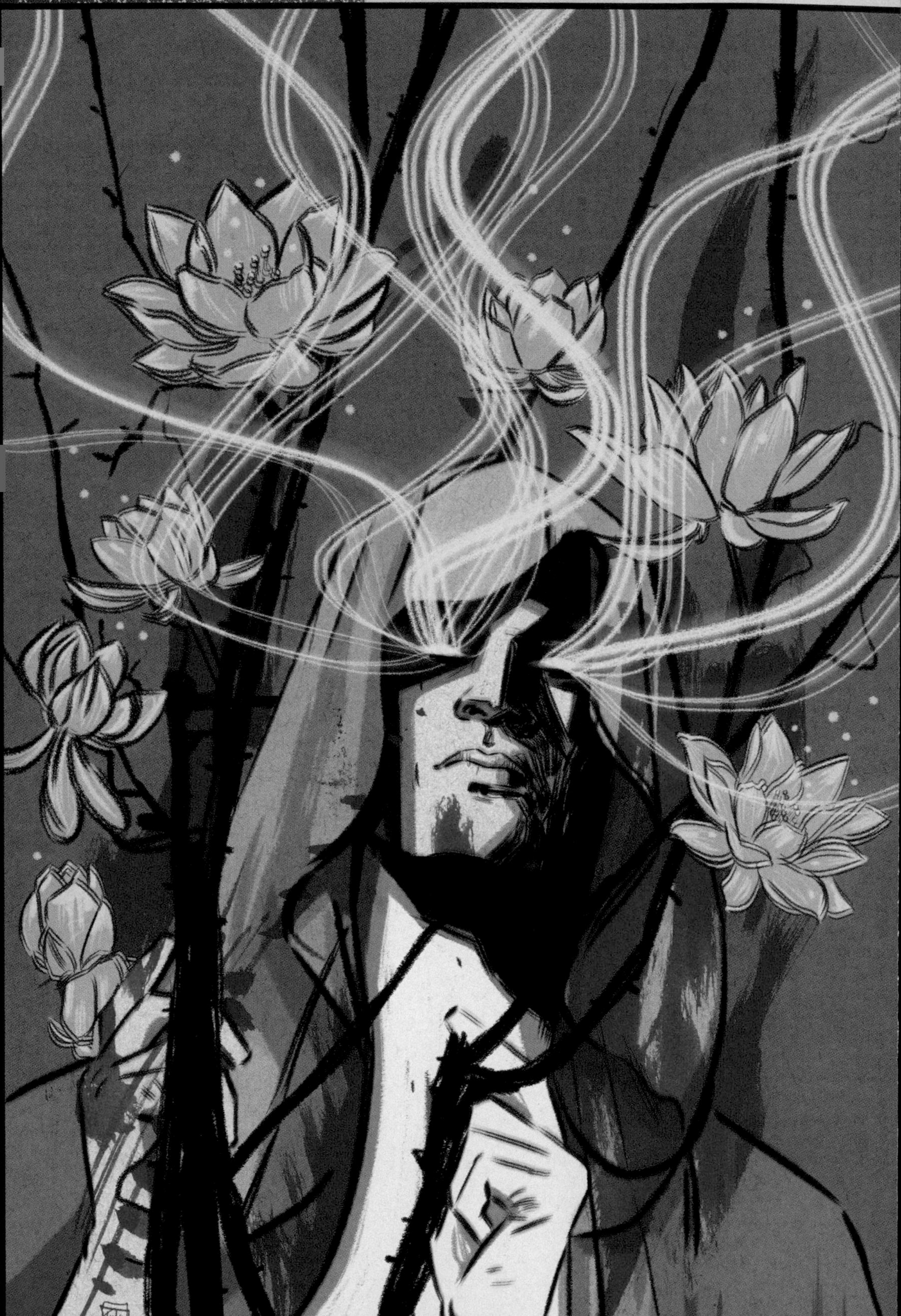

ISSUE #3 COVER BY **TULA LOTAY**

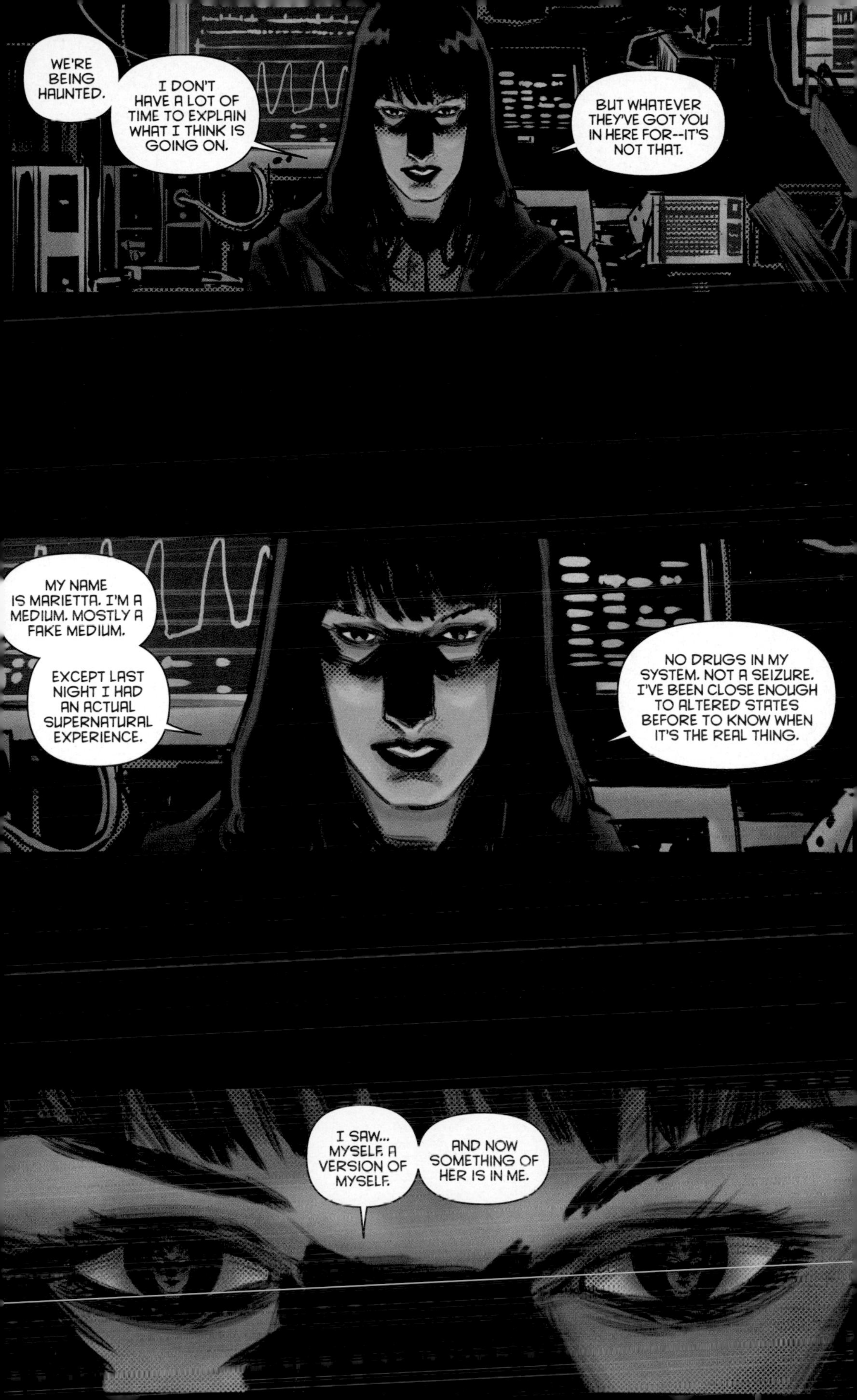
WE'RE BEING HAUNTED.
I DON'T HAVE A LOT OF TIME TO EXPLAIN WHAT I THINK IS GOING ON.
BUT WHATEVER THEY'VE GOT YOU IN HERE FOR--IT'S NOT THAT.
MY NAME IS MARIETTA. I'M A MEDIUM. MOSTLY A FAKE MEDIUM.
EXCEPT LAST NIGHT I HAD AN ACTUAL SUPERNATURAL EXPERIENCE.
NO DRUGS IN MY SYSTEM. NOT A SEIZURE. I'VE BEEN CLOSE ENOUGH TO ALTERED STATES BEFORE TO KNOW WHEN IT'S THE REAL THING.
I SAW... MYSELF. A VERSION OF MYSELF.
AND NOW SOMETHING OF HER IS IN ME.

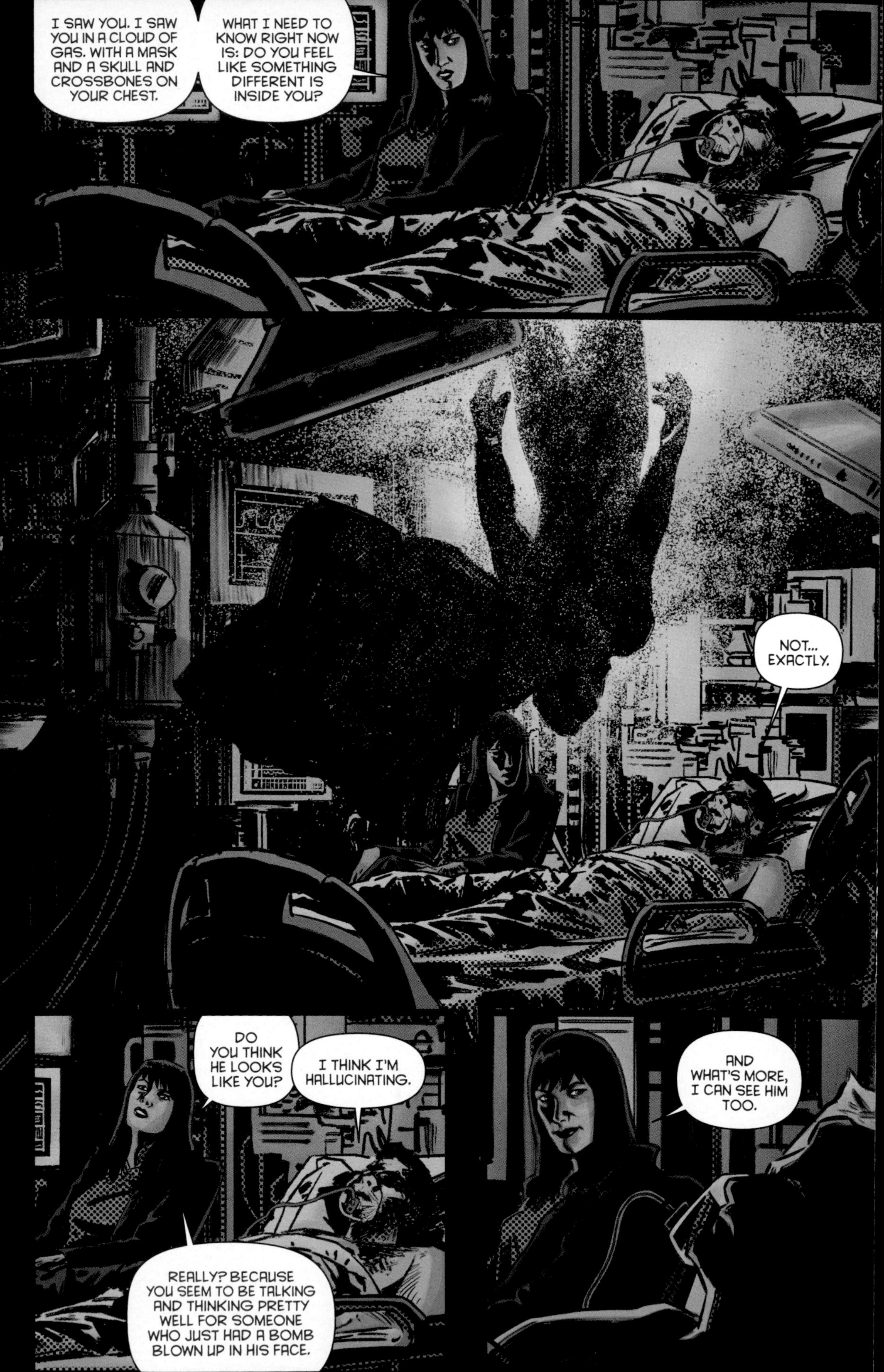
I SAW YOU. I SAW YOU IN A CLOUD OF GAS. WITH A MASK AND A SKULL AND CROSSBONES ON YOUR CHEST.
WHAT I NEED TO KNOW RIGHT NOW IS: DO YOU FEEL LIKE SOMETHING DIFFERENT IS INSIDE YOU?
NOT... EXACTLY.
DO YOU THINK HE LOOKS LIKE YOU?
I THINK I'M HALLUCINATING.
REALLY? BECAUSE YOU SEEM TO BE TALKING AND THINKING PRETTY WELL FOR SOMEONE WHO JUST HAD A BOMB BLOWN UP IN HIS FACE.
AND WHAT'S MORE, I CAN SEE HIM TOO.

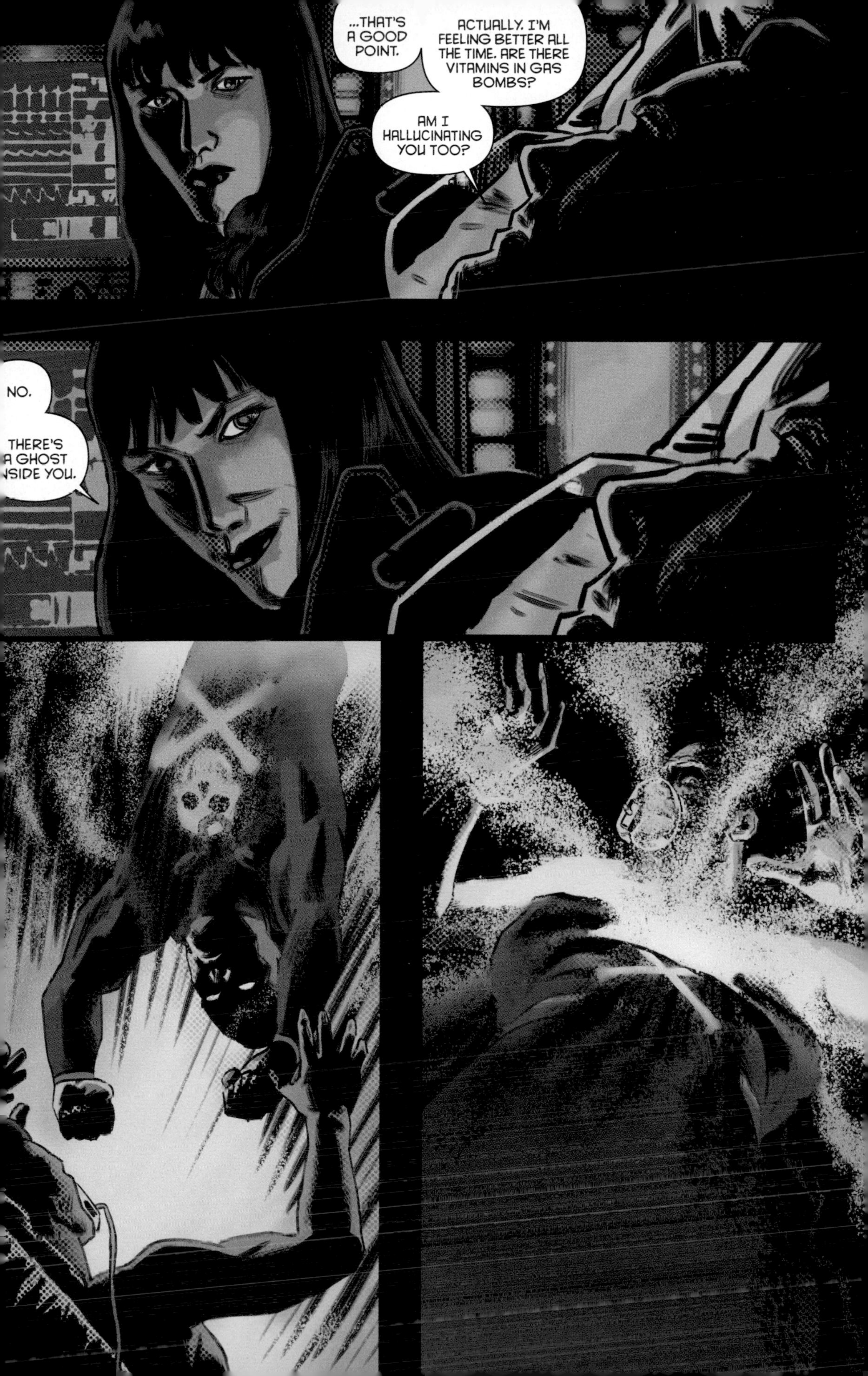
...THAT'S A GOOD POINT.
ACTUALLY. I'M FEELING BETTER ALL THE TIME. ARE THERE VITAMINS IN GAS BOMBS?
AM I HALLUCINATING YOU TOO?
NO.
THERE'S A GHOST NSIDE YOU.

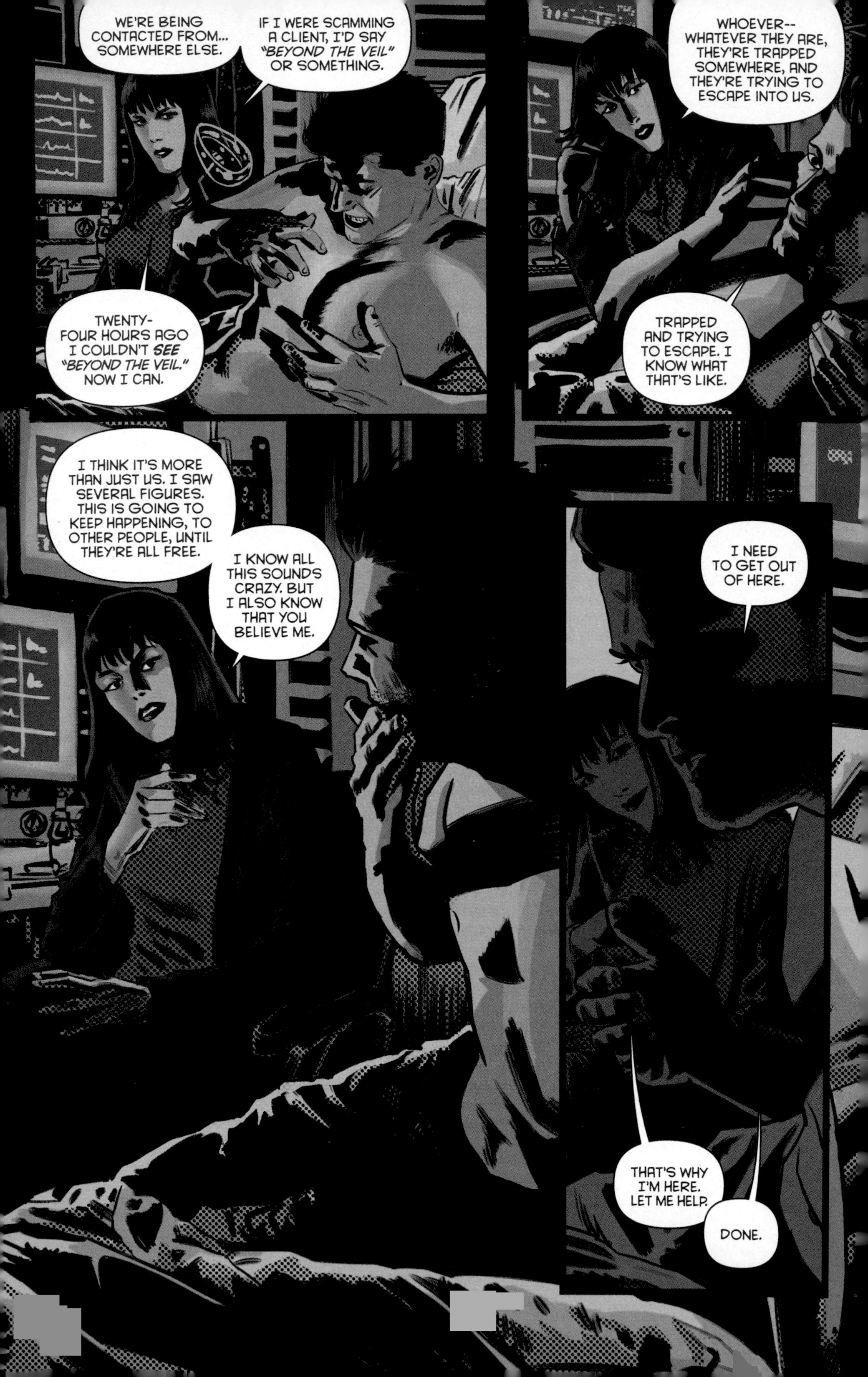
WE'RE BEING CONTACTED FROM... SOMEWHERE ELSE.
IF I WERE SCAMMING A CLIENT, I'D SAY "BEYOND THE VEIL" OR SOMETHING.
TWENTY-FOUR HOURS AGO I COULDN'T SEE "BEYOND THE VEIL." NOW I CAN.
WHOEVER--WHATEVER THEY ARE, THEY'RE TRAPPED SOMEWHERE, AND THEY'RE TRYING TO ESCAPE INTO US.
TRAPPED AND TRYING TO ESCAPE. I KNOW WHAT THAT'S LIKE.
I THINK IT'S MORE THAN JUST US. I SAW SEVERAL FIGURES. THIS IS GOING TO KEEP HAPPENING, TO OTHER PEOPLE, UNTIL THEY'RE ALL FREE.
I KNOW ALL THIS SOUNDS CRAZY. BUT I ALSO KNOW THAT YOU BELIEVE ME.
I NEED TO GET OUT OF HERE.
THAT'S WHY I'M HERE. LET ME HELP.
DONE.

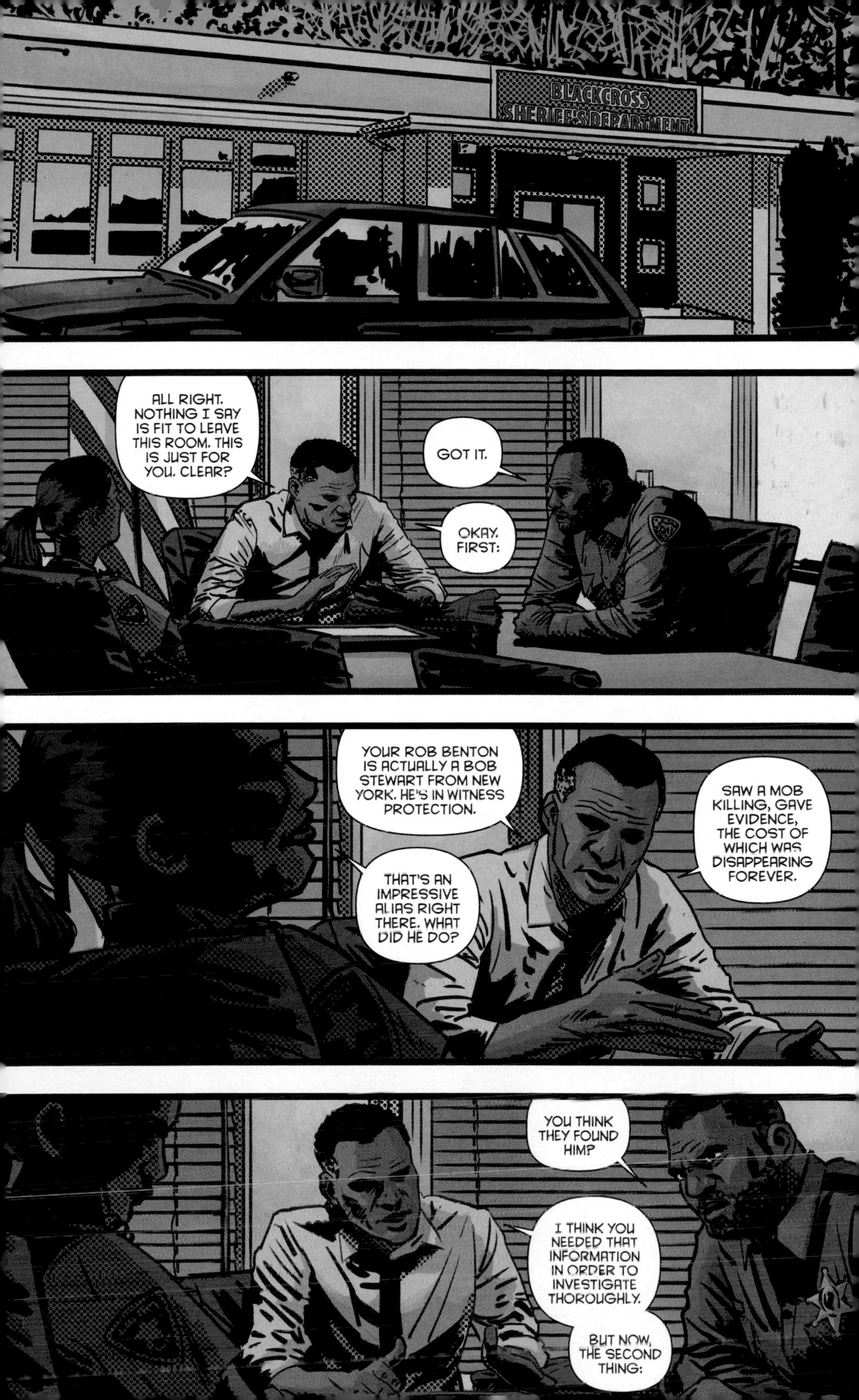
BLACKCROSS SHERIFF'S DEPARTMENT
ALL RIGHT. NOTHING I SAY IS FIT TO LEAVE THIS ROOM. THIS IS JUST FOR YOU. CLEAR?
GOT IT.
OKAY. FIRST:
YOUR ROB BENTON IS ACTUALLY A BOB STEWART FROM NEW YORK. HE'S IN WITNESS PROTECTION.
THAT'S AN IMPRESSIVE ALIAS RIGHT THERE. WHAT DID HE DO?
SAW A MOB KILLING, GAVE EVIDENCE, THE COST OF WHICH WAS DISAPPEARING FOREVER.
YOU THINK THEY FOUND HIM?
I THINK YOU NEEDED THAT INFORMATION IN ORDER TO INVESTIGATE THOROUGHLY.
BUT NOW, THE SECOND THING:

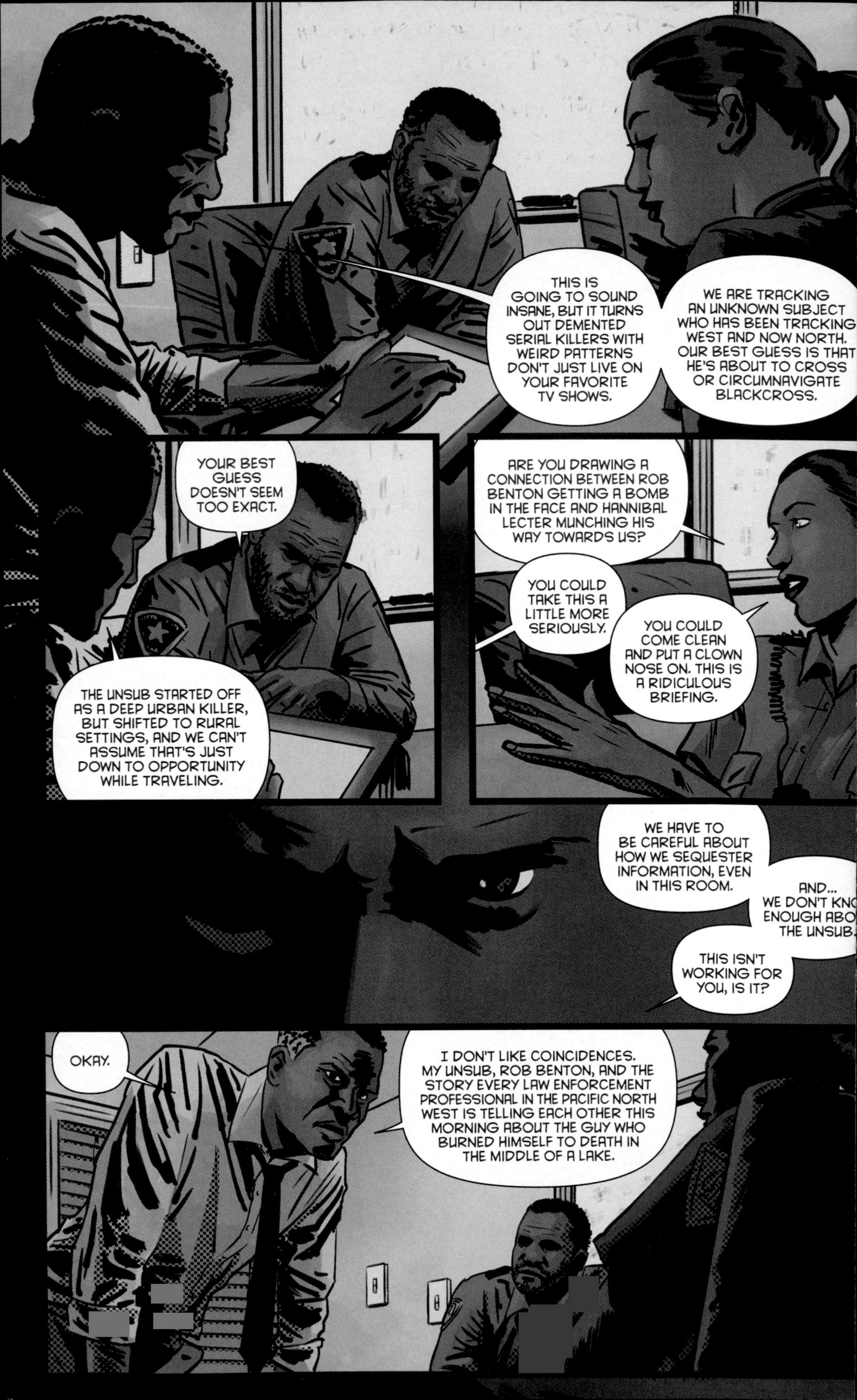
THIS IS GOING TO SOUND INSANE, BUT IT TURNS OUT DEMENTED SERIAL KILLERS WITH WEIRD PATTERNS DON'T JUST LIVE ON YOUR FAVORITE TV SHOWS.
WE ARE TRACKING AN UNKNOWN SUBJECT WHO HAS BEEN TRACKING WEST AND NOW NORTH. OUR BEST GUESS IS THAT HE'S ABOUT TO CROSS OR CIRCUMNAVIGATE BLACKCROSS.
YOUR BEST GUESS DOESN'T SEEM TOO EXACT.
THE UNSUB STARTED OFF AS A DEEP URBAN KILLER, BUT SHIFTED TO RURAL SETTINGS, AND WE CAN'T ASSUME THAT'S JUST DOWN TO OPPORTUNITY WHILE TRAVELING.
ARE YOU DRAWING A CONNECTION BETWEEN ROB BENTON GETTING A BOMB IN THE FACE AND HANNIBAL LECTER MUNCHING HIS WAY TOWARDS US?
YOU COULD TAKE THIS A LITTLE MORE SERIOUSLY.
YOU COULD COME CLEAN AND PUT A CLOWN NOSE ON. THIS IS A RIDICULOUS BRIEFING.
WE HAVE TO BE CAREFUL ABOUT HOW WE SEQUESTER INFORMATION, EVEN IN THIS ROOM.
AND... WE DON'T KNO ENOUGH ABO THE UNSUB.
THIS ISN'T WORKING FOR YOU, IS IT?
OKAY.
I DON'T LIKE COINCIDENCES. MY UNSUB, ROB BENTON, AND THE STORY EVERY LAW ENFORCEMENT PROFESSIONAL IN THE PACIFIC NORTH WEST IS TELLING EACH OTHER THIS MORNING ABOUT THE GUY WHO BURNED HIMSELF TO DEATH IN THE MIDDLE OF A LAKE.

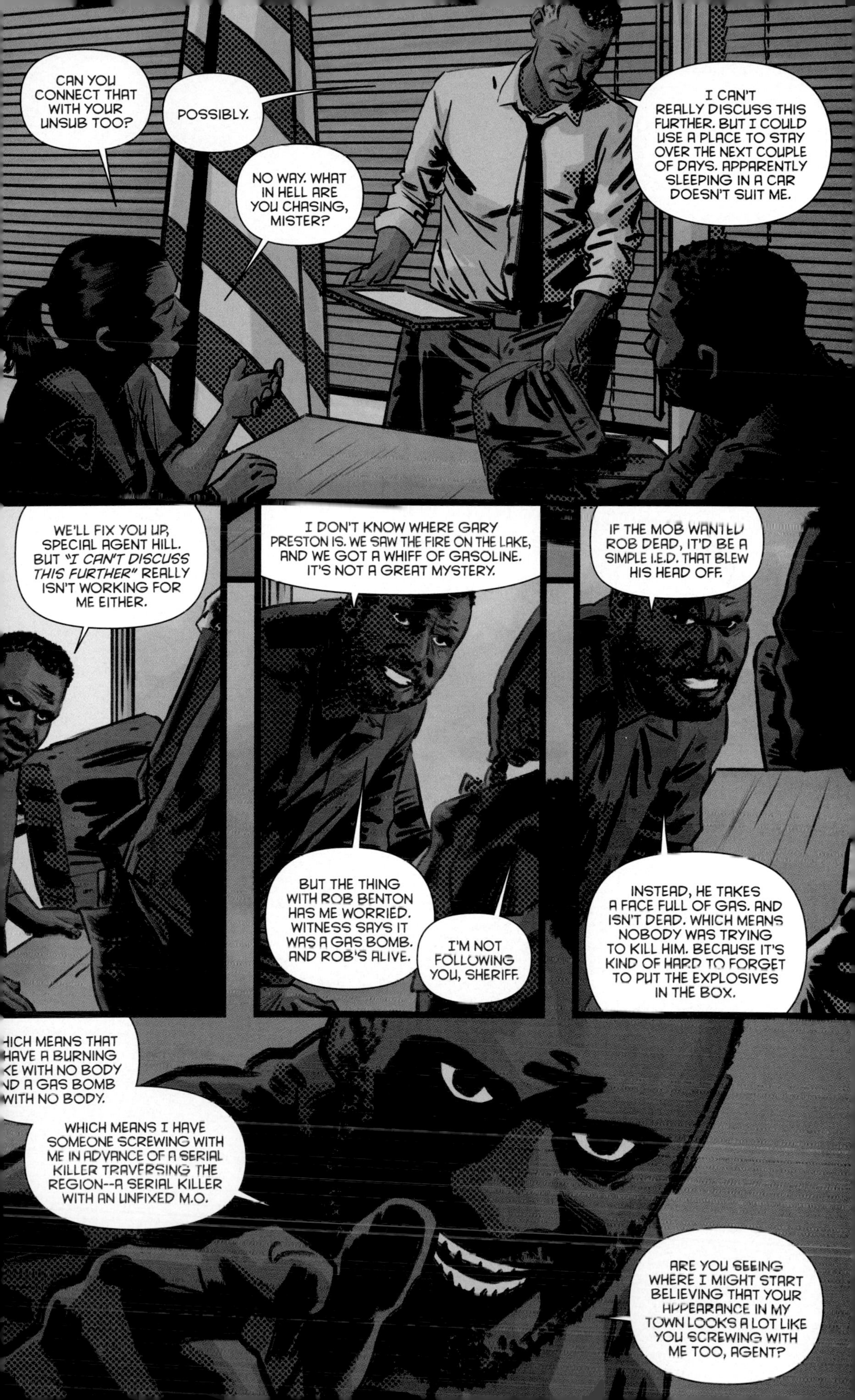
CAN YOU CONNECT THAT WITH YOUR UNSUB TOO?
POSSIBLY.
NO WAY. WHAT IN HELL ARE YOU CHASING, MISTER?
I CAN'T REALLY DISCUSS THIS FURTHER. BUT I COULD USE A PLACE TO STAY OVER THE NEXT COUPLE OF DAYS. APPARENTLY SLEEPING IN A CAR DOESN'T SUIT ME.
WE'LL FIX YOU UP, SPECIAL AGENT HILL. BUT *"I CAN'T DISCUSS THIS FURTHER"* REALLY ISN'T WORKING FOR ME EITHER.
I DON'T KNOW WHERE GARY PRESTON IS. WE SAW THE FIRE ON THE LAKE, AND WE GOT A WHIFF OF GASOLINE. IT'S NOT A GREAT MYSTERY.
BUT THE THING WITH ROB BENTON HAS ME WORRIED. WITNESS SAYS IT WAS A GAS BOMB. AND ROB'S ALIVE.
I'M NOT FOLLOWING YOU, SHERIFF.
IF THE MOB WANTED ROB DEAD, IT'D BE A SIMPLE I.E.D. THAT BLEW HIS HEAD OFF.
INSTEAD, HE TAKES A FACE FULL OF GAS. AND ISN'T DEAD. WHICH MEANS NOBODY WAS TRYING TO KILL HIM. BECAUSE IT'S KIND OF HARD TO FORGET TO PUT THE EXPLOSIVES IN THE BOX.
HICH MEANS THAT HAVE A BURNING KE WITH NO BODY ND A GAS BOMB WITH NO BODY.
WHICH MEANS I HAVE SOMEONE SCREWING WITH ME IN ADVANCE OF A SERIAL KILLER TRAVERSING THE REGION--A SERIAL KILLER WITH AN UNFIXED M.O.
ARE YOU SEEING WHERE I MIGHT START BELIEVING THAT YOUR APPEARANCE IN MY TOWN LOOKS A LOT LIKE YOU SCREWING WITH ME TOO, AGENT?

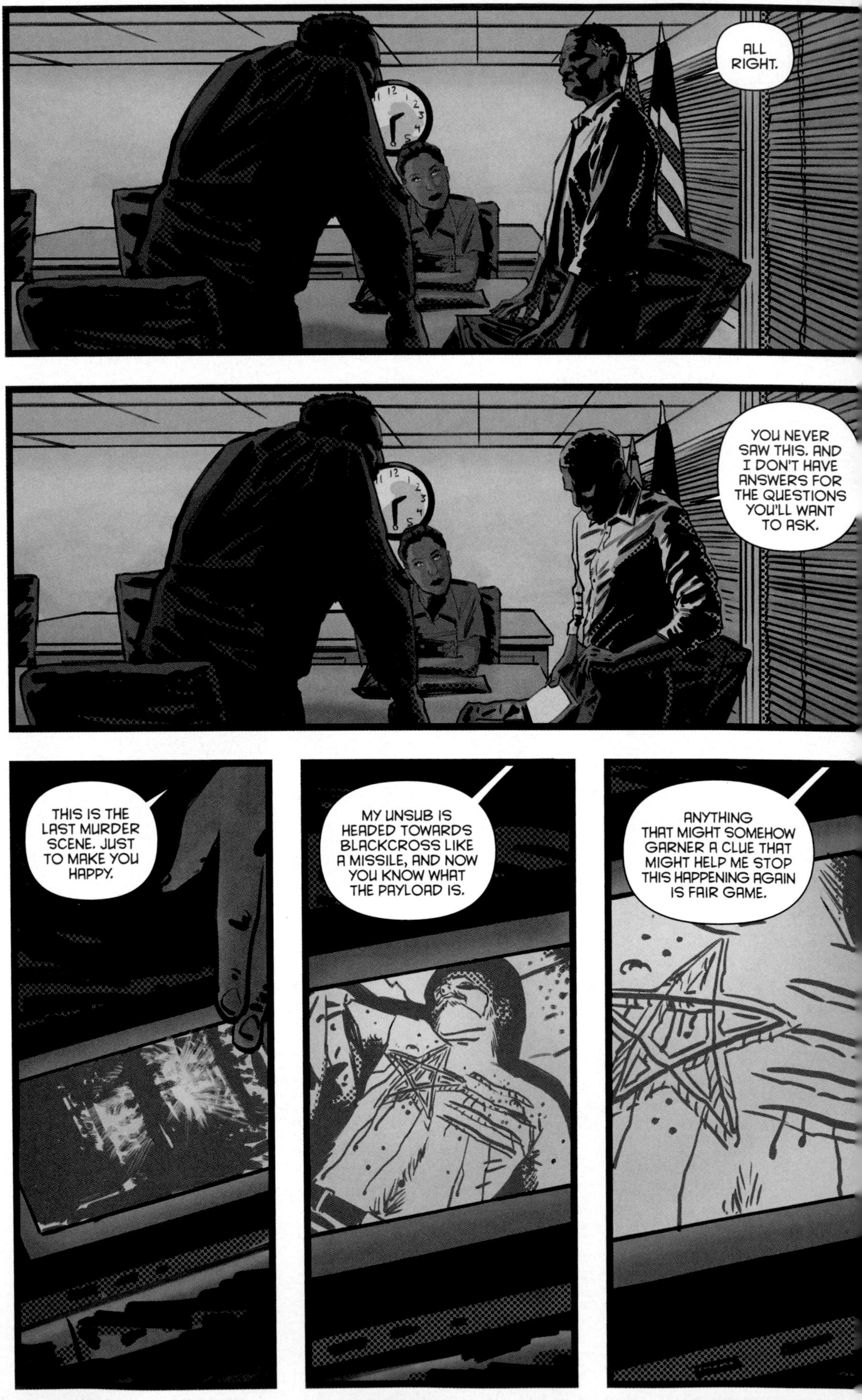
ALL RIGHT.
YOU NEVER SAW THIS. AND I DON'T HAVE ANSWERS FOR THE QUESTIONS YOU'LL WANT TO ASK.
THIS IS THE LAST MURDER SCENE. JUST TO MAKE YOU HAPPY.
MY UNSUB IS HEADED TOWARDS BLACKCROSS LIKE A MISSILE, AND NOW YOU KNOW WHAT THE PAYLOAD IS.
ANYTHING THAT MIGHT SOMEHOW GARNER A CLUE THAT MIGHT HELP ME STOP THIS HAPPENING AGAIN IS FAIR GAME.

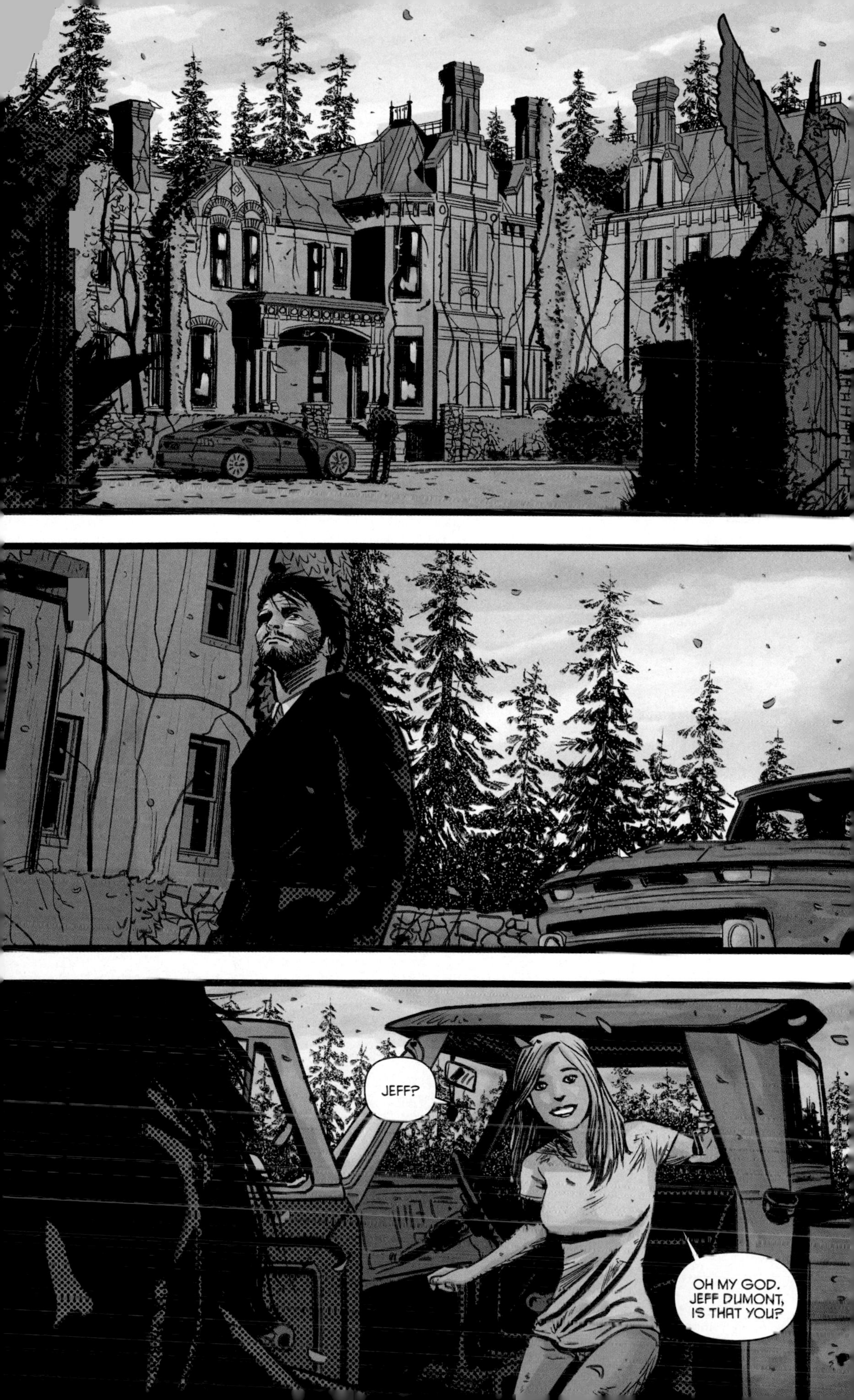
JEFF?
OH MY GOD. JEFF DUMONT, IS THAT YOU?

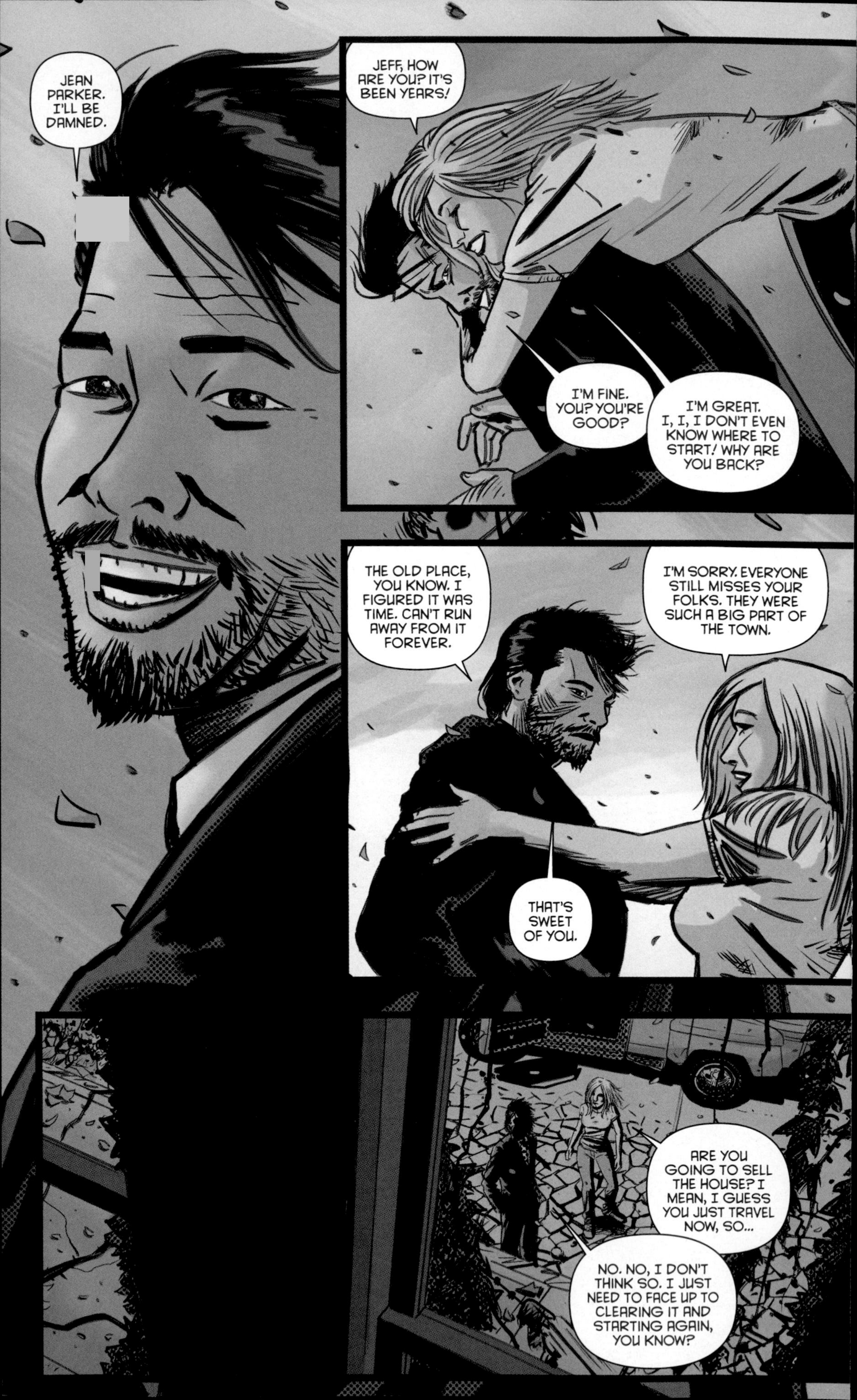
JEAN PARKER. I'LL BE DAMNED.
JEFF, HOW ARE YOU? IT'S BEEN YEARS!
I'M FINE. YOU? YOU'RE GOOD?
I'M GREAT. I, I, I DON'T EVEN KNOW WHERE TO START! WHY ARE YOU BACK?
THE OLD PLACE, YOU KNOW. I FIGURED IT WAS TIME. CAN'T RUN AWAY FROM IT FOREVER.
I'M SORRY. EVERYONE STILL MISSES YOUR FOLKS. THEY WERE SUCH A BIG PART OF THE TOWN.
THAT'S SWEET OF YOU.
ARE YOU GOING TO SELL THE HOUSE? I MEAN, I GUESS YOU JUST TRAVEL NOW, SO...
NO. NO, I DON'T THINK SO. I JUST NEED TO FACE UP TO CLEARING IT AND STARTING AGAIN, YOU KNOW?

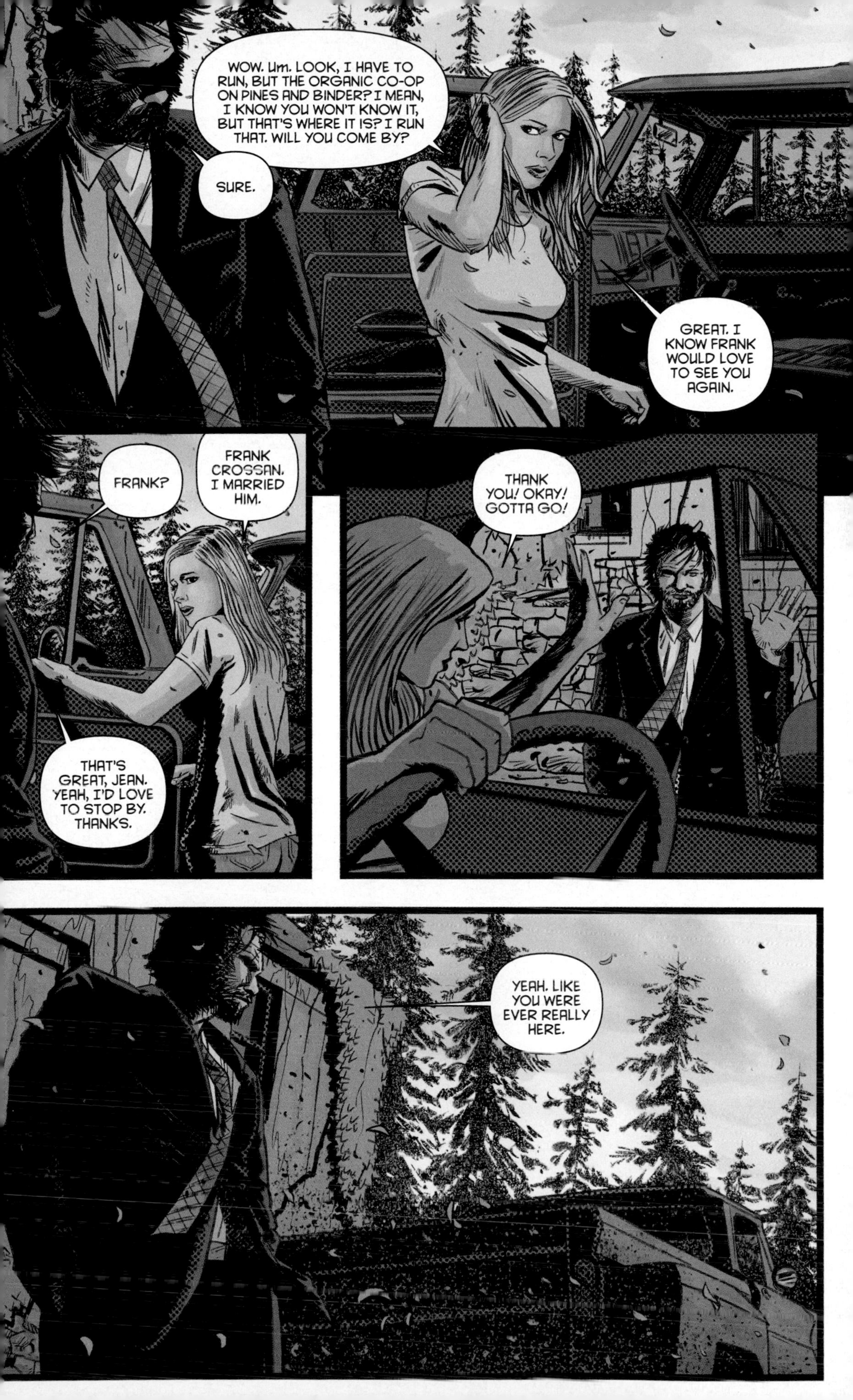
WOW. Um. LOOK, I HAVE TO RUN, BUT THE ORGANIC CO-OP ON PINES AND BINDER? I MEAN, I KNOW YOU WON'T KNOW IT, BUT THAT'S WHERE IT IS? I RUN THAT. WILL YOU COME BY?
SURE.
GREAT. I KNOW FRANK WOULD LOVE TO SEE YOU AGAIN.
FRANK?
FRANK CROSSAN. I MARRIED HIM.
THAT'S GREAT, JEAN. YEAH, I'D LOVE TO STOP BY. THANKS.
THANK YOU! OKAY! GOTTA GO!
YEAH. LIKE YOU WERE EVER REALLY HERE.

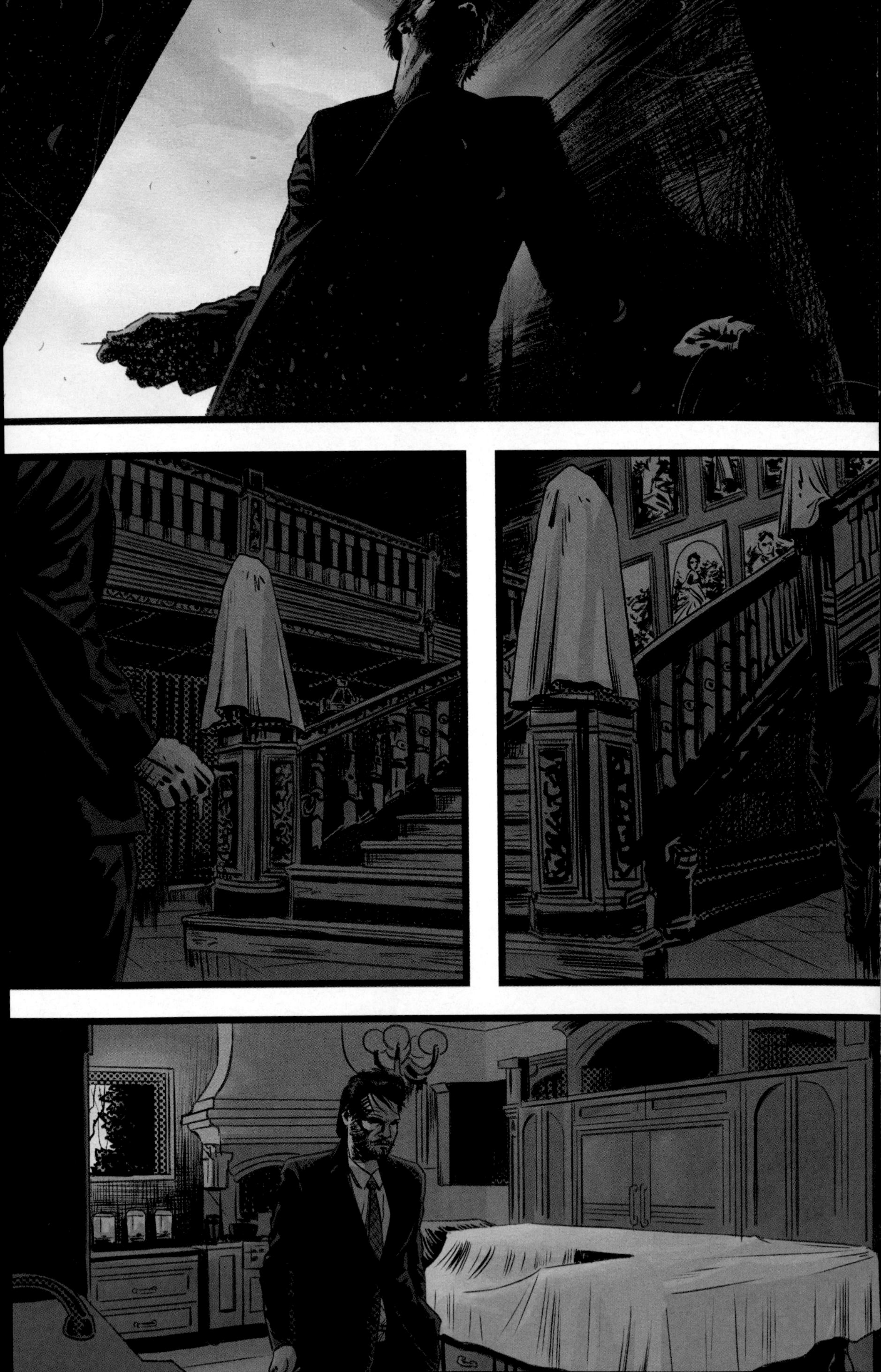

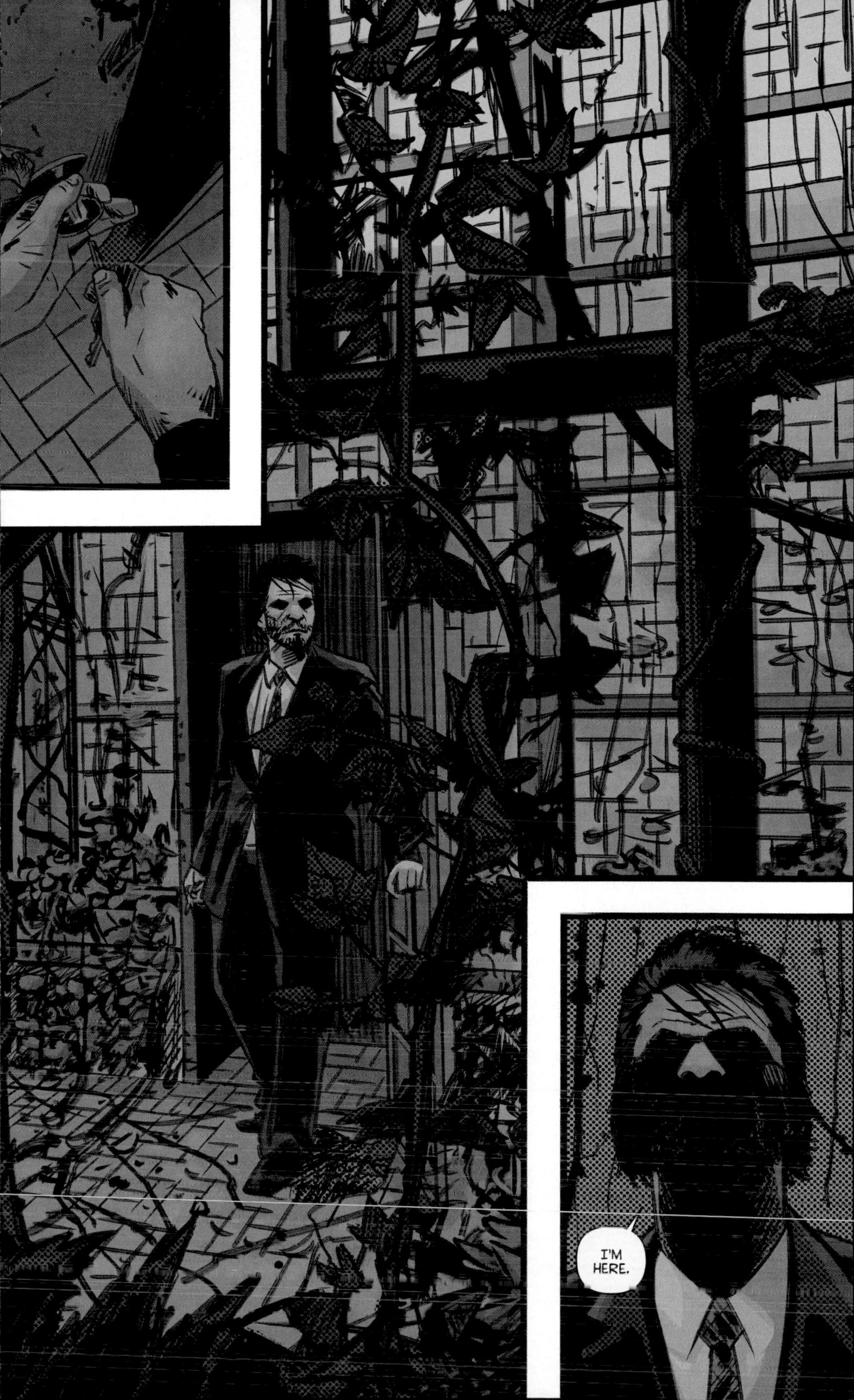
I'M HERE.

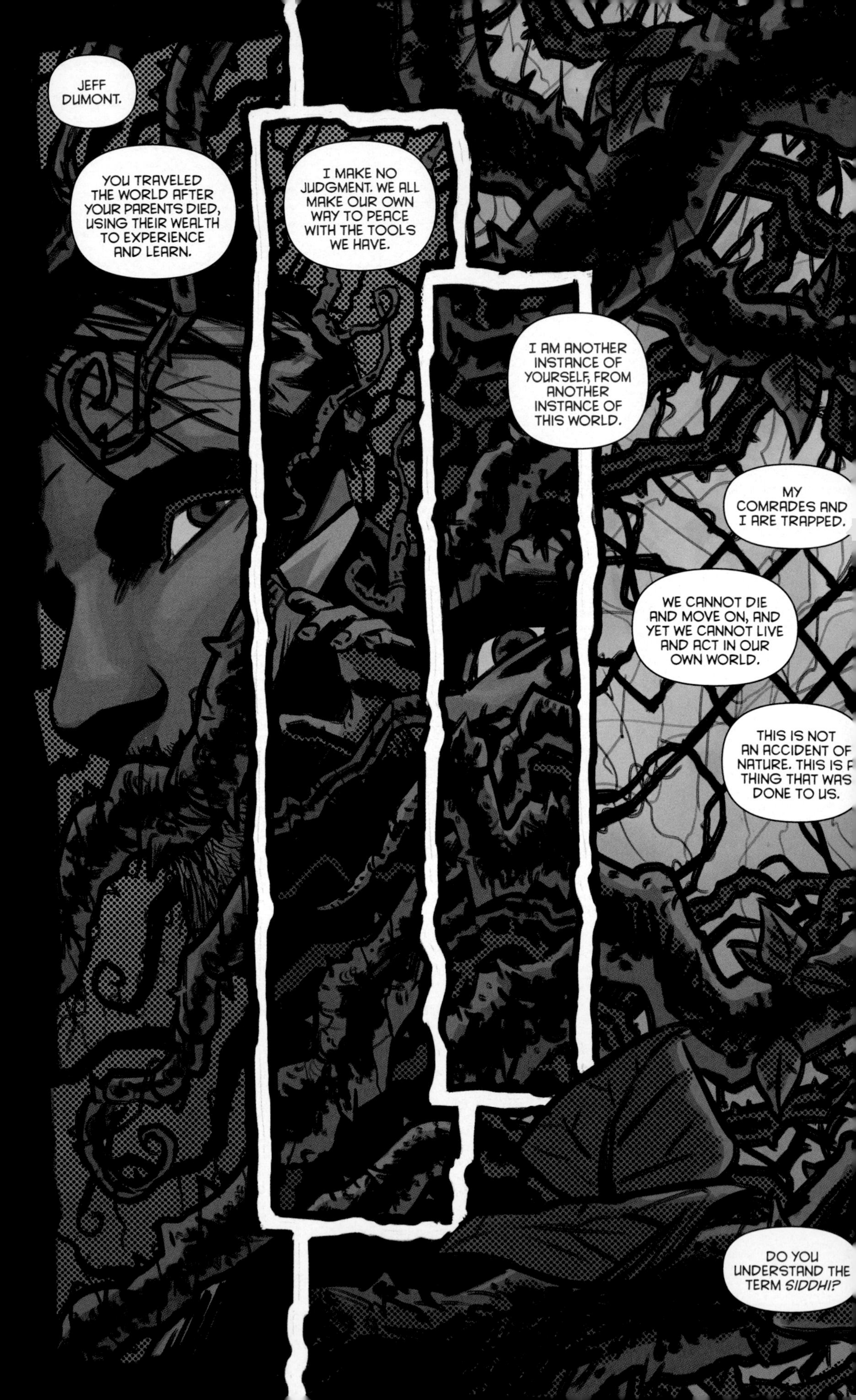
JEFF DUMONT.
YOU TRAVELED THE WORLD AFTER YOUR PARENTS DIED, USING THEIR WEALTH TO EXPERIENCE AND LEARN.
I MAKE NO JUDGMENT. WE ALL MAKE OUR OWN WAY TO PEACE WITH THE TOOLS WE HAVE.
I AM ANOTHER INSTANCE OF YOURSELF, FROM ANOTHER INSTANCE OF THIS WORLD.
MY COMRADES AND I ARE TRAPPED.
WE CANNOT DIE AND MOVE ON, AND YET WE CANNOT LIVE AND ACT IN OUR OWN WORLD.
THIS IS NOT AN ACCIDENT OF NATURE. THIS IS A THING THAT WAS DONE TO US.
DO YOU UNDERSTAND THE TERM *SIDDHI?*

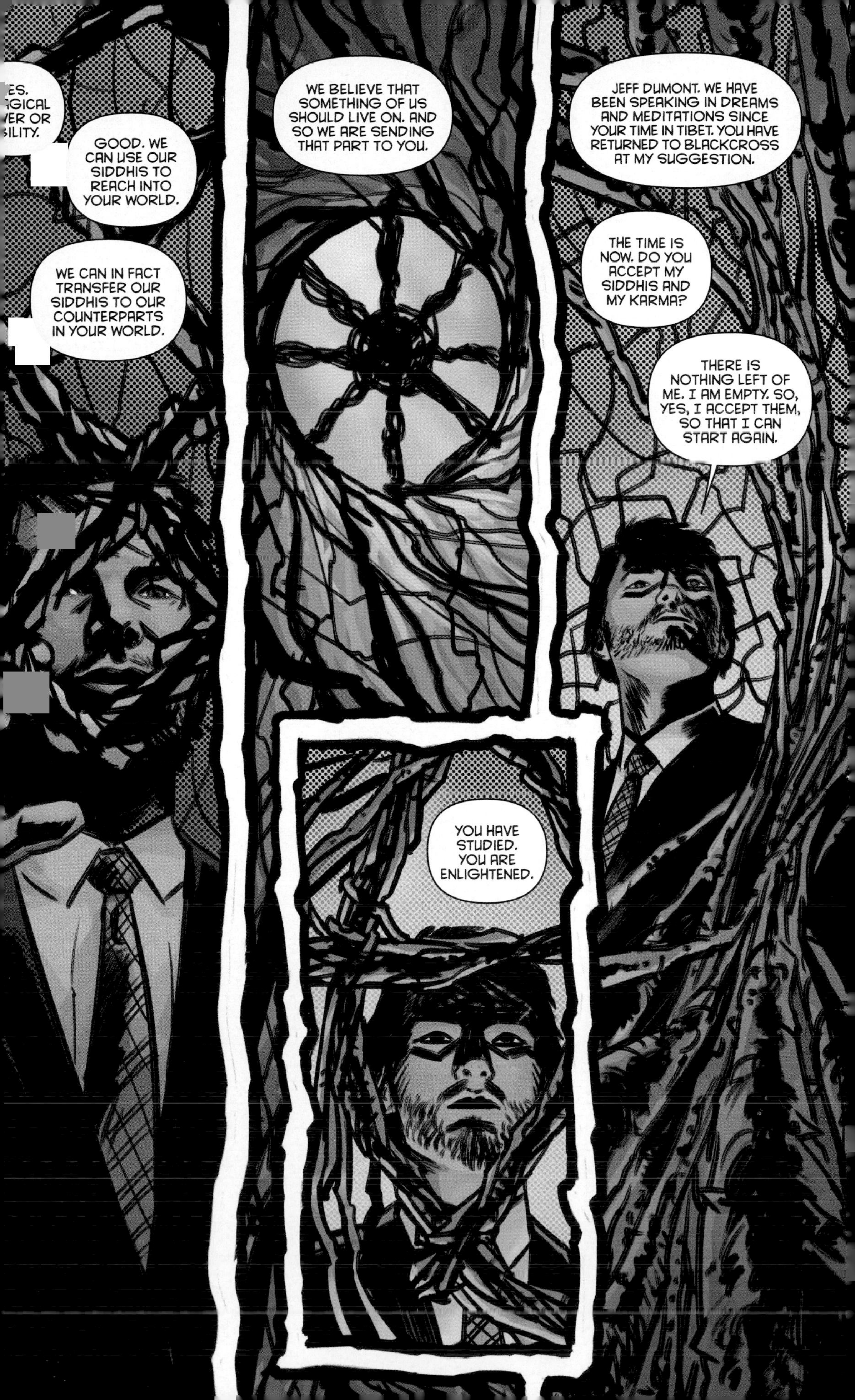
GOOD. WE CAN USE OUR SIDDHIS TO REACH INTO YOUR WORLD.
WE CAN IN FACT TRANSFER OUR SIDDHIS TO OUR COUNTERPARTS IN YOUR WORLD.
WE BELIEVE THAT SOMETHING OF US SHOULD LIVE ON. AND SO WE ARE SENDING THAT PART TO YOU.
YOU HAVE STUDIED. YOU ARE ENLIGHTENED.
JEFF DUMONT. WE HAVE BEEN SPEAKING IN DREAMS AND MEDITATIONS SINCE YOUR TIME IN TIBET. YOU HAVE RETURNED TO BLACKCROSS AT MY SUGGESTION.
THE TIME IS NOW. DO YOU ACCEPT MY SIDDHIS AND MY KARMA?
THERE IS NOTHING LEFT OF ME. I AM EMPTY. SO, YES, I ACCEPT THEM, SO THAT I CAN START AGAIN.

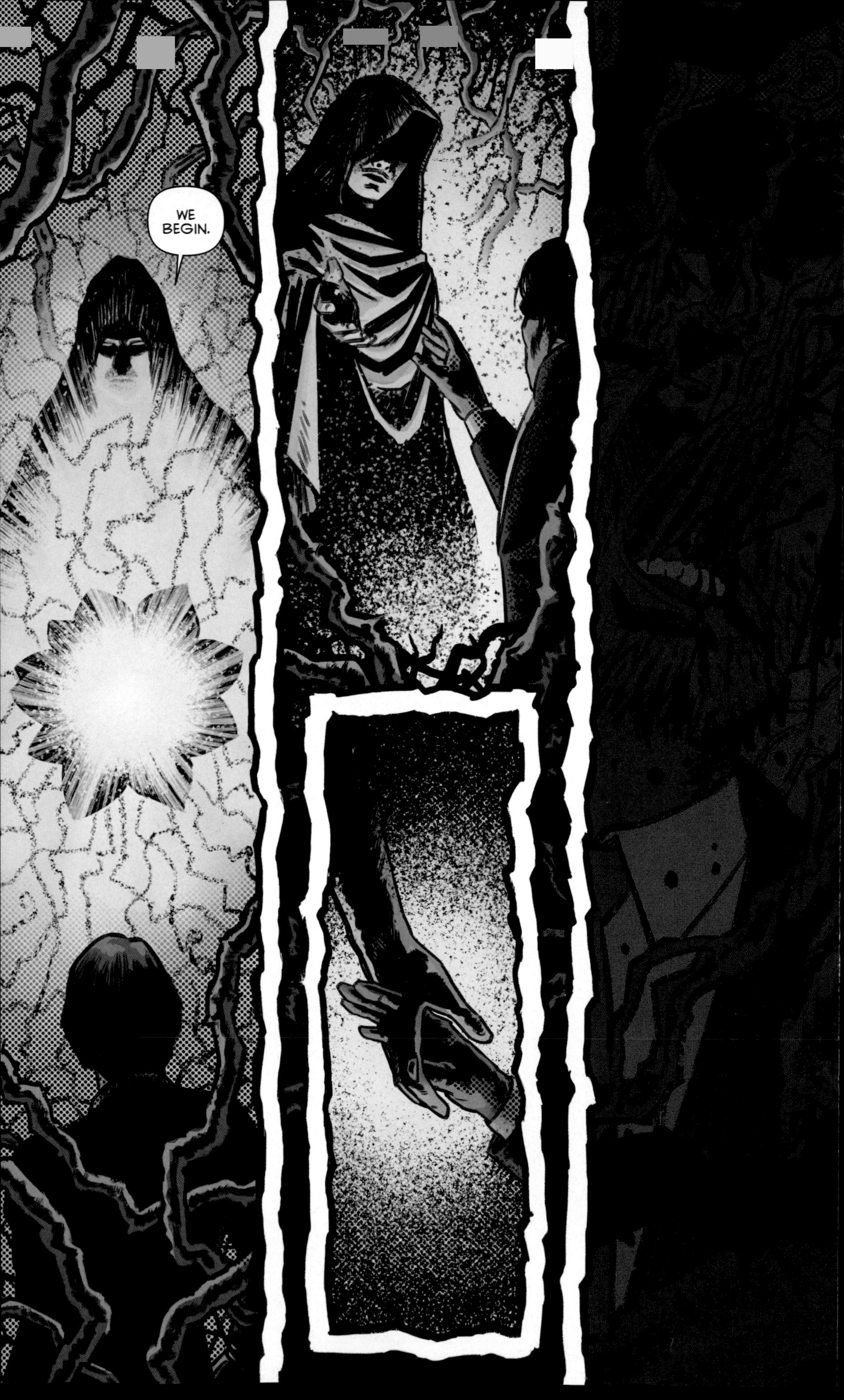
WE BEGIN.

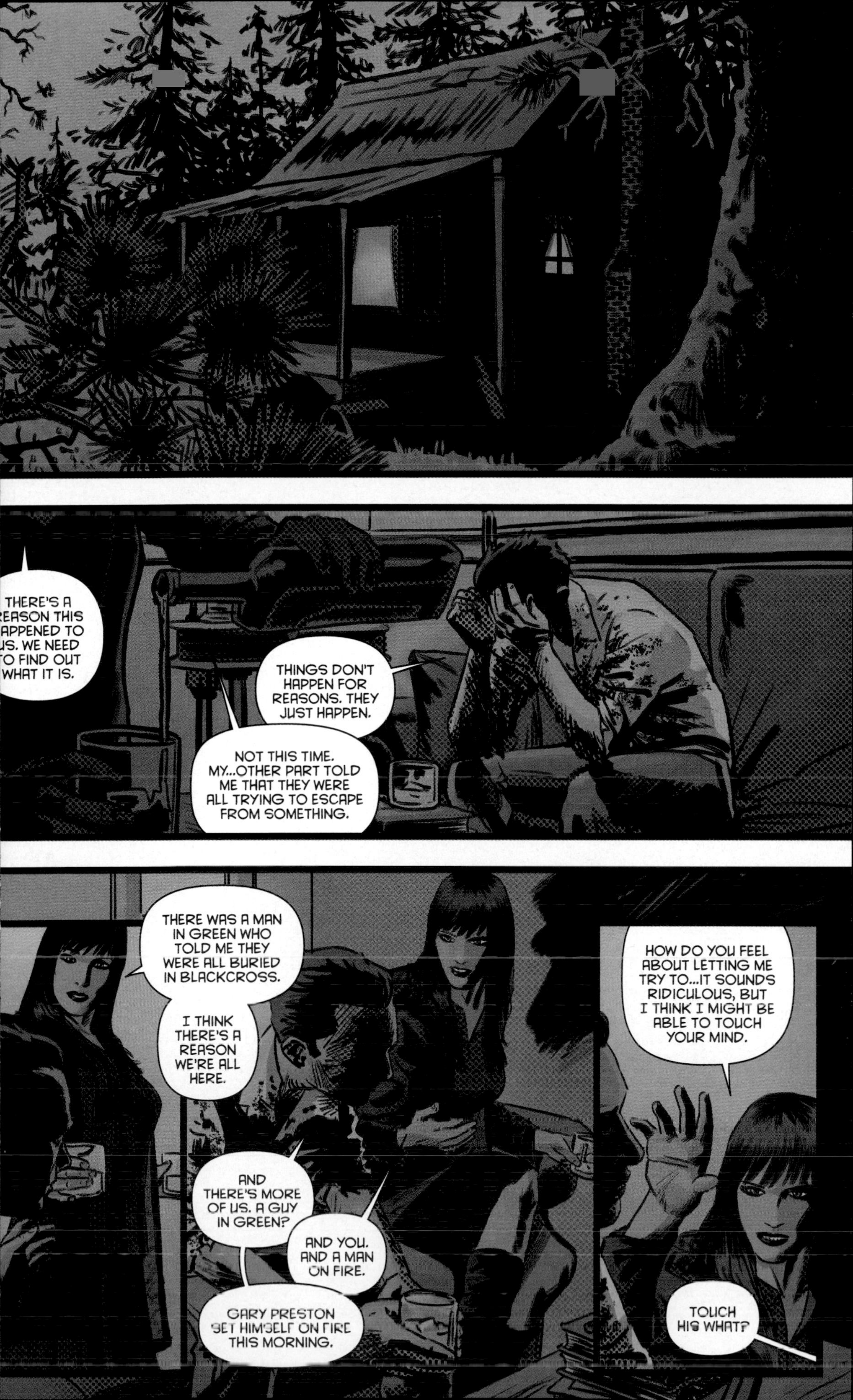
THERE'S A EASON THIS APPENED TO JS. WE NEED O FIND OUT WHAT IT IS.
THINGS DON'T HAPPEN FOR REASONS. THEY JUST HAPPEN.
NOT THIS TIME. MY...OTHER PART TOLD ME THAT THEY WERE ALL TRYING TO ESCAPE FROM SOMETHING.
THERE WAS A MAN IN GREEN WHO TOLD ME THEY WERE ALL BURIED IN BLACKCROSS.
I THINK THERE'S A REASON WE'RE ALL HERE.
AND THERE'S MORE OF US. A GUY IN GREEN?
AND YOU. AND A MAN ON FIRE.
GARY PRESTON SET HIMSELF ON FIRE THIS MORNING.
HOW DO YOU FEEL ABOUT LETTING ME TRY TO...IT SOUNDS RIDICULOUS, BUT I THINK I MIGHT BE ABLE TO TOUCH YOUR MIND.
TOUCH HIS WHAT?

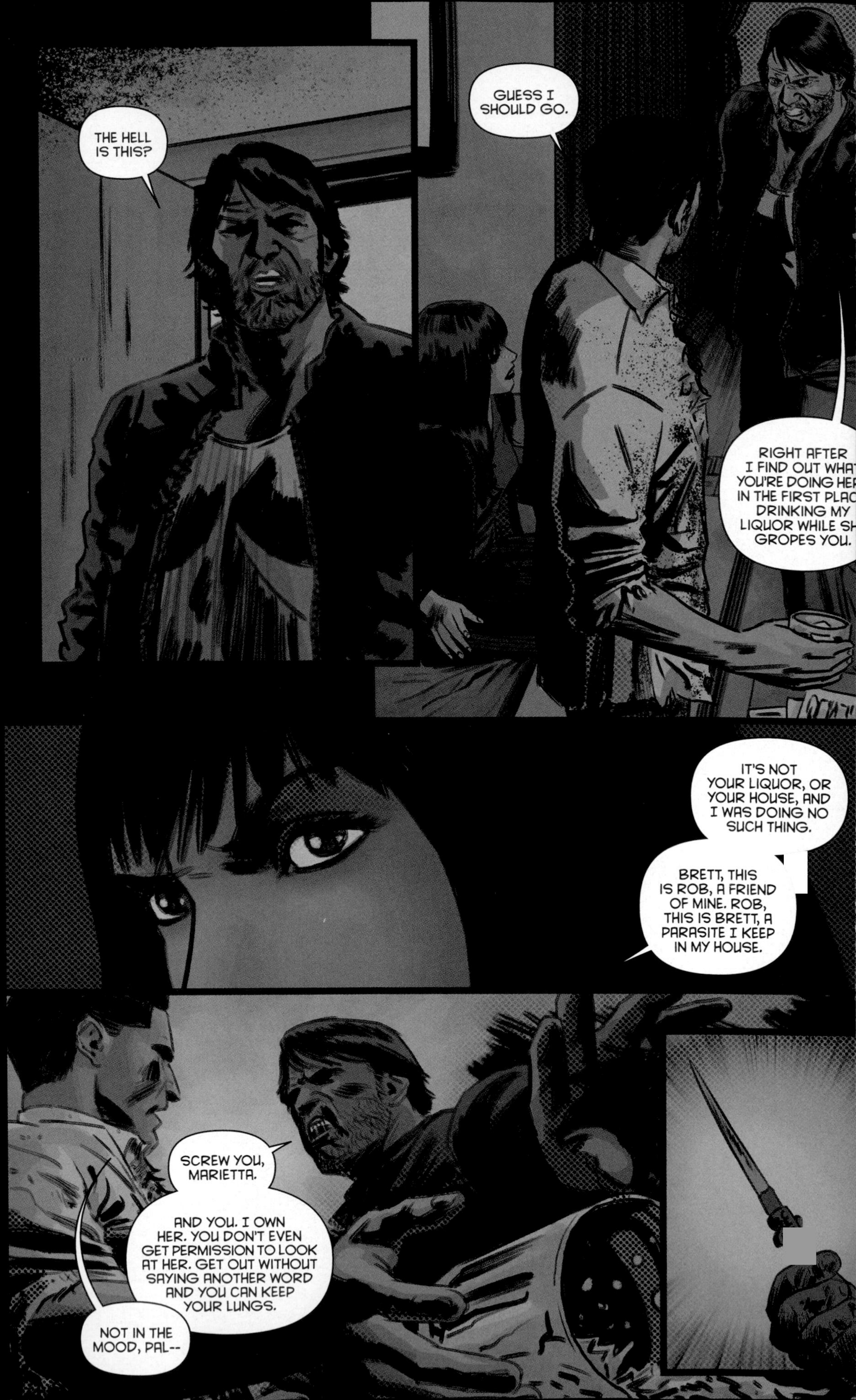
THE HELL IS THIS?
GUESS I SHOULD GO.
RIGHT AFTER I FIND OUT WHA YOU'RE DOING HE IN THE FIRST PLAC DRINKING MY LIQUOR WHILE S GROPES YOU.
IT'S NOT YOUR LIQUOR, OR YOUR HOUSE, AND I WAS DOING NO SUCH THING.
BRETT, THIS IS ROB, A FRIEND OF MINE. ROB, THIS IS BRETT, A PARASITE I KEEP IN MY HOUSE.
SCREW YOU, MARIETTA.
AND YOU. I OWN HER. YOU DON'T EVEN GET PERMISSION TO LOOK AT HER. GET OUT WITHOUT SAYING ANOTHER WORD AND YOU CAN KEEP YOUR LUNGS.
NOT IN THE MOOD, PAL--

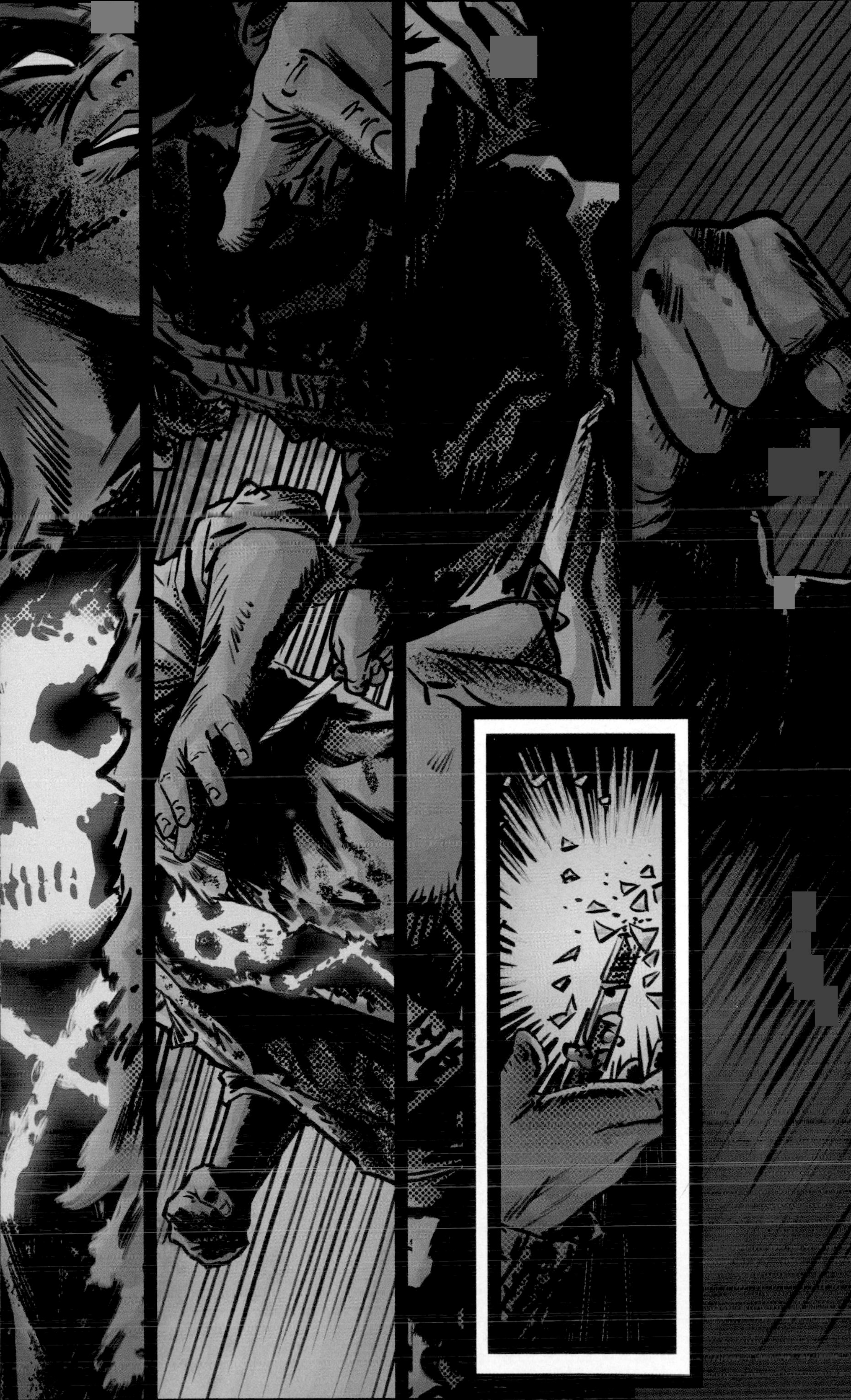

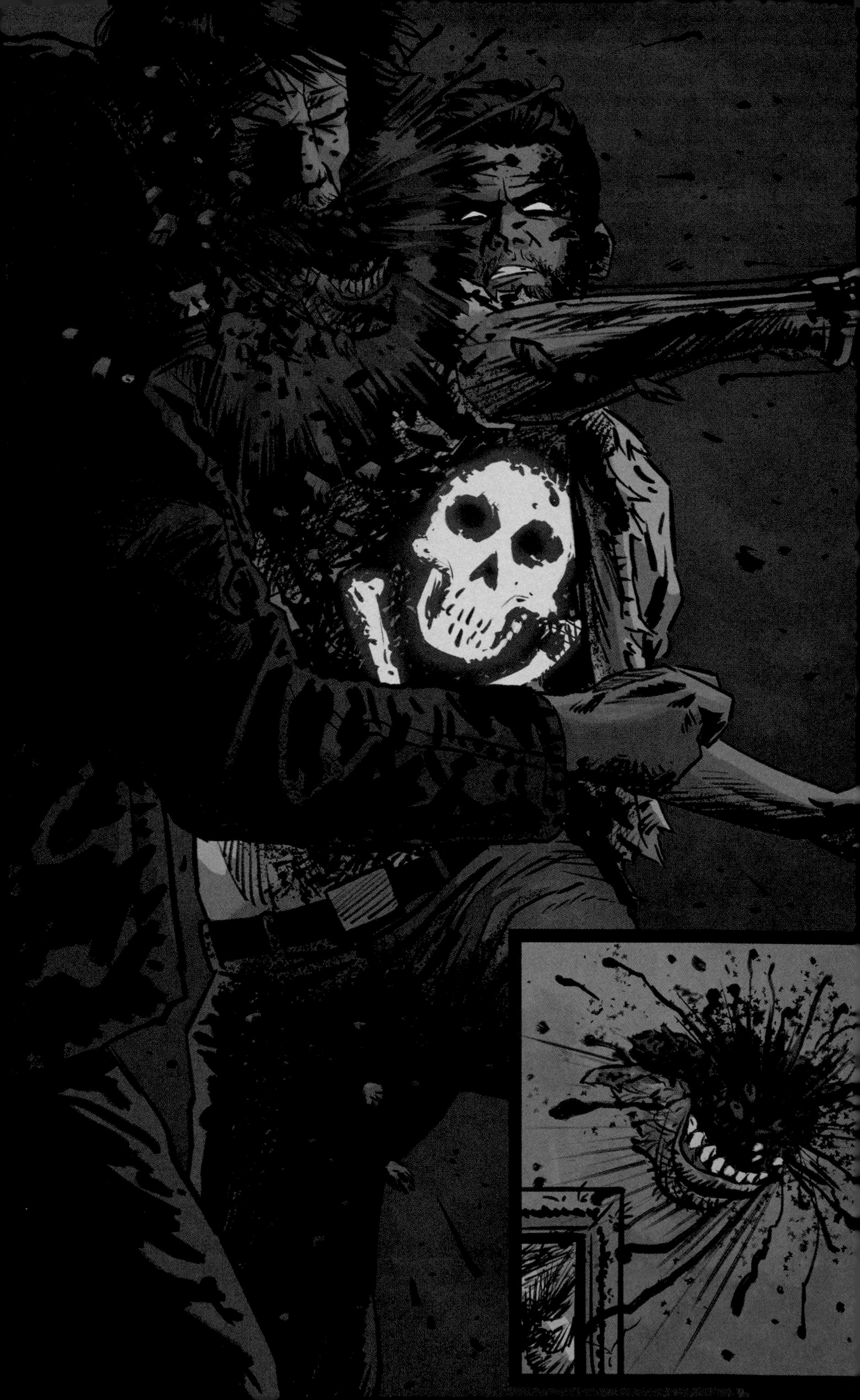

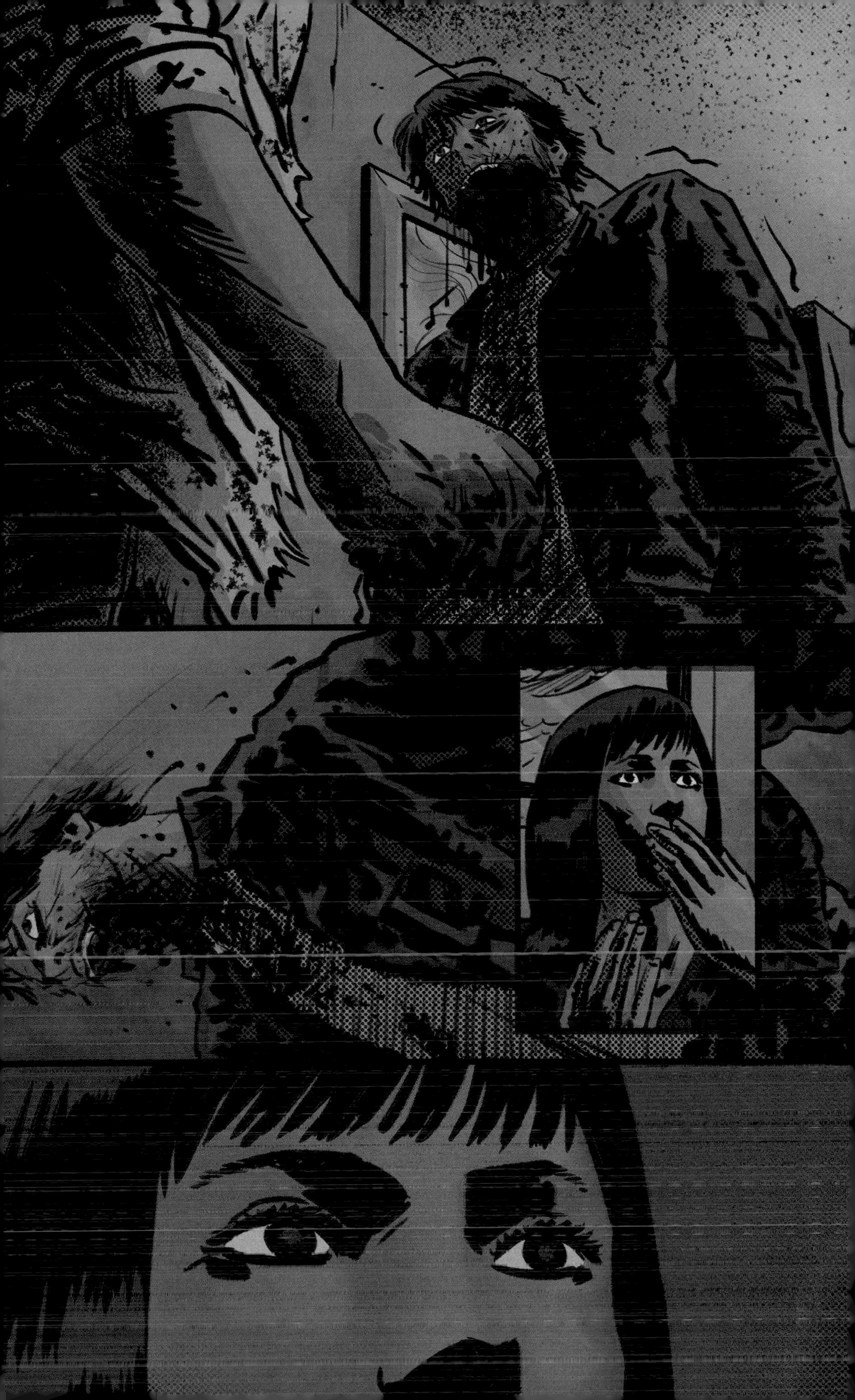

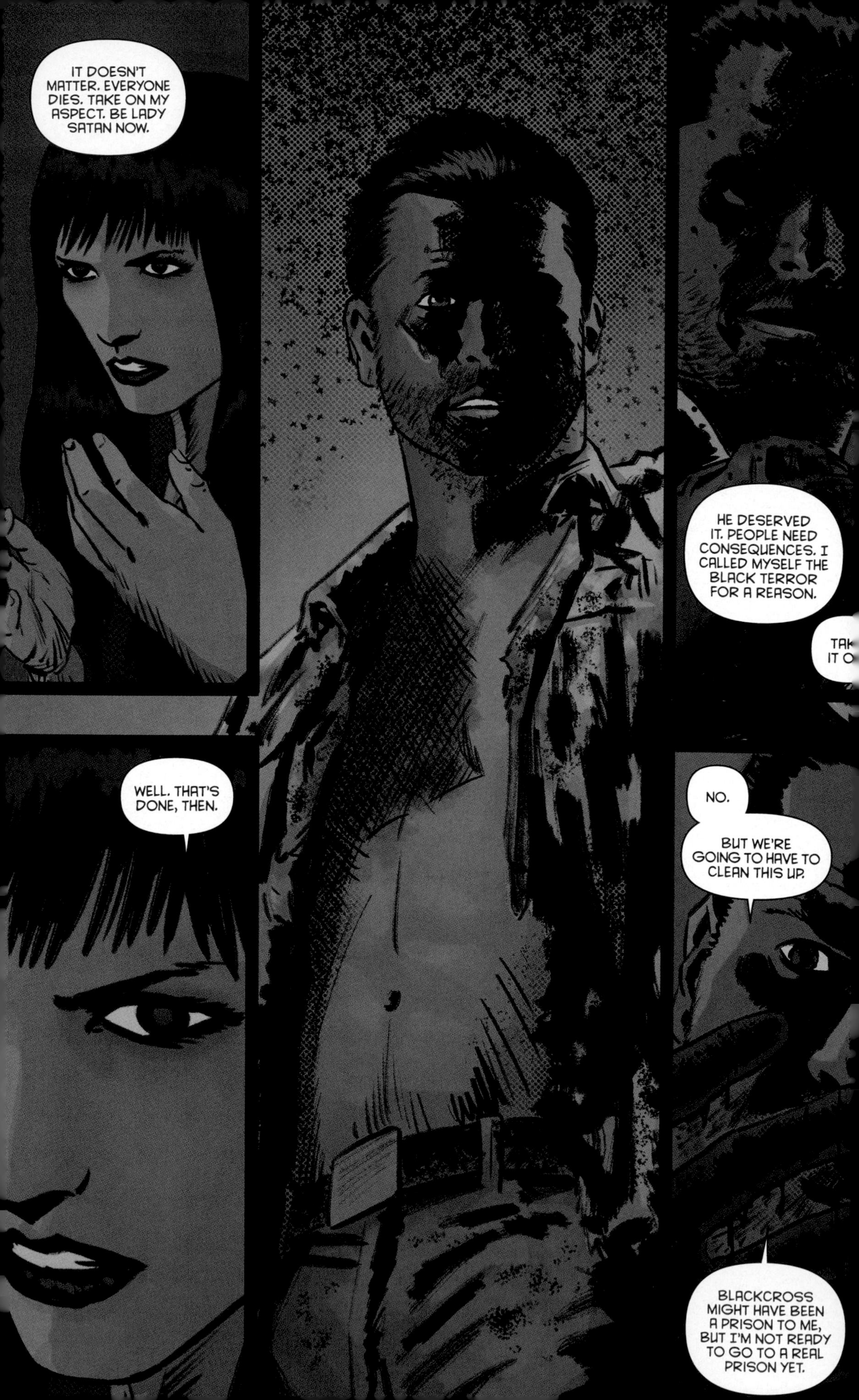

IT DOESN'T MATTER. EVERYONE DIES. TAKE ON MY ASPECT. BE LADY SATAN NOW.
HE DESERVED IT. PEOPLE NEED CONSEQUENCES. I CALLED MYSELF THE BLACK TERROR FOR A REASON.
WELL. THAT'S DONE, THEN.
NO.
BUT WE'RE GOING TO HAVE TO CLEAN THIS UP.
BLACKCROSS MIGHT HAVE BEEN A PRISON TO ME, BUT I'M NOT READY TO GO TO A REAL PRISON YET.

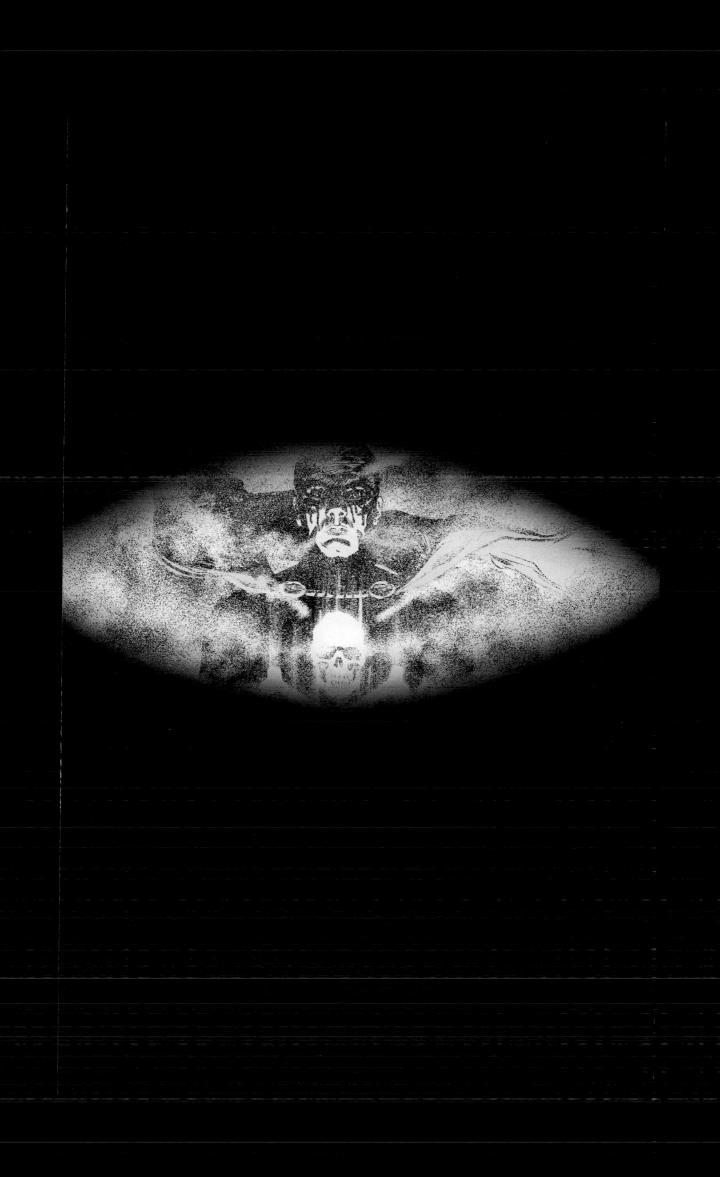

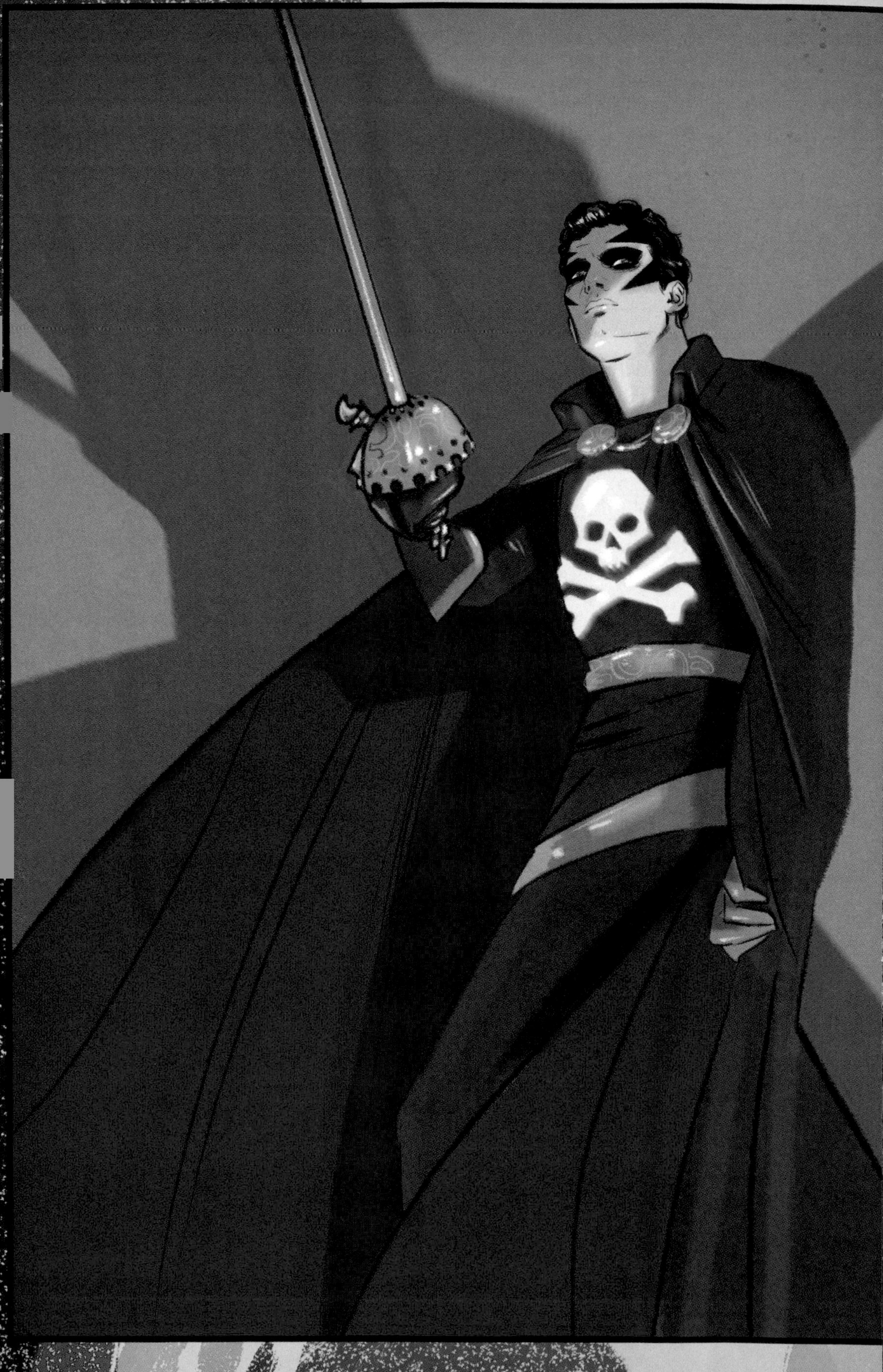

ISSUE #4 COVER BY TULA LOTAY

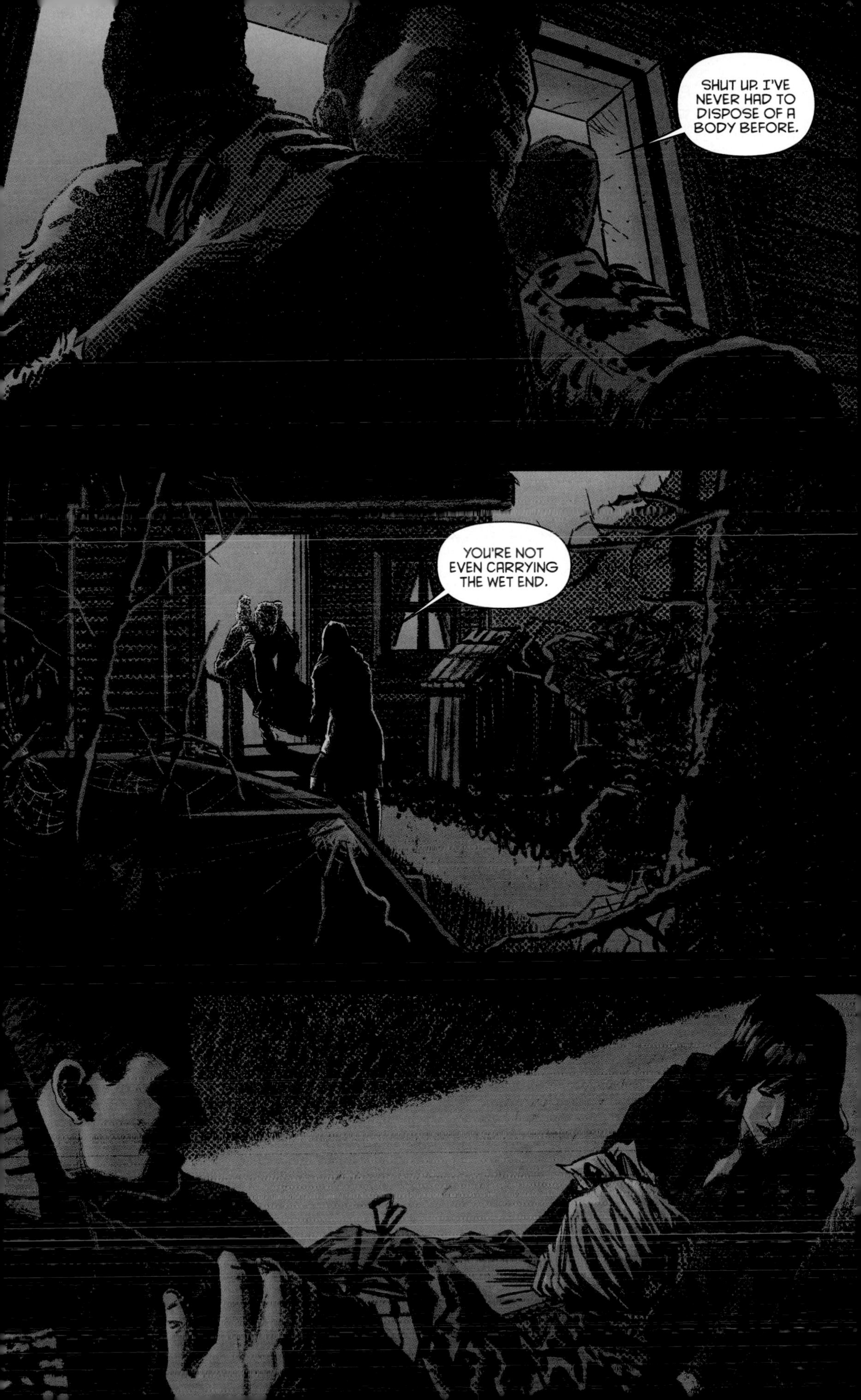
SHUT UP. I'VE NEVER HAD TO DISPOSE OF A BODY BEFORE.
YOU'RE NOT EVEN CARRYING THE WET END.

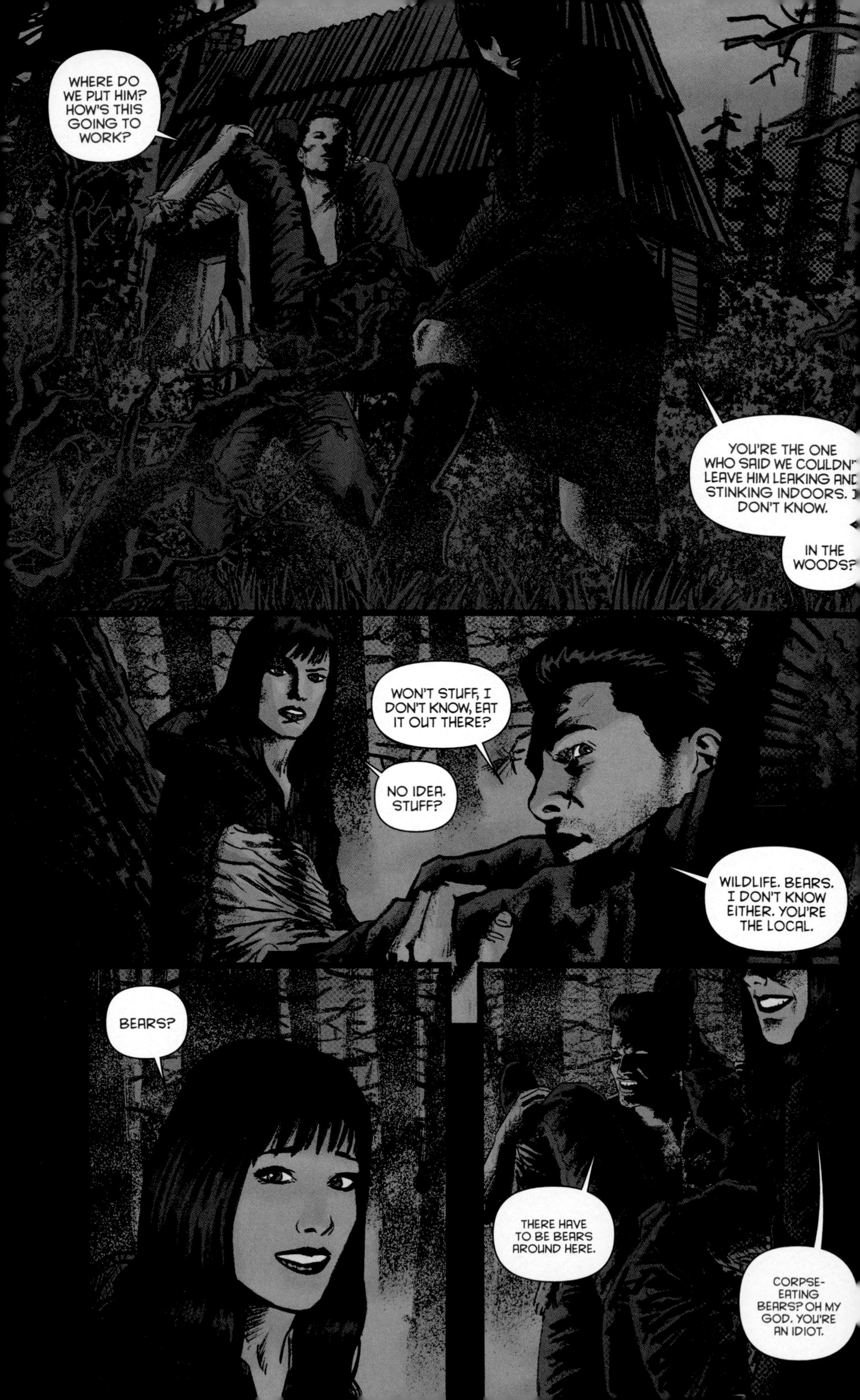
WHERE DO WE PUT HIM? HOW'S THIS GOING TO WORK?
YOU'RE THE ONE WHO SAID WE COULDN'T LEAVE HIM LEAKING AND STINKING INDOORS. I DON'T KNOW.
IN THE WOODS?
WON'T STUFF, I DON'T KNOW, EAT IT OUT THERE?
NO IDEA. STUFF?
WILDLIFE. BEARS. I DON'T KNOW EITHER. YOU'RE THE LOCAL.
BEARS?
THERE HAVE TO BE BEARS AROUND HERE.
CORPSE-EATING BEARS? OH MY GOD. YOU'RE AN IDIOT.

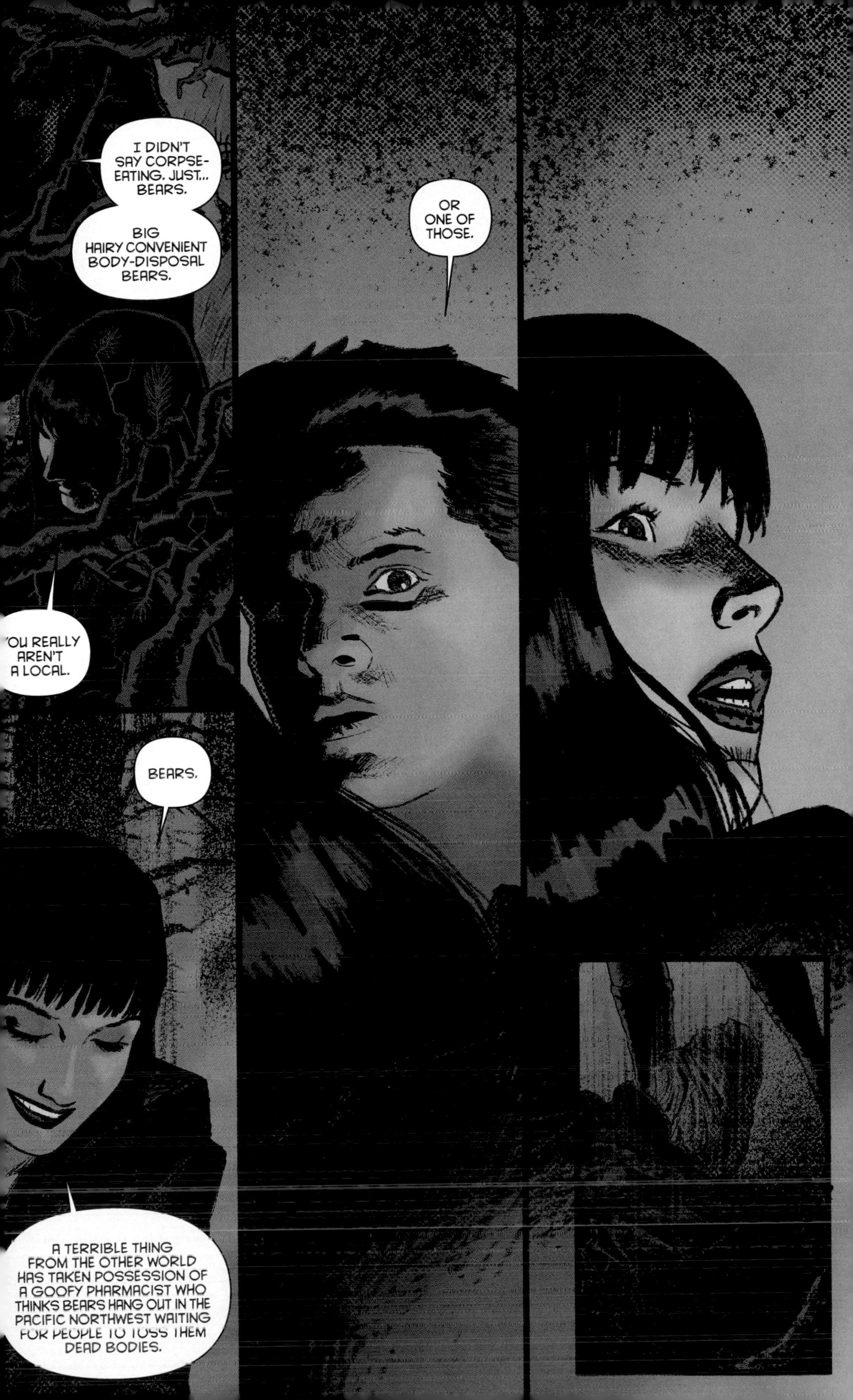
I DIDN'T SAY CORPSE-EATING. JUST... BEARS.
BIG HAIRY CONVENIENT BODY-DISPOSAL BEARS.
OR ONE OF THOSE.
OU REALLY AREN'T A LOCAL.
BEARS.
A TERRIBLE THING FROM THE OTHER WORLD HAS TAKEN POSSESSION OF A GOOFY PHARMACIST WHO THINKS BEARS HANG OUT IN THE PACIFIC NORTHWEST WAITING FOR PEOPLE TO TOSS THEM DEAD BODIES.

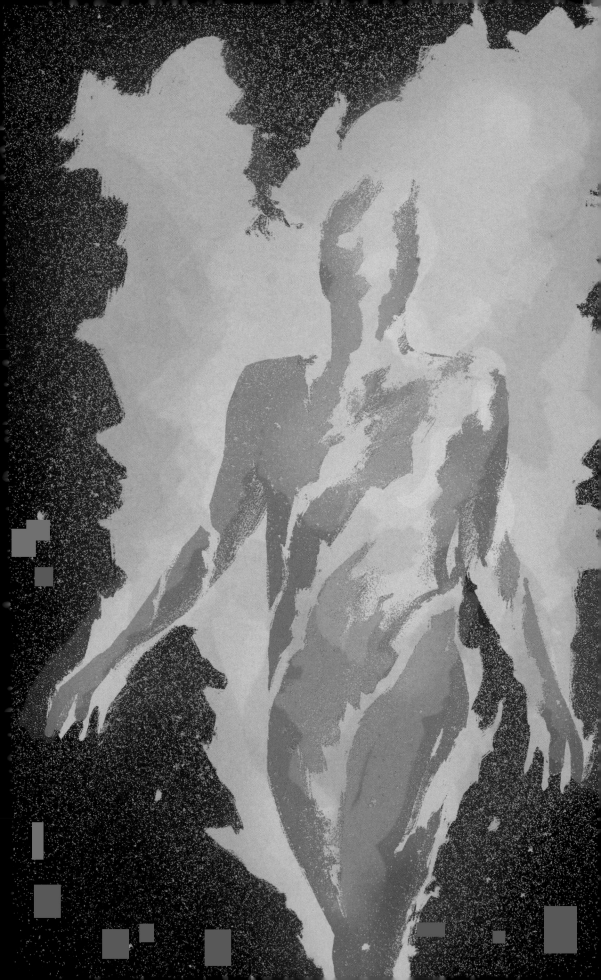

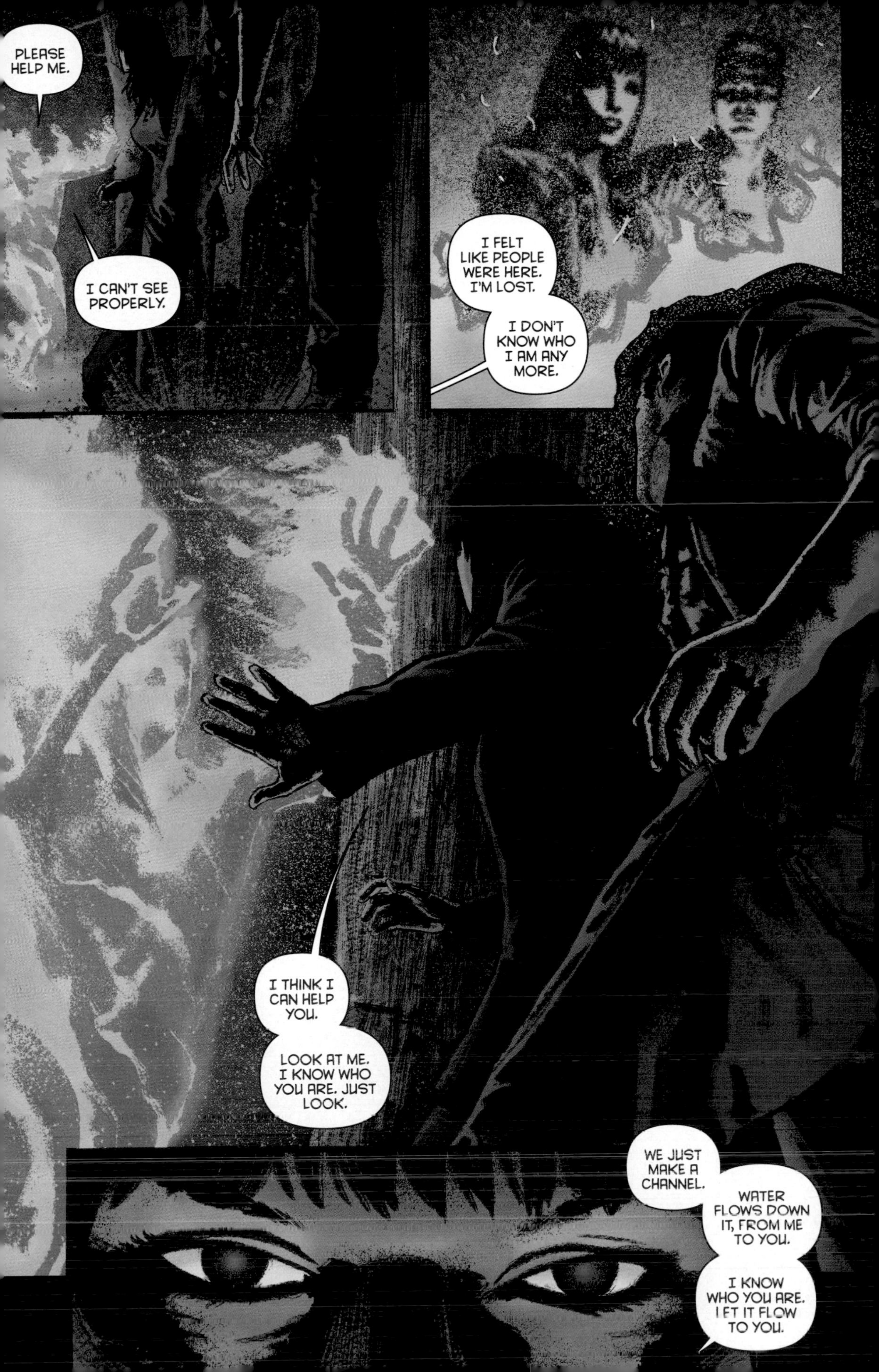
PLEASE HELP ME.
I CAN'T SEE PROPERLY.
I FELT LIKE PEOPLE WERE HERE. I'M LOST.
I DON'T KNOW WHO I AM ANY MORE.
I THINK I CAN HELP YOU.
LOOK AT ME. I KNOW WHO YOU ARE. JUST LOOK.
WE JUST MAKE A CHANNEL.
WATER FLOWS DOWN IT, FROM ME TO YOU.
I KNOW WHO YOU ARE. LET IT FLOW TO YOU.

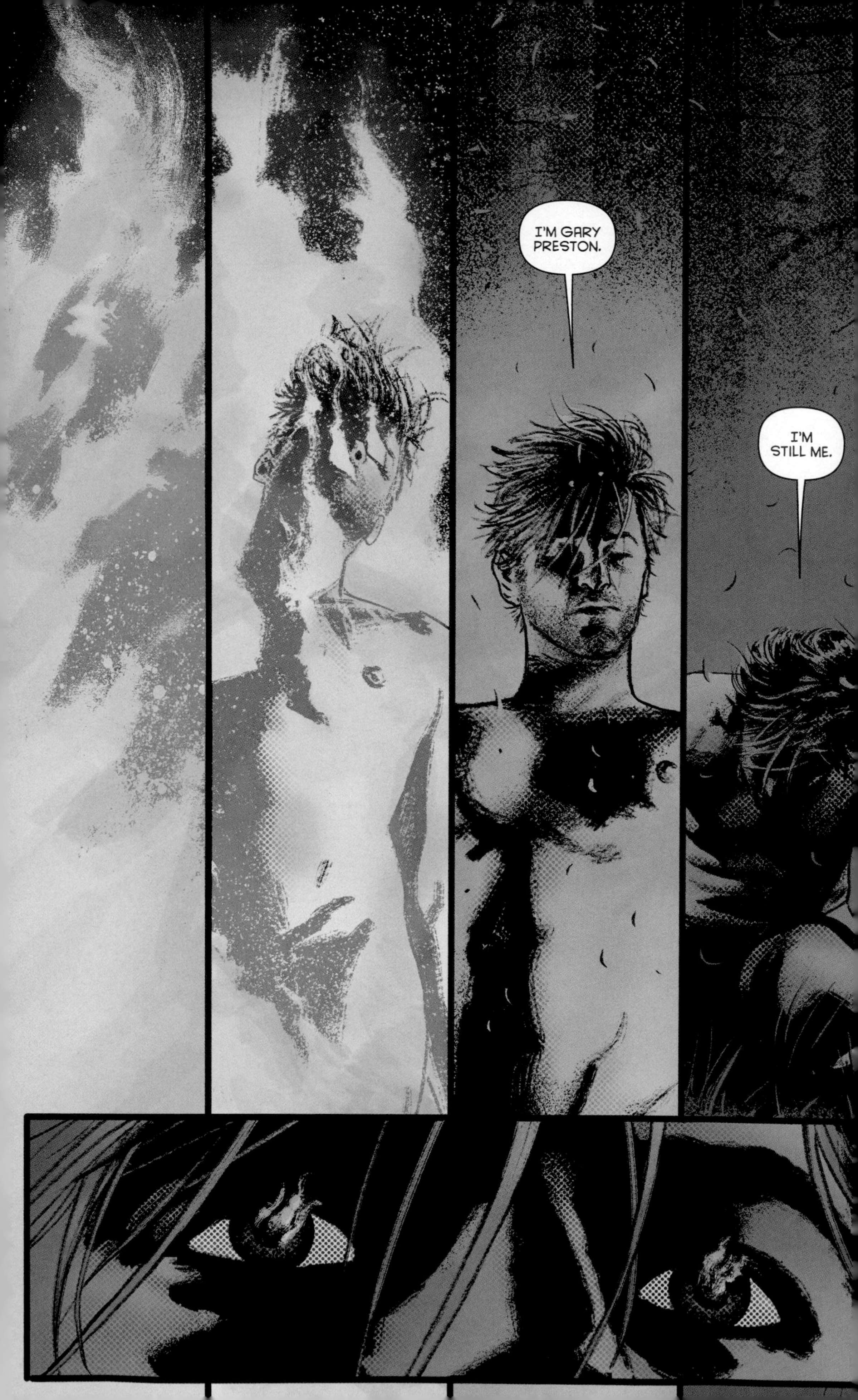
I'M GARY PRESTON.
I'M STILL ME.

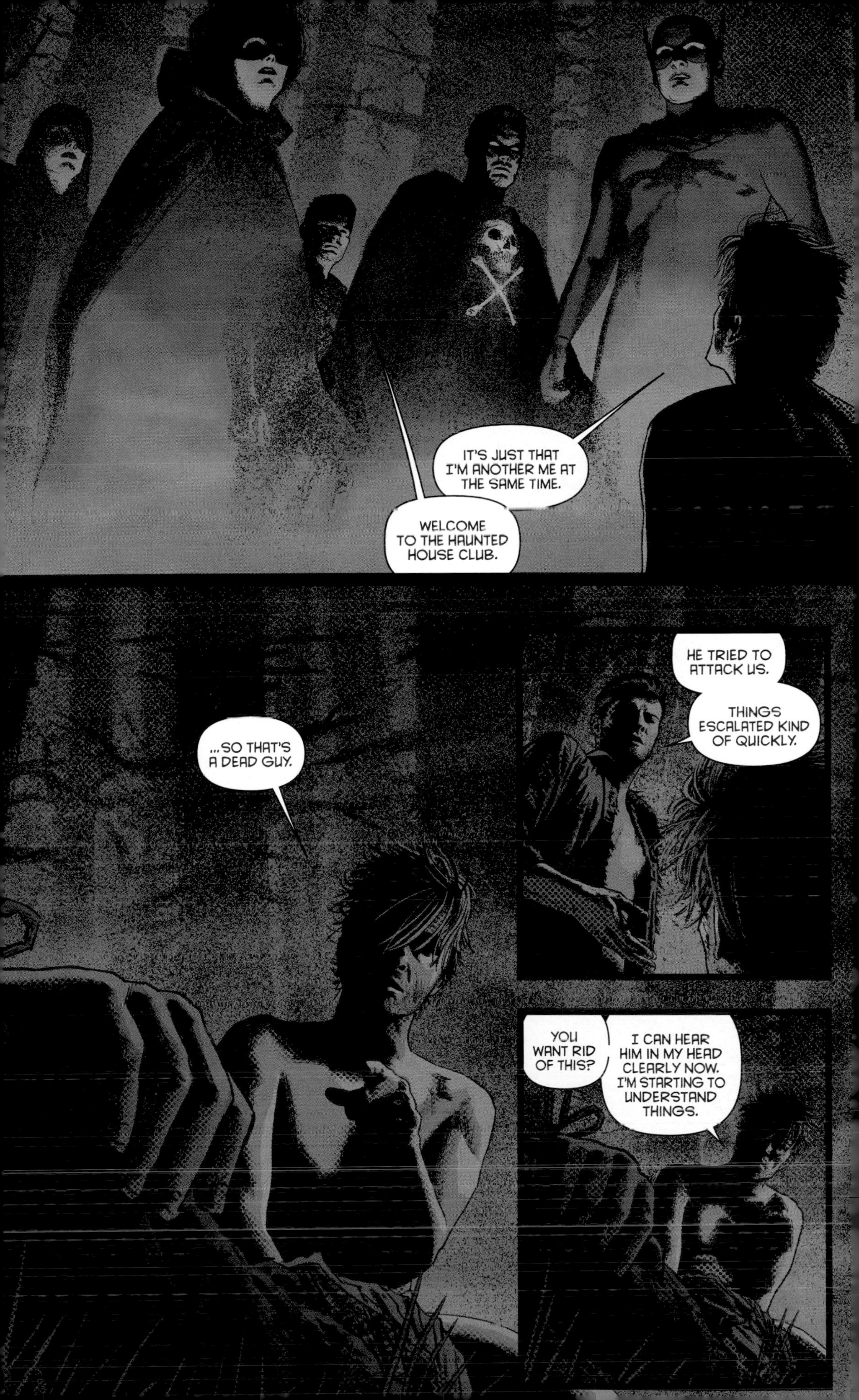
IT'S JUST THAT I'M ANOTHER ME AT THE SAME TIME.
WELCOME TO THE HAUNTED HOUSE CLUB.
...SO THAT'S A DEAD GUY.
HE TRIED TO ATTACK US.
THINGS ESCALATED KIND OF QUICKLY.
YOU WANT RID OF THIS?
I CAN HEAR HIM IN MY HEAD CLEARLY NOW. I'M STARTING TO UNDERSTAND THINGS.

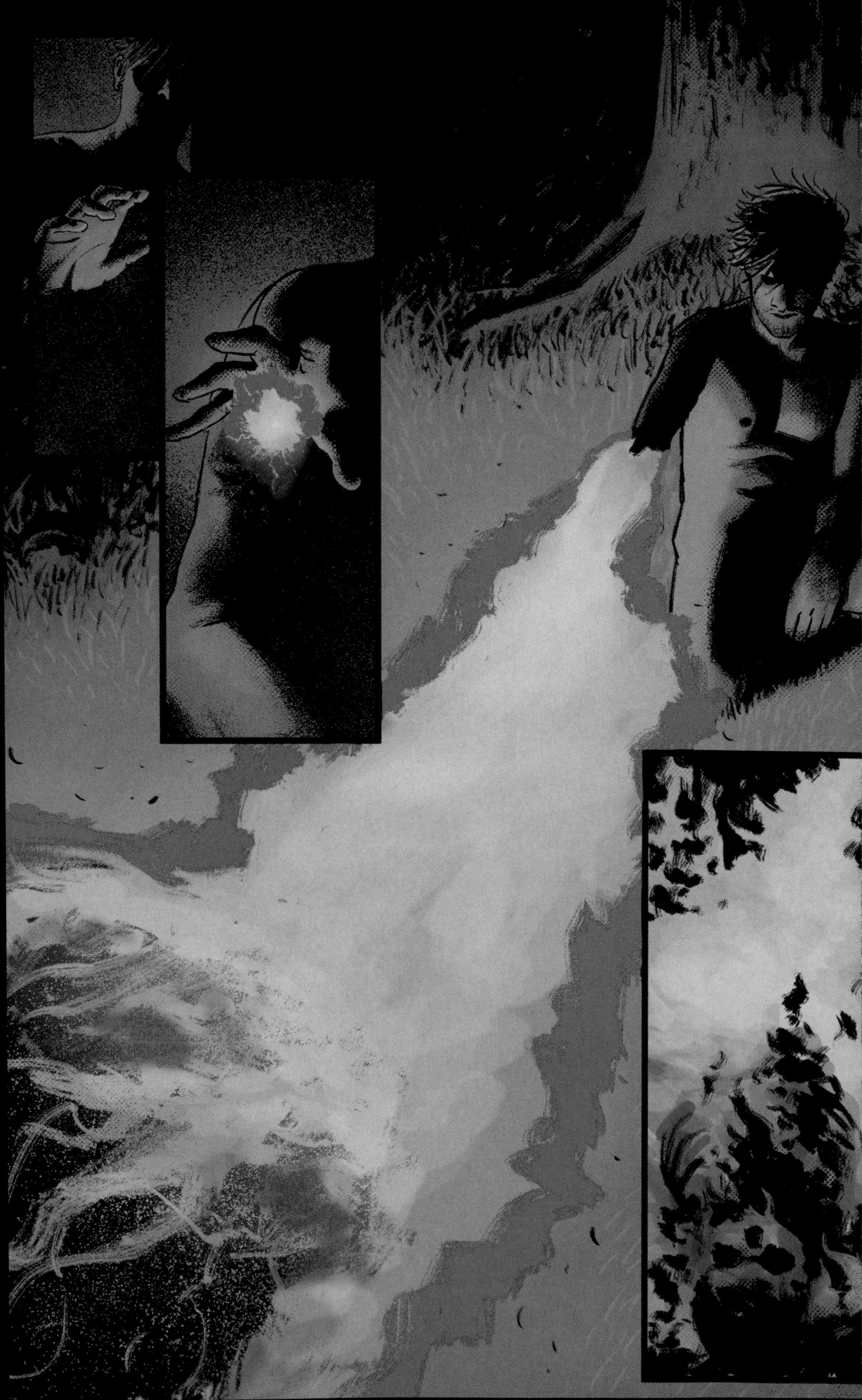

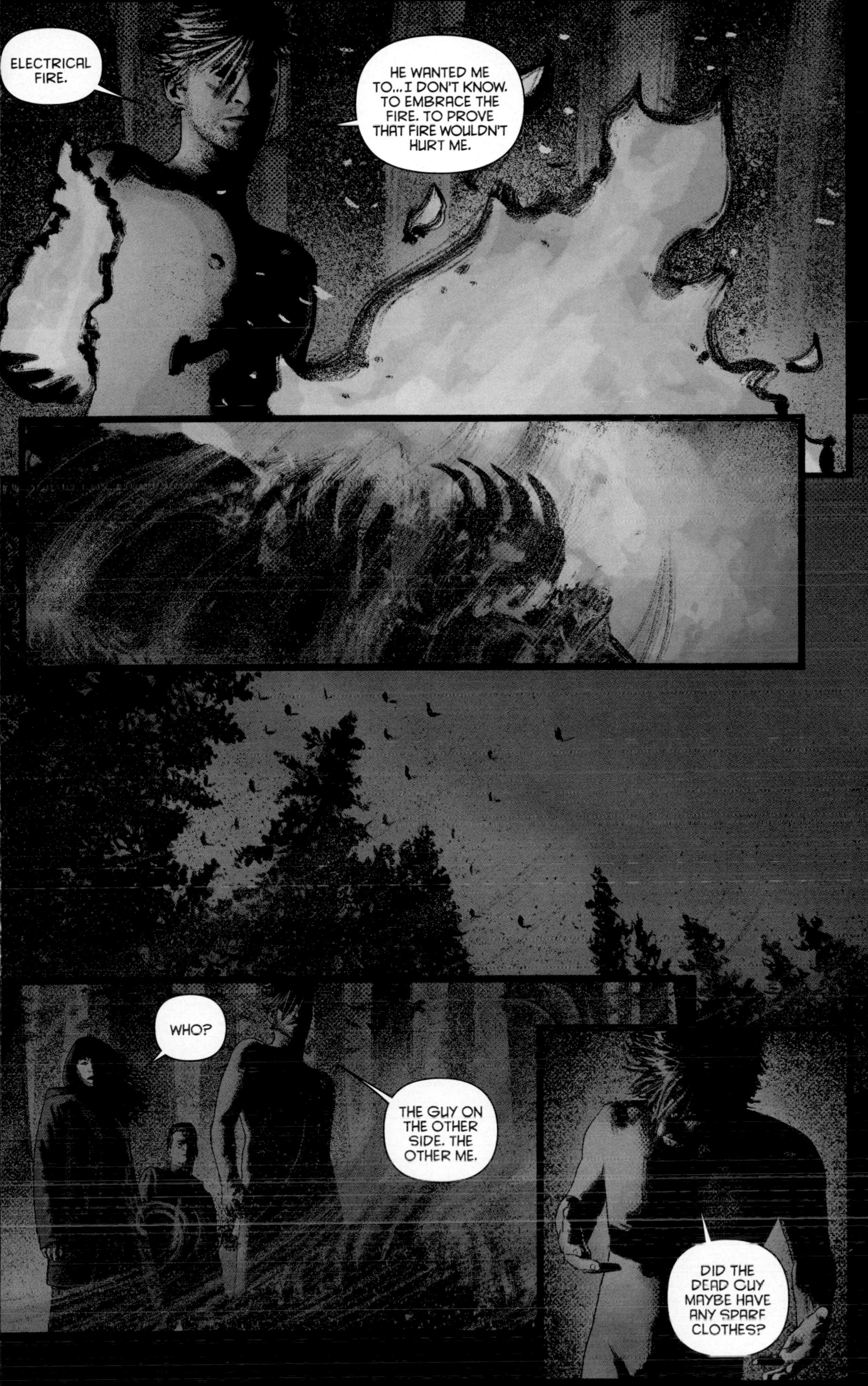
ELECTRICAL FIRE.
HE WANTED ME TO...I DON'T KNOW. TO EMBRACE THE FIRE. TO PROVE THAT FIRE WOULDN'T HURT ME.
WHO?
THE GUY ON THE OTHER SIDE. THE OTHER ME.
DID THE DEAD GUY MAYBE HAVE ANY SPARE CLOTHES?

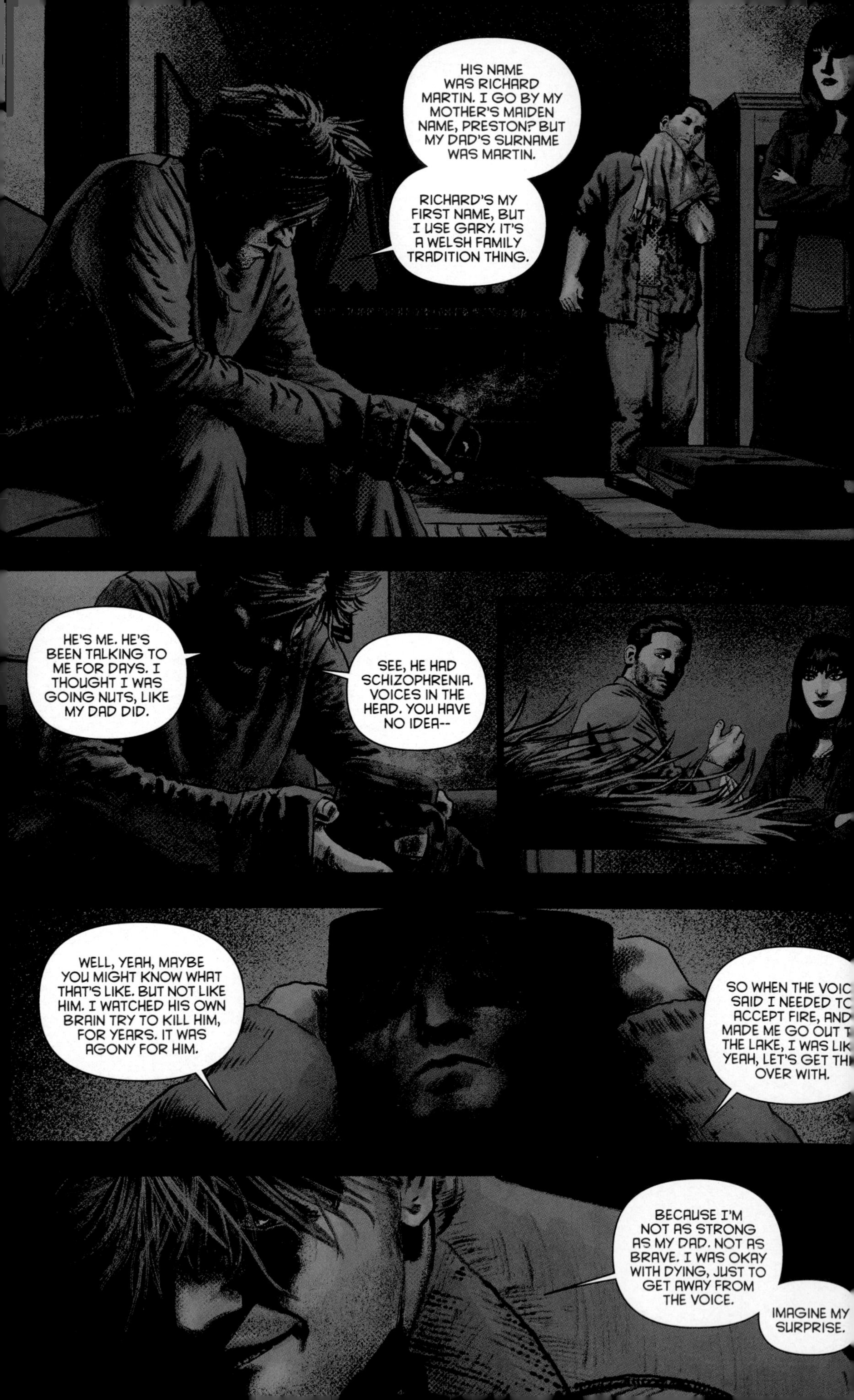
HIS NAME WAS RICHARD MARTIN. I GO BY MY MOTHER'S MAIDEN NAME, PRESTON? BUT MY DAD'S SURNAME WAS MARTIN.
RICHARD'S MY FIRST NAME, BUT I USE GARY. IT'S A WELSH FAMILY TRADITION THING.
HE'S ME. HE'S BEEN TALKING TO ME FOR DAYS. I THOUGHT I WAS GOING NUTS, LIKE MY DAD DID.
SEE, HE HAD SCHIZOPHRENIA. VOICES IN THE HEAD. YOU HAVE NO IDEA--
WELL, YEAH, MAYBE YOU MIGHT KNOW WHAT THAT'S LIKE. BUT NOT LIKE HIM. I WATCHED HIS OWN BRAIN TRY TO KILL HIM, FOR YEARS. IT WAS AGONY FOR HIM.
BECAUSE I'M NOT AS STRONG AS MY DAD. NOT AS BRAVE. I WAS OKAY WITH DYING, JUST TO GET AWAY FROM THE VOICE.
IMAGINE MY SURPRISE.

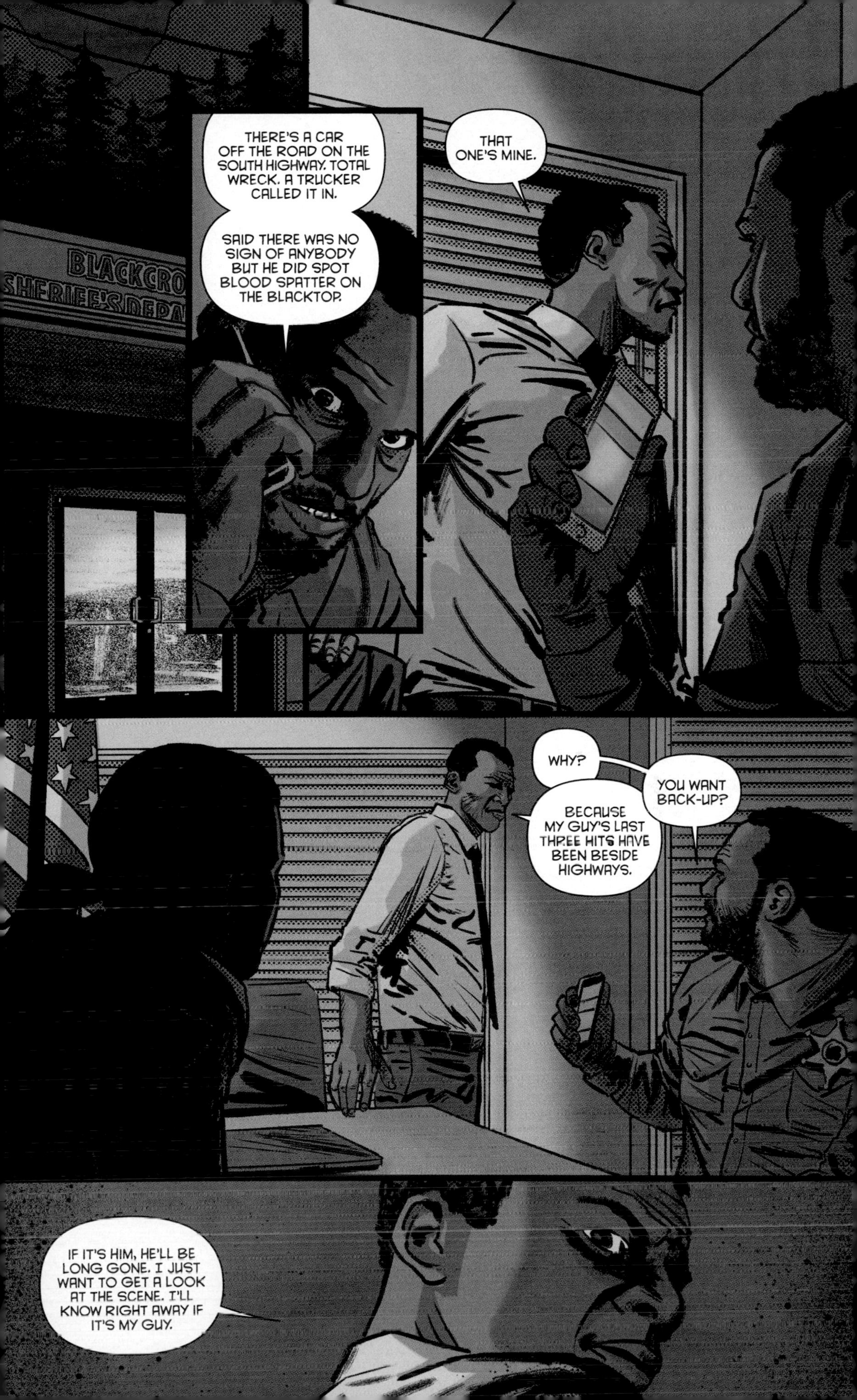
THERE'S A CAR OFF THE ROAD ON THE SOUTH HIGHWAY. TOTAL WRECK. A TRUCKER CALLED IT IN.
SAID THERE WAS NO SIGN OF ANYBODY BUT HE DID SPOT BLOOD SPATTER ON THE BLACKTOP.
THAT ONE'S MINE.
WHY?
YOU WANT BACK-UP?
BECAUSE MY GUY'S LAST THREE HITS HAVE BEEN BESIDE HIGHWAYS.
IF IT'S HIM, HE'LL BE LONG GONE. I JUST WANT TO GET A LOOK AT THE SCENE. I'LL KNOW RIGHT AWAY IF IT'S MY GUY.

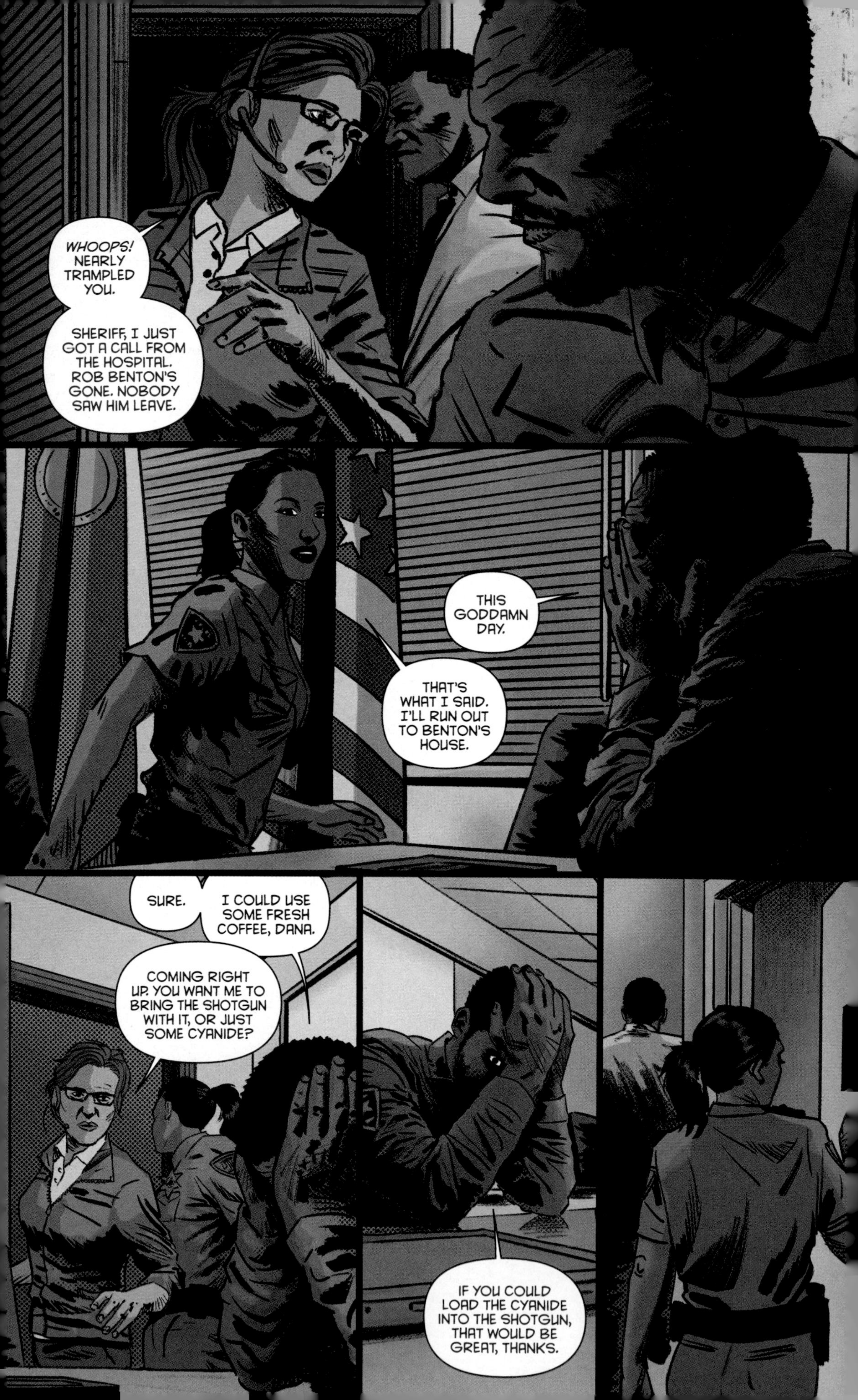
WHOOPS! NEARLY TRAMPLED YOU.
SHERIFF, I JUST GOT A CALL FROM THE HOSPITAL. ROB BENTON'S GONE. NOBODY SAW HIM LEAVE.
THIS GODDAMN DAY.
THAT'S WHAT I SAID. I'LL RUN OUT TO BENTON'S HOUSE.
SURE.
I COULD USE SOME FRESH COFFEE, DANA.
COMING RIGHT UP. YOU WANT ME TO BRING THE SHOTGUN WITH IT, OR JUST SOME CYANIDE?
IF YOU COULD LOAD THE CYANIDE INTO THE SHOTGUN, THAT WOULD BE GREAT, THANKS.

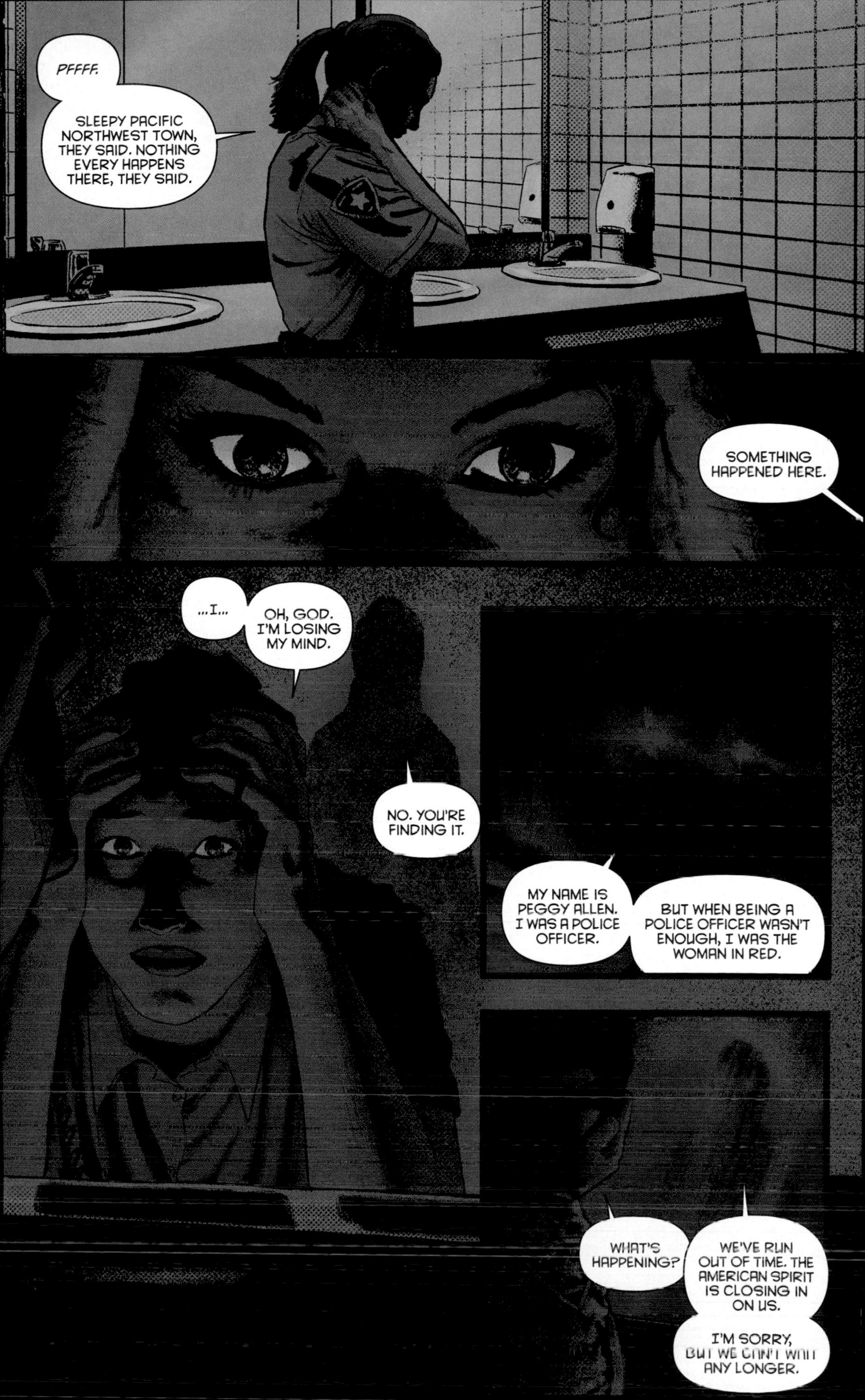
PFFFF.
SLEEPY PACIFIC NORTHWEST TOWN, THEY SAID. NOTHING EVERY HAPPENS THERE, THEY SAID.
SOMETHING HAPPENED HERE.
...I...
OH, GOD. I'M LOSING MY MIND.
NO. YOU'RE FINDING IT.
MY NAME IS PEGGY ALLEN. I WAS A POLICE OFFICER.
BUT WHEN BEING A POLICE OFFICER WASN'T ENOUGH, I WAS THE WOMAN IN RED.
WHAT'S HAPPENING?
WE'VE RUN OUT OF TIME. THE AMERICAN SPIRIT IS CLOSING IN ON US.
I'M SORRY, BUT WE CAN'T WAIT ANY LONGER.

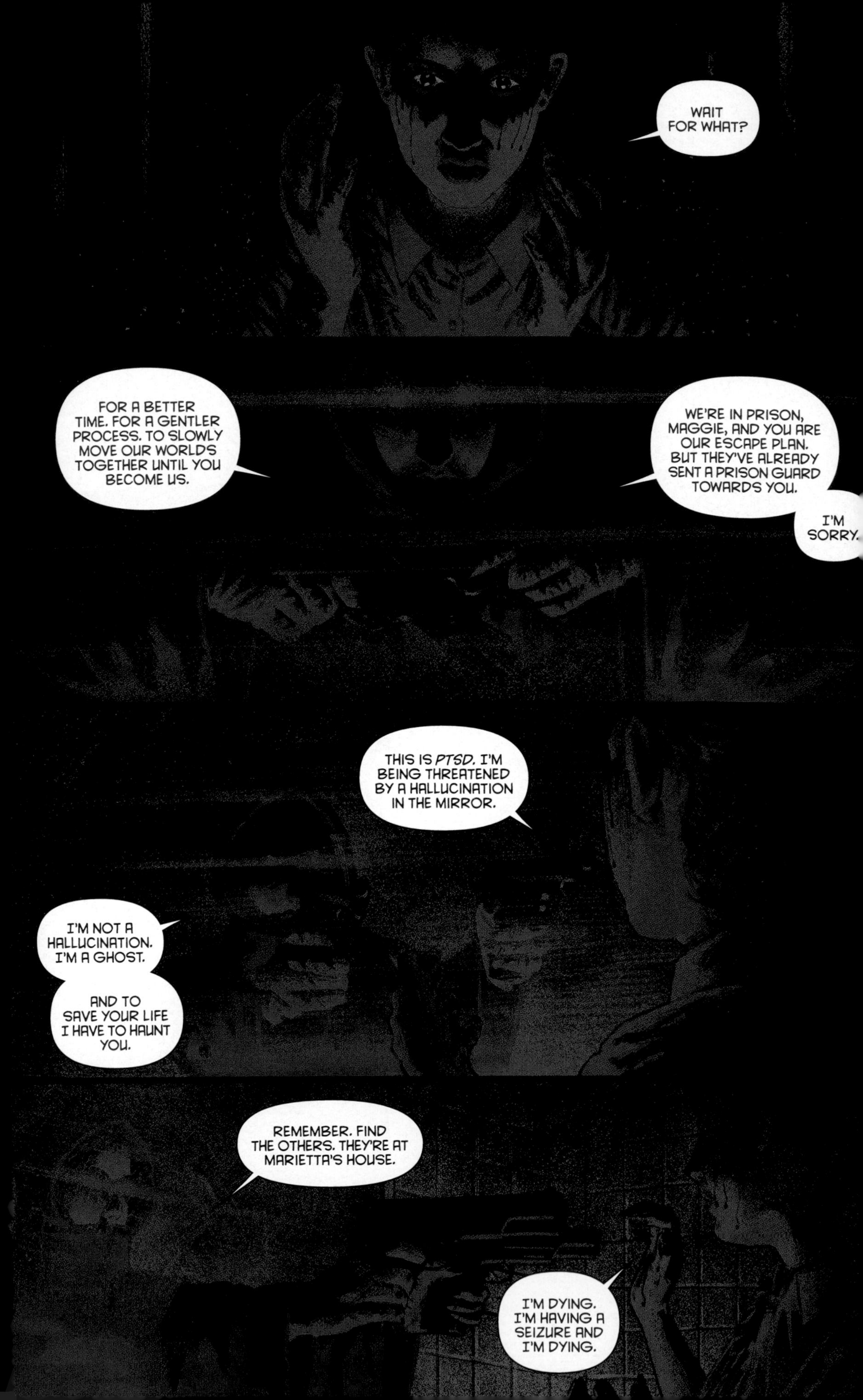
WAIT FOR WHAT?
FOR A BETTER TIME. FOR A GENTLER PROCESS. TO SLOWLY MOVE OUR WORLDS TOGETHER UNTIL YOU BECOME US.
WE'RE IN PRISON, MAGGIE, AND YOU ARE OUR ESCAPE PLAN. BUT THEY'VE ALREADY SENT A PRISON GUARD TOWARDS YOU.
I'M SORRY.
THIS IS *PTSD*. I'M BEING THREATENED BY A HALLUCINATION IN THE MIRROR.
I'M NOT A HALLUCINATION. I'M A GHOST.
AND TO SAVE YOUR LIFE I HAVE TO HAUNT YOU.
REMEMBER. FIND THE OTHERS. THEY'RE AT MARIETTA'S HOUSE.
I'M DYING. I'M HAVING A SEIZURE AND I'M DYING.

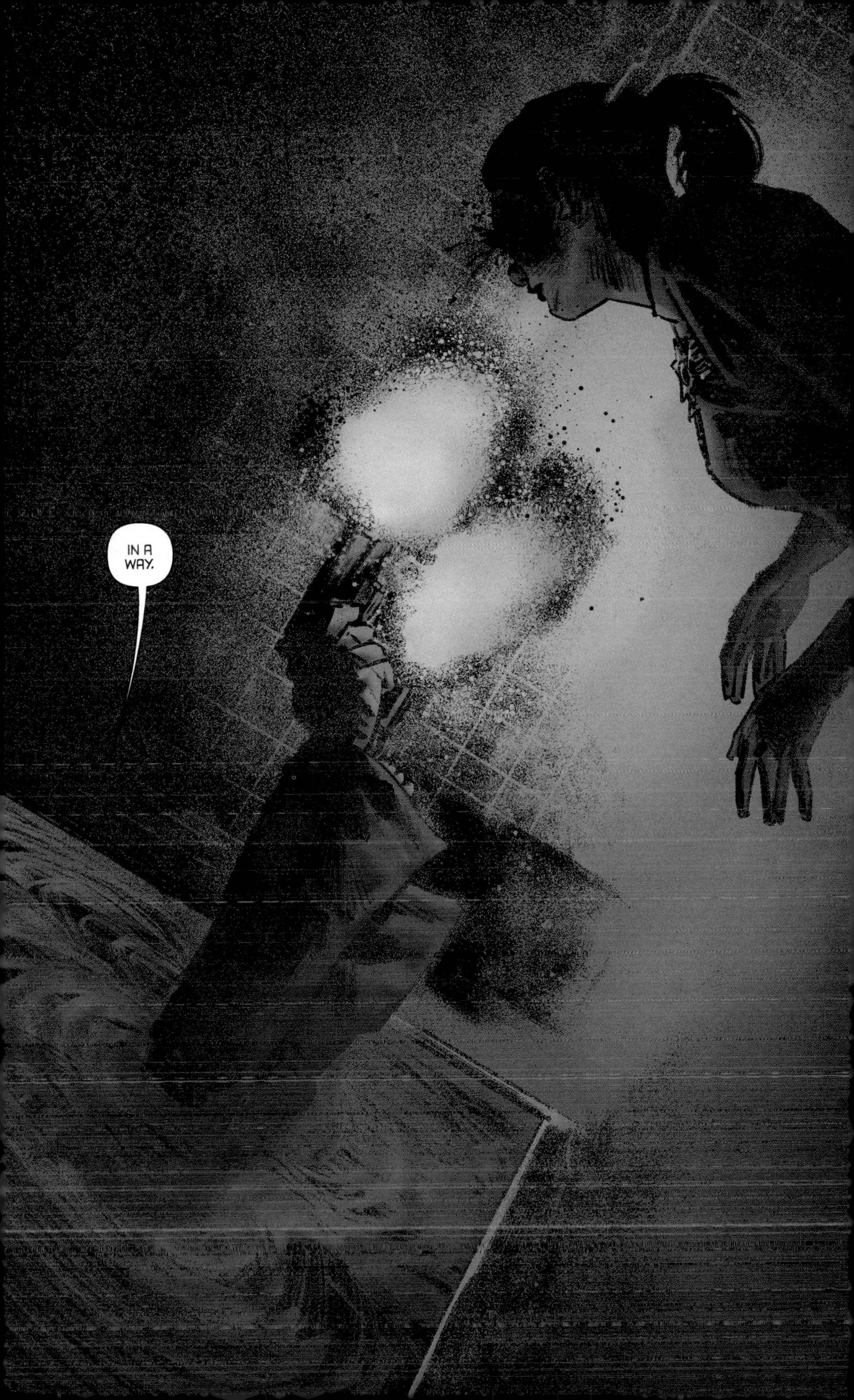
IN A WAY.

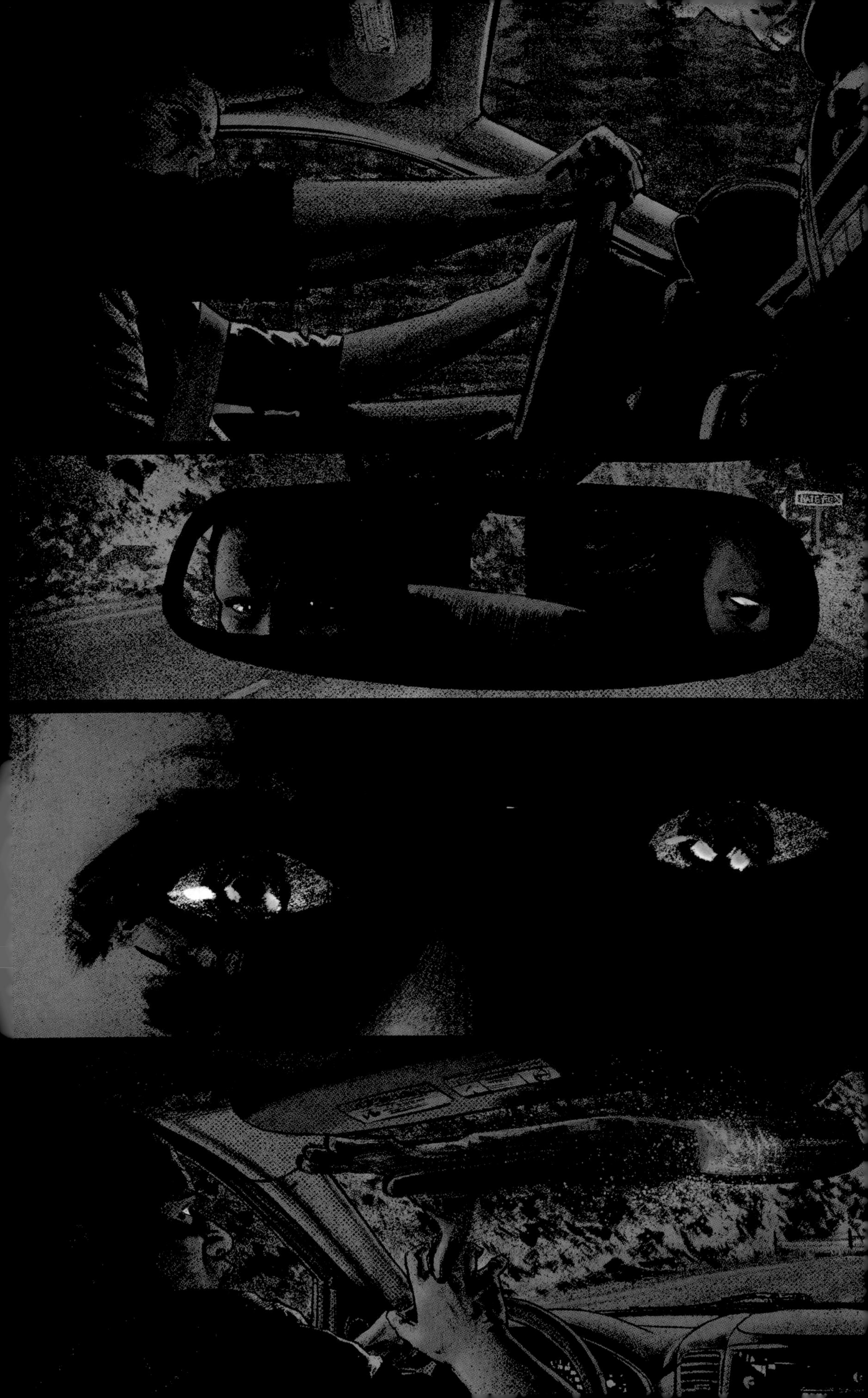

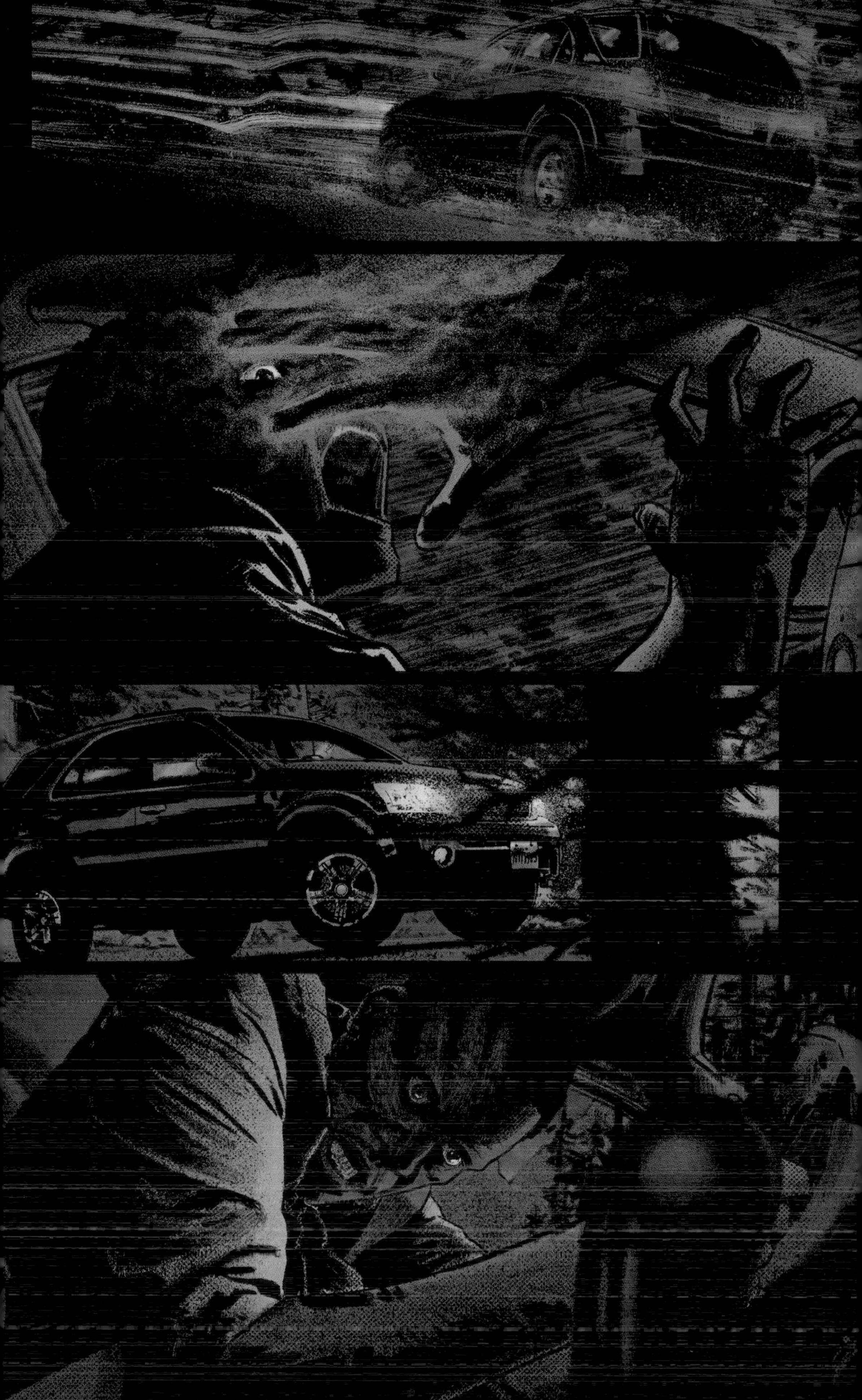

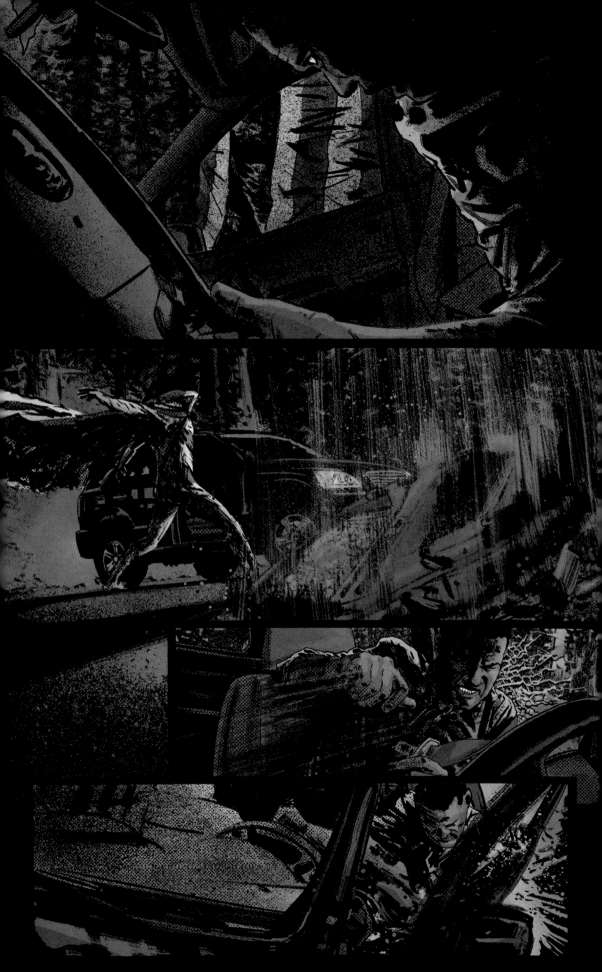

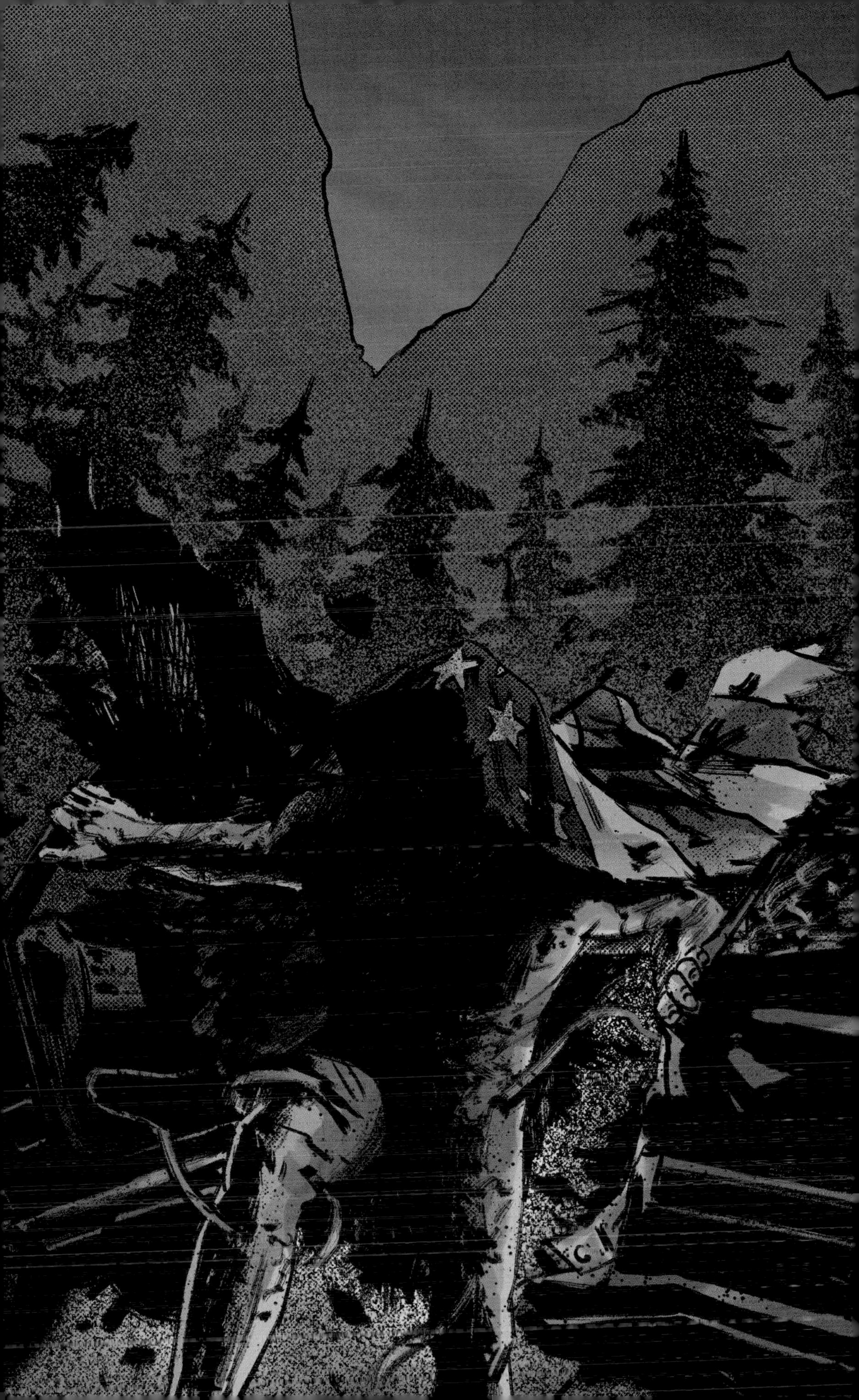

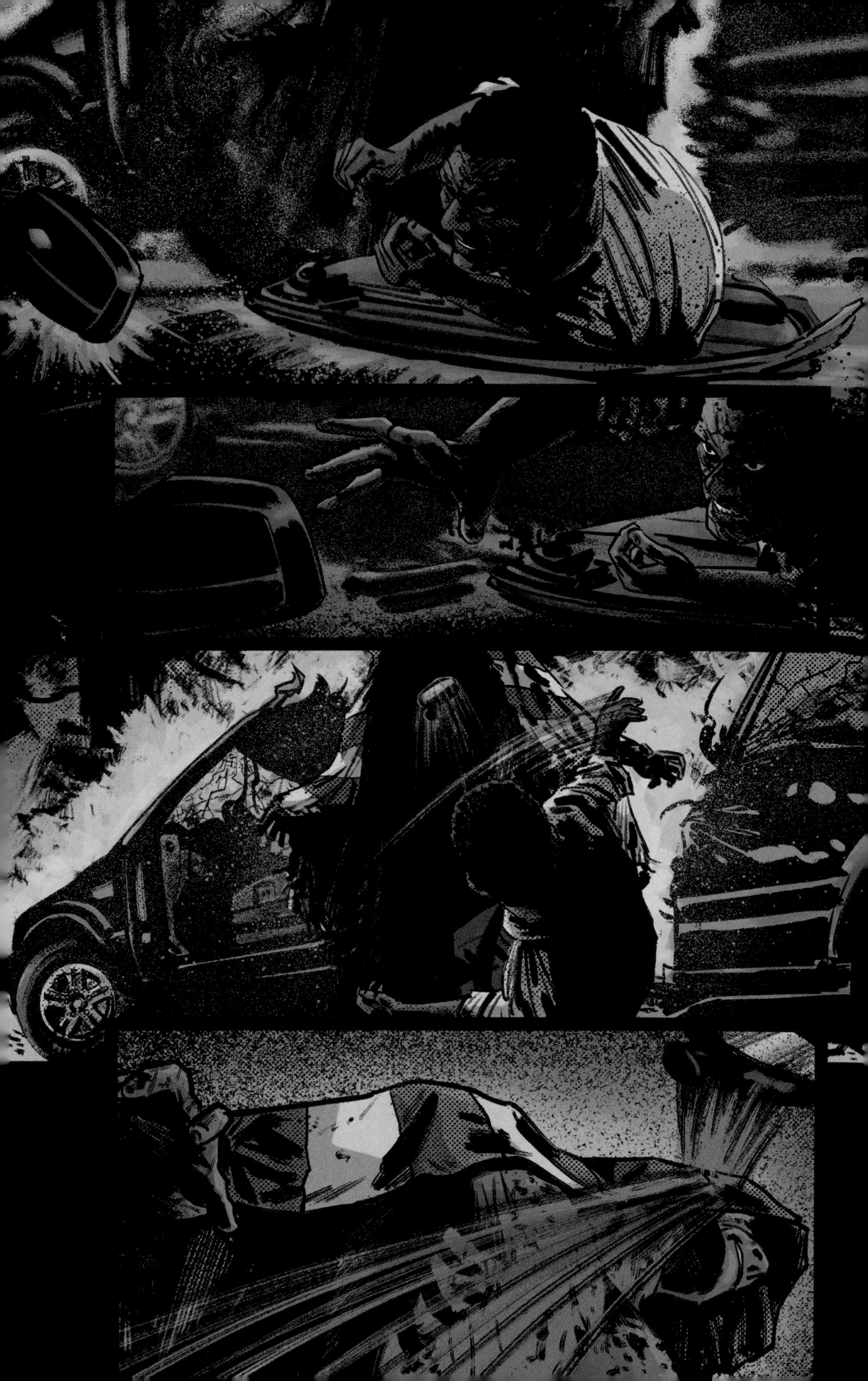

LET ME HELP YOU BE SAFE.

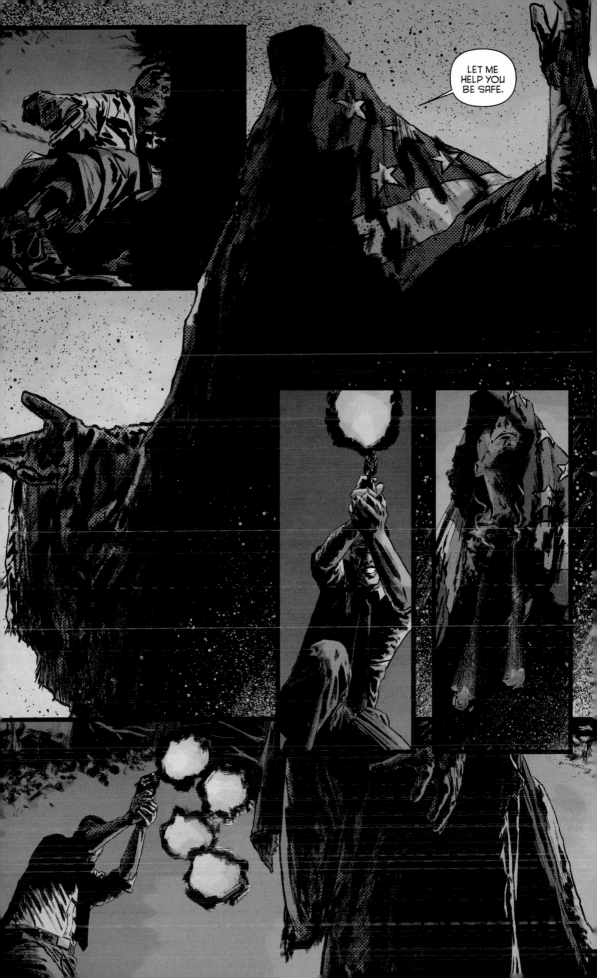

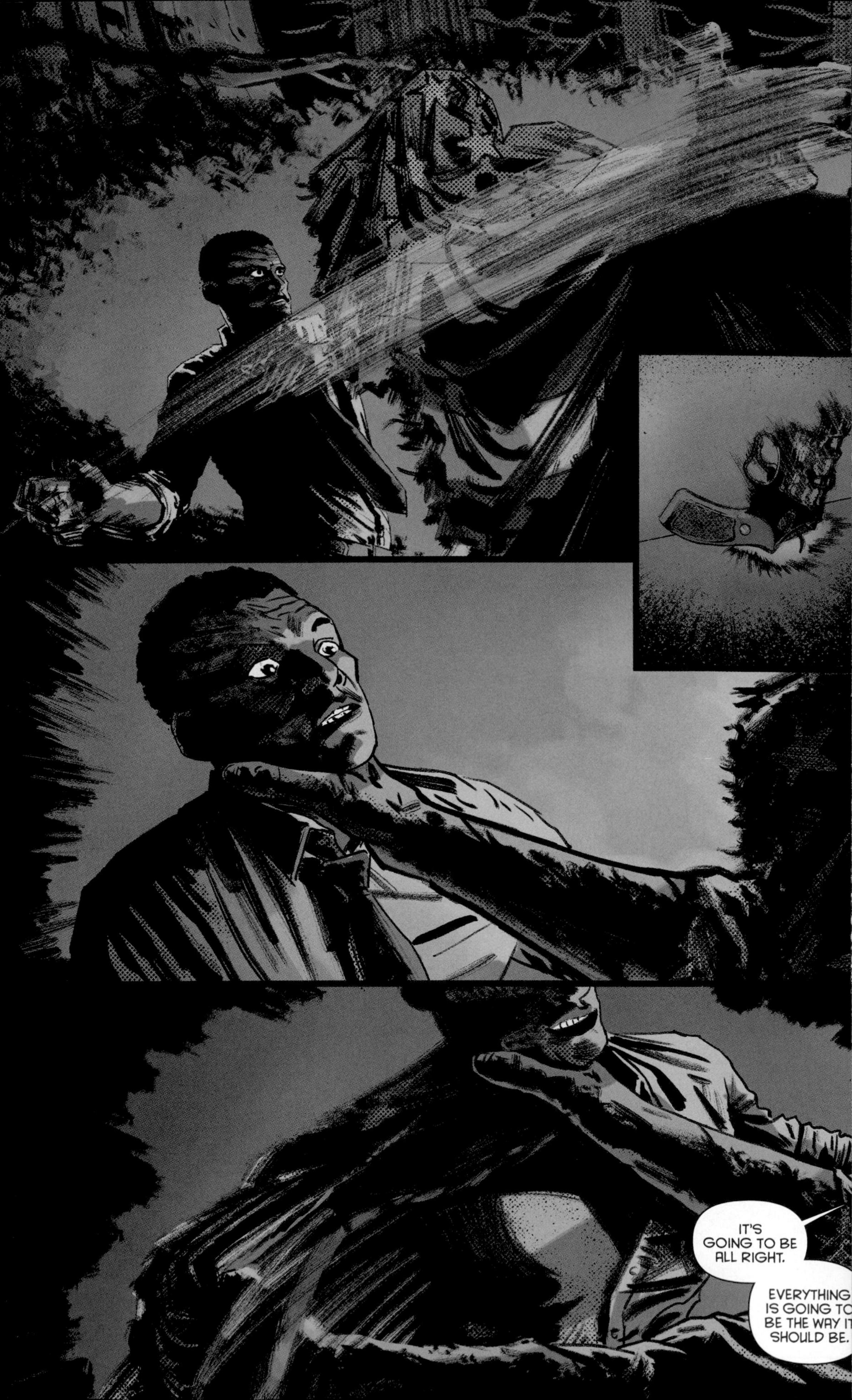
IT'S GOING TO BE ALL RIGHT.
EVERYTHING IS GOING TO BE THE WAY IT SHOULD BE.

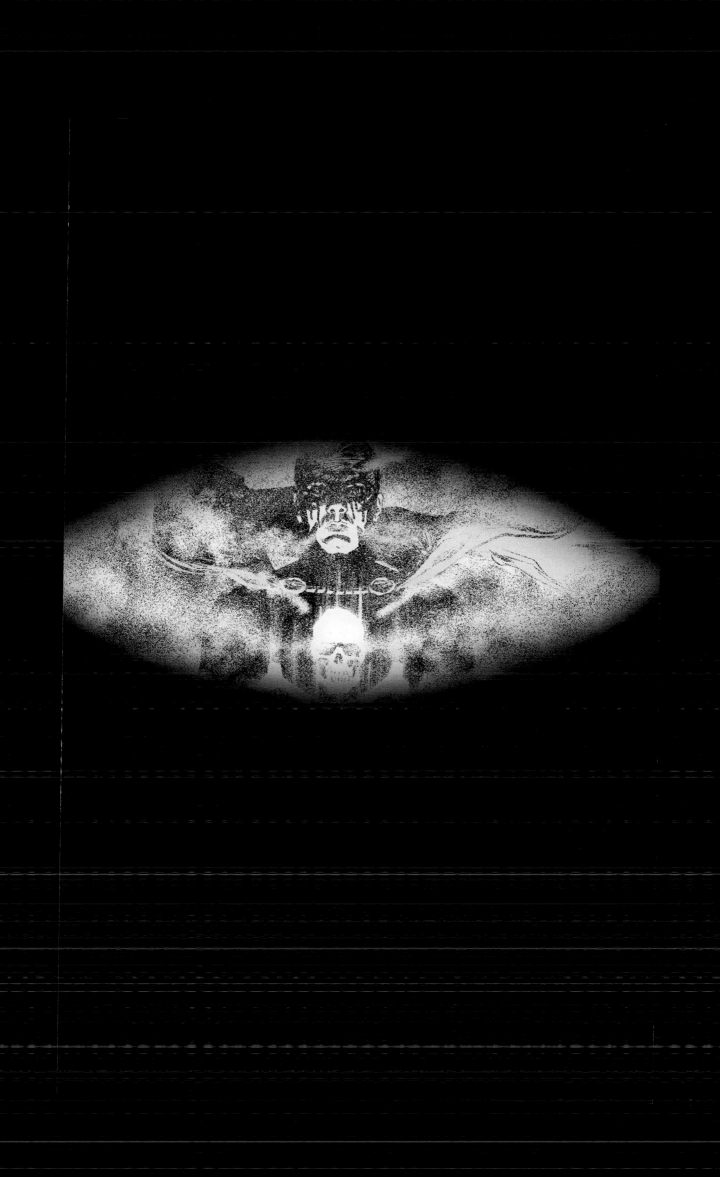

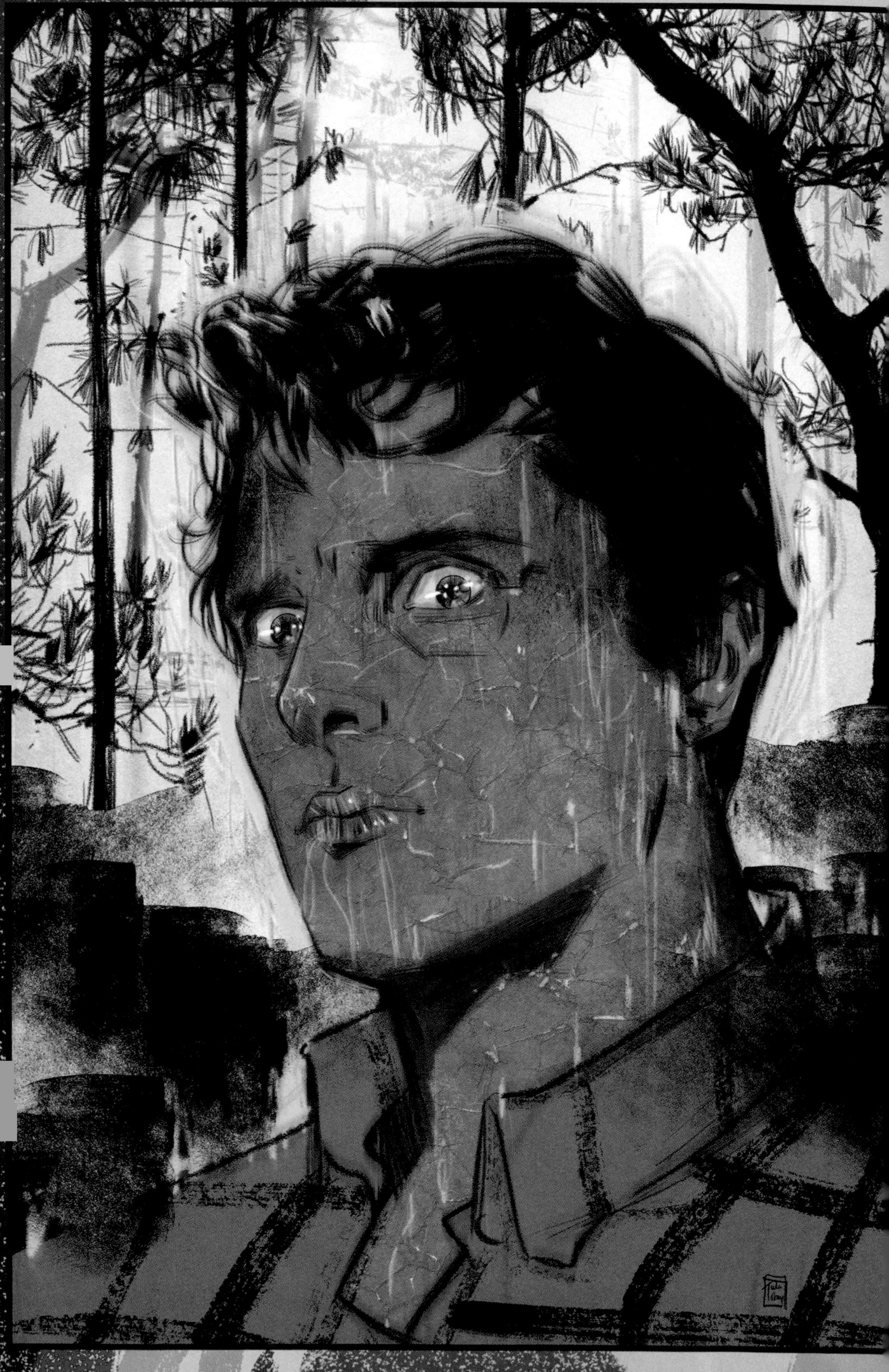

ISSUE #5 COVER BY TULA LOTAY

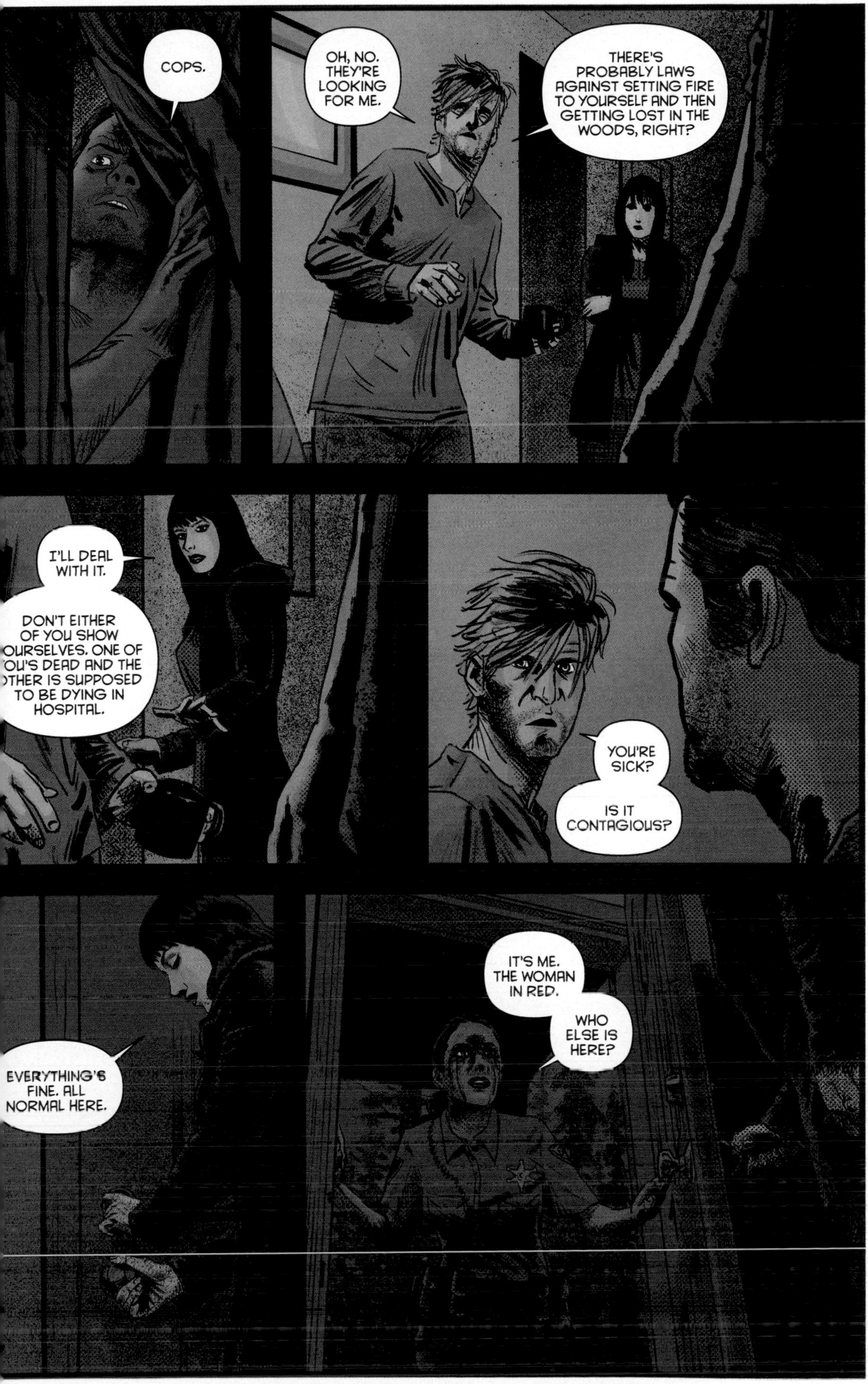
COPS.
OH, NO. THEY'RE LOOKING FOR ME.
THERE'S PROBABLY LAWS AGAINST SETTING FIRE TO YOURSELF AND THEN GETTING LOST IN THE WOODS, RIGHT?
I'LL DEAL WITH IT.
DON'T EITHER OF YOU SHOW OURSELVES. ONE OF OU'S DEAD AND THE THER IS SUPPOSED TO BE DYING IN HOSPITAL.
YOU'RE SICK?
IS IT CONTAGIOUS?
IT'S ME. THE WOMAN IN RED.
WHO ELSE IS HERE?
EVERYTHING'S FINE. ALL NORMAL HERE.

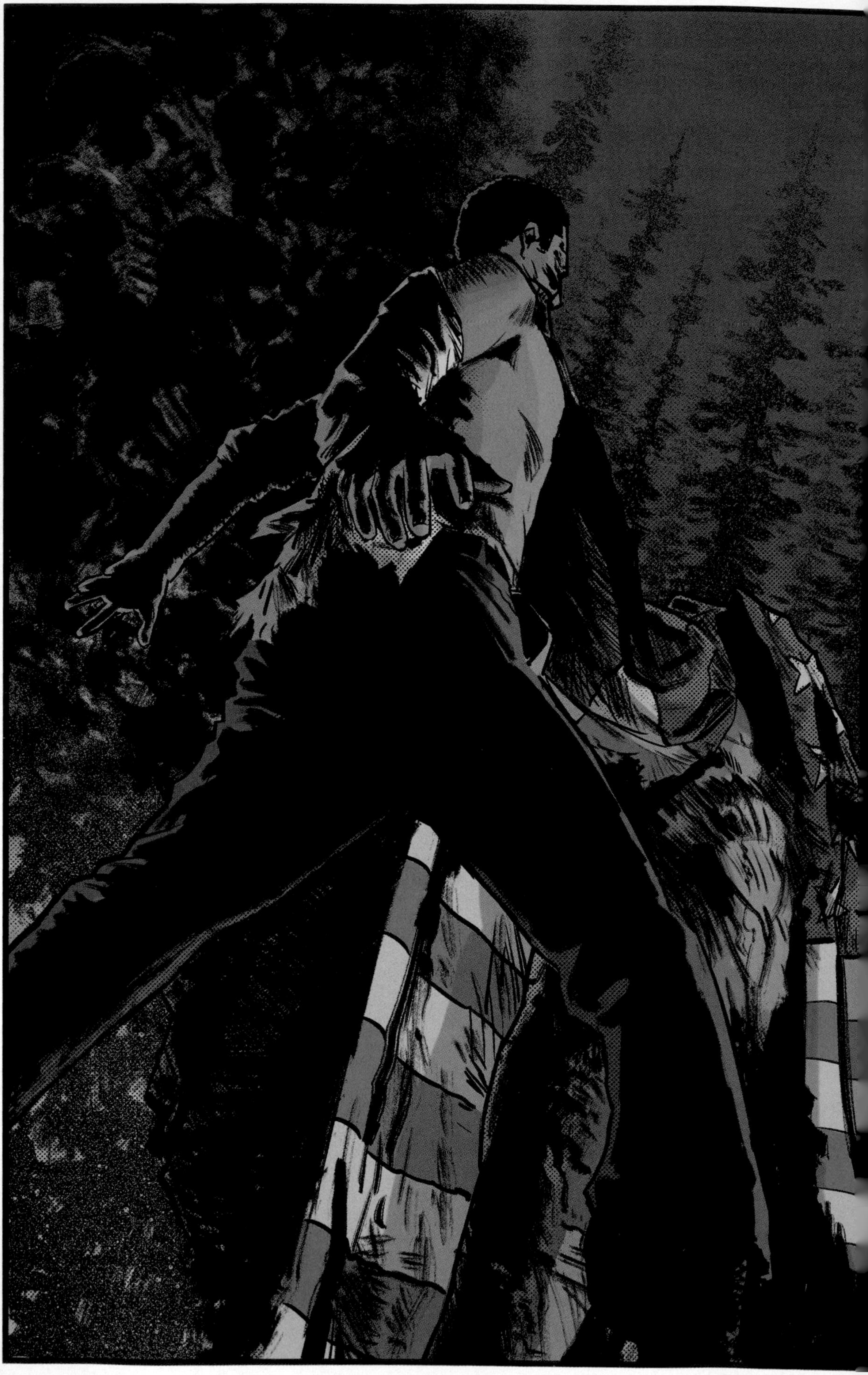

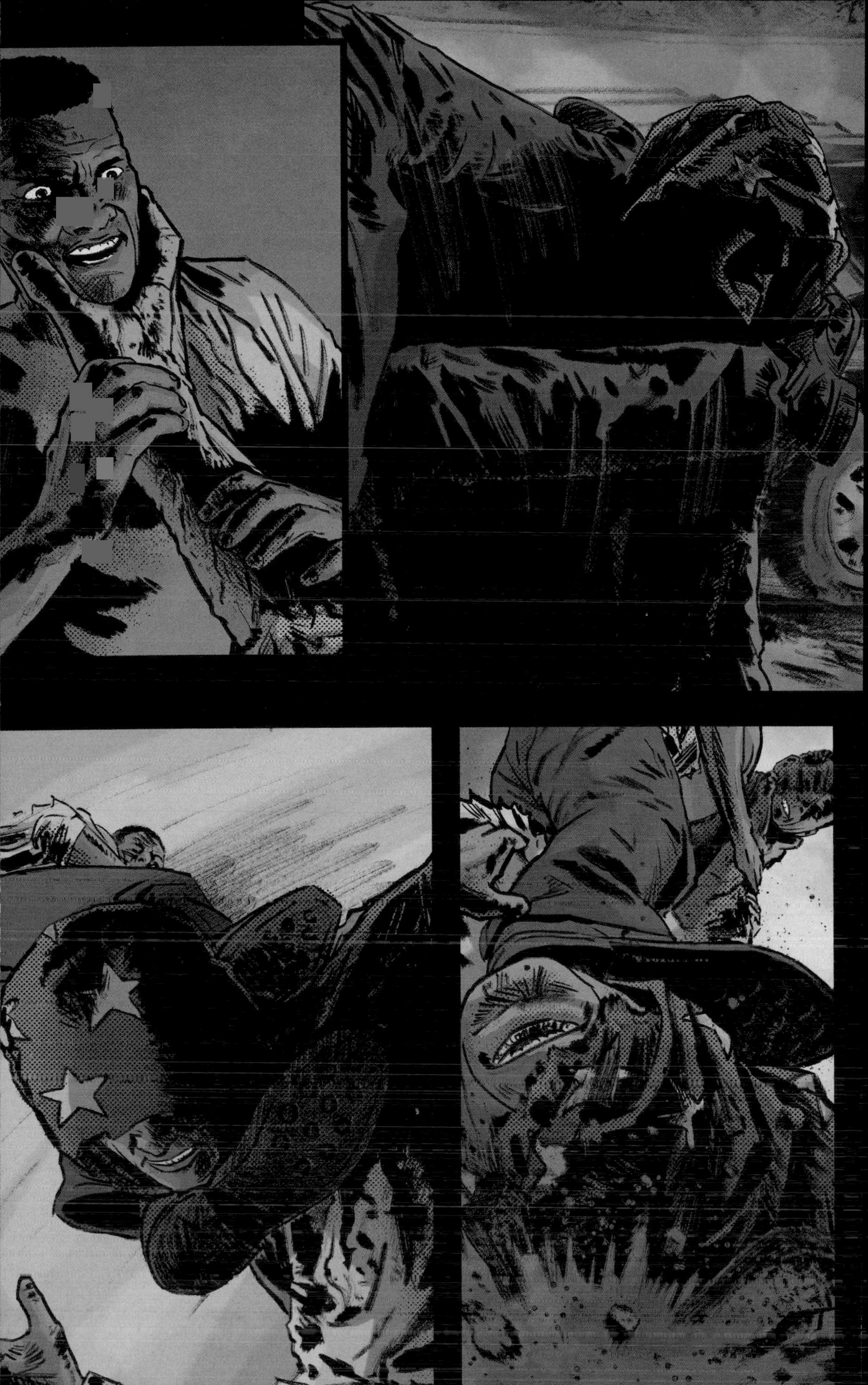

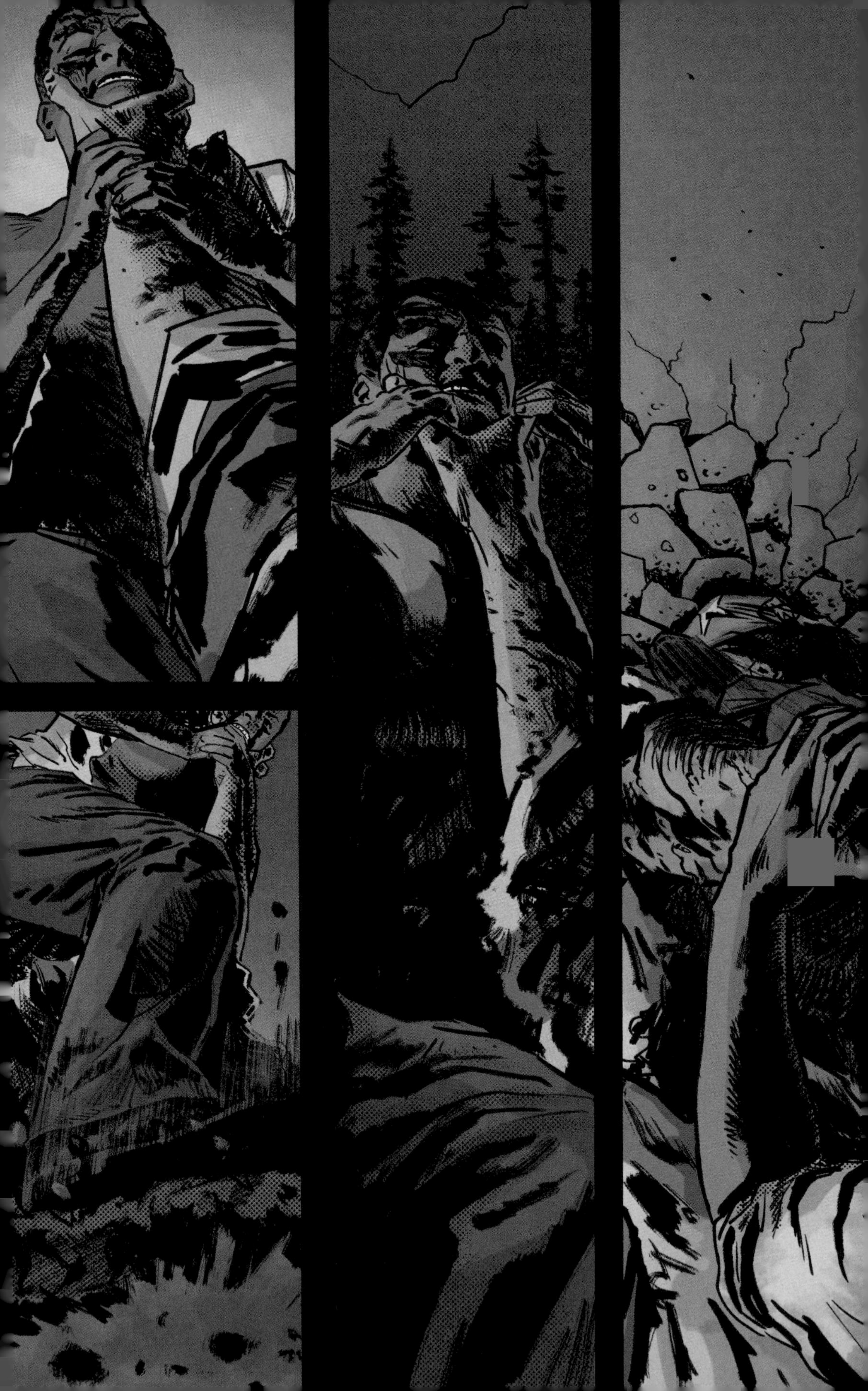

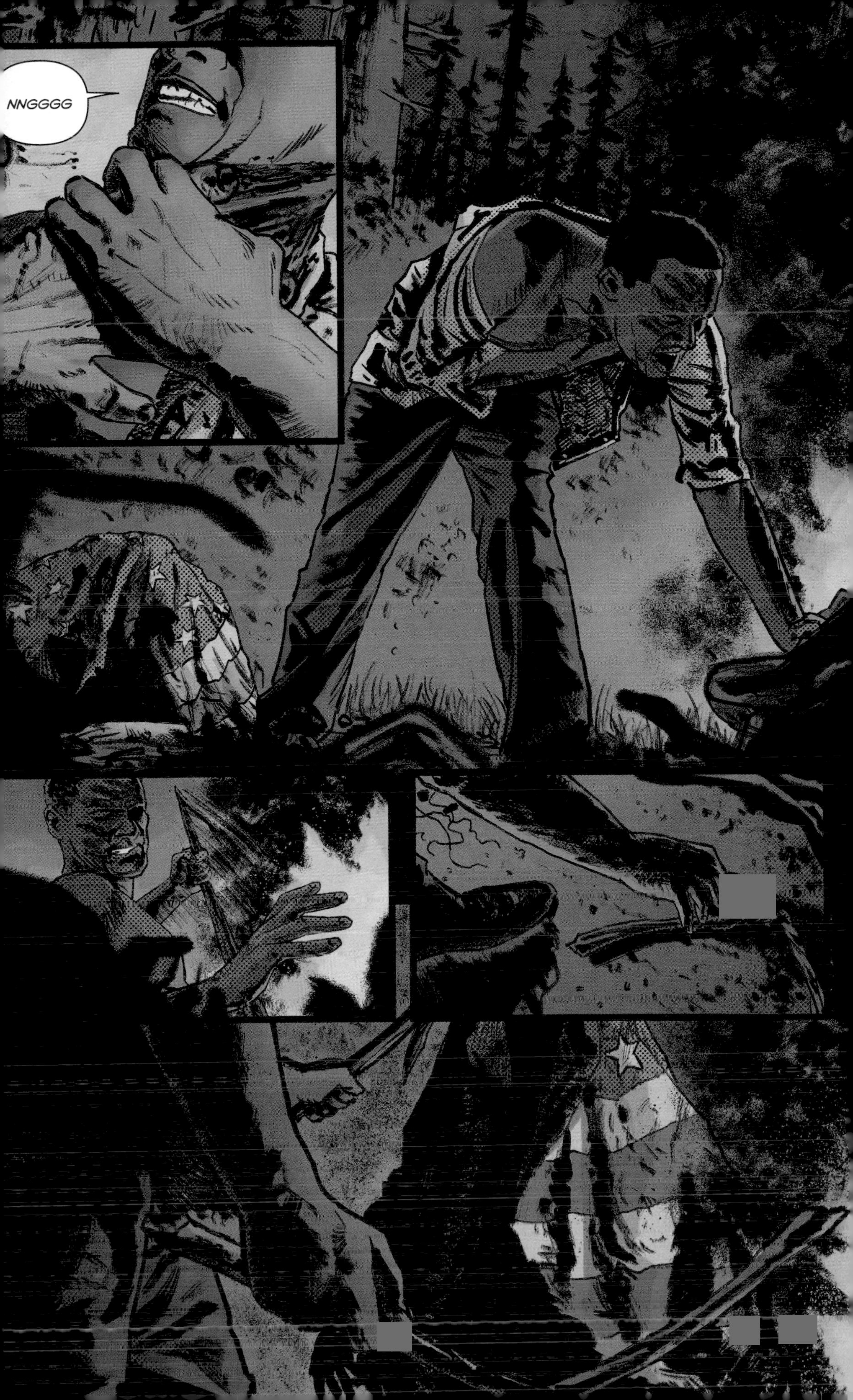
NNGGGG

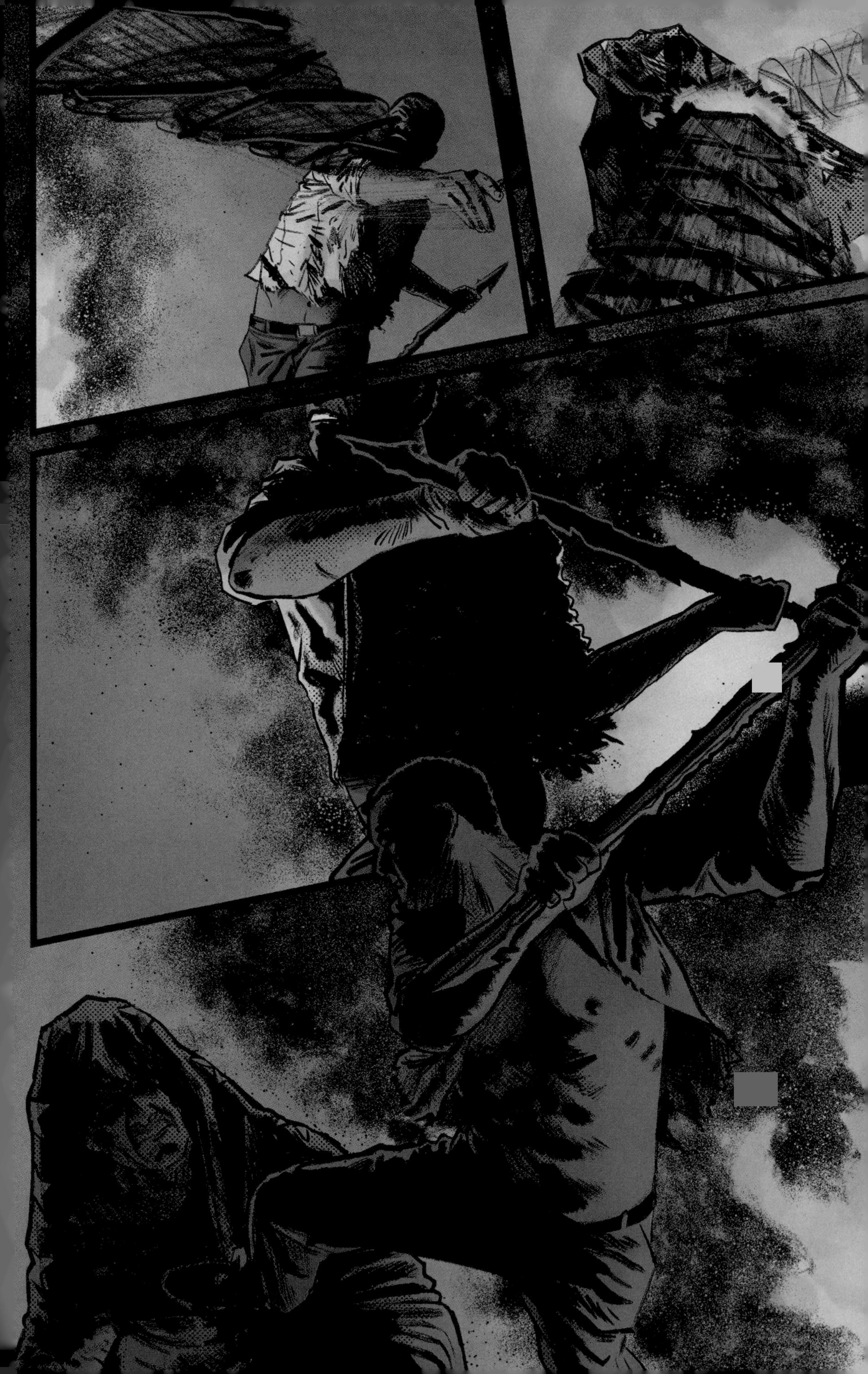

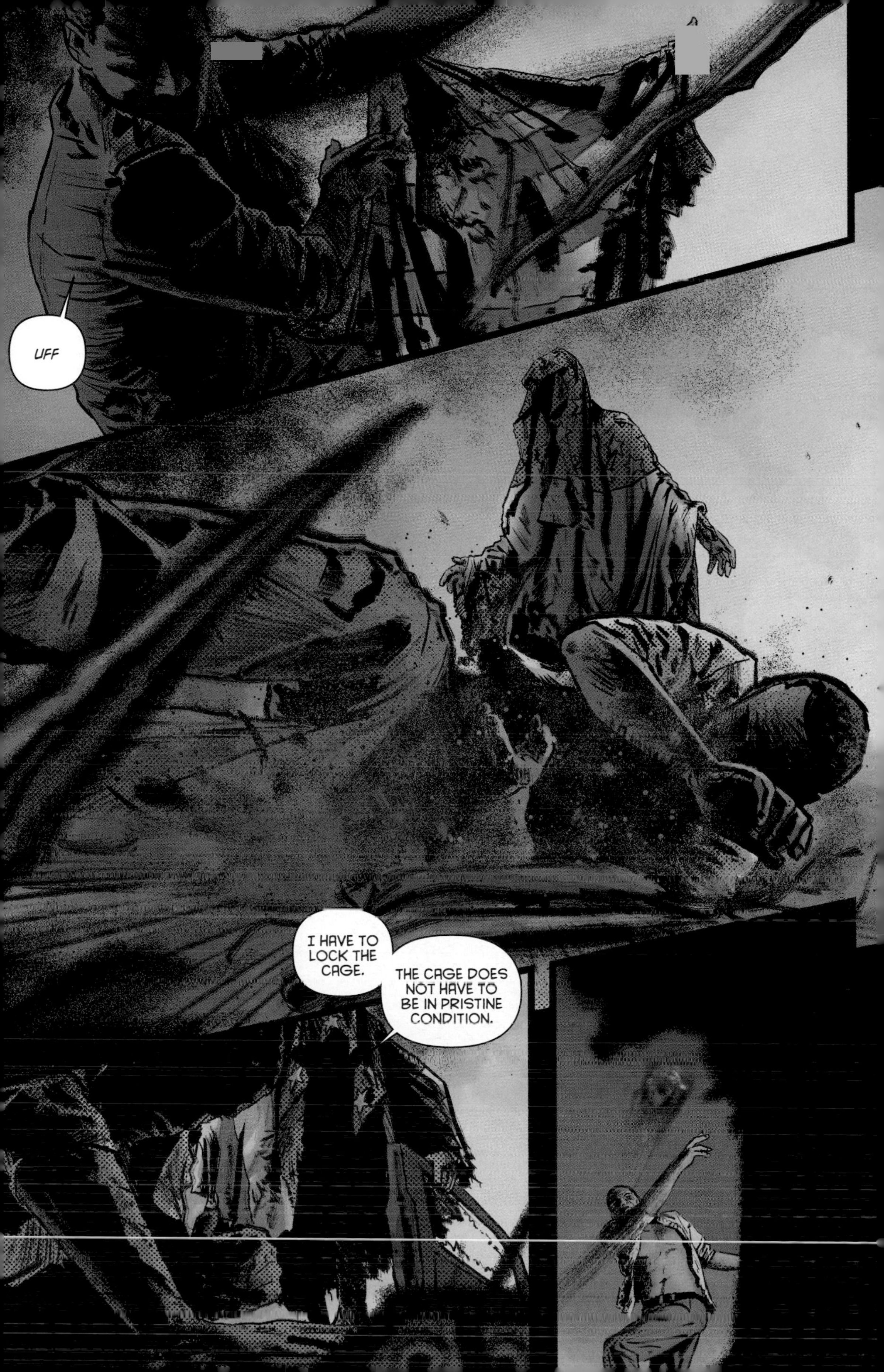
UFF
I HAVE TO LOCK THE CAGE.
THE CAGE DOES NOT HAVE TO BE IN PRISTINE CONDITION.

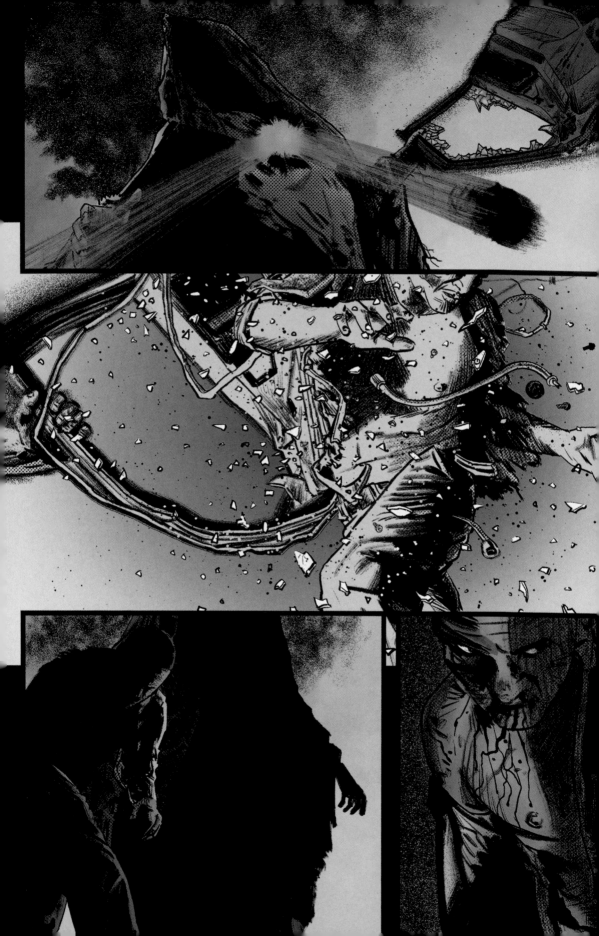

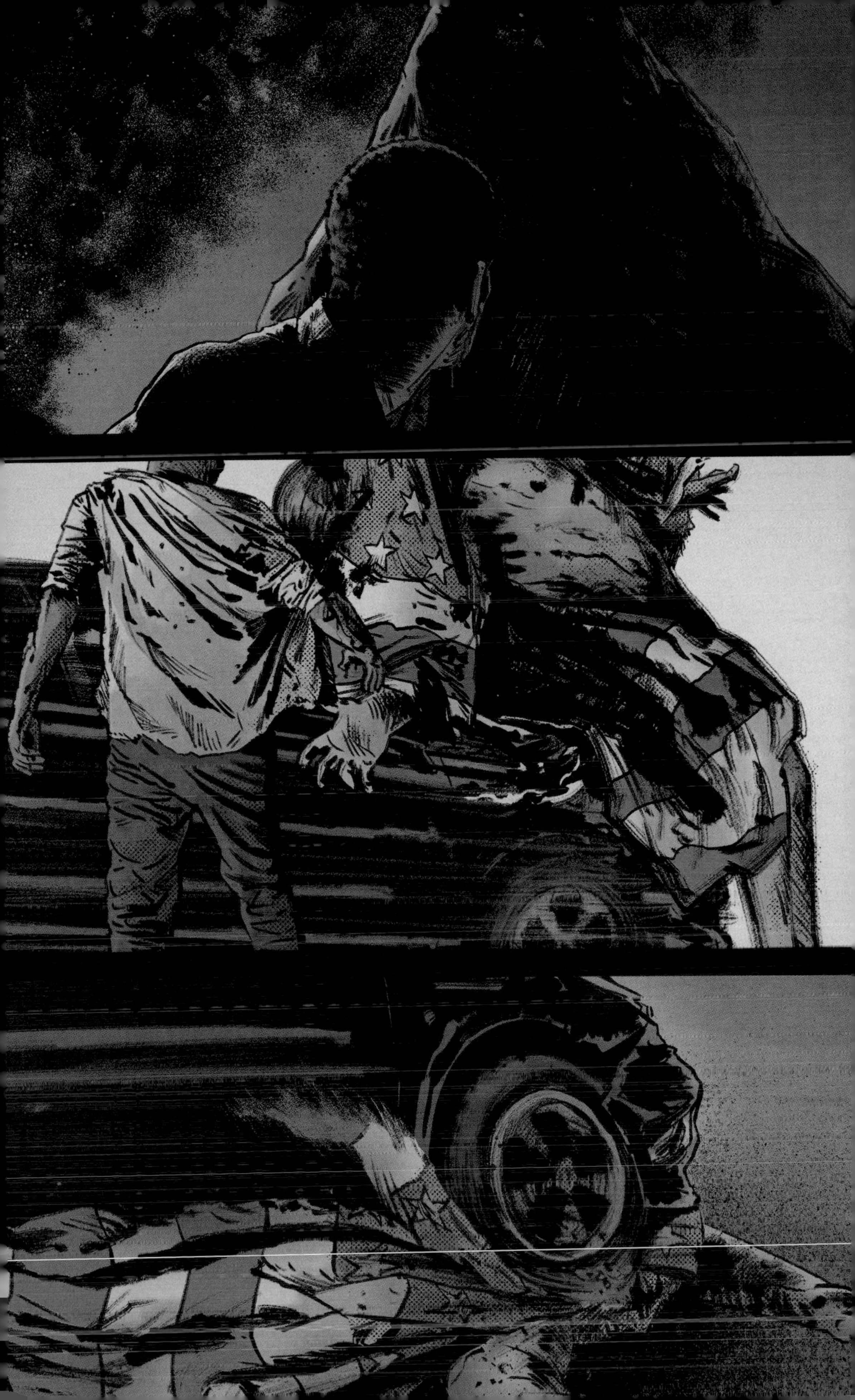

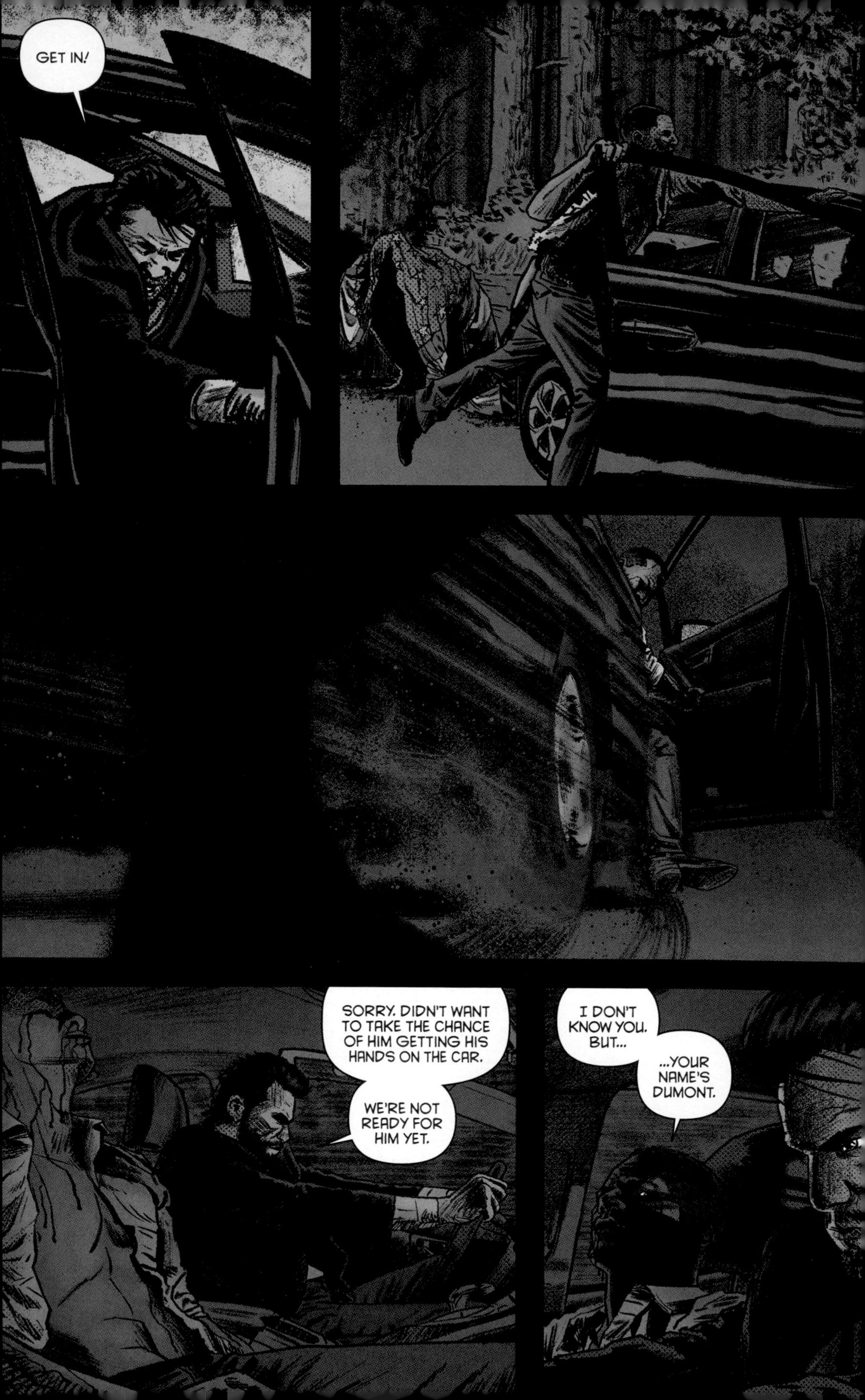
GET IN!
SORRY. DIDN'T WANT TO TAKE THE CHANCE OF HIM GETTING HIS HANDS ON THE CAR.
WE'RE NOT READY FOR HIM YET.
I DON'T KNOW YOU. BUT...
...YOUR NAME'S DUMONT.

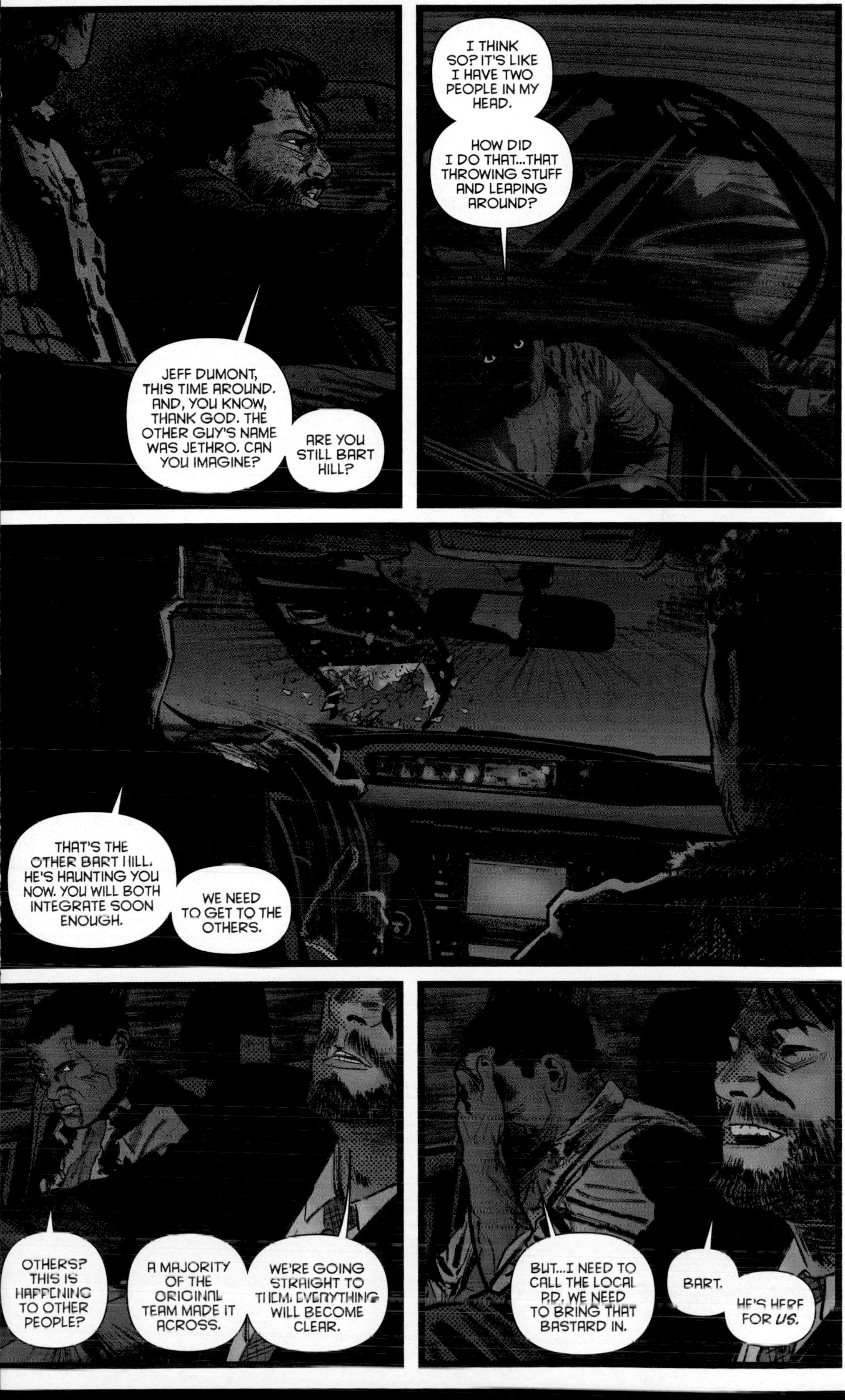
JEFF DUMONT, THIS TIME AROUND. AND, YOU KNOW, THANK GOD. THE OTHER GUY'S NAME WAS JETHRO. CAN YOU IMAGINE?
ARE YOU STILL BART HILL?
I THINK SO? IT'S LIKE I HAVE TWO PEOPLE IN MY HEAD.
HOW DID I DO THAT...THAT THROWING STUFF AND LEAPING AROUND?
THAT'S THE OTHER BART HILL. HE'S HAUNTING YOU NOW. YOU WILL BOTH INTEGRATE SOON ENOUGH.
WE NEED TO GET TO THE OTHERS.
OTHERS? THIS IS HAPPENING TO OTHER PEOPLE?
A MAJORITY OF THE ORIGINAL TEAM MADE IT ACROSS.
WE'RE GOING STRAIGHT TO THEM. EVERYTHING WILL BECOME CLEAR.
BUT...I NEED TO CALL THE LOCAL P.D. WE NEED TO BRING THAT BASTARD IN.
BART.
HE'S HERE FOR *US*.

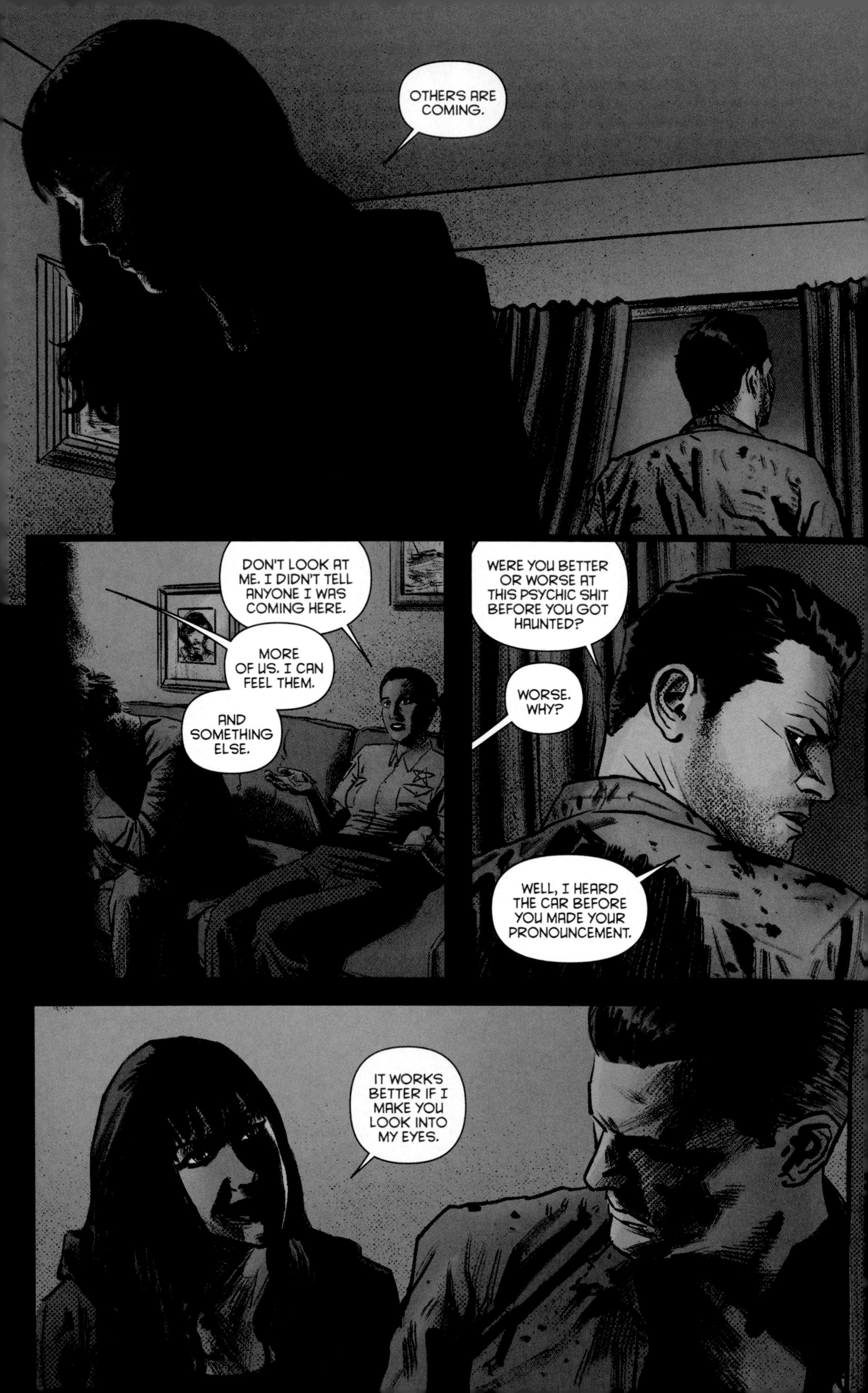
OTHERS ARE COMING.
DON'T LOOK AT ME. I DIDN'T TELL ANYONE I WAS COMING HERE.
MORE OF US. I CAN FEEL THEM.
AND SOMETHING ELSE.
WERE YOU BETTER OR WORSE AT THIS PSYCHIC SHIT BEFORE YOU GOT HAUNTED?
WORSE. WHY?
WELL, I HEARD THE CAR BEFORE YOU MADE YOUR PRONOUNCEMENT.
IT WORKS BETTER IF I MAKE YOU LOOK INTO MY EYES.

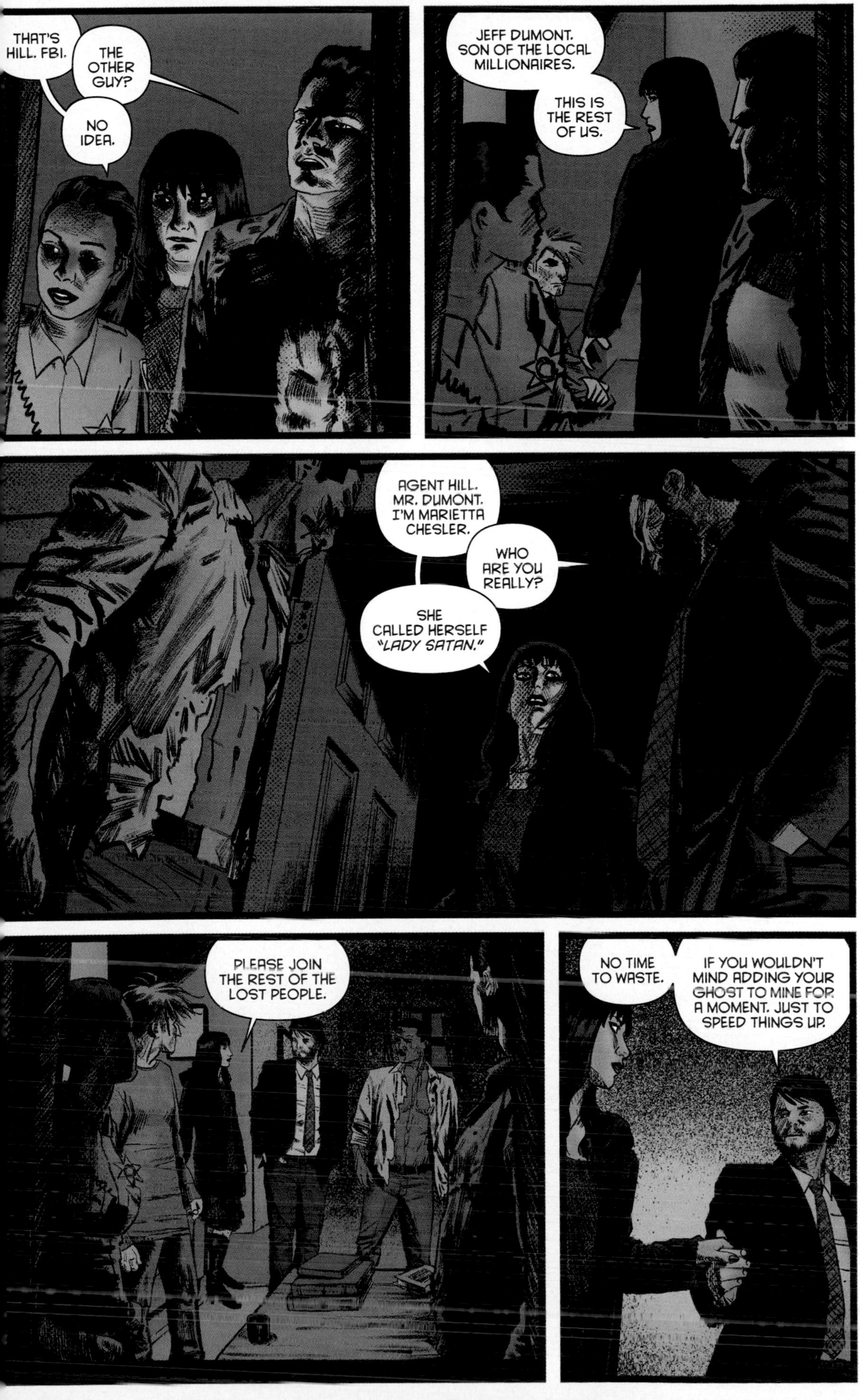
THAT'S HILL. FBI.
THE OTHER GUY?
NO IDEA.
JEFF DUMONT. SON OF THE LOCAL MILLIONAIRES.
THIS IS THE REST OF US.
AGENT HILL. MR. DUMONT. I'M MARIETTA CHESLER.
WHO ARE YOU REALLY?
SHE CALLED HERSELF "LADY SATAN."
PLEASE JOIN THE REST OF THE LOST PEOPLE.
NO TIME TO WASTE.
IF YOU WOULDN'T MIND ADDING YOUR GHOST TO MINE FOR A MOMENT. JUST TO SPEED THINGS UP.

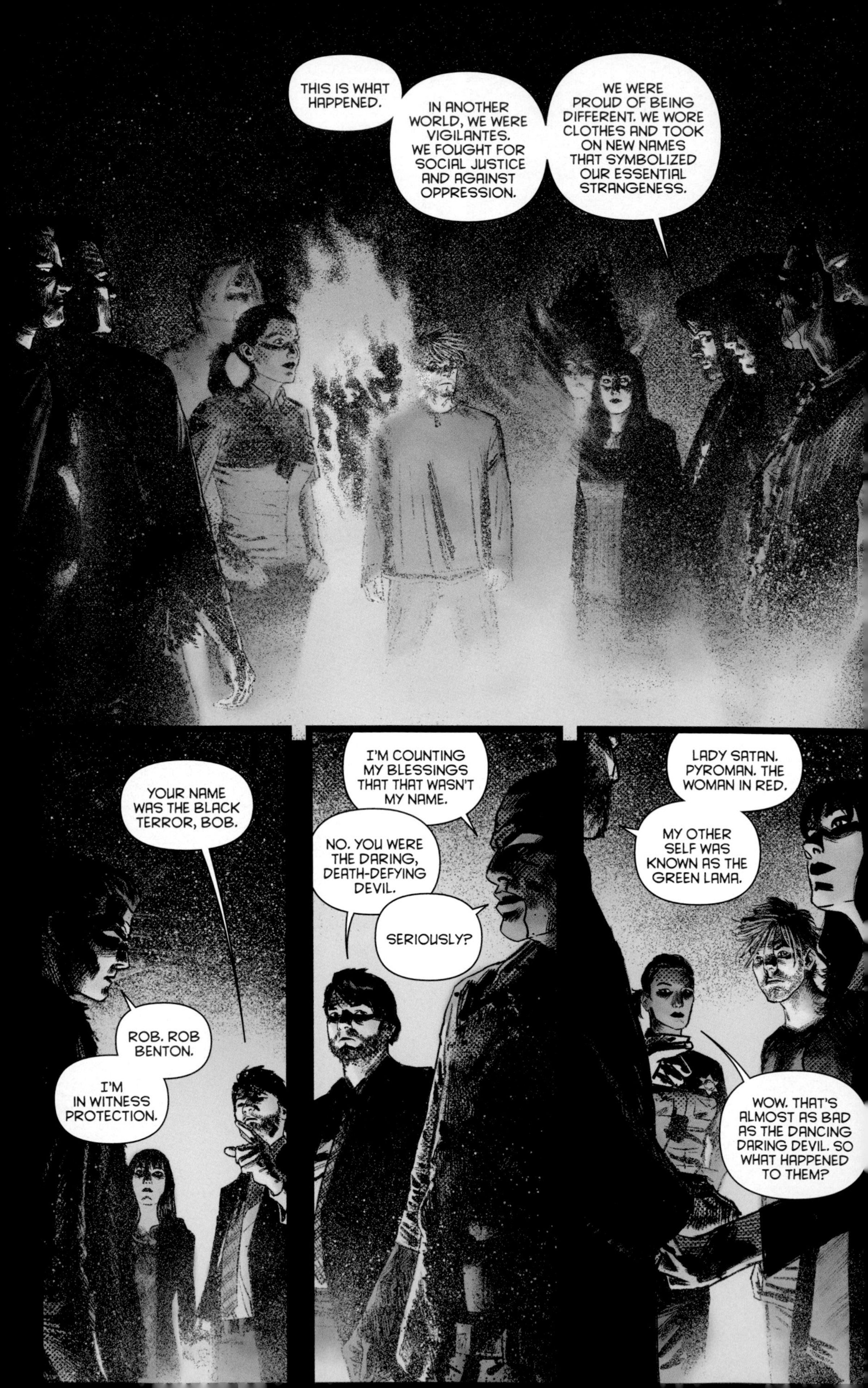
THIS IS WHAT HAPPENED.
IN ANOTHER WORLD, WE WERE VIGILANTES. WE FOUGHT FOR SOCIAL JUSTICE AND AGAINST OPPRESSION.
WE WERE PROUD OF BEING DIFFERENT. WE WORE CLOTHES AND TOOK ON NEW NAMES THAT SYMBOLIZED OUR ESSENTIAL STRANGENESS.
YOUR NAME WAS THE BLACK TERROR, BOB.
ROB. ROB BENTON.
I'M IN WITNESS PROTECTION.
I'M COUNTING MY BLESSINGS THAT THAT WASN'T MY NAME.
NO. YOU WERE THE DARING, DEATH-DEFYING DEVIL.
SERIOUSLY?
LADY SATAN. PYROMAN. THE WOMAN IN RED.
MY OTHER SELF WAS KNOWN AS THE GREEN LAMA.
WOW. THAT'S ALMOST AS BAD AS THE DANCING DARING DEVIL. SO WHAT HAPPENED TO THEM?

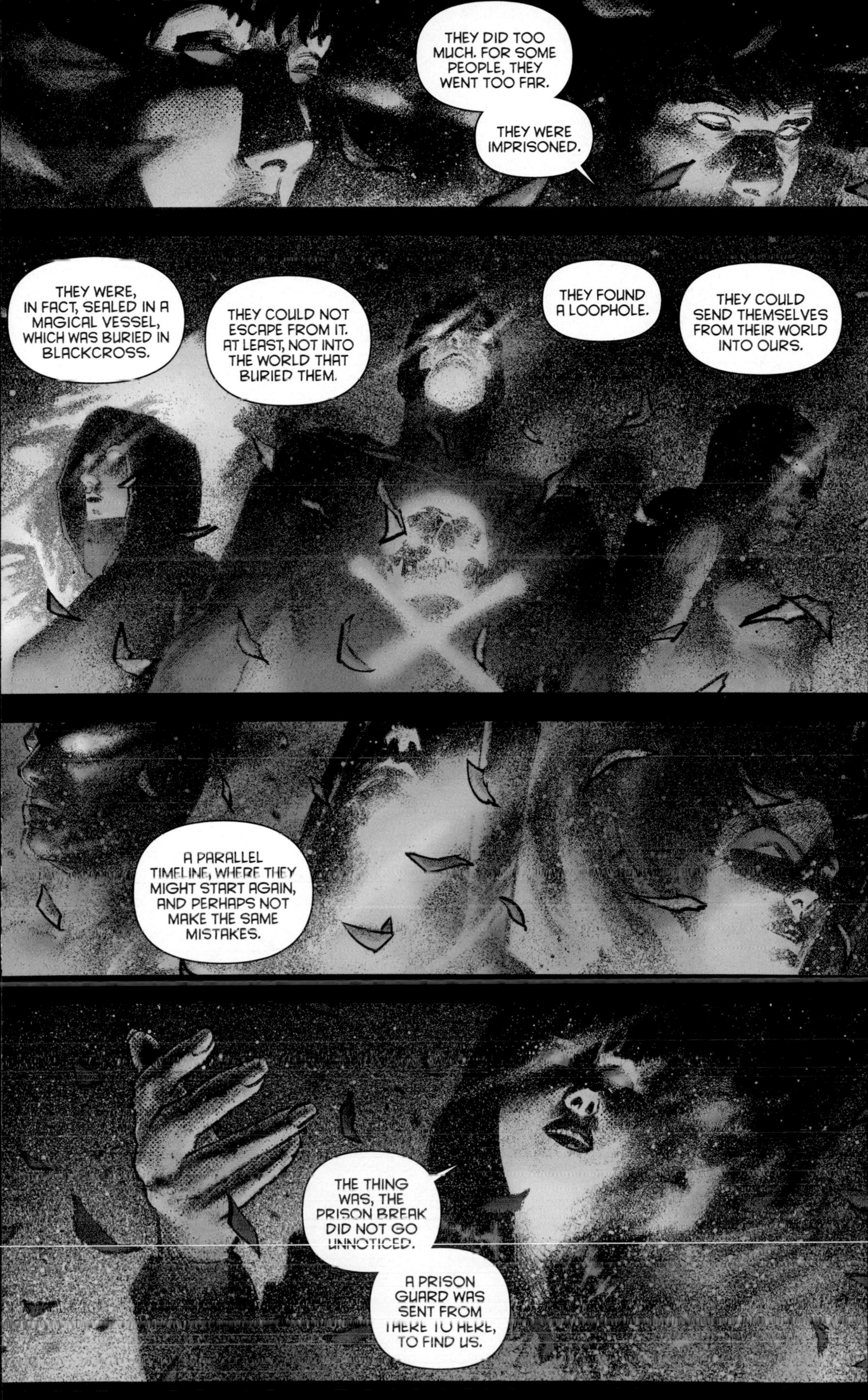
THEY DID TOO MUCH. FOR SOME PEOPLE, THEY WENT TOO FAR.
THEY WERE IMPRISONED.
THEY WERE, IN FACT, SEALED IN A MAGICAL VESSEL, WHICH WAS BURIED IN BLACKCROSS.
THEY COULD NOT ESCAPE FROM IT. AT LEAST, NOT INTO THE WORLD THAT BURIED THEM.
THEY FOUND A LOOPHOLE.
THEY COULD SEND THEMSELVES FROM THEIR WORLD INTO OURS.
A PARALLEL TIMELINE, WHERE THEY MIGHT START AGAIN, AND PERHAPS NOT MAKE THE SAME MISTAKES.
THE THING WAS, THE PRISON BREAK DID NOT GO UNNOTICED.
A PRISON GUARD WAS SENT FROM THERE TO HERE, TO FIND US.

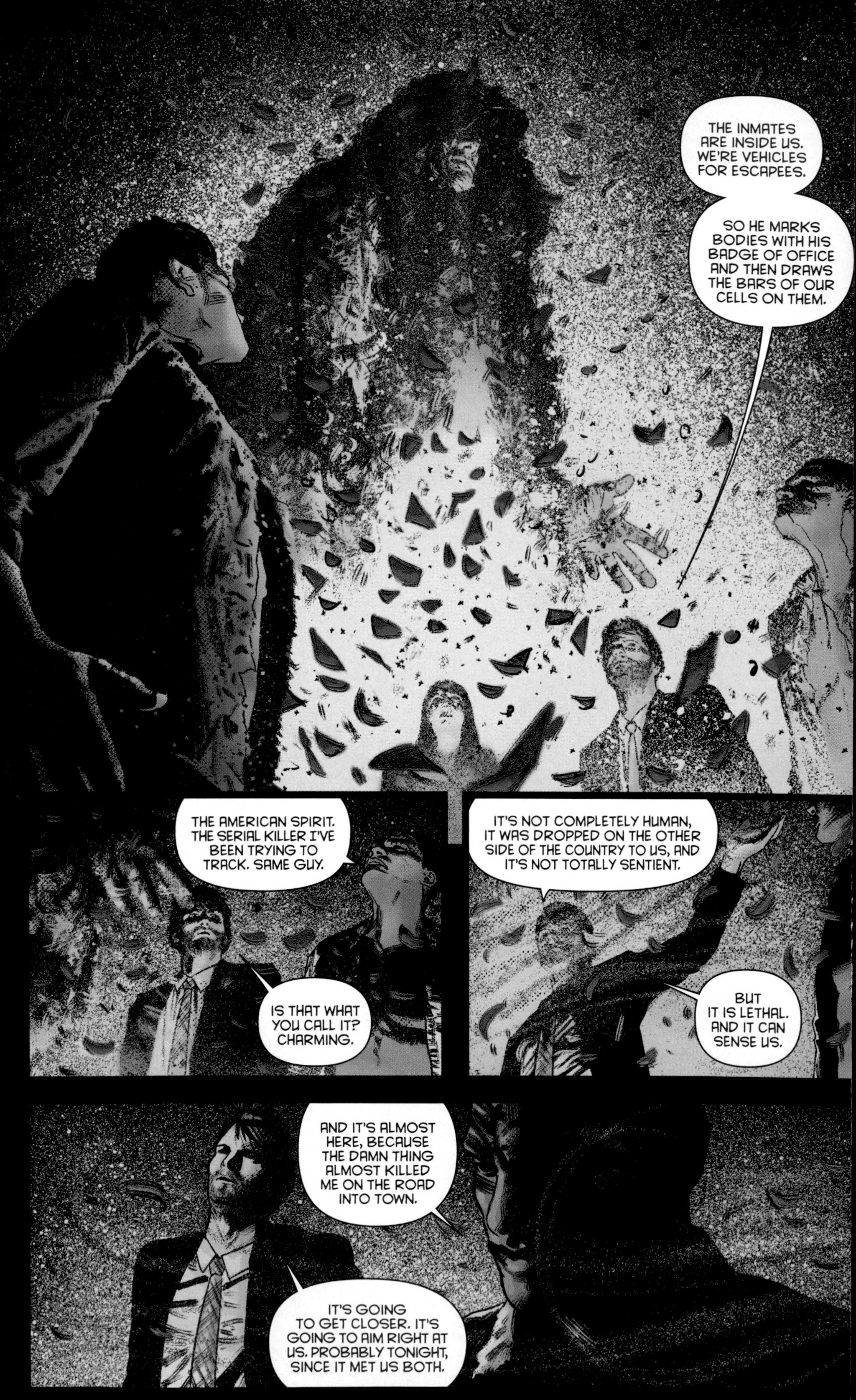
THE INMATES ARE INSIDE US. WE'RE VEHICLES FOR ESCAPEES.
SO HE MARKS BODIES WITH HIS BADGE OF OFFICE AND THEN DRAWS THE BARS OF OUR CELLS ON THEM.
THE AMERICAN SPIRIT. THE SERIAL KILLER I'VE BEEN TRYING TO TRACK. SAME GUY.
IS THAT WHAT YOU CALL IT? CHARMING.
IT'S NOT COMPLETELY HUMAN, IT WAS DROPPED ON THE OTHER SIDE OF THE COUNTRY TO US, AND IT'S NOT TOTALLY SENTIENT.
BUT IT IS LETHAL. AND IT CAN SENSE US.
AND IT'S ALMOST HERE, BECAUSE THE DAMN THING ALMOST KILLED ME ON THE ROAD INTO TOWN.
IT'S GOING TO GET CLOSER. IT'S GOING TO AIM RIGHT AT US. PROBABLY TONIGHT, SINCE IT MET US BOTH.

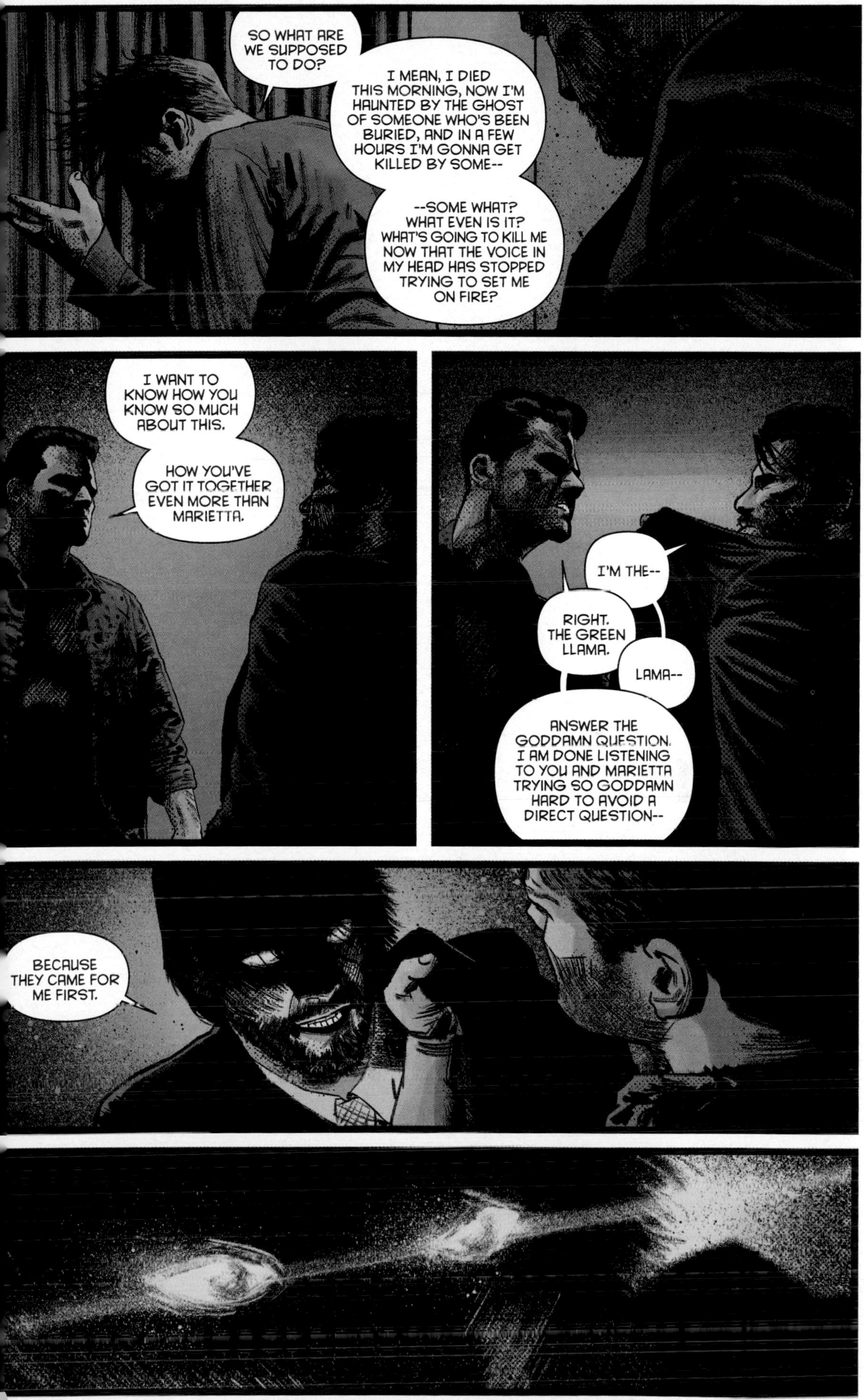
SO WHAT ARE WE SUPPOSED TO DO?
I MEAN, I DIED THIS MORNING, NOW I'M HAUNTED BY THE GHOST OF SOMEONE WHO'S BEEN BURIED, AND IN A FEW HOURS I'M GONNA GET KILLED BY SOME--
--SOME WHAT? WHAT EVEN IS IT? WHAT'S GOING TO KILL ME NOW THAT THE VOICE IN MY HEAD HAS STOPPED TRYING TO SET ME ON FIRE?
I WANT TO KNOW HOW YOU KNOW SO MUCH ABOUT THIS.
HOW YOU'VE GOT IT TOGETHER EVEN MORE THAN MARIETTA.
I'M THE--
RIGHT. THE GREEN LLAMA.
LAMA--
ANSWER THE GODDAMN QUESTION. I AM DONE LISTENING TO YOU AND MARIETTA TRYING SO GODDAMN HARD TO AVOID A DIRECT QUESTION--
BECAUSE THEY CAME FOR ME FIRST.

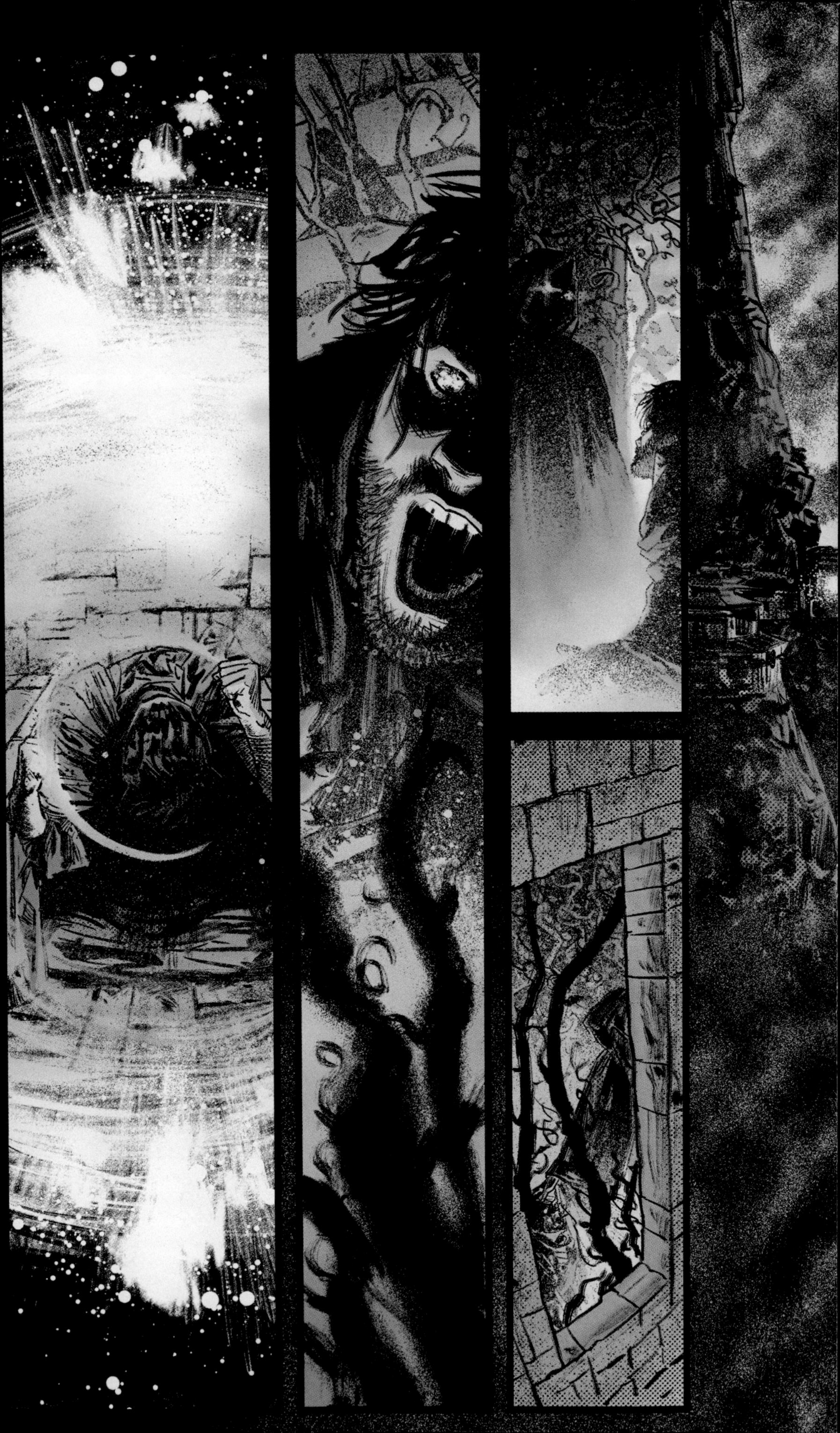

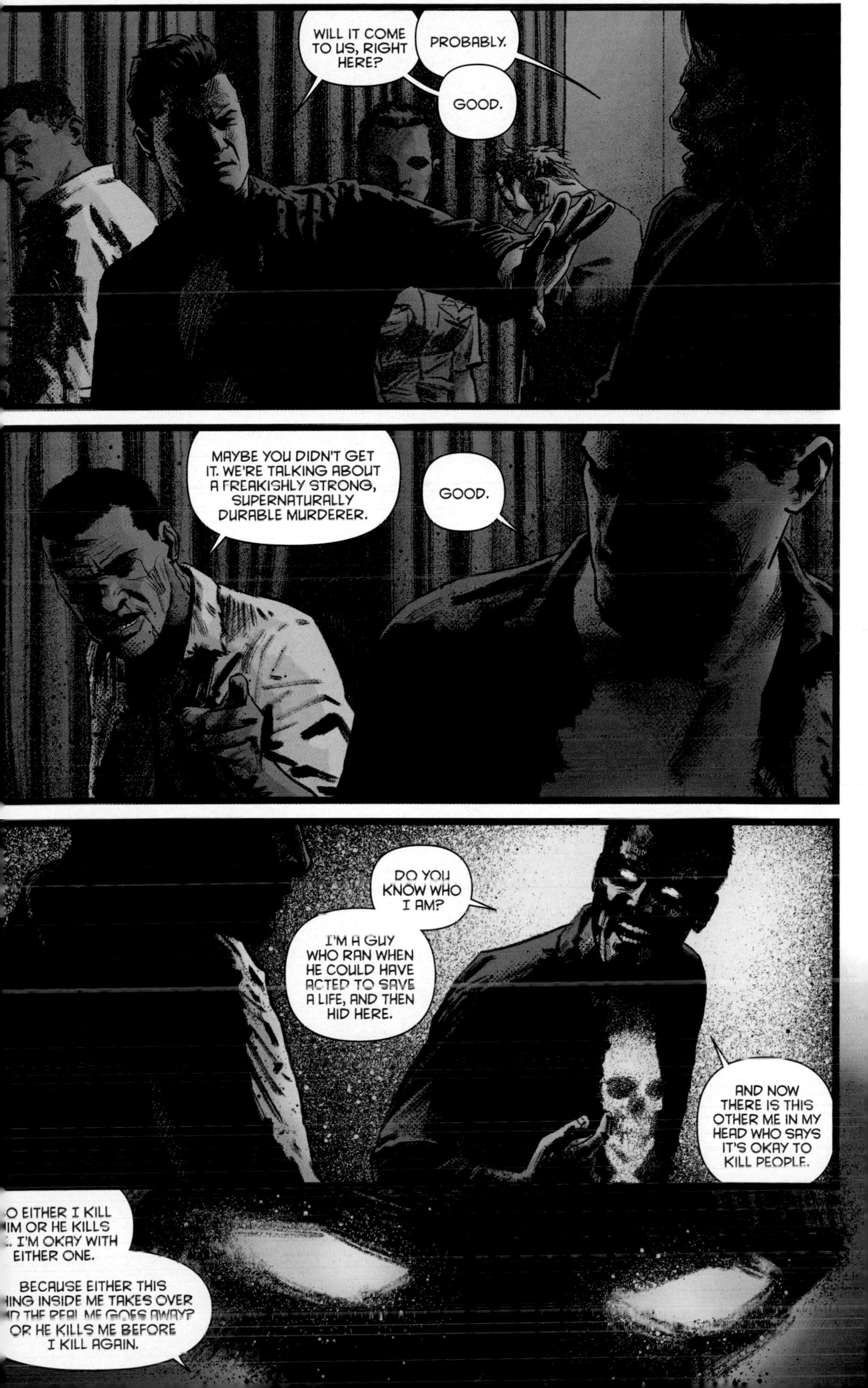
WILL IT COME TO US, RIGHT HERE?
PROBABLY.
GOOD.
MAYBE YOU DIDN'T GET IT. WE'RE TALKING ABOUT A FREAKISHLY STRONG, SUPERNATURALLY DURABLE MURDERER.
GOOD.
DO YOU KNOW WHO I AM?
I'M A GUY WHO RAN WHEN HE COULD HAVE ACTED TO SAVE A LIFE, AND THEN HID HERE.
AND NOW THERE IS THIS OTHER ME IN MY HEAD WHO SAYS IT'S OKAY TO KILL PEOPLE.
EITHER I KILL HIM OR HE KILLS I'M OKAY WITH EITHER ONE.
BECAUSE EITHER THIS INSIDE ME TAKES OVER THE REAL ME GOES AWAY? OR HE KILLS ME BEFORE I KILL AGAIN.

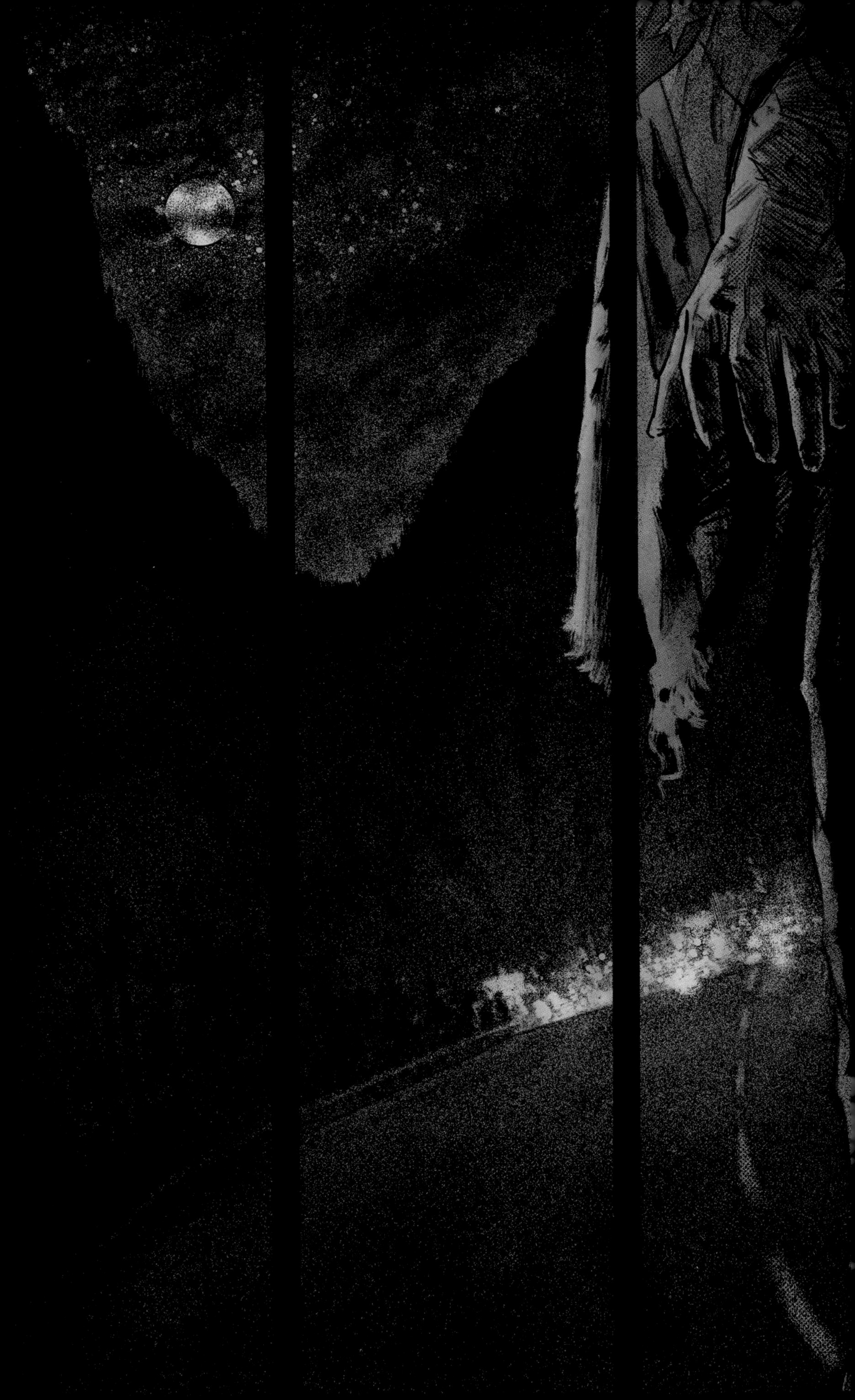

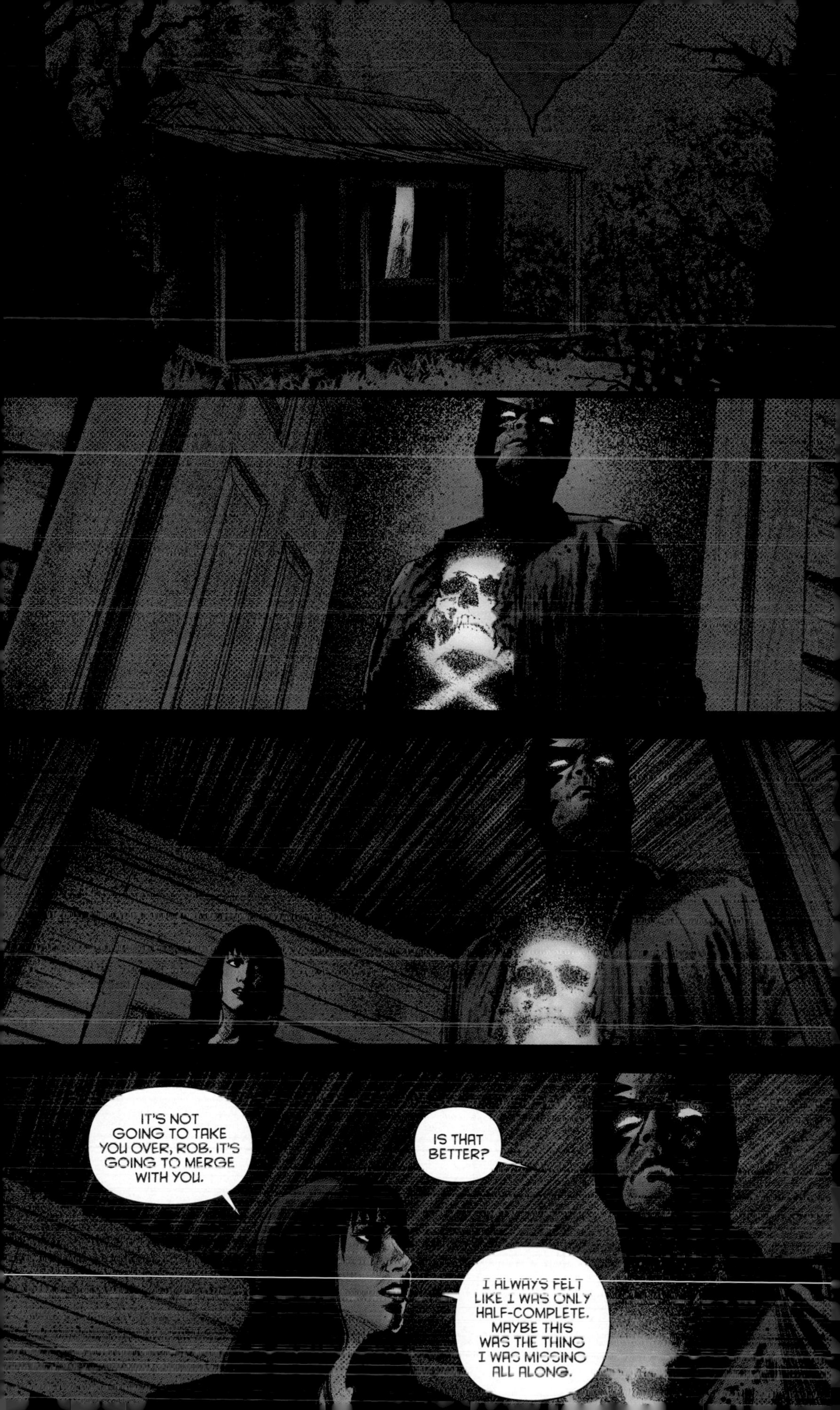
IT'S NOT GOING TO TAKE YOU OVER, ROB. IT'S GOING TO MERGE WITH YOU.
IS THAT BETTER?
I ALWAYS FELT LIKE I WAS ONLY HALF-COMPLETE. MAYBE THIS WAS THE THING I WAS MISSING ALL ALONG.

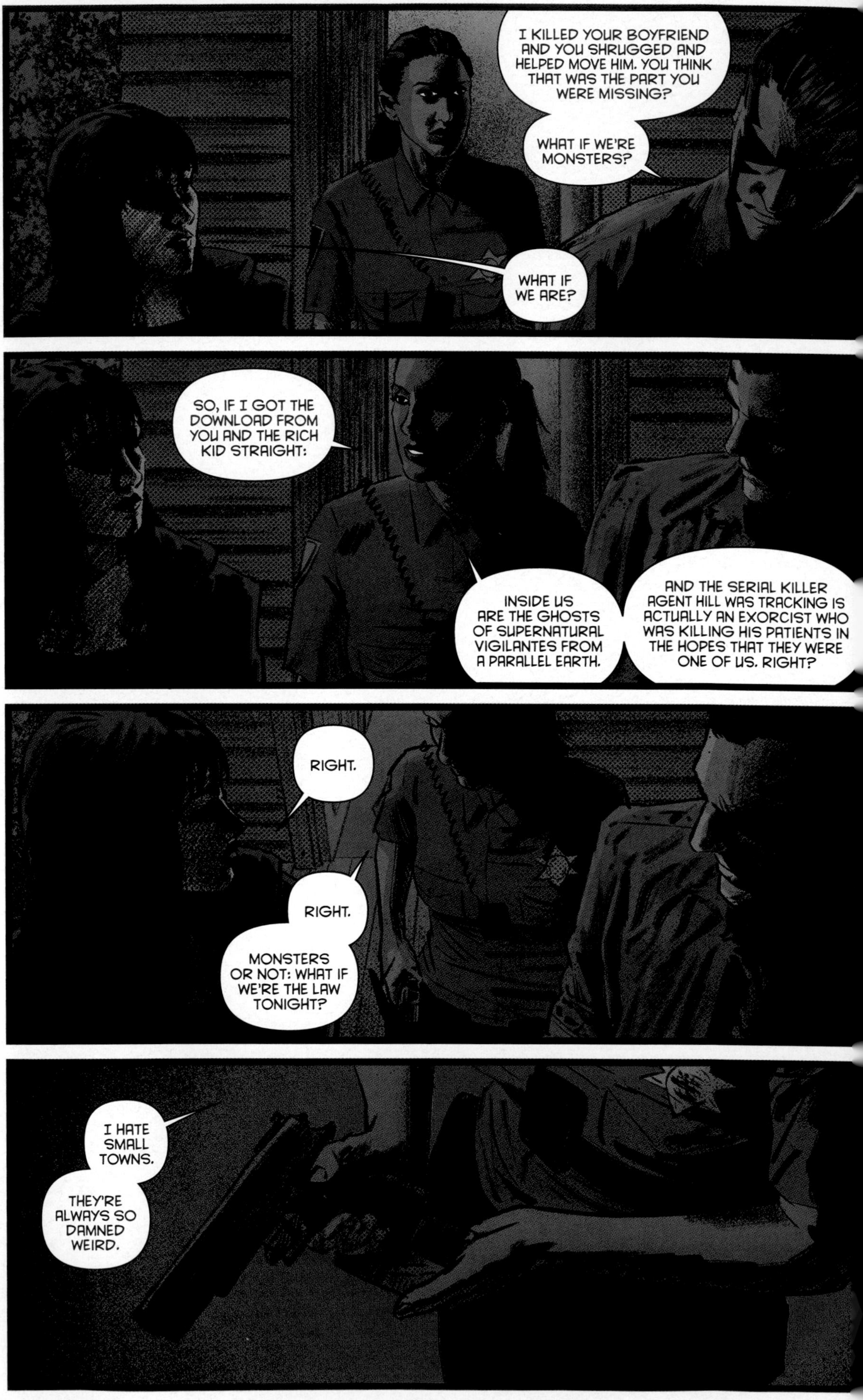
I KILLED YOUR BOYFRIEND AND YOU SHRUGGED AND HELPED MOVE HIM. YOU THINK THAT WAS THE PART YOU WERE MISSING?
WHAT IF WE'RE MONSTERS?
WHAT IF WE ARE?
SO, IF I GOT THE DOWNLOAD FROM YOU AND THE RICH KID STRAIGHT:
INSIDE US ARE THE GHOSTS OF SUPERNATURAL VIGILANTES FROM A PARALLEL EARTH.
AND THE SERIAL KILLER AGENT HILL WAS TRACKING IS ACTUALLY AN EXORCIST WHO WAS KILLING HIS PATIENTS IN THE HOPES THAT THEY WERE ONE OF US. RIGHT?
RIGHT.
RIGHT.
MONSTERS OR NOT: WHAT IF WE'RE THE LAW TONIGHT?
I HATE SMALL TOWNS.
THEY'RE ALWAYS SO DAMNED WEIRD.

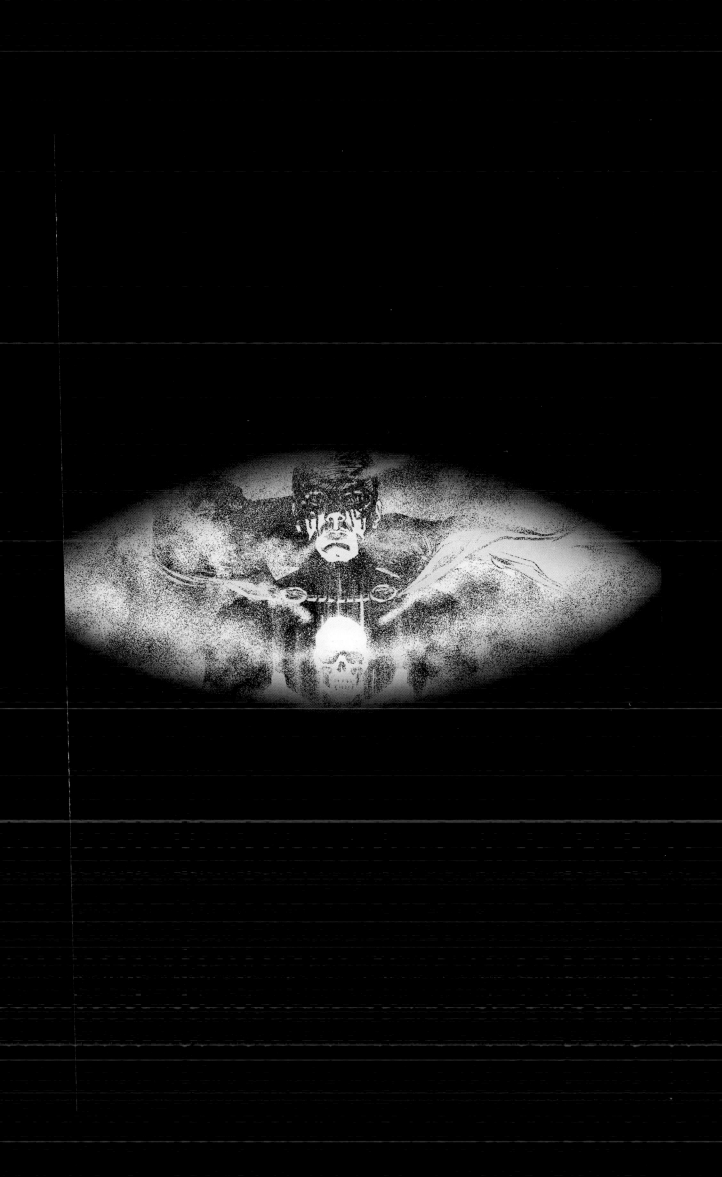

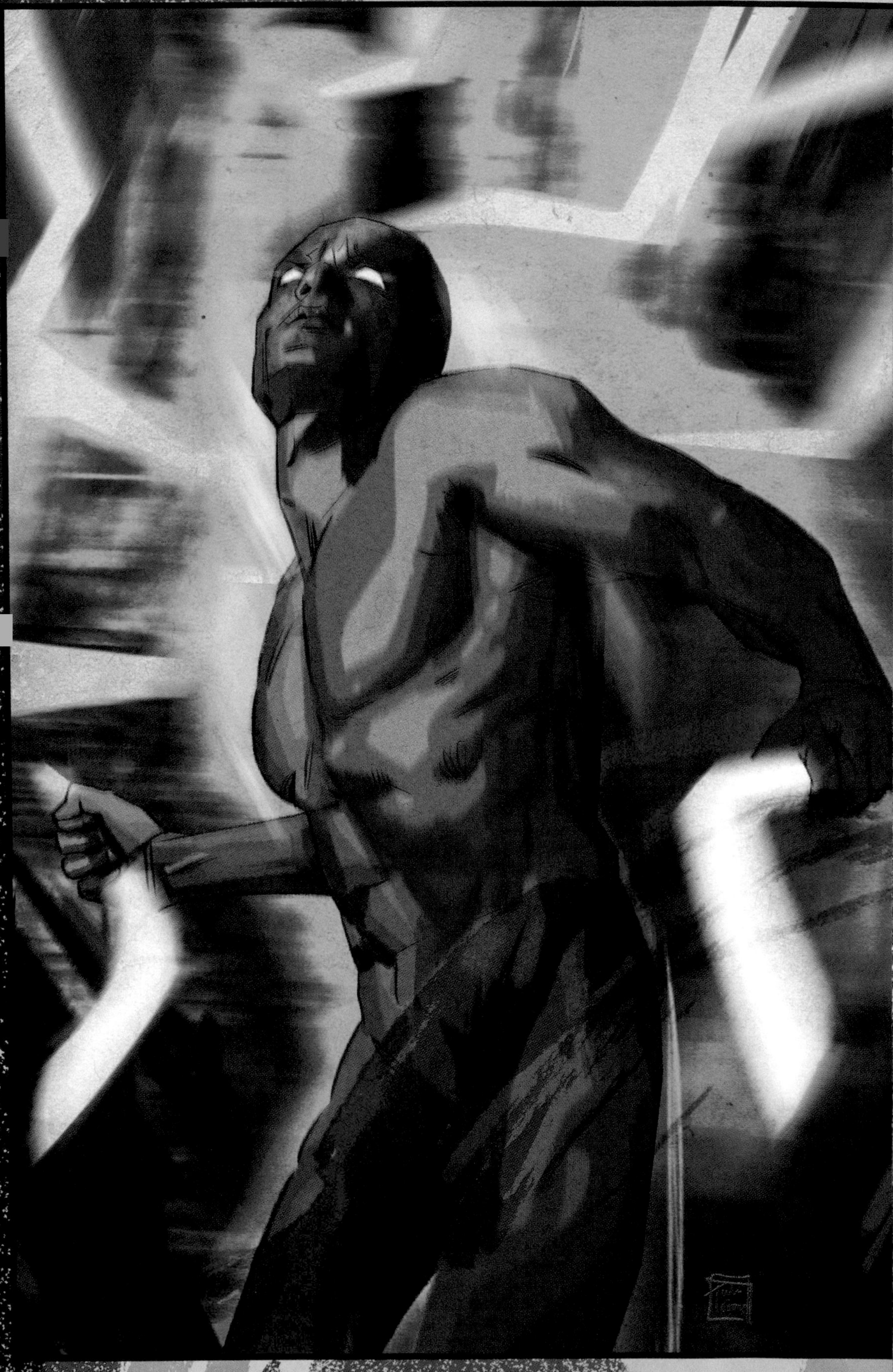

ISSUE #6 COVER BY TULA LOTAY

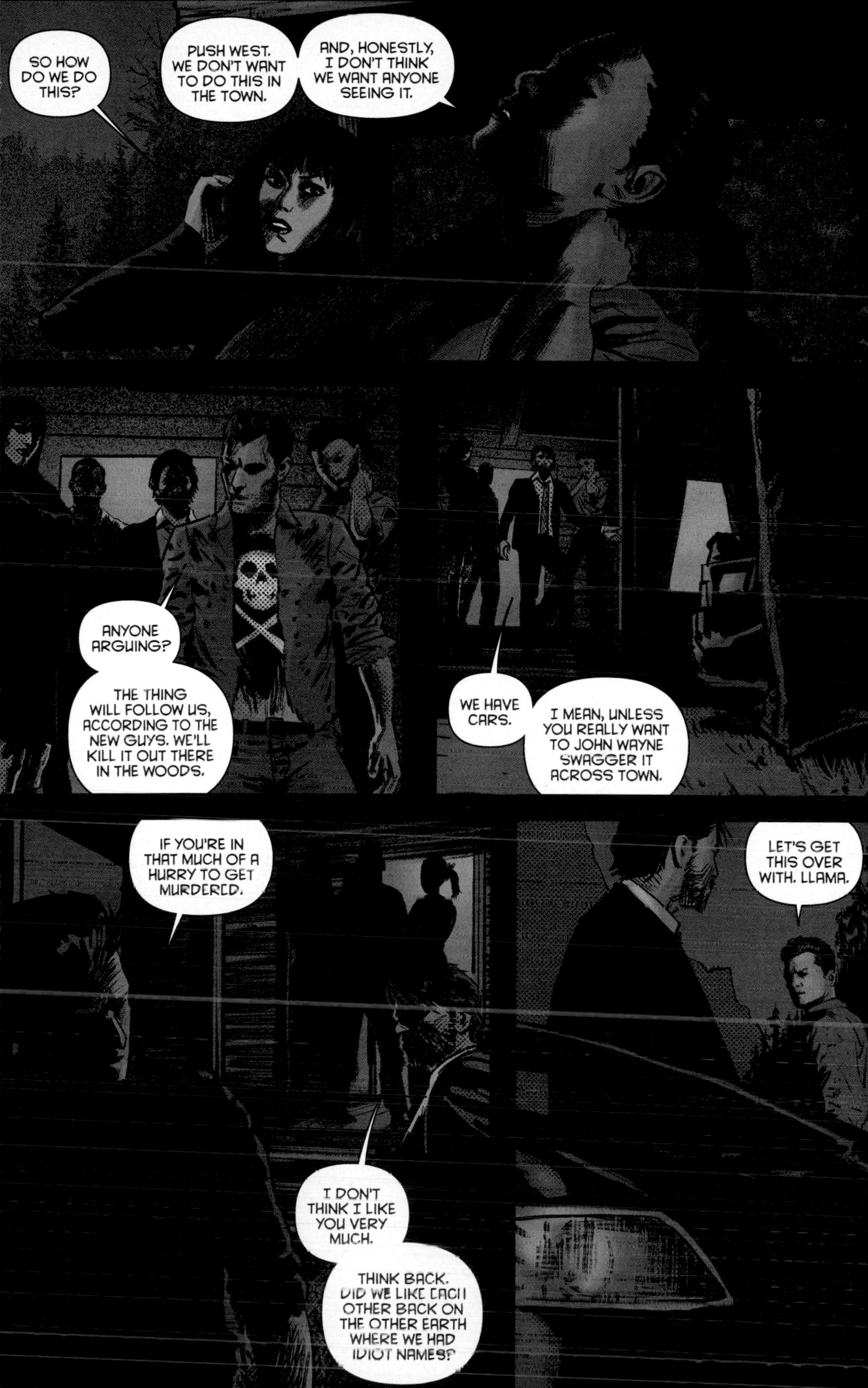
SO HOW DO WE DO THIS?
PUSH WEST. WE DON'T WANT TO DO THIS IN THE TOWN.
AND, HONESTLY, I DON'T THINK WE WANT ANYONE SEEING IT.
ANYONE ARGUING?
THE THING WILL FOLLOW US, ACCORDING TO THE NEW GUYS. WE'LL KILL IT OUT THERE IN THE WOODS.
WE HAVE CARS.
I MEAN, UNLESS YOU REALLY WANT TO JOHN WAYNE SWAGGER IT ACROSS TOWN.
IF YOU'RE IN THAT MUCH OF A HURRY TO GET MURDERED.
LET'S GET THIS OVER WITH. LLAMA.
I DON'T THINK I LIKE YOU VERY MUCH.
THINK BACK. DID WE LIKE EACH OTHER BACK ON THE OTHER EARTH WHERE WE HAD IDIOT NAMES?

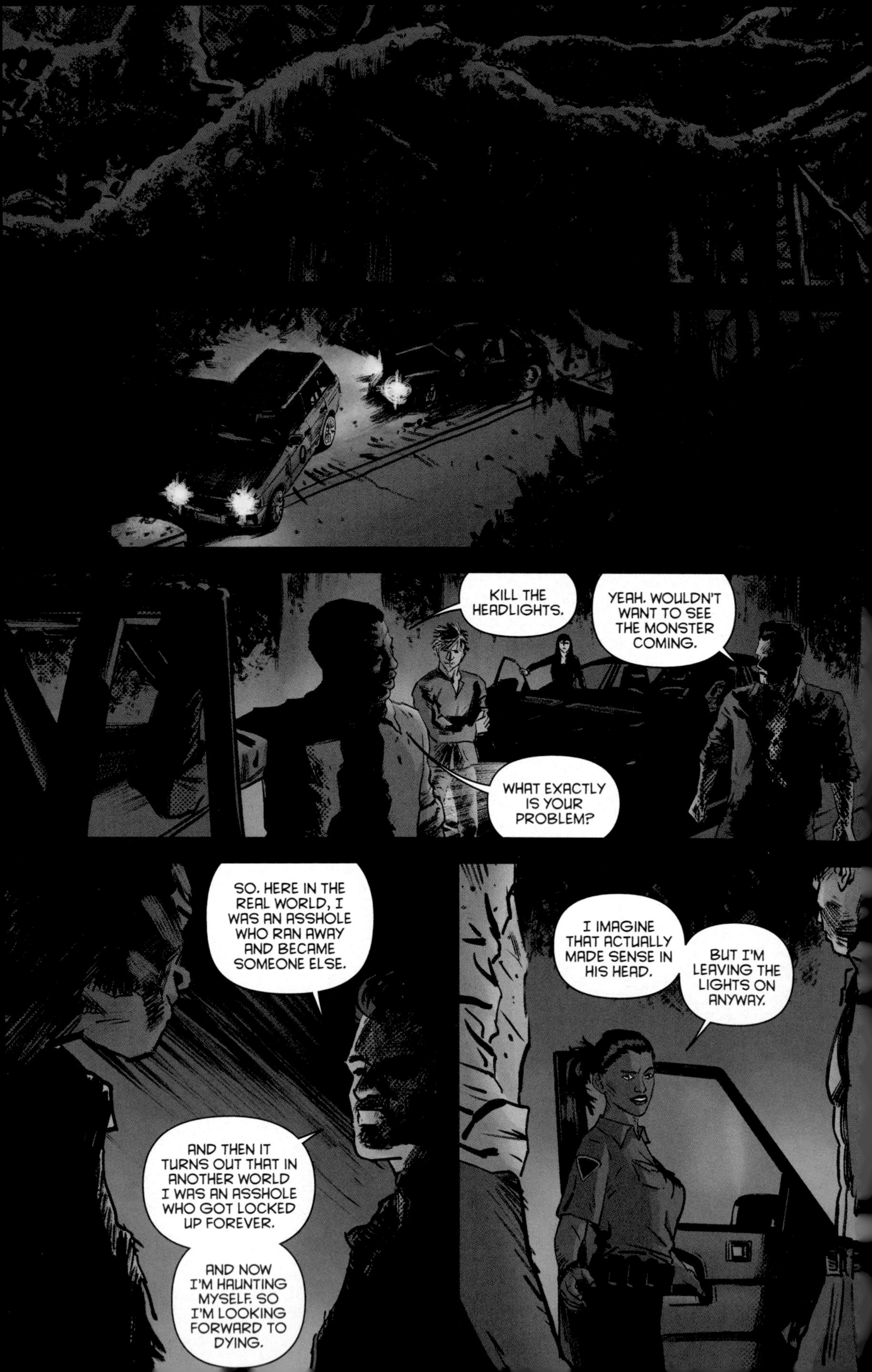
KILL THE HEADLIGHTS.
YEAH. WOULDN'T WANT TO SEE THE MONSTER COMING.
WHAT EXACTLY IS YOUR PROBLEM?
SO. HERE IN THE REAL WORLD, I WAS AN ASSHOLE WHO RAN AWAY AND BECAME SOMEONE ELSE.
AND THEN IT TURNS OUT THAT IN ANOTHER WORLD I WAS AN ASSHOLE WHO GOT LOCKED UP FOREVER.
AND NOW I'M HAUNTING MYSELF. SO I'M LOOKING FORWARD TO DYING.
I IMAGINE THAT ACTUALLY MADE SENSE IN HIS HEAD.
BUT I'M LEAVING THE LIGHTS ON ANYWAY.

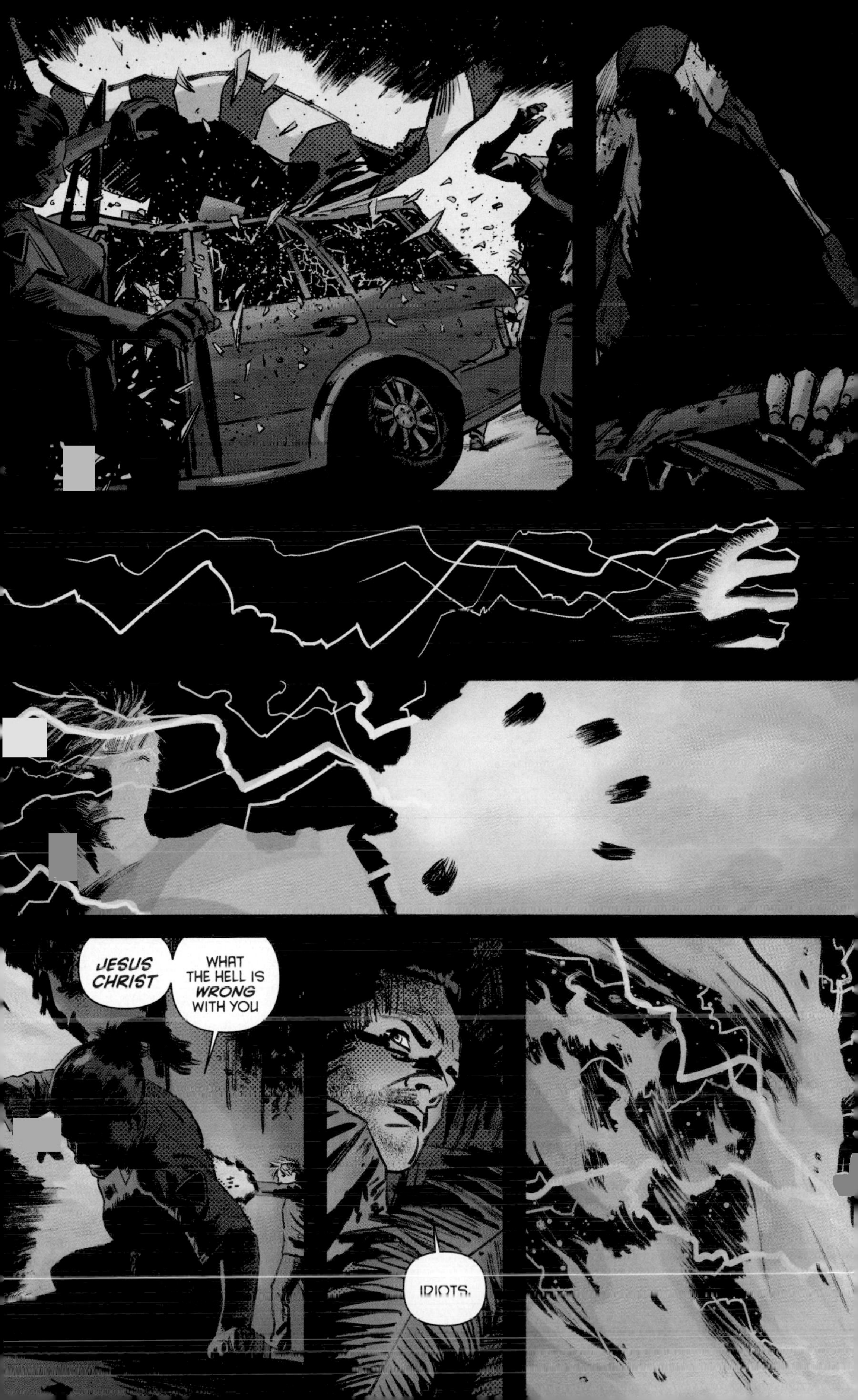
JESUS CHRIST
WHAT THE HELL IS WRONG WITH YOU
IDIOTS.

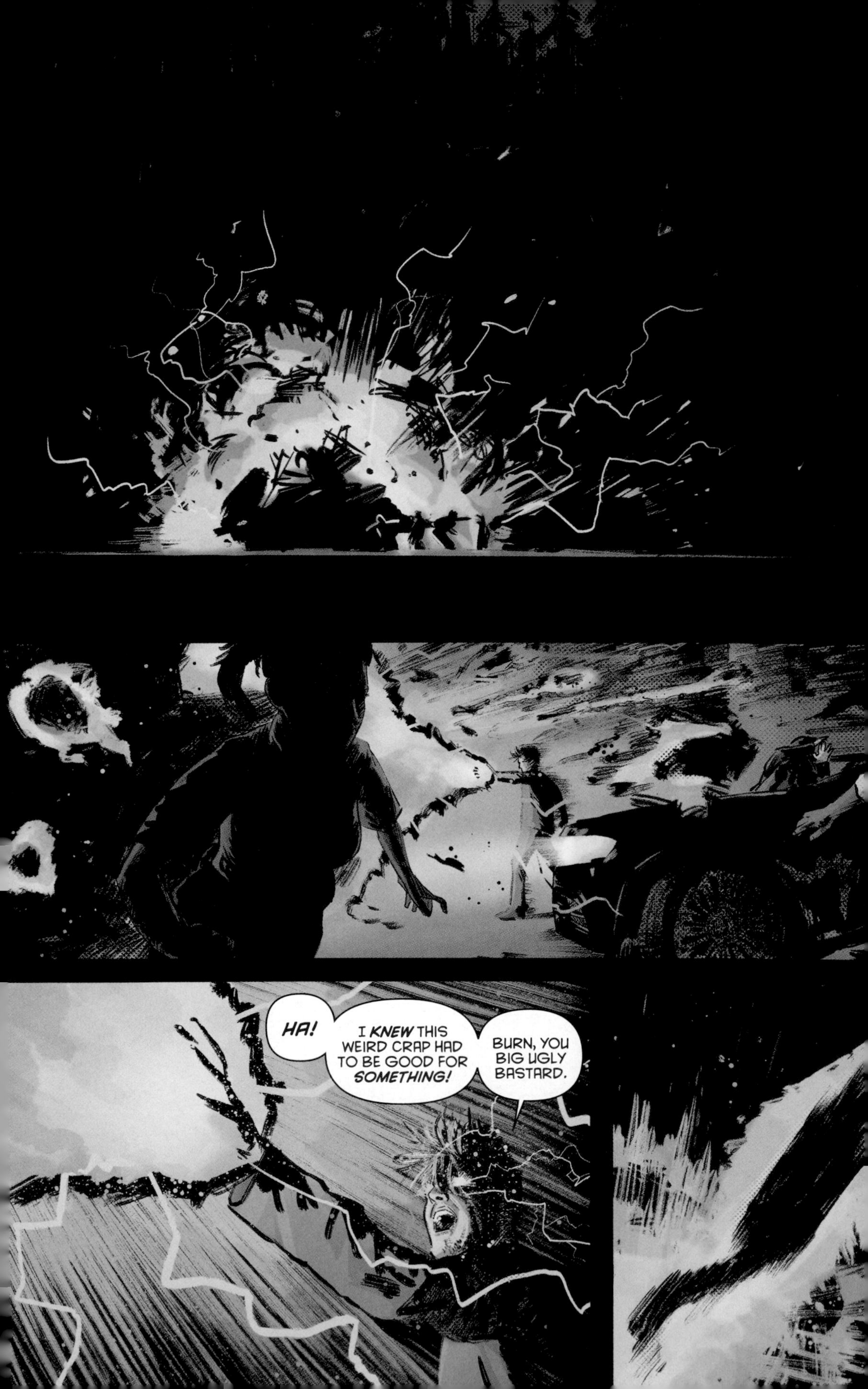
HA!
I KNEW THIS WEIRD CRAP HAD TO BE GOOD FOR SOMETHING!
BURN, YOU BIG UGLY BASTARD.

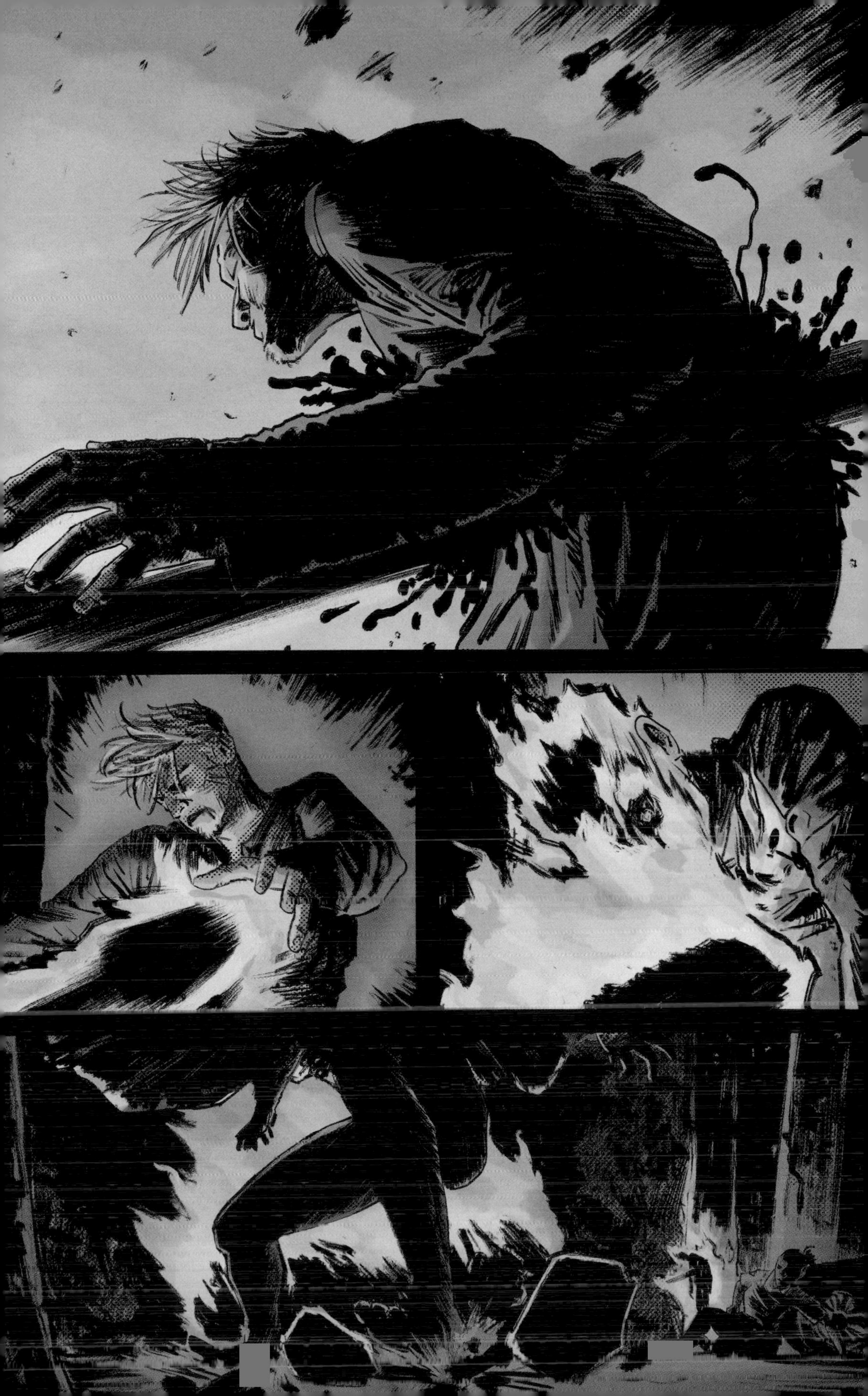

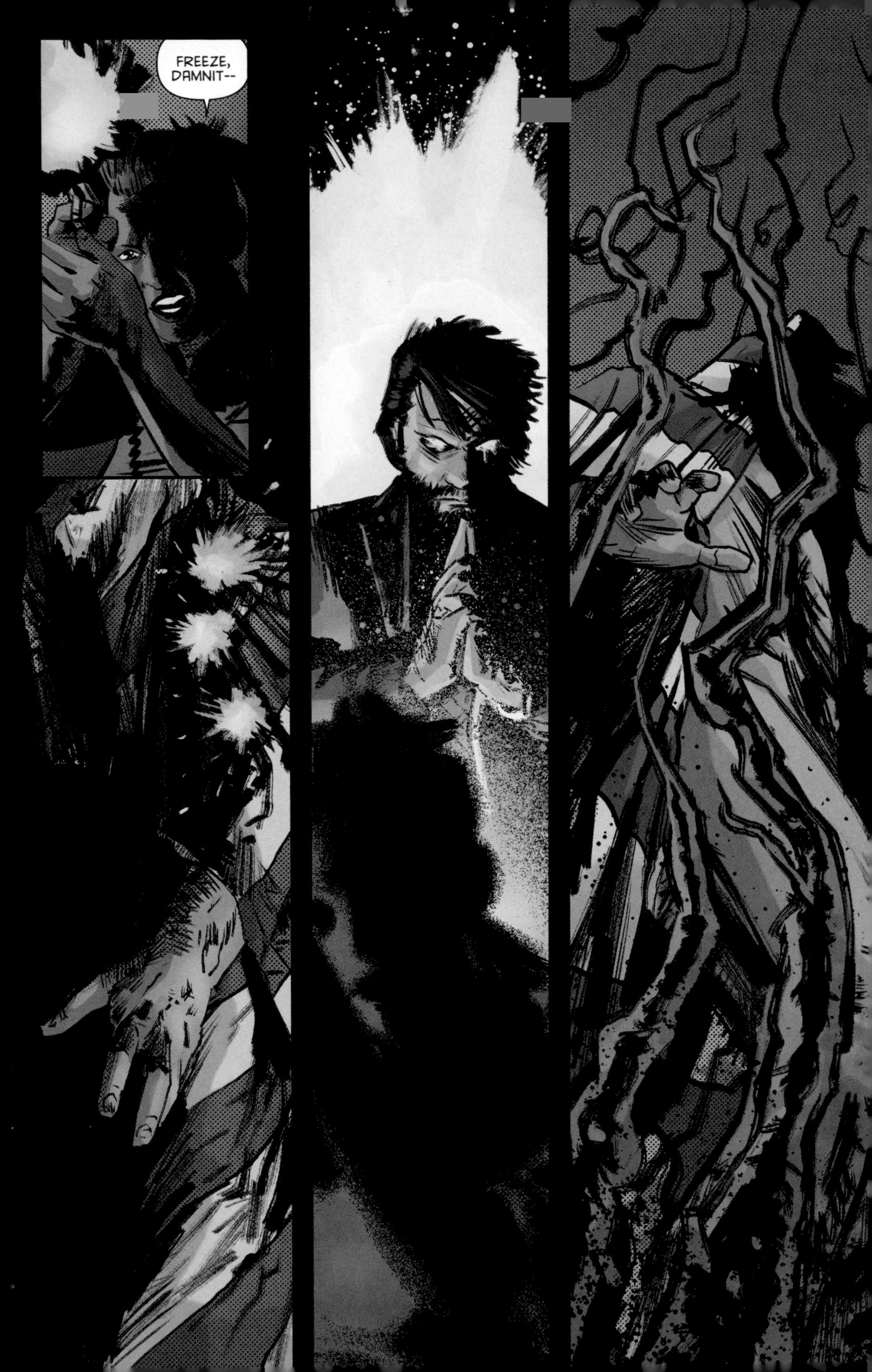
FREEZE, DAMNIT--

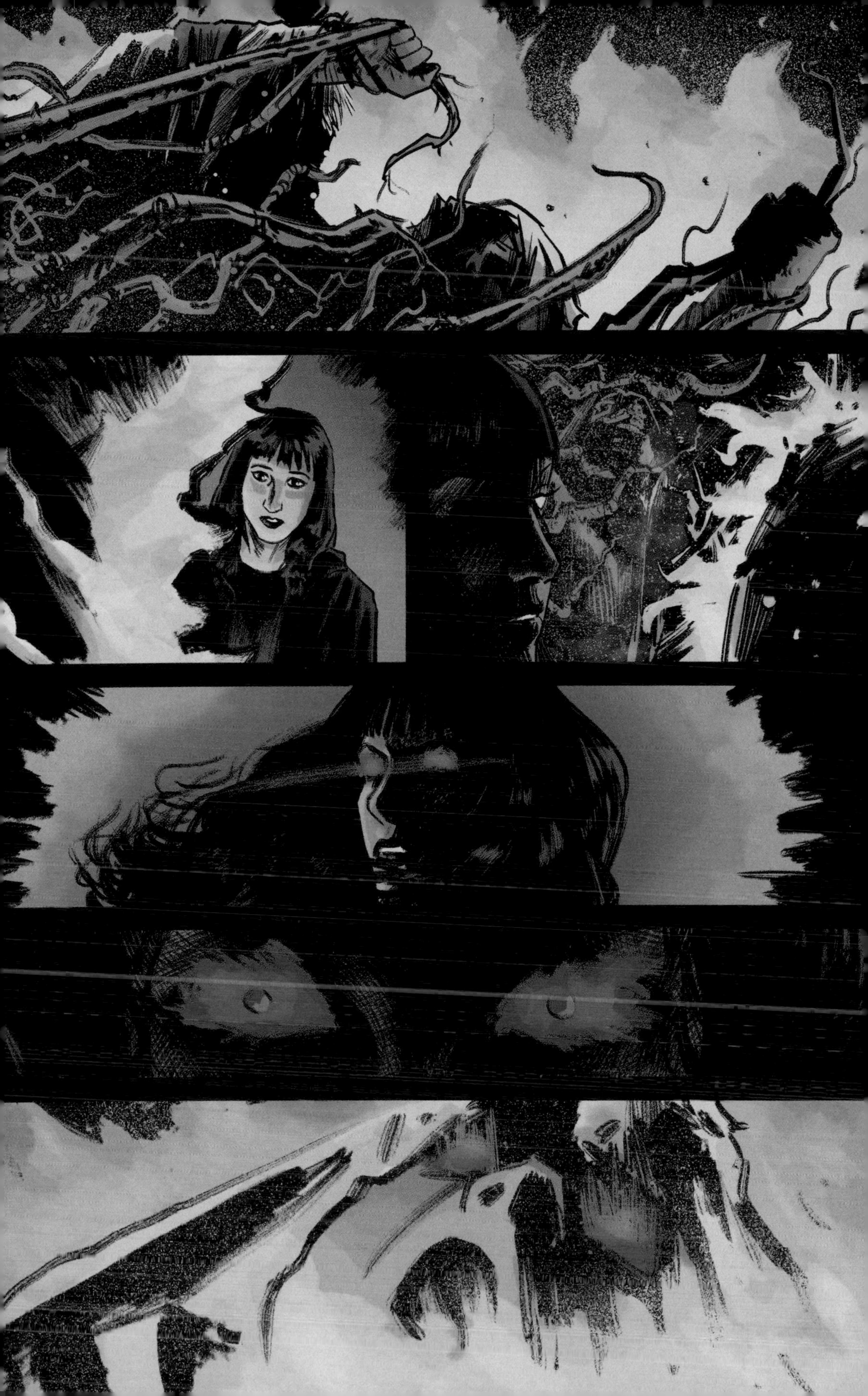

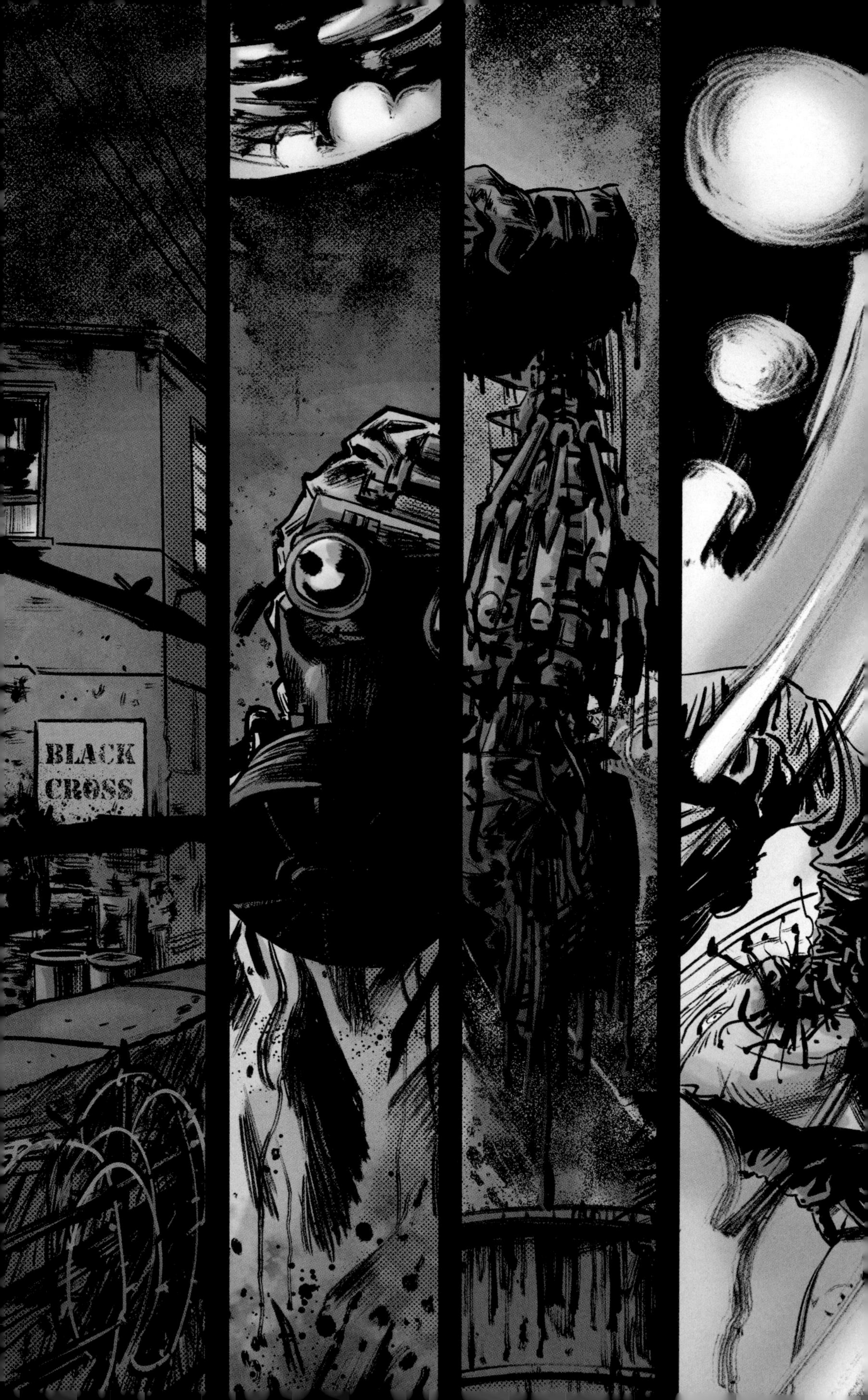
BLACK CROSS

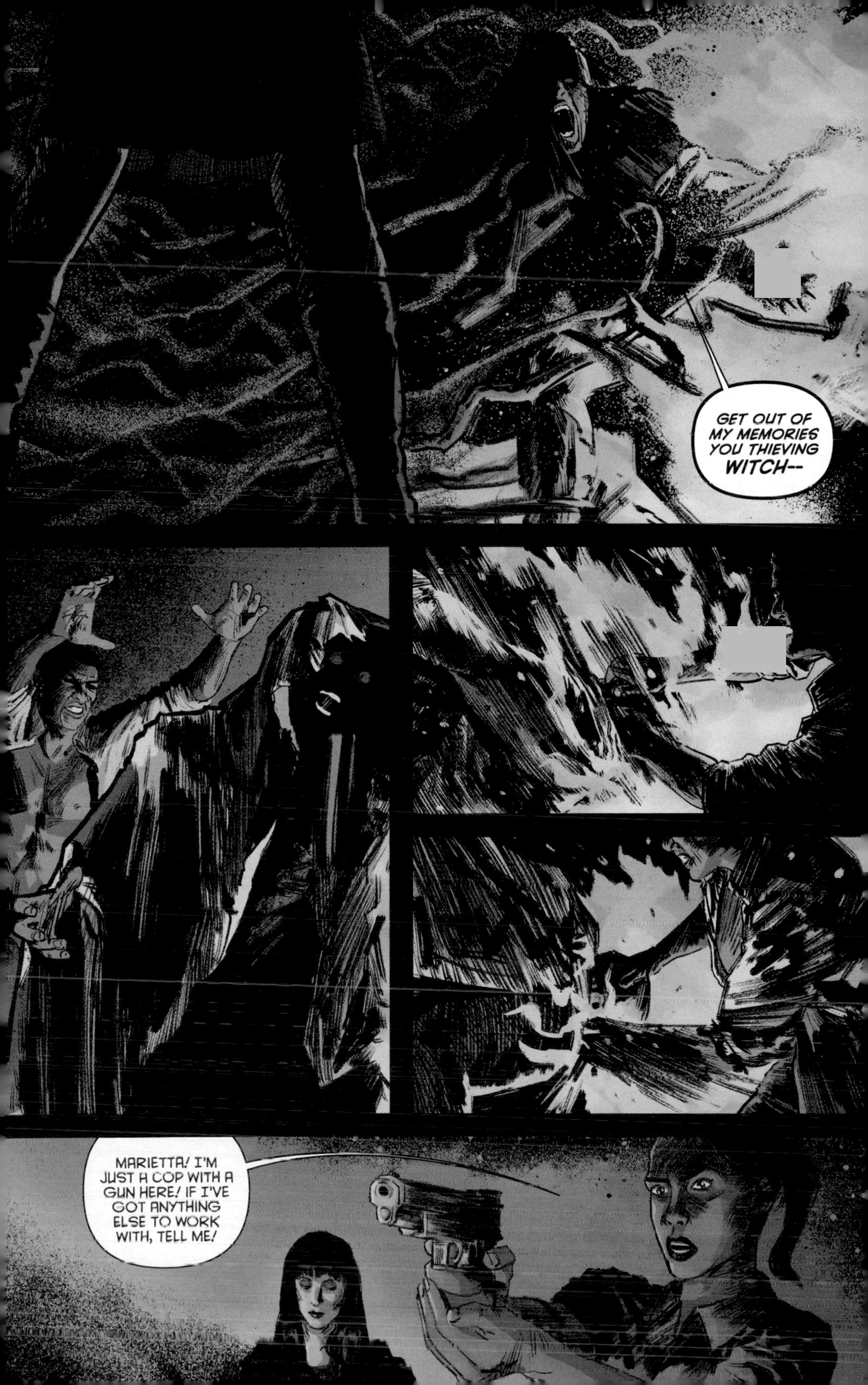

GET OUT OF MY MEMORIES YOU THIEVING WITCH--
MARIETTA! I'M JUST A COP WITH A GUN HERE! IF I'VE GOT ANYTHING ELSE TO WORK WITH, TELL ME!

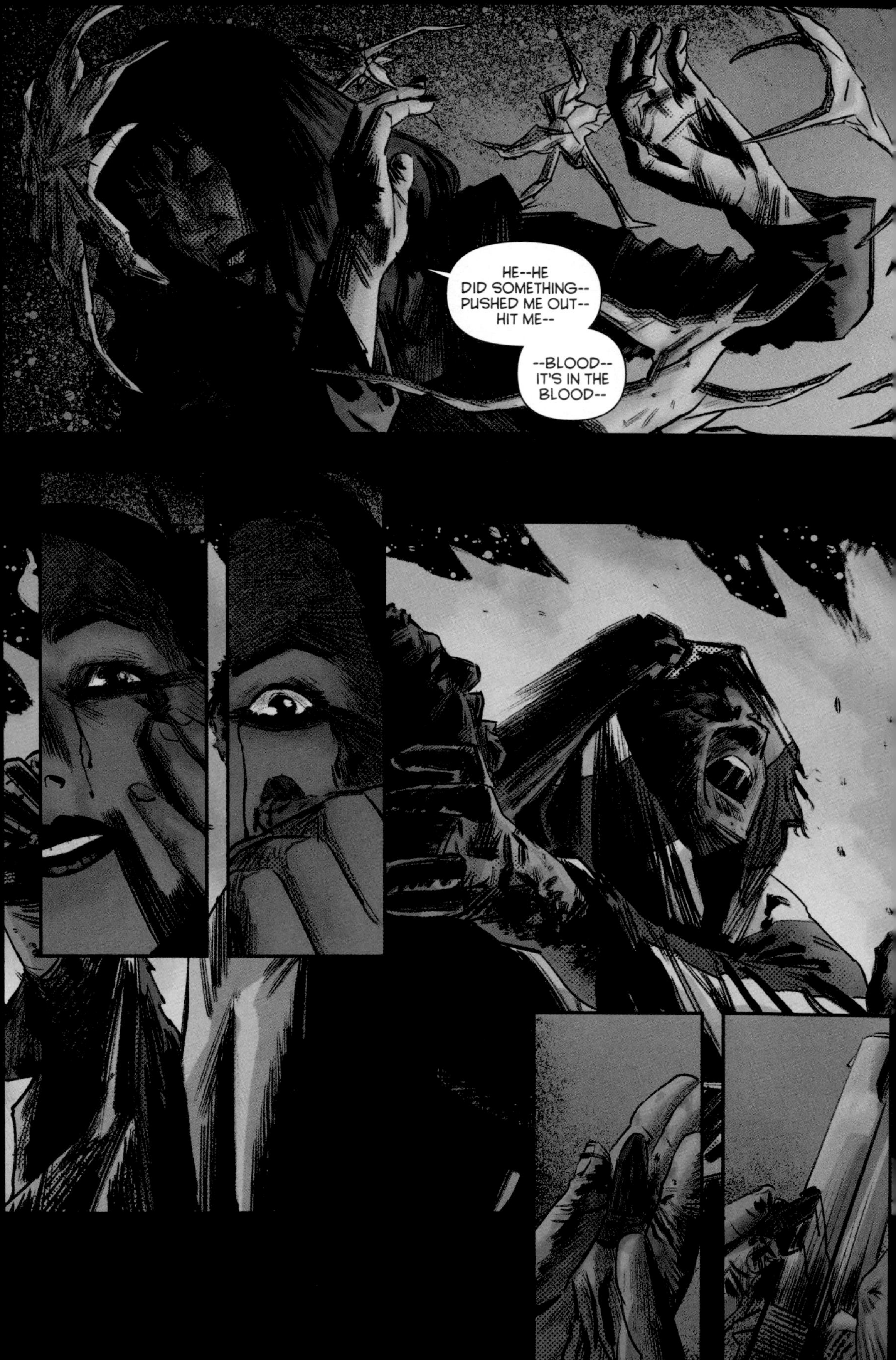
HE--HE DID SOMETHING-- PUSHED ME OUT-- HIT ME--
--BLOOD-- IT'S IN THE BLOOD--

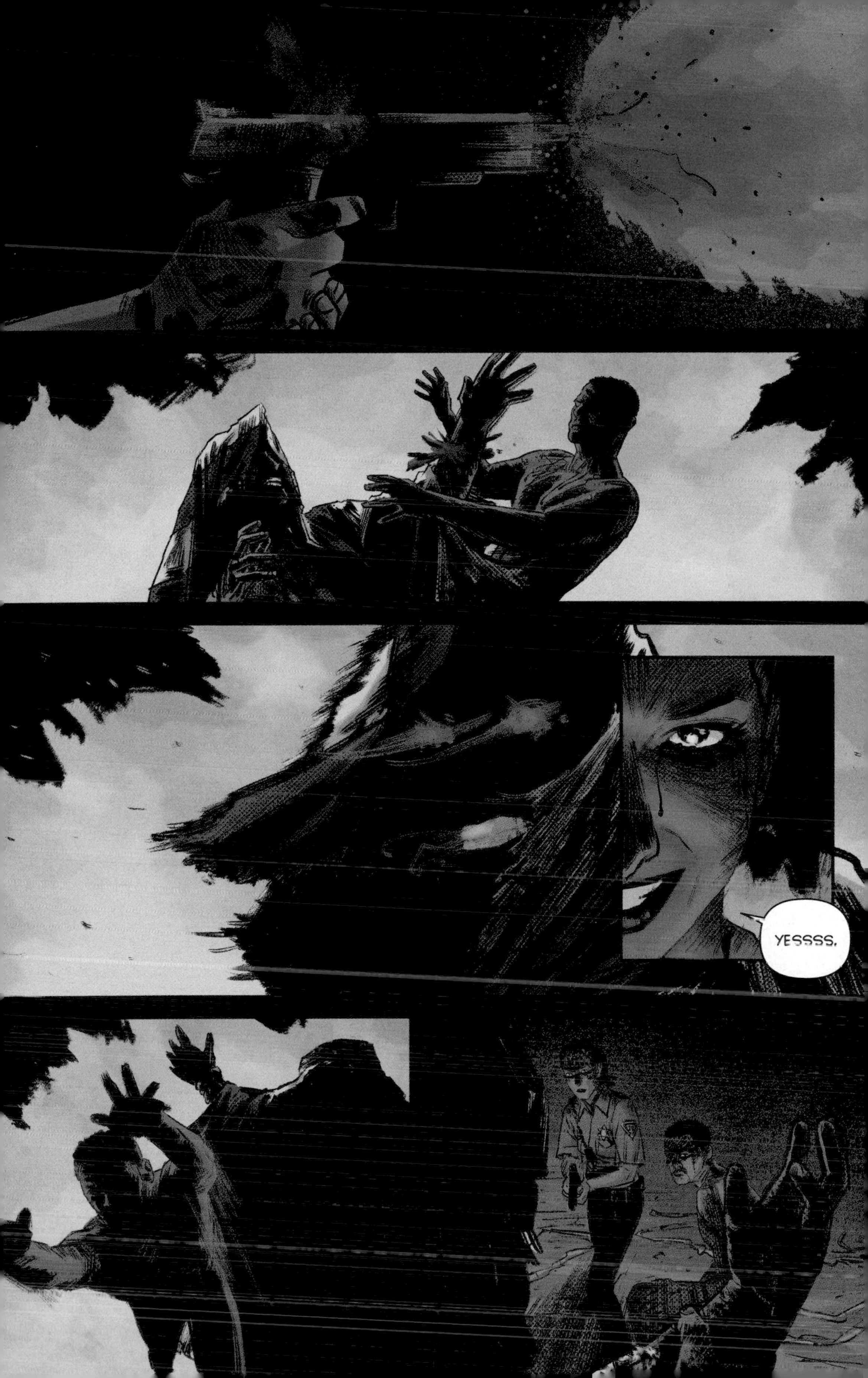
YESSSS.

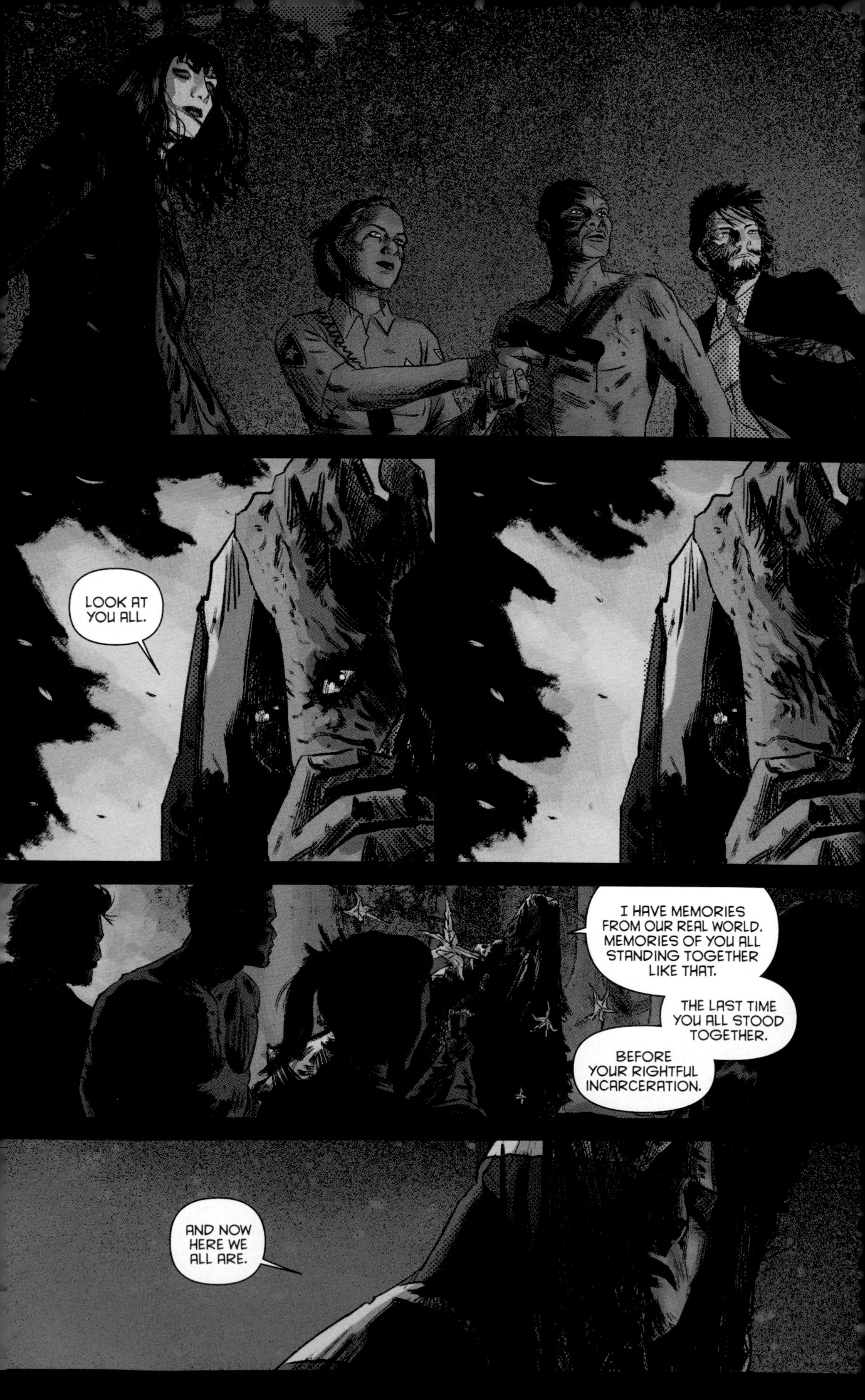
LOOK AT YOU ALL.
I HAVE MEMORIES FROM OUR REAL WORLD. MEMORIES OF YOU ALL STANDING TOGETHER LIKE THAT.
THE LAST TIME YOU ALL STOOD TOGETHER.
BEFORE YOUR RIGHTFUL INCARCERATION.
AND NOW HERE WE ALL ARE.

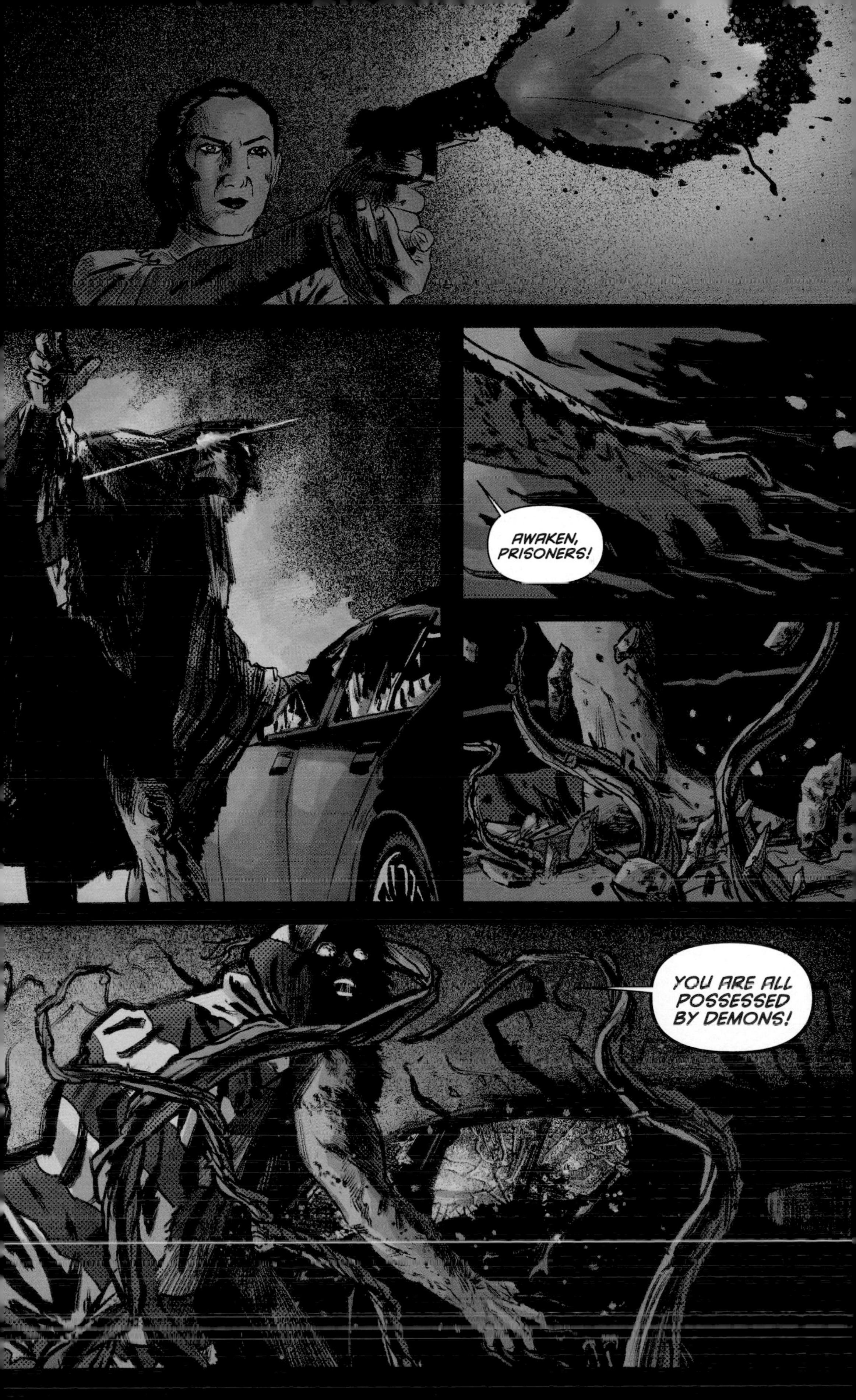
AWAKEN, PRISONERS!
YOU ARE ALL POSSESSED BY DEMONS!

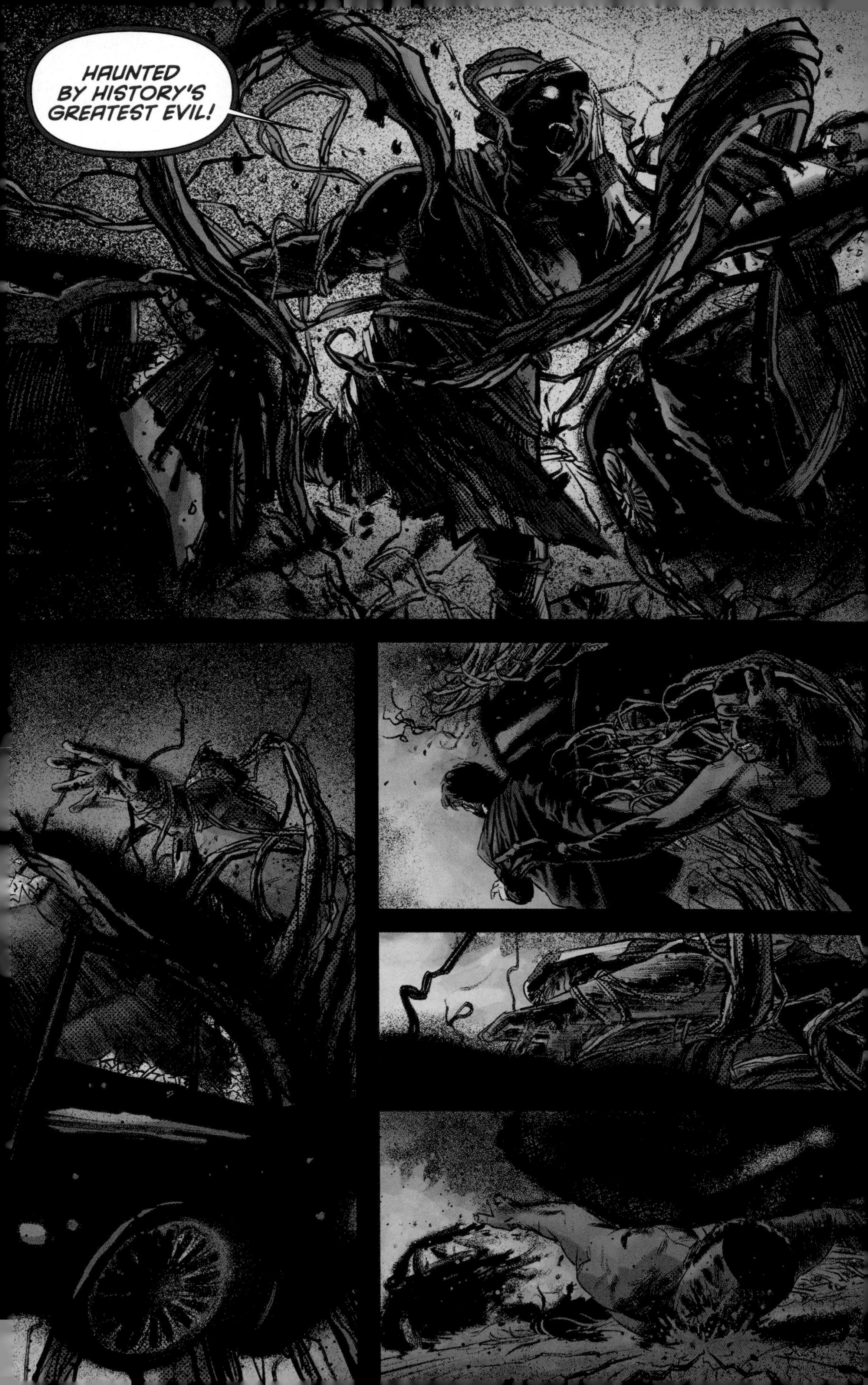
HAUNTED BY HISTORY'S GREATEST EVIL!

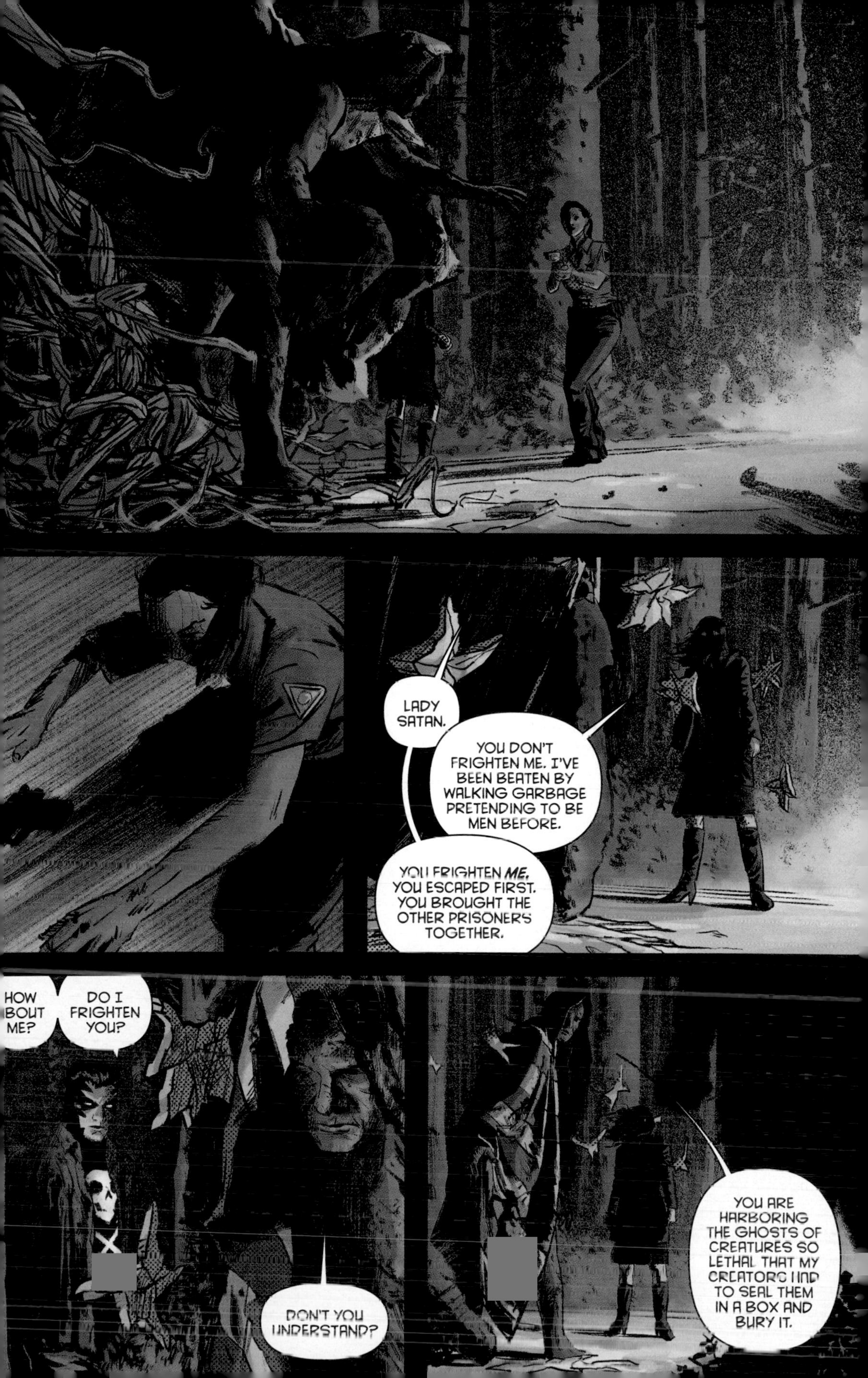
LADY SATAN.
YOU DON'T FRIGHTEN ME. I'VE BEEN BEATEN BY WALKING GARBAGE PRETENDING TO BE MEN BEFORE.
YOU FRIGHTEN *ME.* YOU ESCAPED FIRST. YOU BROUGHT THE OTHER PRISONERS TOGETHER.
HOW BOUT ME?
DO I FRIGHTEN YOU?
DON'T YOU UNDERSTAND?
YOU ARE HARBORING THE GHOSTS OF CREATURES SO LETHAL THAT MY CREATORS HAD TO SEAL THEM IN A BOX AND BURY IT.

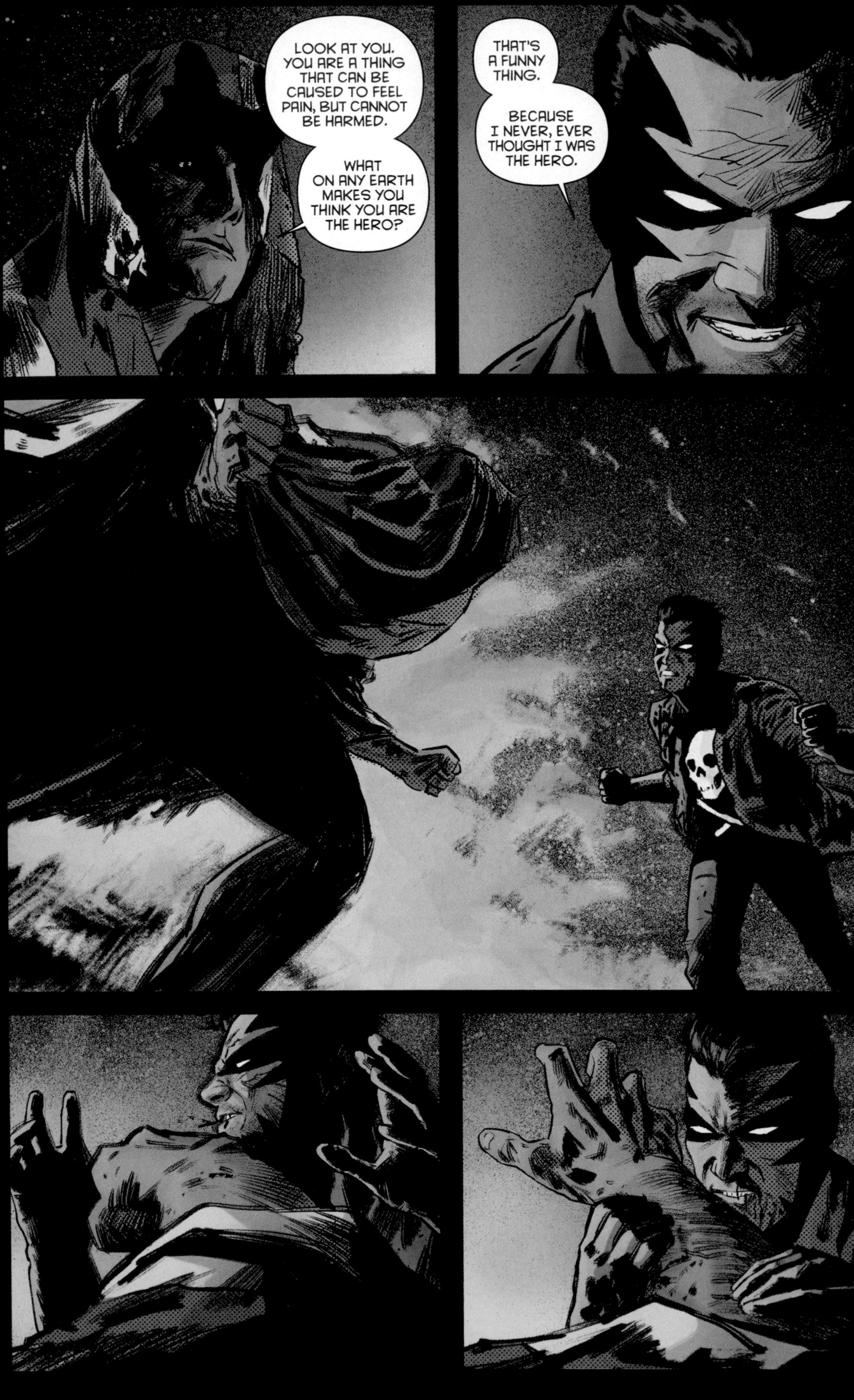
LOOK AT YOU. YOU ARE A THING THAT CAN BE CAUSED TO FEEL PAIN, BUT CANNOT BE HARMED.
WHAT ON ANY EARTH MAKES YOU THINK YOU ARE THE HERO?
THAT'S A FUNNY THING.
BECAUSE I NEVER, EVER THOUGHT I WAS THE HERO.

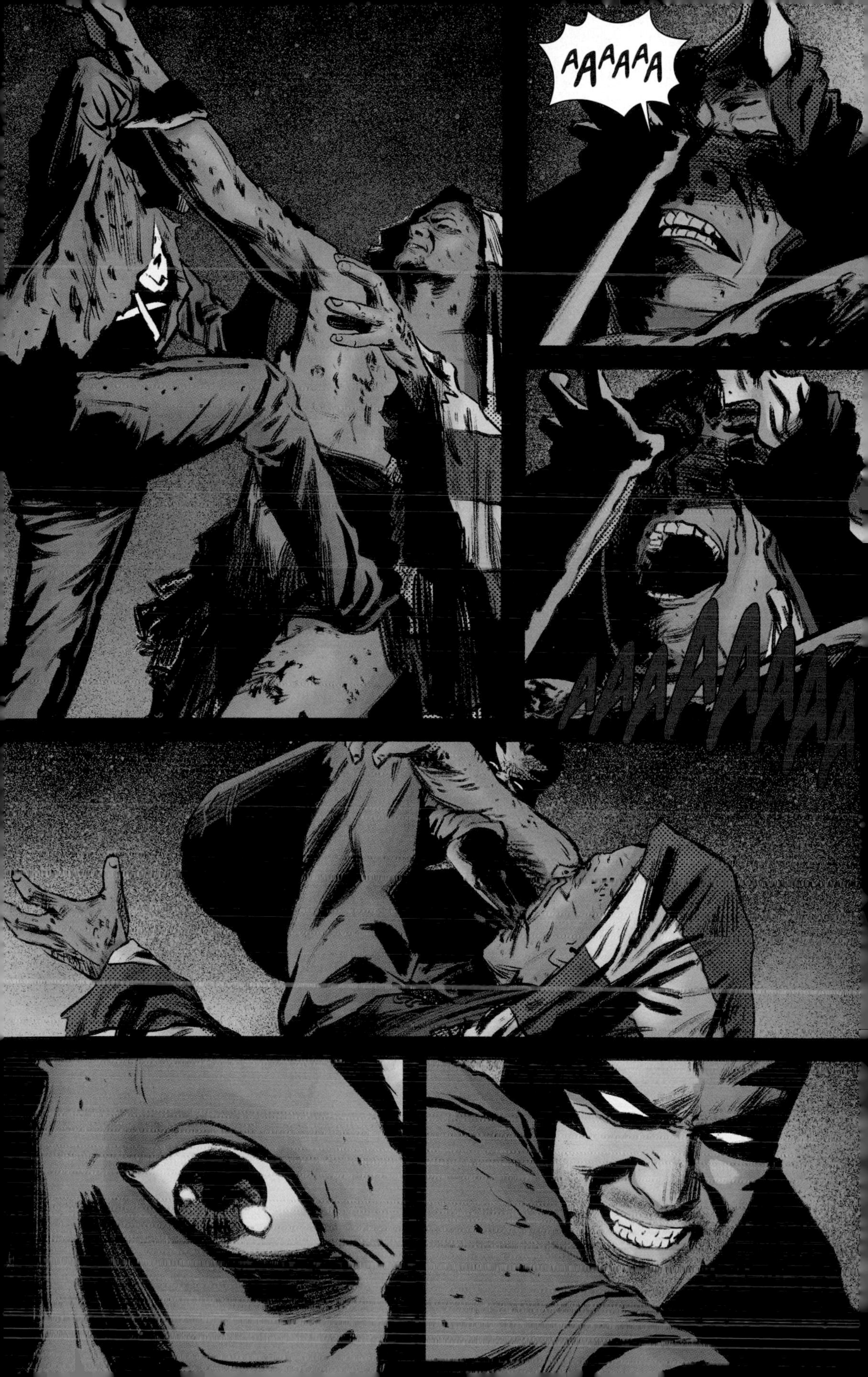
AAAAA
AAAAAAAA

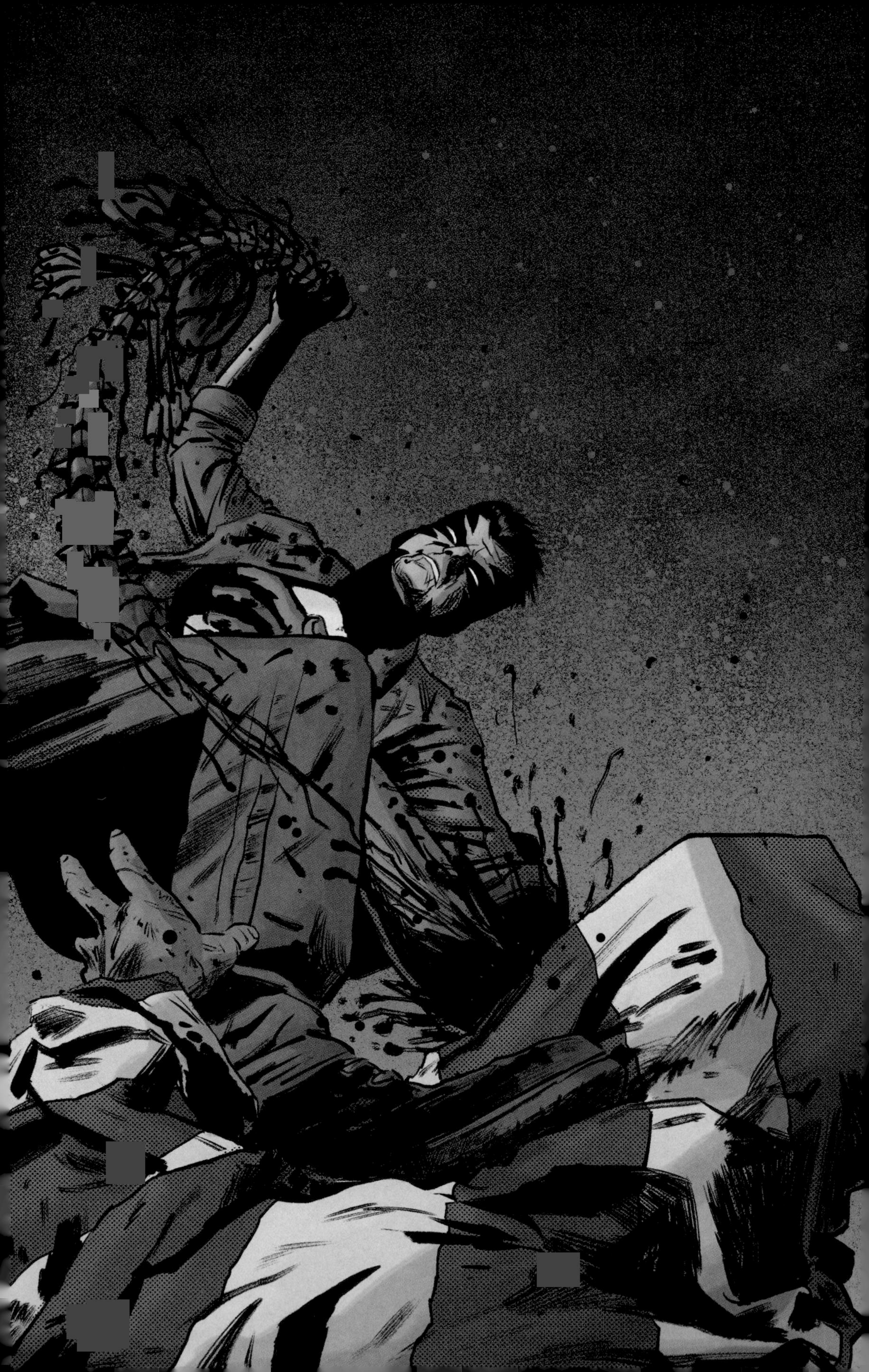

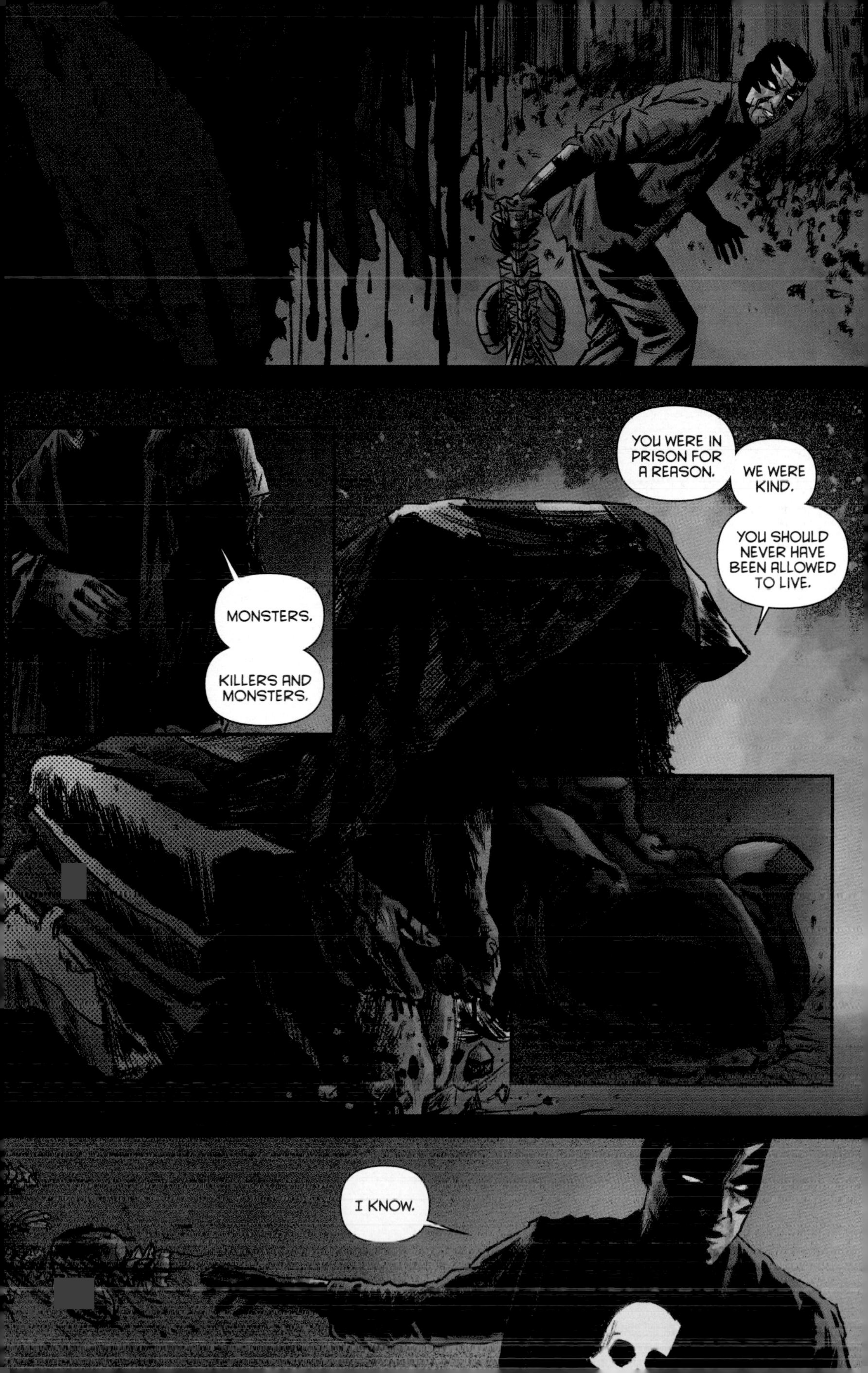
MONSTERS.
KILLERS AND MONSTERS.
YOU WERE IN PRISON FOR A REASON.
WE WERE KIND.
YOU SHOULD NEVER HAVE BEEN ALLOWED TO LIVE.
I KNOW.

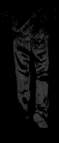

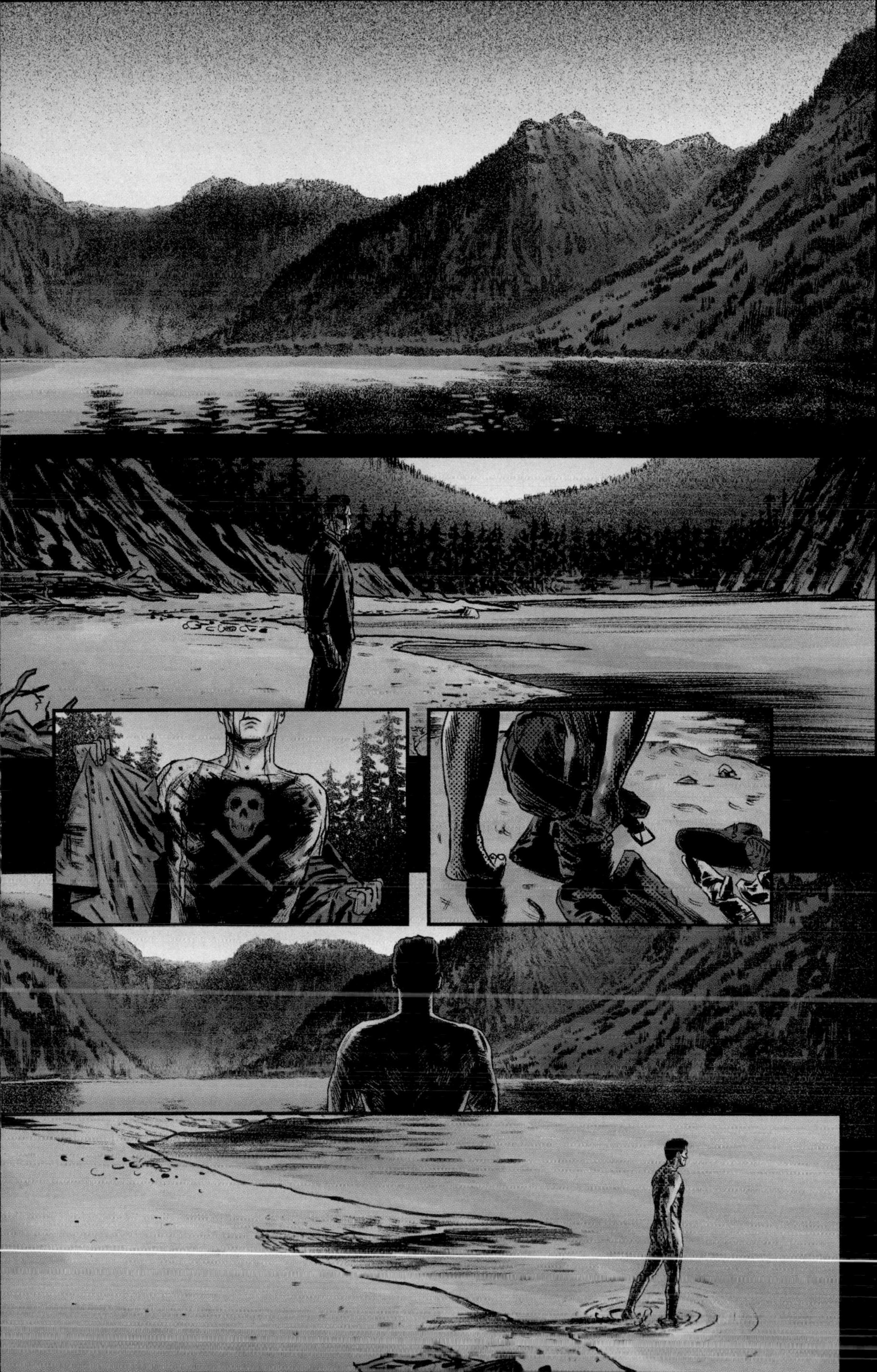

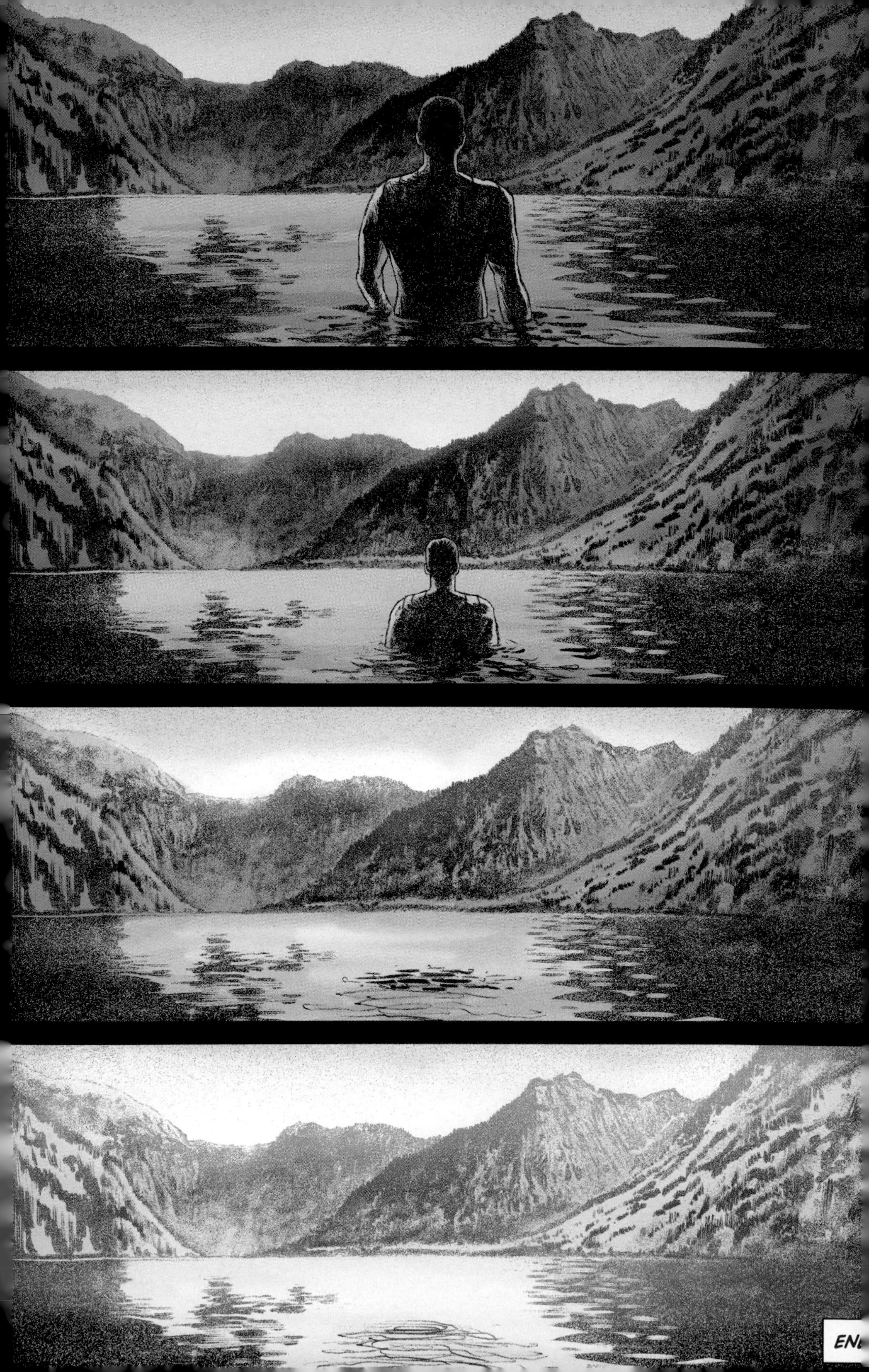
EN

ALTERNATE
COVER GALLERY

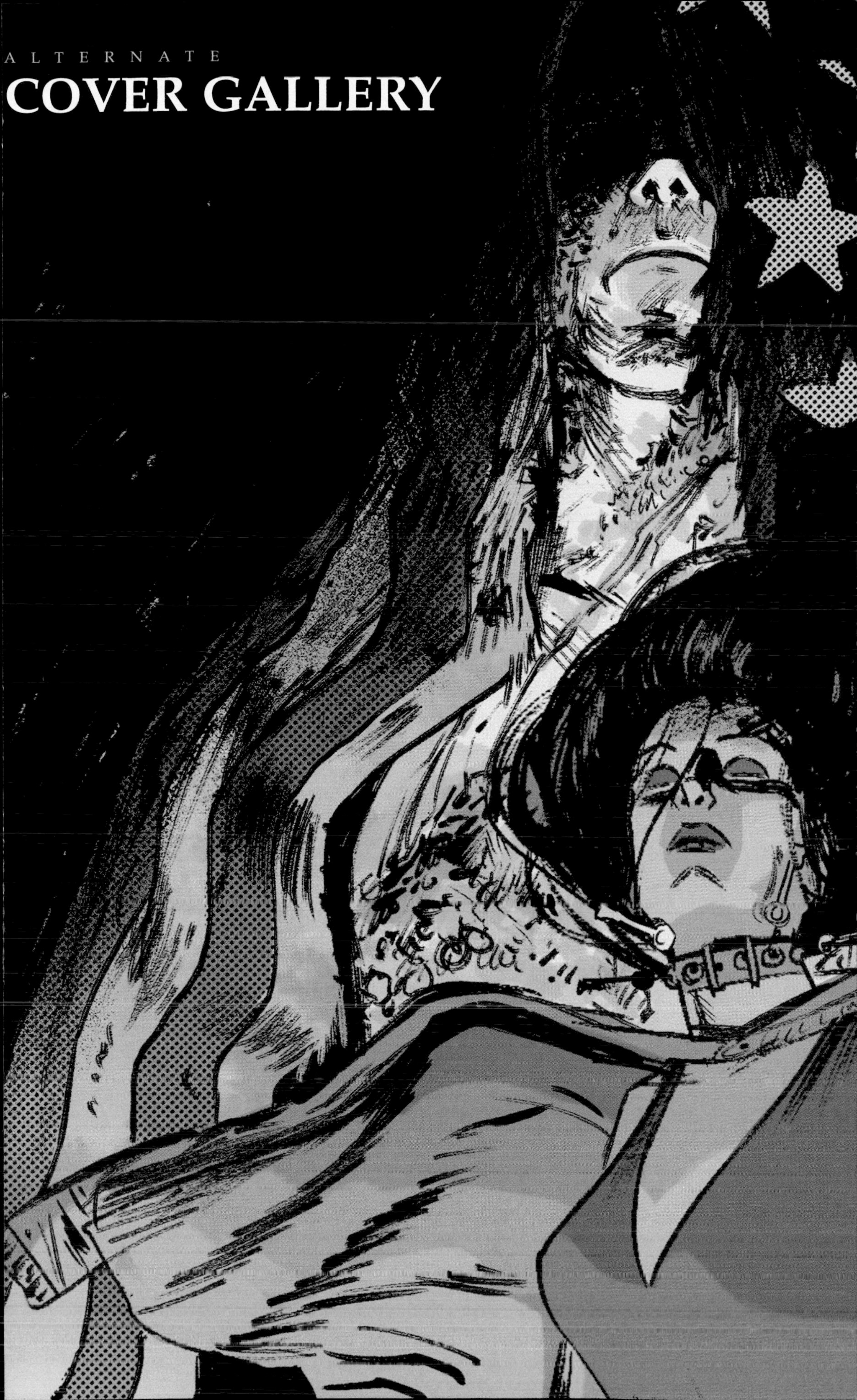

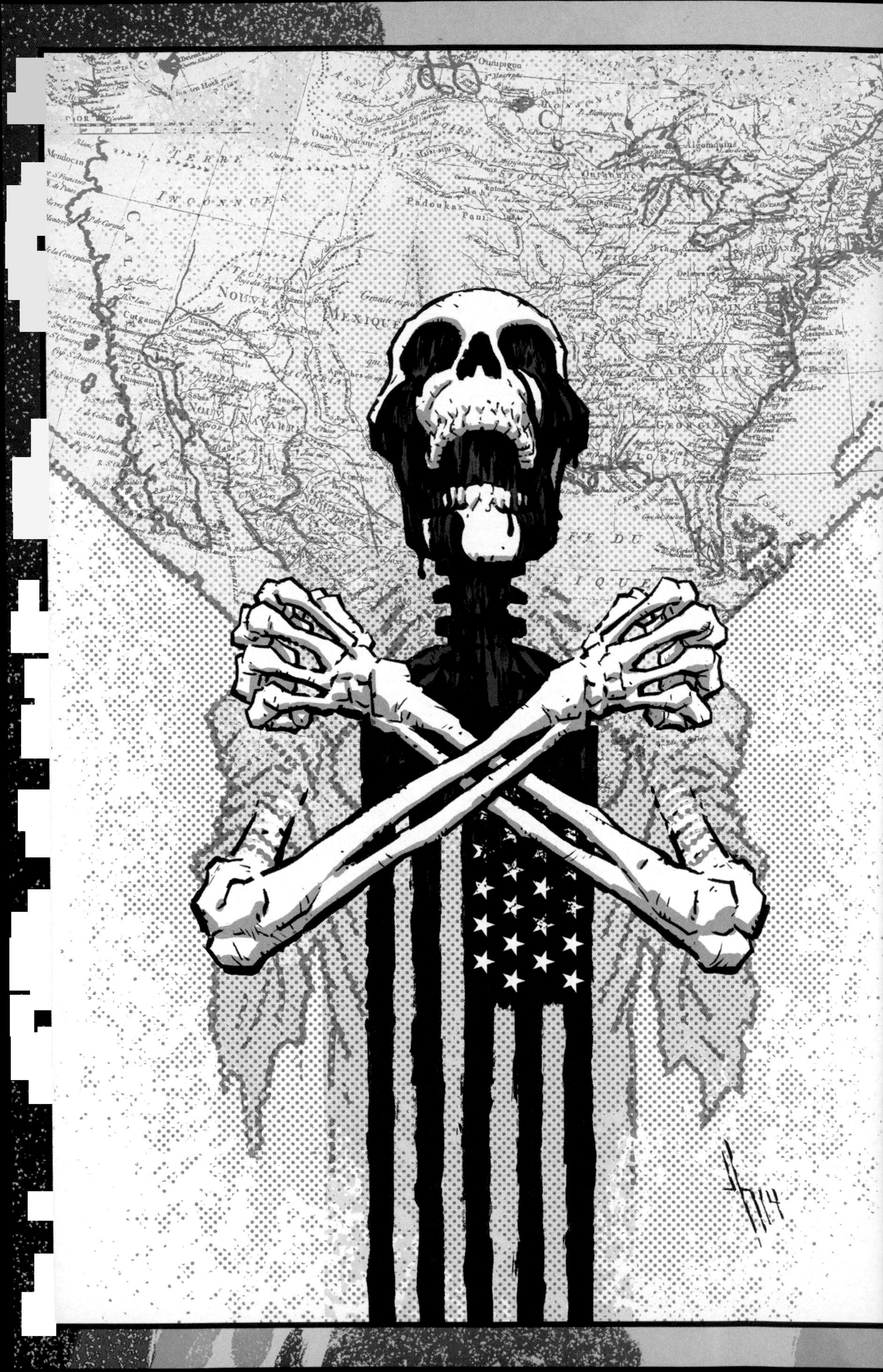
TERRE
INCONNUE
NOUVEAU
MEXIQUE
Padoukas

ISSUE #1 COVER BY **JASON HOWARD**

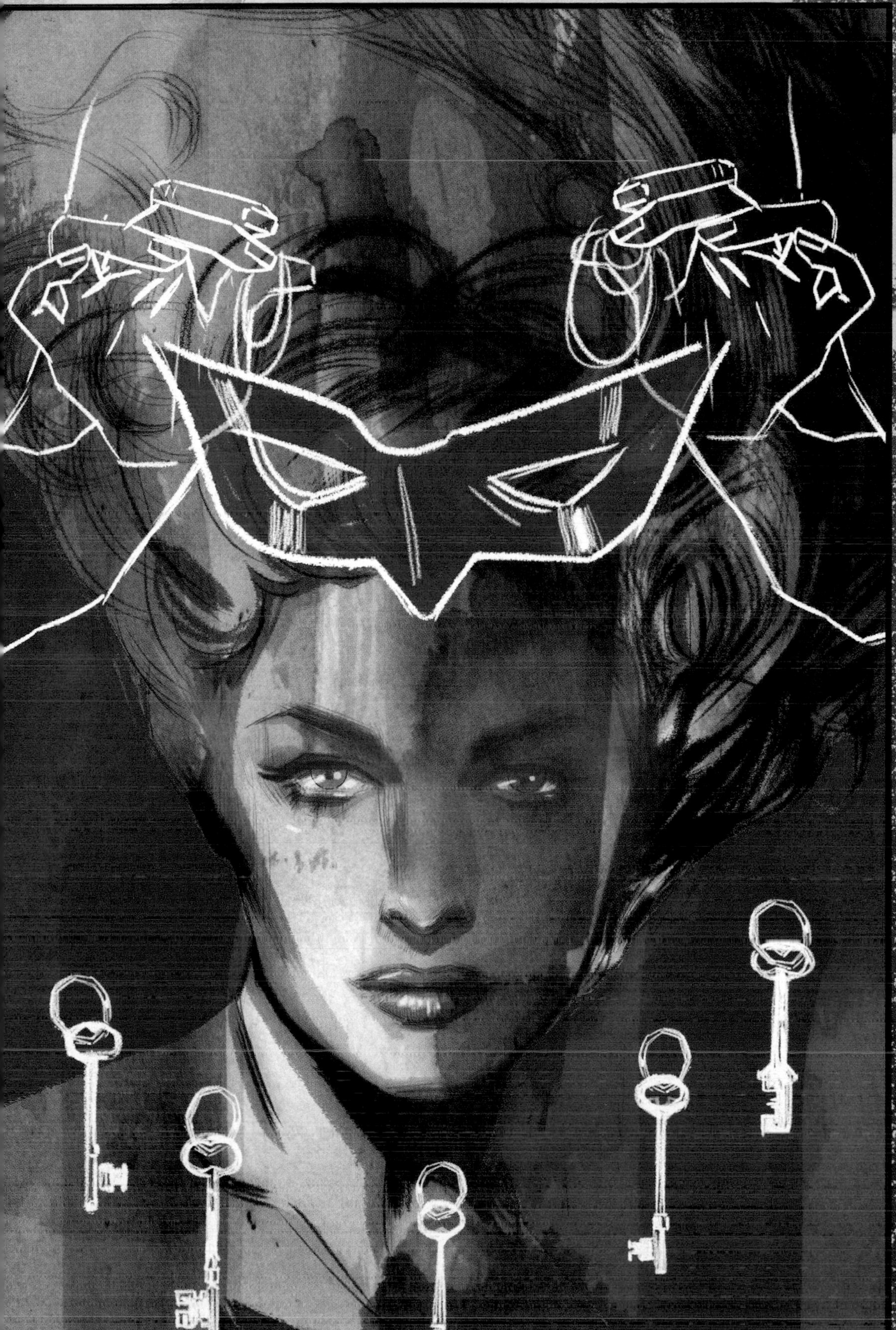

ISSUE #1 COVER BY TULA LOTAY

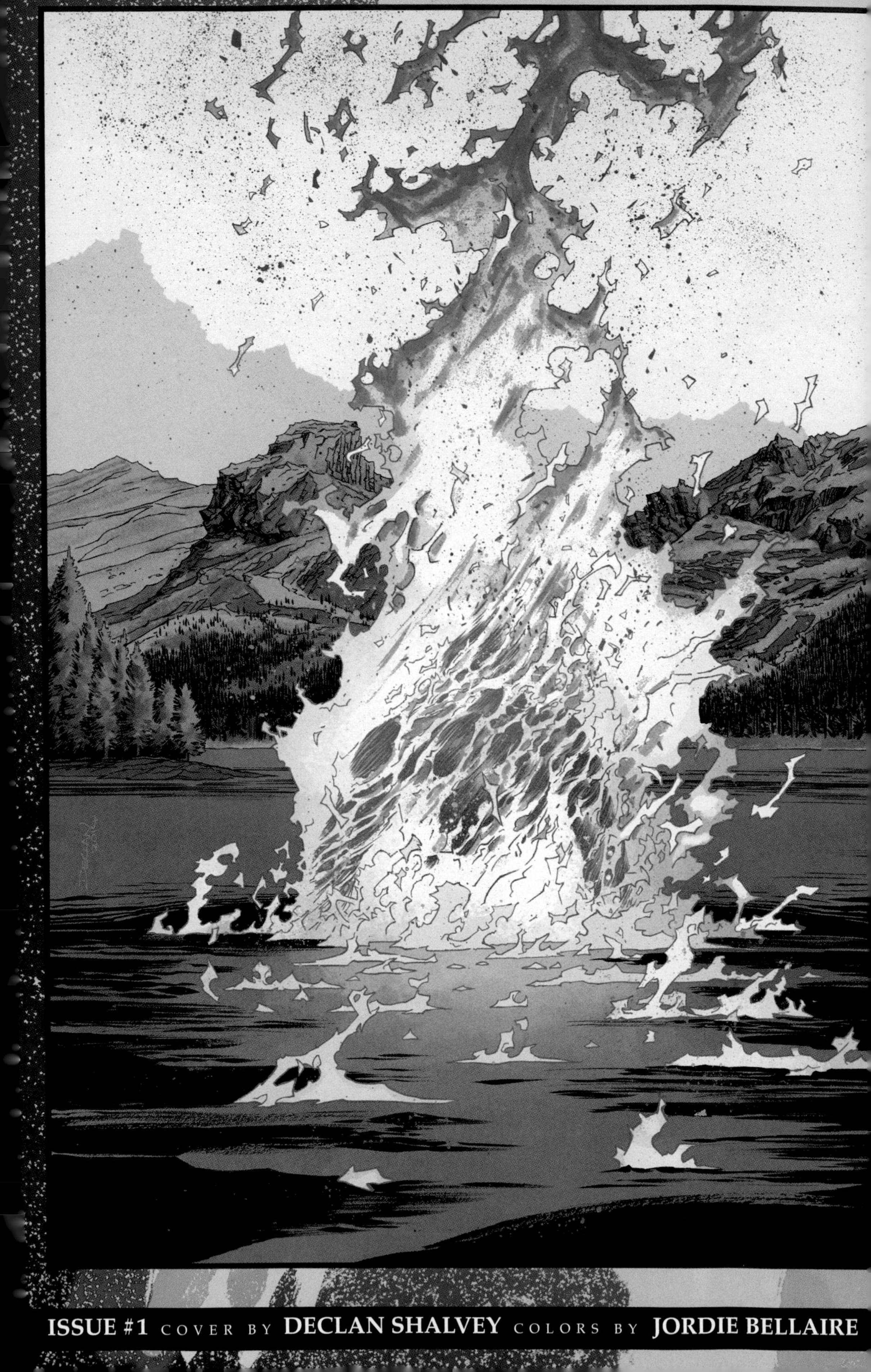

ISSUE #1 COVER BY **DECLAN SHALVEY** COLORS BY **JORDIE BELLAIRE**

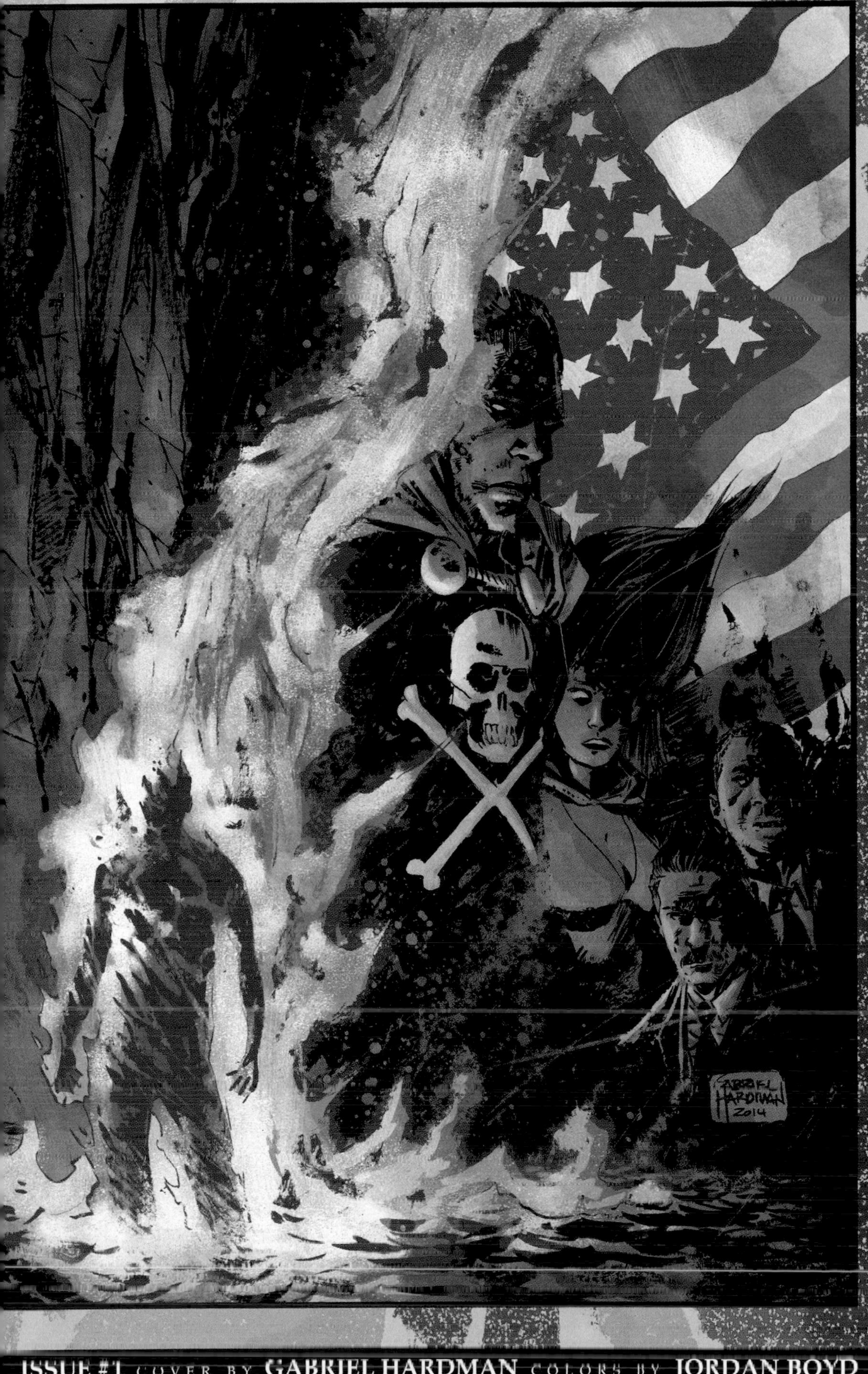

ISSUE #1 COVER BY GABRIEL HARDMAN COLORS BY JORDAN BOYD

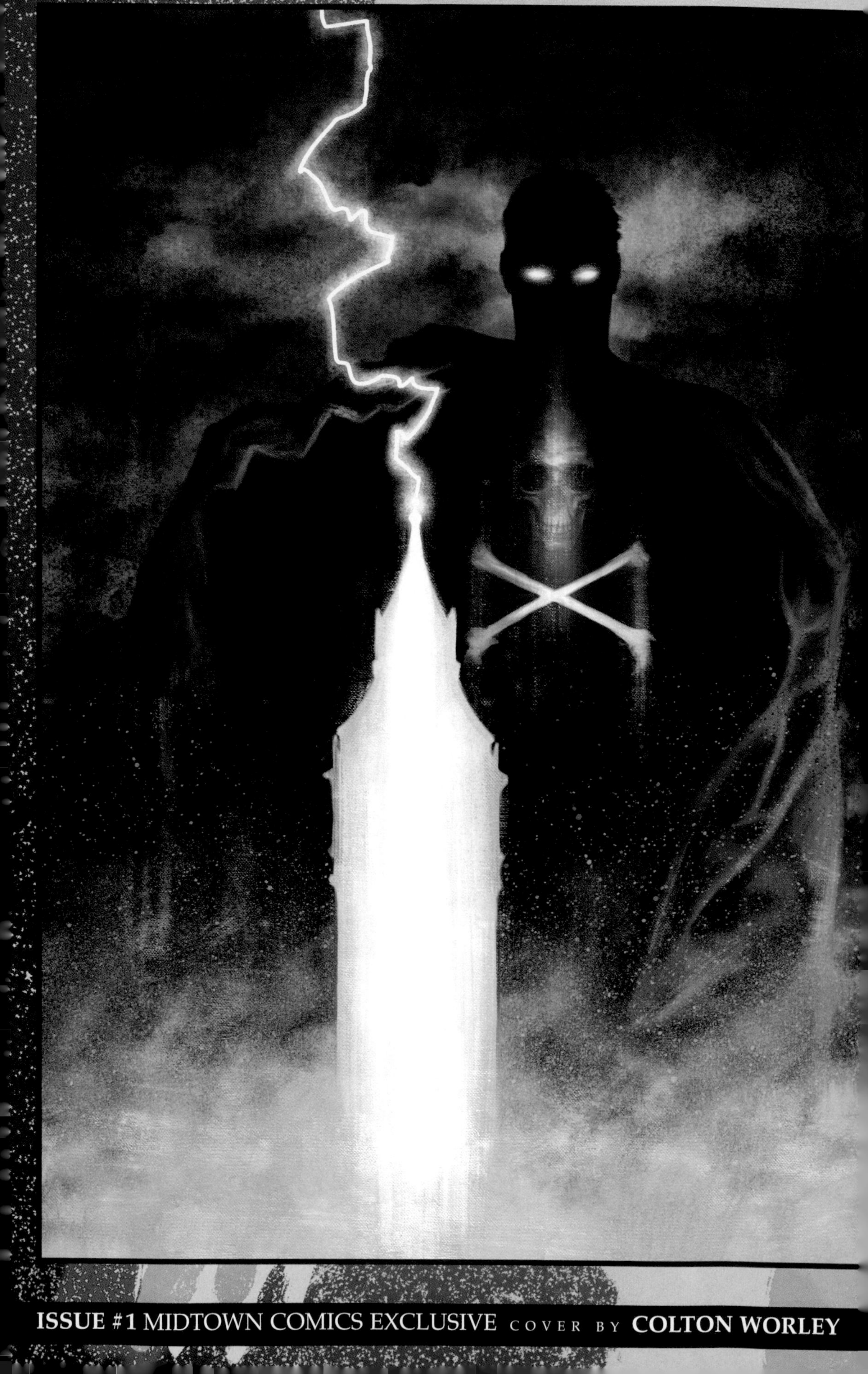

ISSUE #1 MIDTOWN COMICS EXCLUSIVE COVER BY COLTON WORLEY

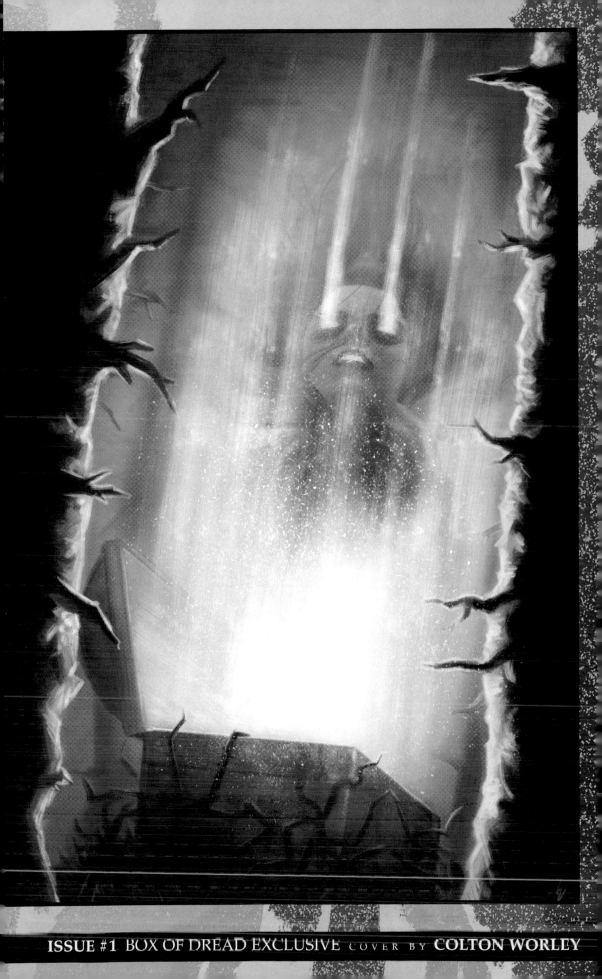

ISSUE #1 BOX OF DREAD EXCLUSIVE COVER BY **COLTON WORLEY**

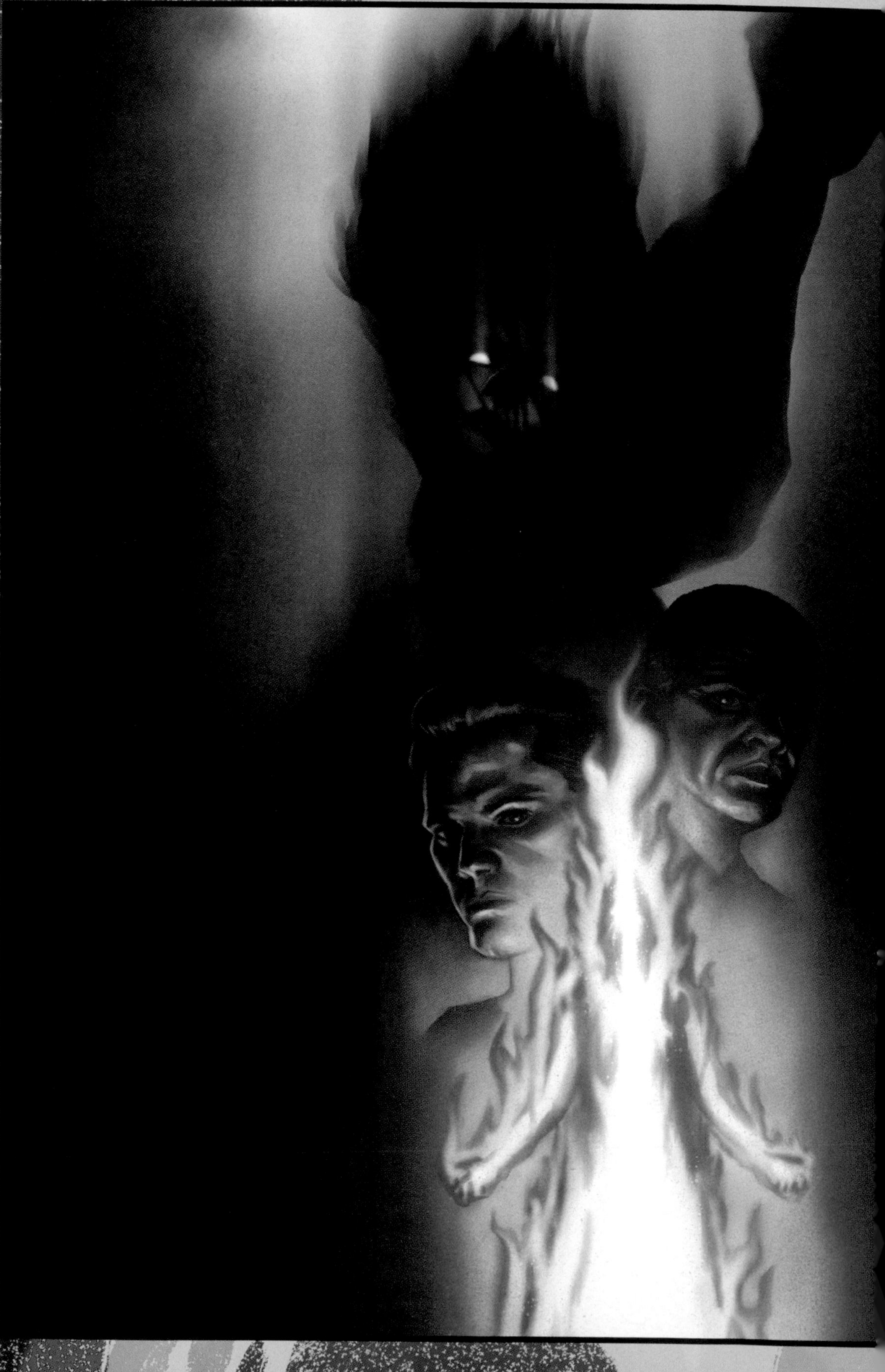

ISSUE #1 COVER BY **COLTON WORLEY**

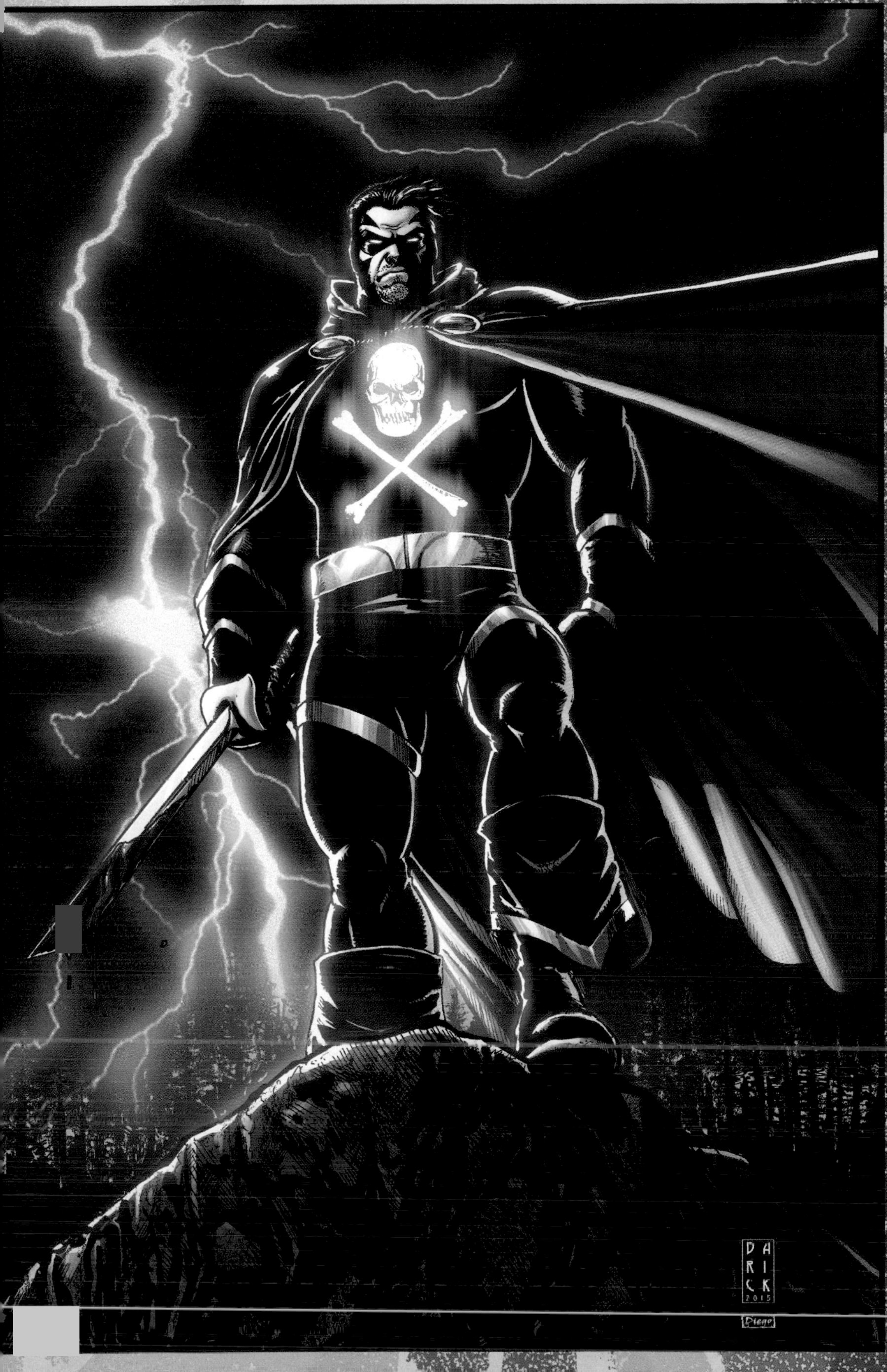

SSUE #1 COVER BY DARICK ROBERTSON COLORS BY DIEGO RODRIGUEZ

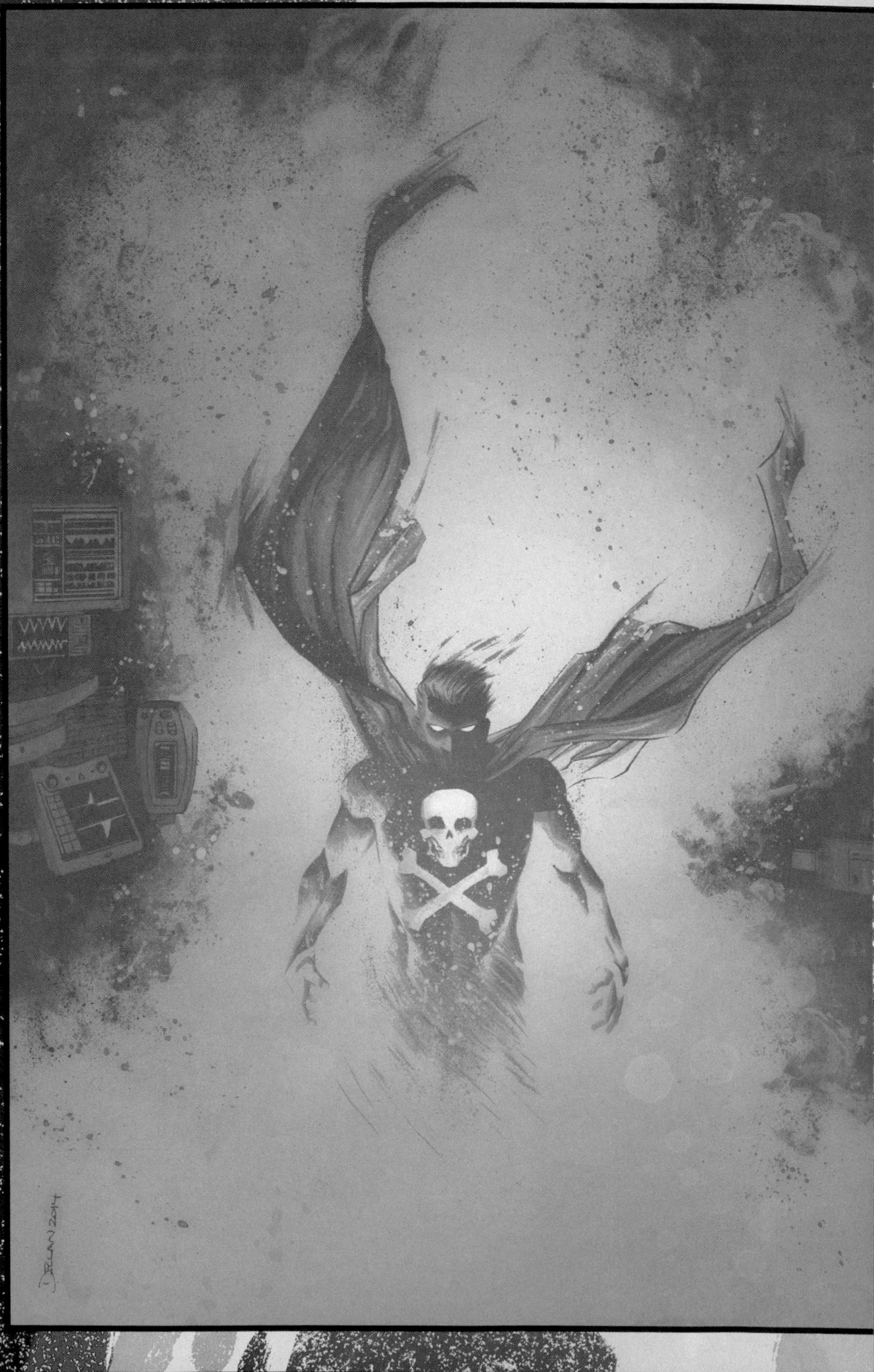
DECLAN 2014

ISSUE #2 COVER BY **DECLAN SHALVEY** COLORS BY **JORDIE BELLAIRE**

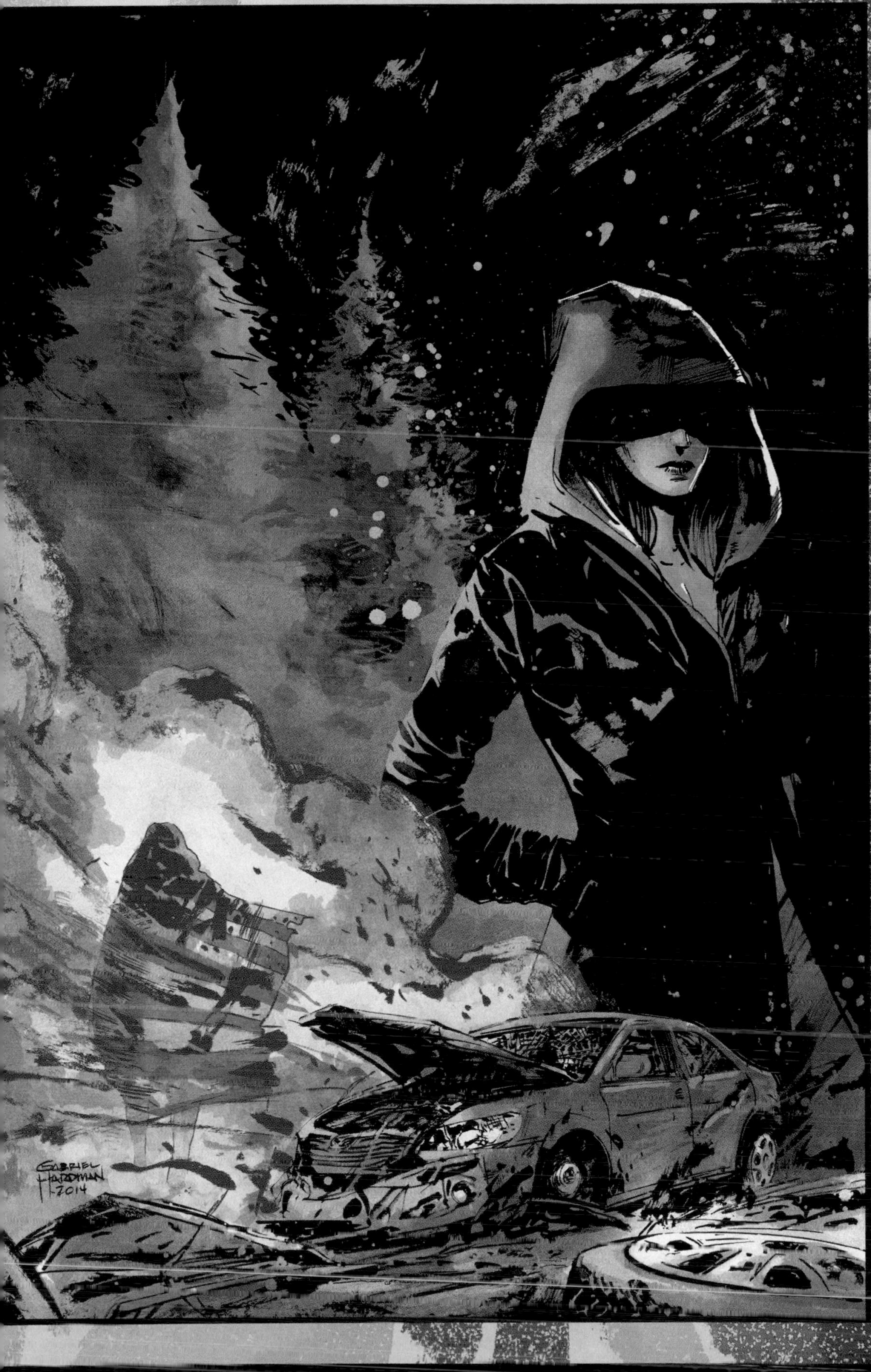
GABRIEL
HARDMAN
2014

ISSUE #2 COVER BY GABRIEL HARDMAN COLORS BY JORDAN BOYD

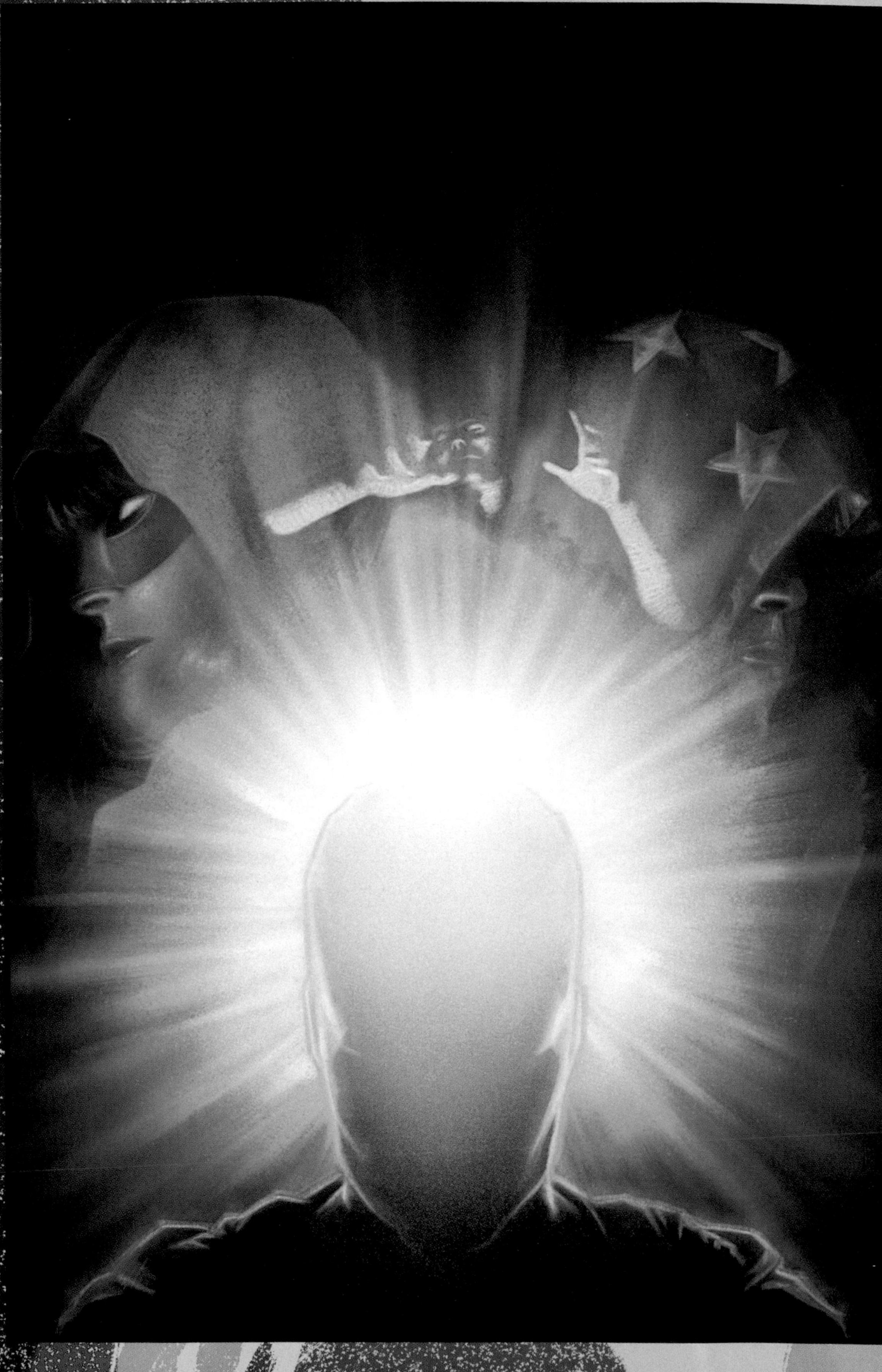

ISSUE #2 COVER BY COLTON WORLEY

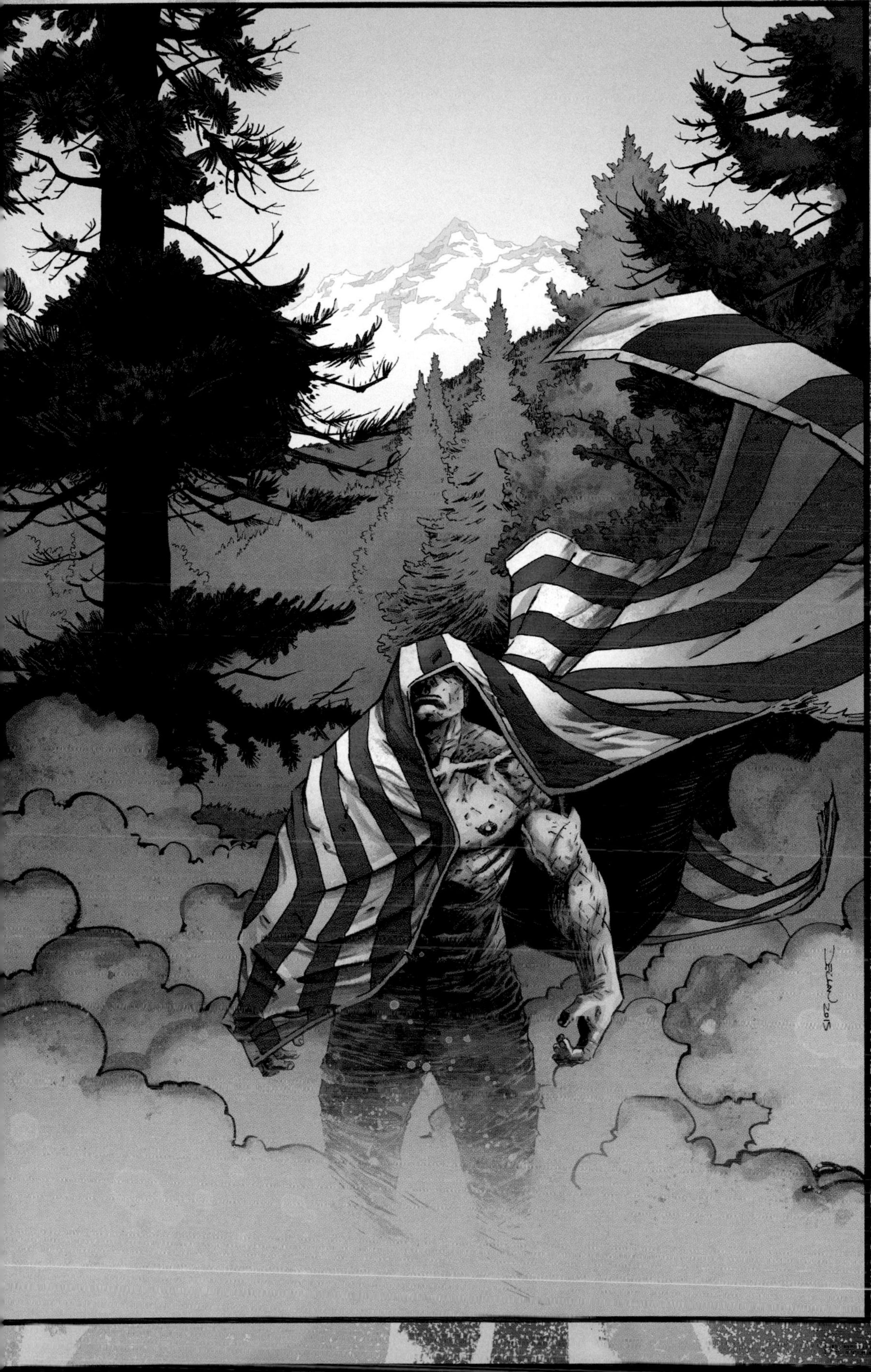
DECLAN 2015

ISSUE #3 COVER BY **DECLAN SHALVEY** COLORS BY **JORDIE BELLAIRE**

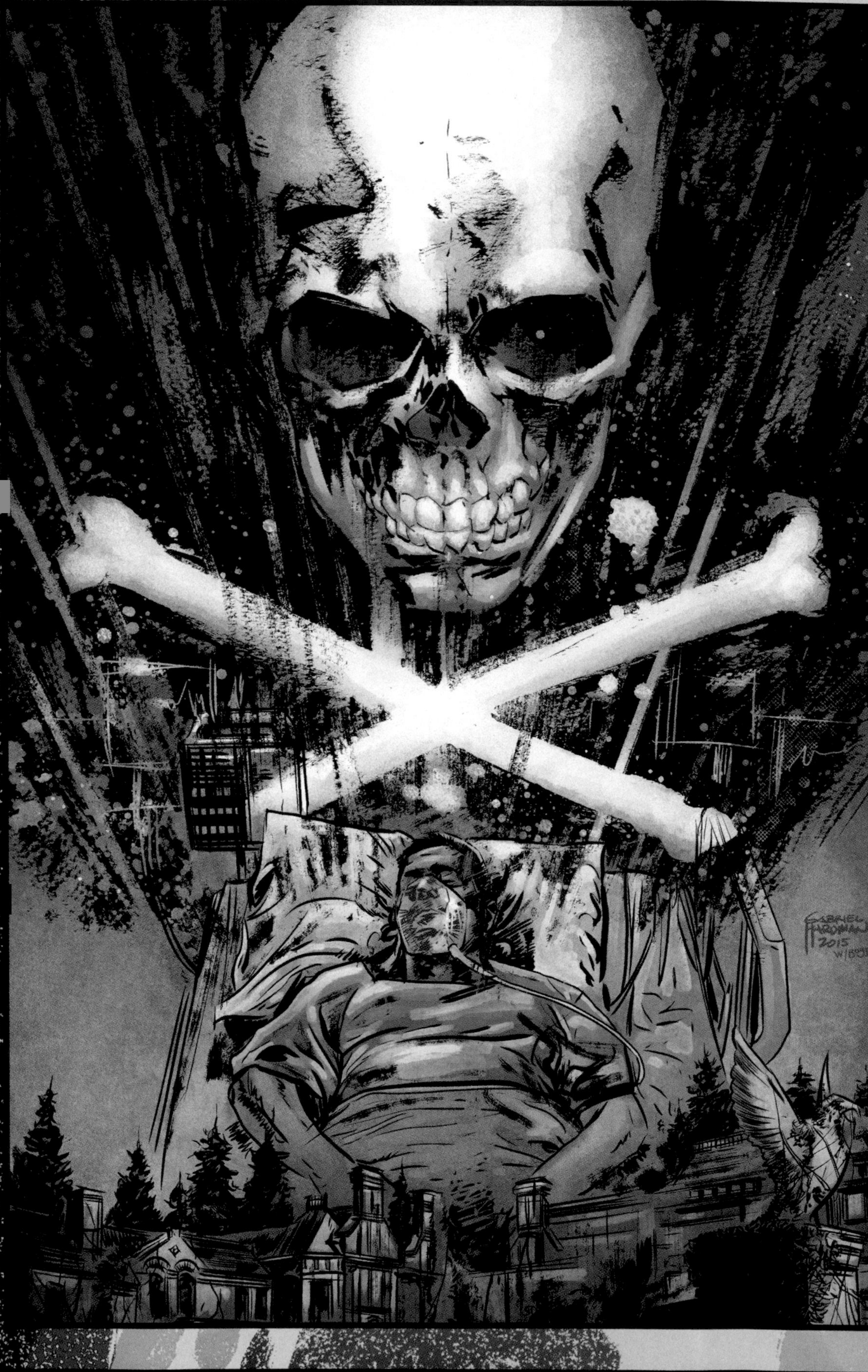

ISSUE #3 COVER BY **GABRIEL HARDMAN** COLORS BY **JORDAN BOYD**

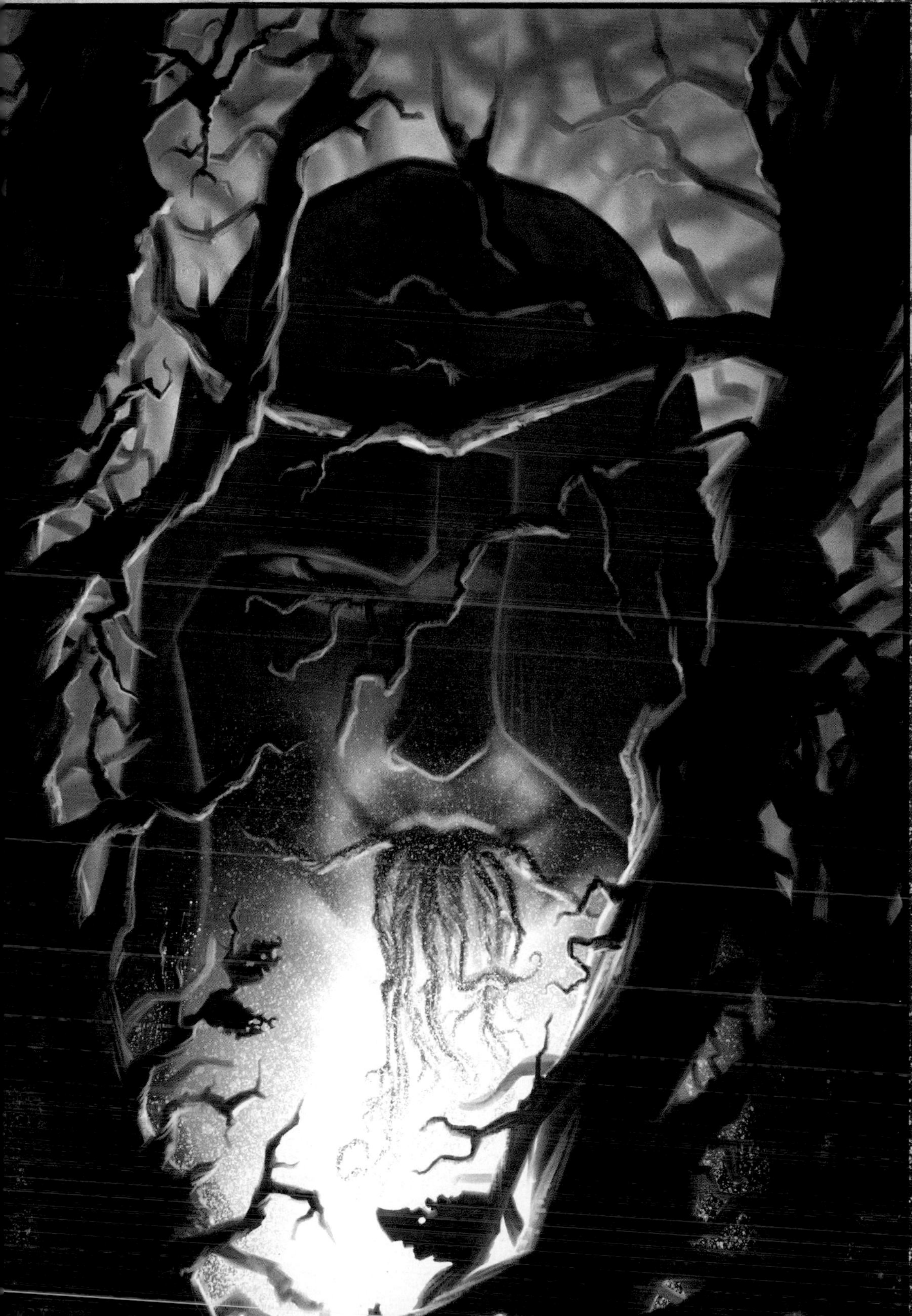

ISSUE #3 COVER BY COLTON WORLEY

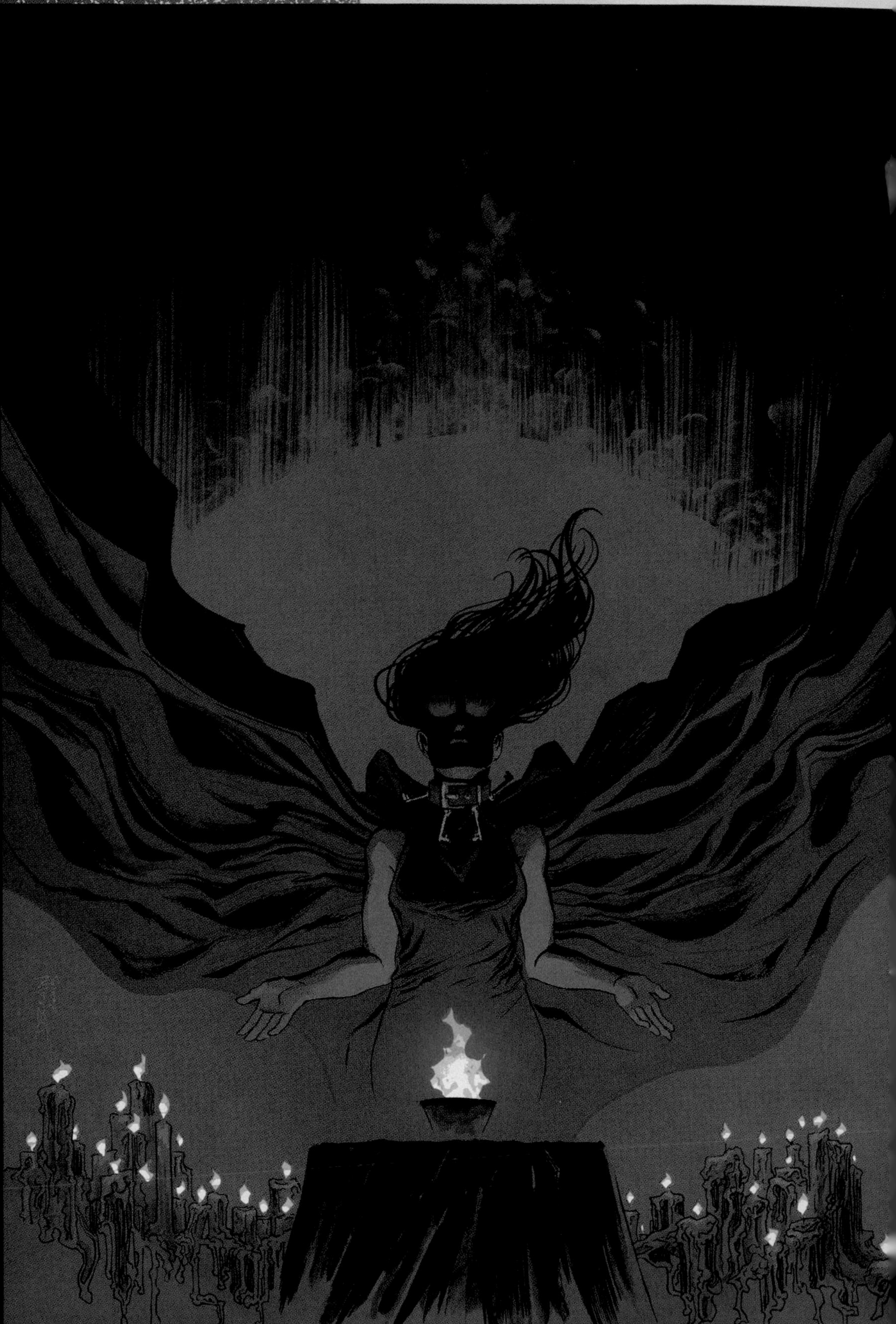

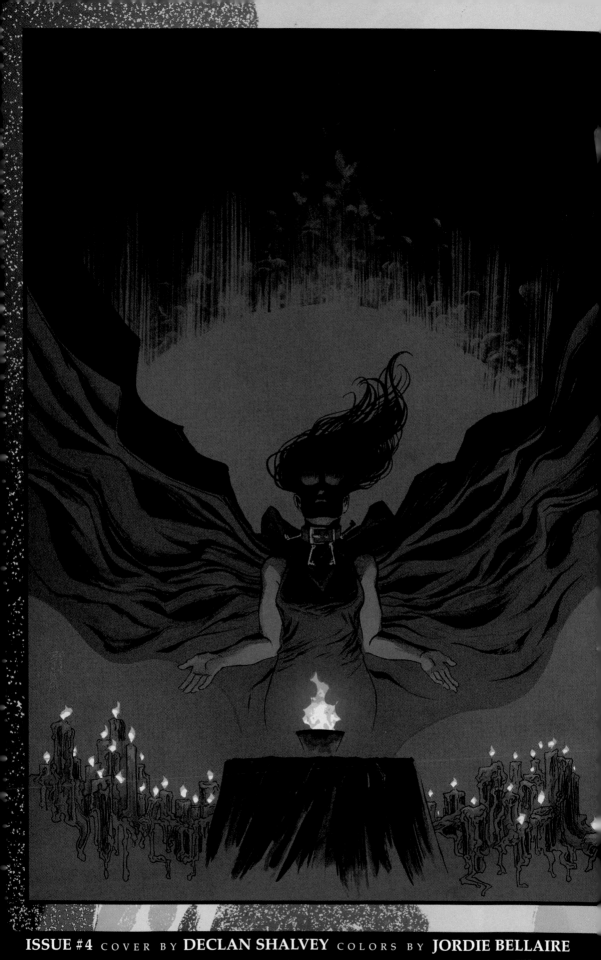

ISSUE #4 COVER BY DECLAN SHALVEY COLORS BY JORDIE BELLAIRE

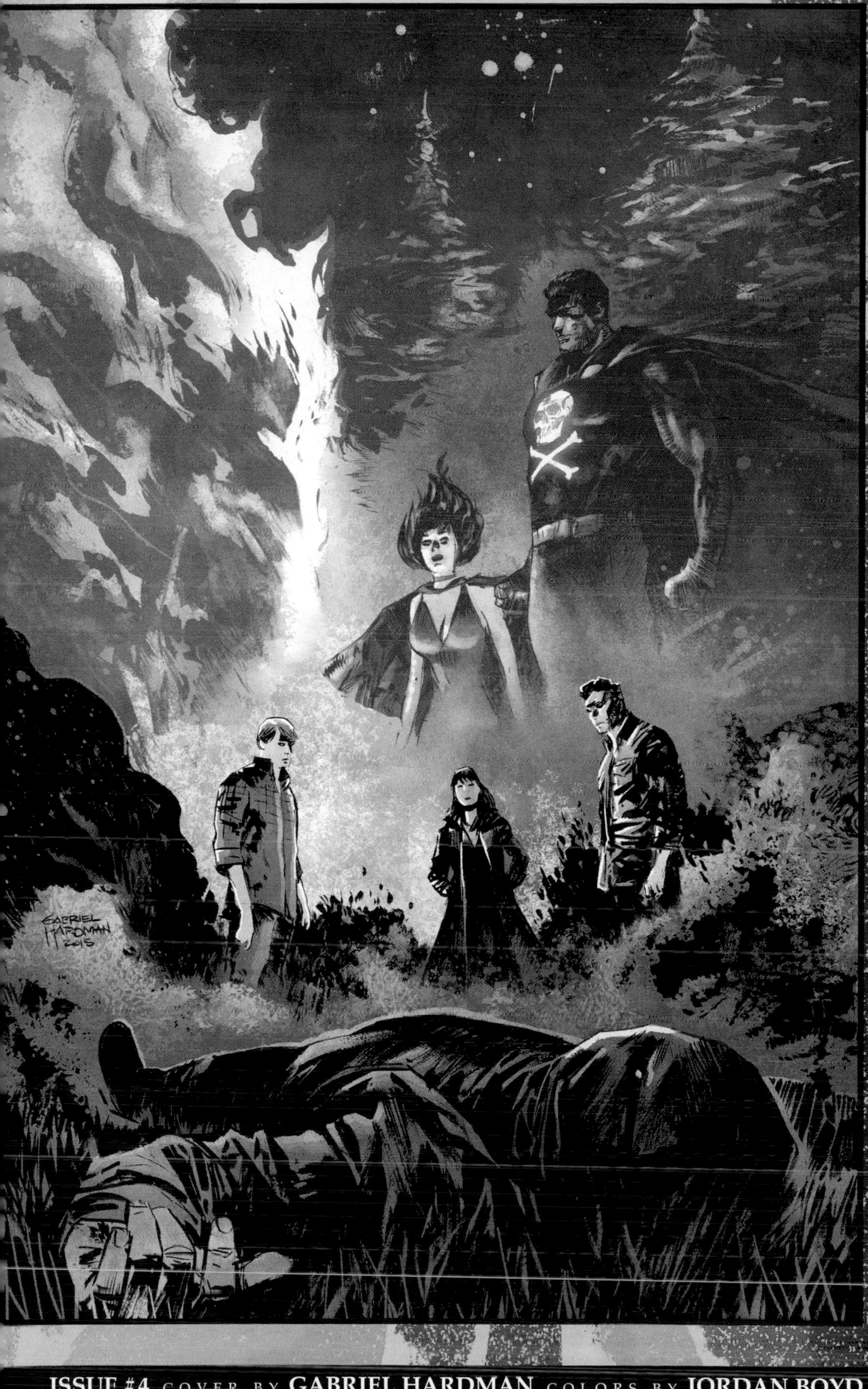

GABRIEL
HARDMAN
2015

ISSUE #4 COVER BY **GABRIEL HARDMAN** COLORS BY **JORDAN BOYD**

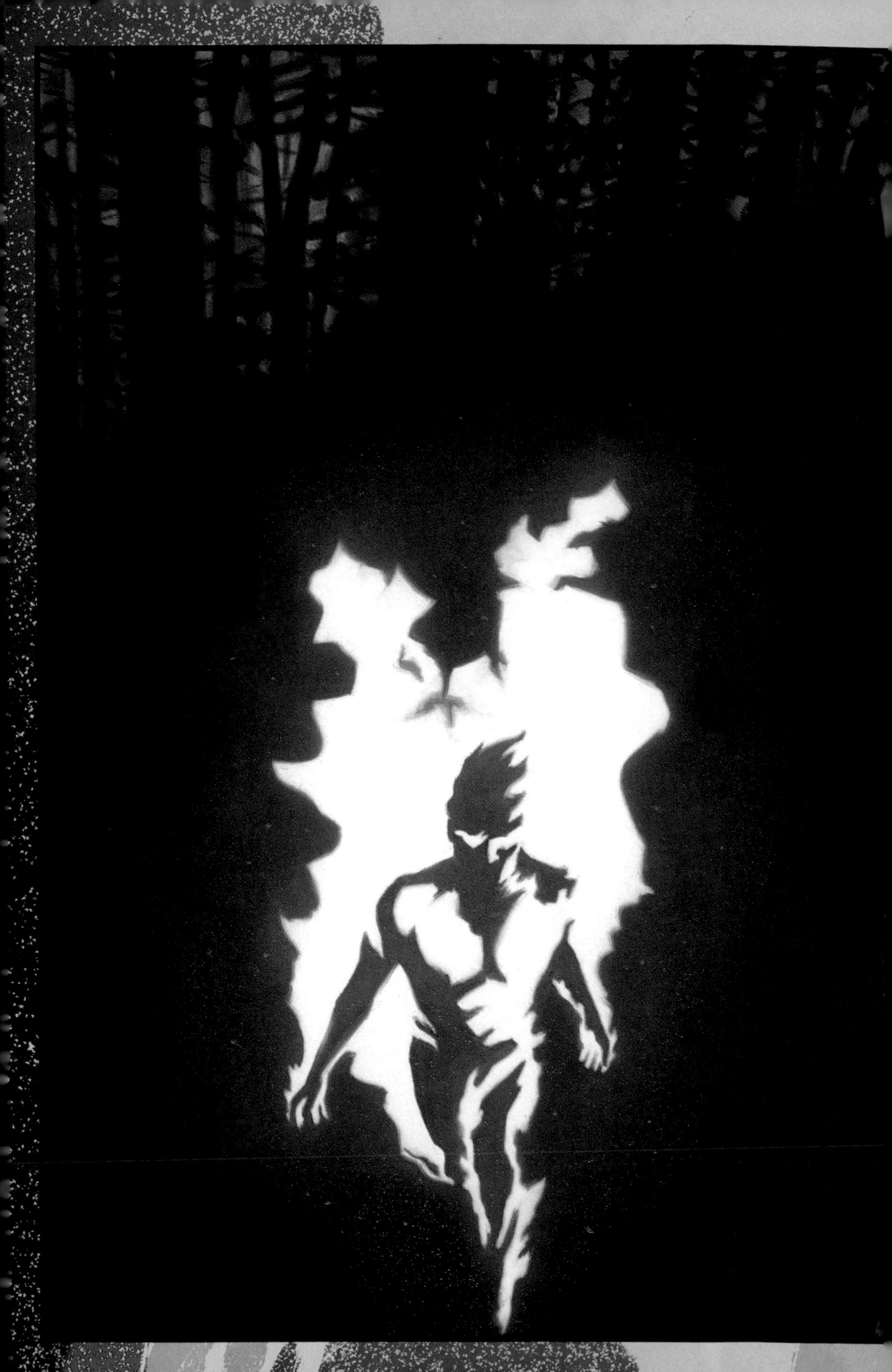

ISSUE #4 COVER BY COLTON WORLEY

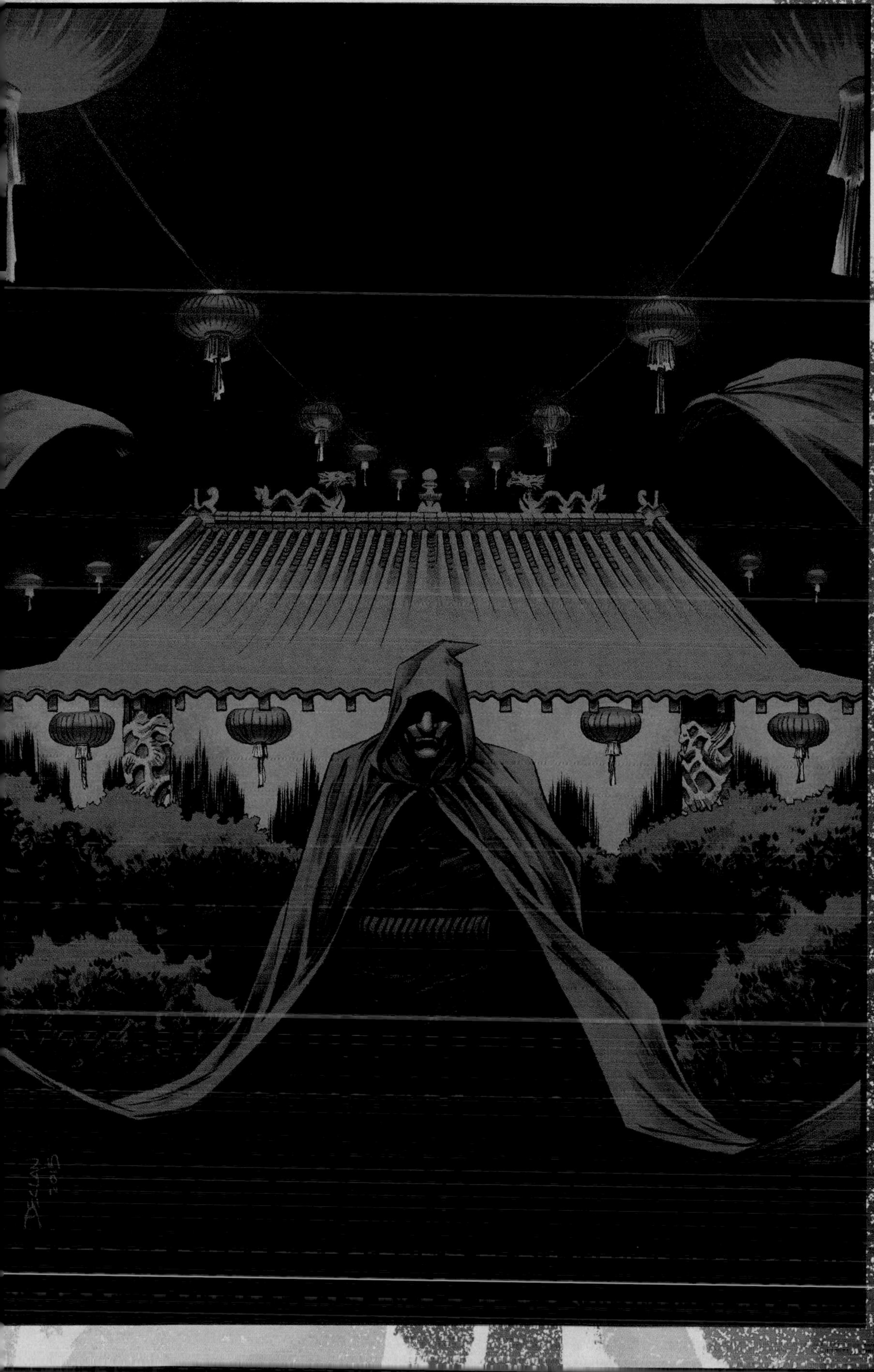
DECLAN
2015

ISSUE #5 COVER BY **DECLAN SHALVEY** COLORS BY **JORDIE BELLAIRE**

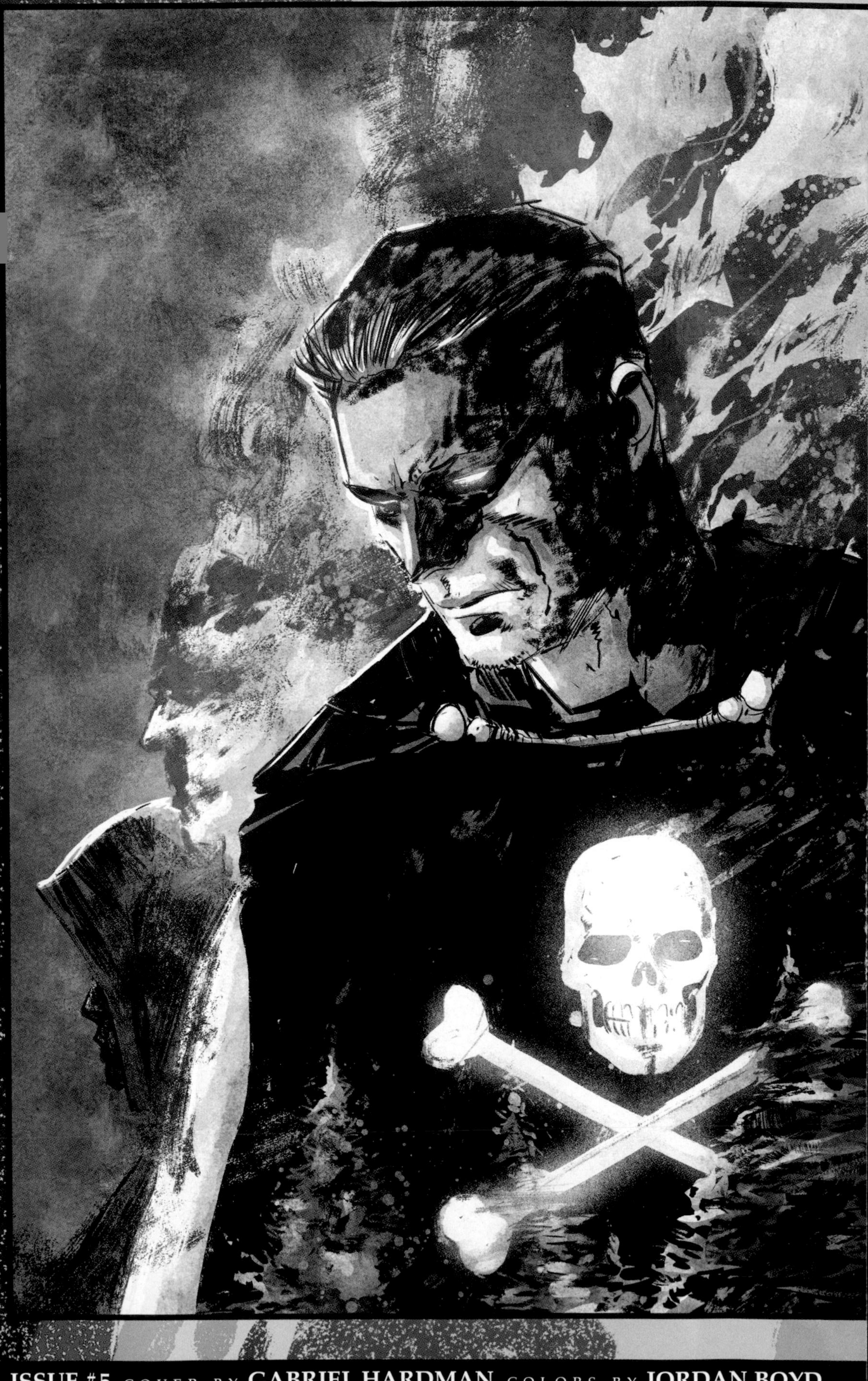

ISSUE #5 COVER BY GABRIEL HARDMAN COLORS BY JORDAN BOYD

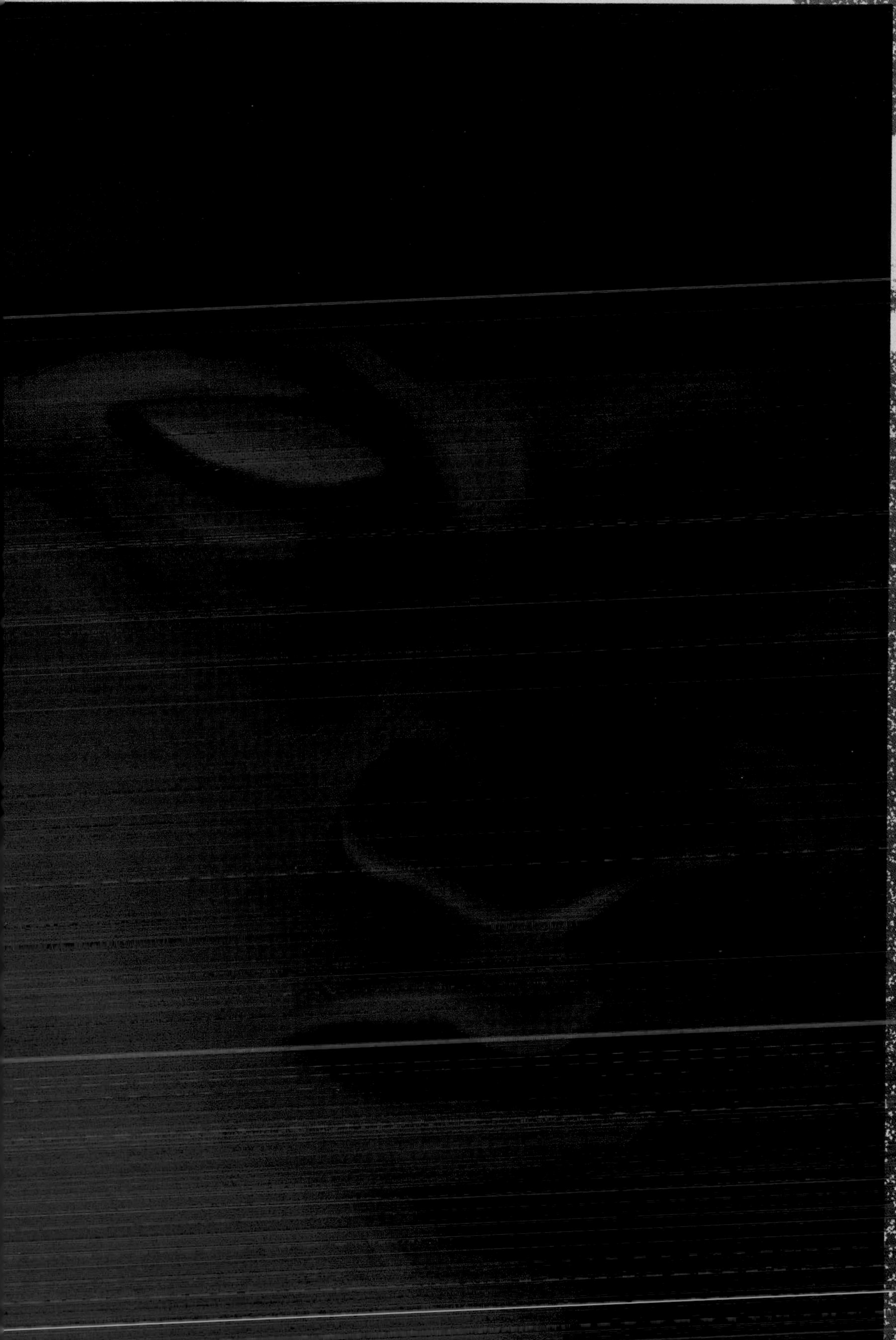

ISSUE #5 COVER BY COLTON WORLEY

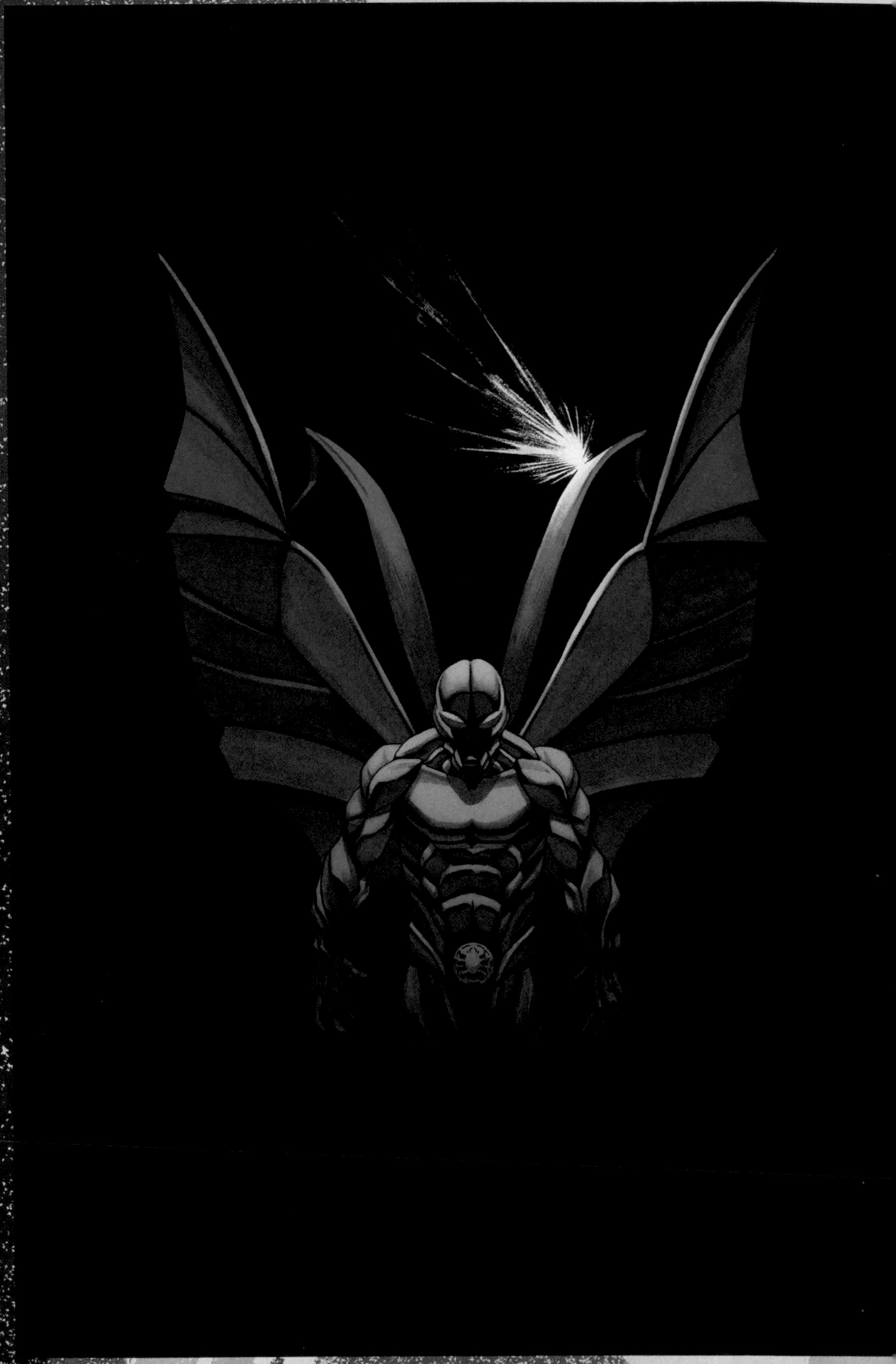

ISSUE #6 COVER BY DECLAN SHALVEY COLORS BY JORDAN BELLAIRE

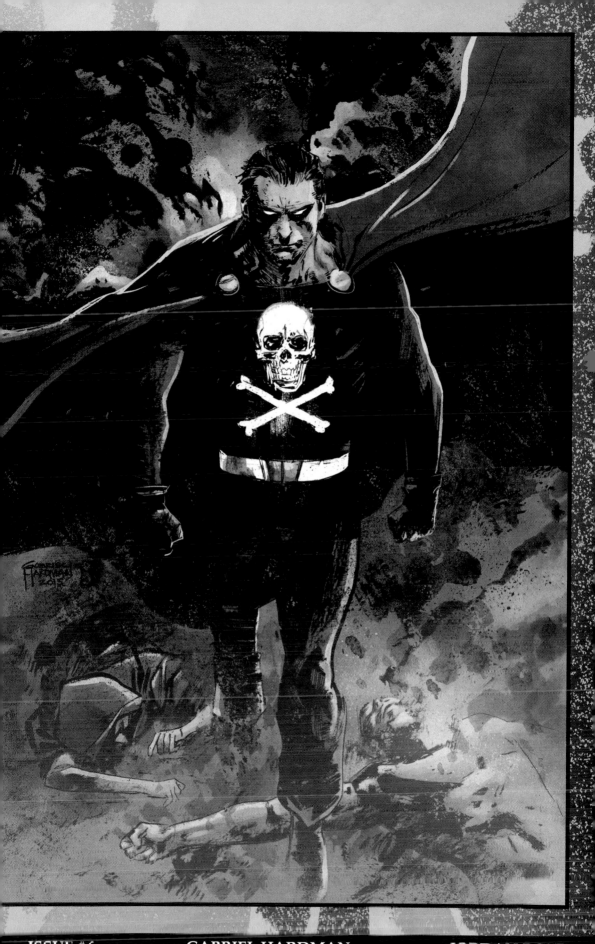

ISSUE #6 COVER BY GABRIEL HARDMAN COLORS BY JORDAN BOYD

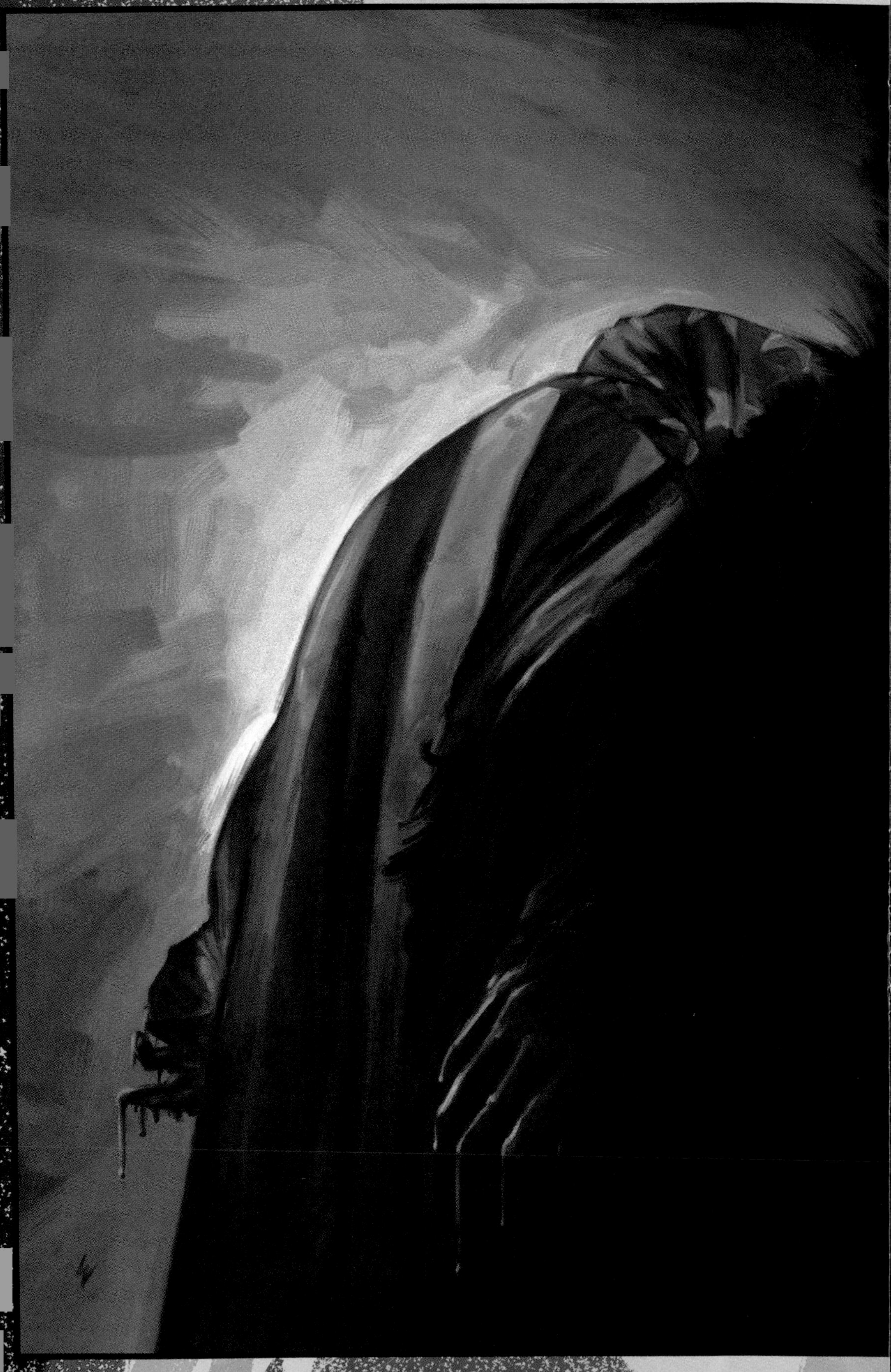

ISSUE #6 COVER BY **COLTON WORLEY**

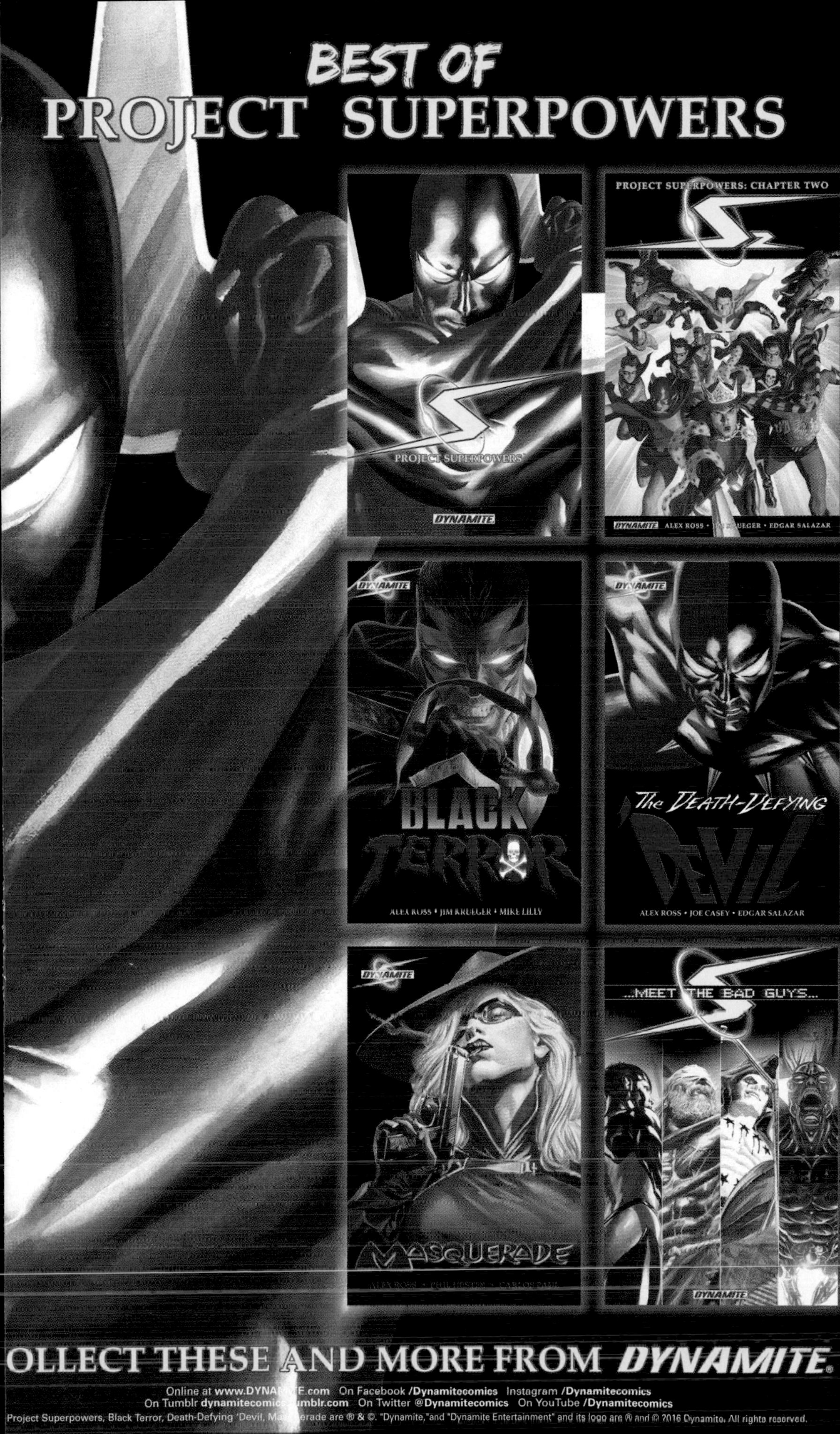
BEST OF
PROJECT SUPERPOWERS
PROJECT SUPERPOWERS
DYNAMITE
PROJECT SUPERPOWERS: CHAPTER TWO
DYNAMITE ALEX ROSS • JIM KRUEGER • EDGAR SALAZAR
DYNAMITE
BLACK TERROR
ALEX ROSS • JIM KRUEGER • MIKE LILLY
DYNAMITE
The DEATH-DEFYING 'DEVIL
ALEX ROSS • JOE CASEY • EDGAR SALAZAR
DYNAMITE
MASQUERADE
...MEET THE BAD GUYS...
DYNAMITE
OLLECT THESE AND MORE FROM DYNAMITE
Online at www.DYNAMITE.com On Facebook /Dynamitecomics Instagram /Dynamitecomics
On Tumblr dynamitecomics.tumblr.com On Twitter @Dynamitecomics On YouTube /Dynamitecomics
Project Superpowers, Black Terror, Death-Defying 'Devil, Masquerade are ® & ©. "Dynamite,"and "Dynamite Entertainment" and its logo are ® and © 2016 Dynamite. All rights reserved.

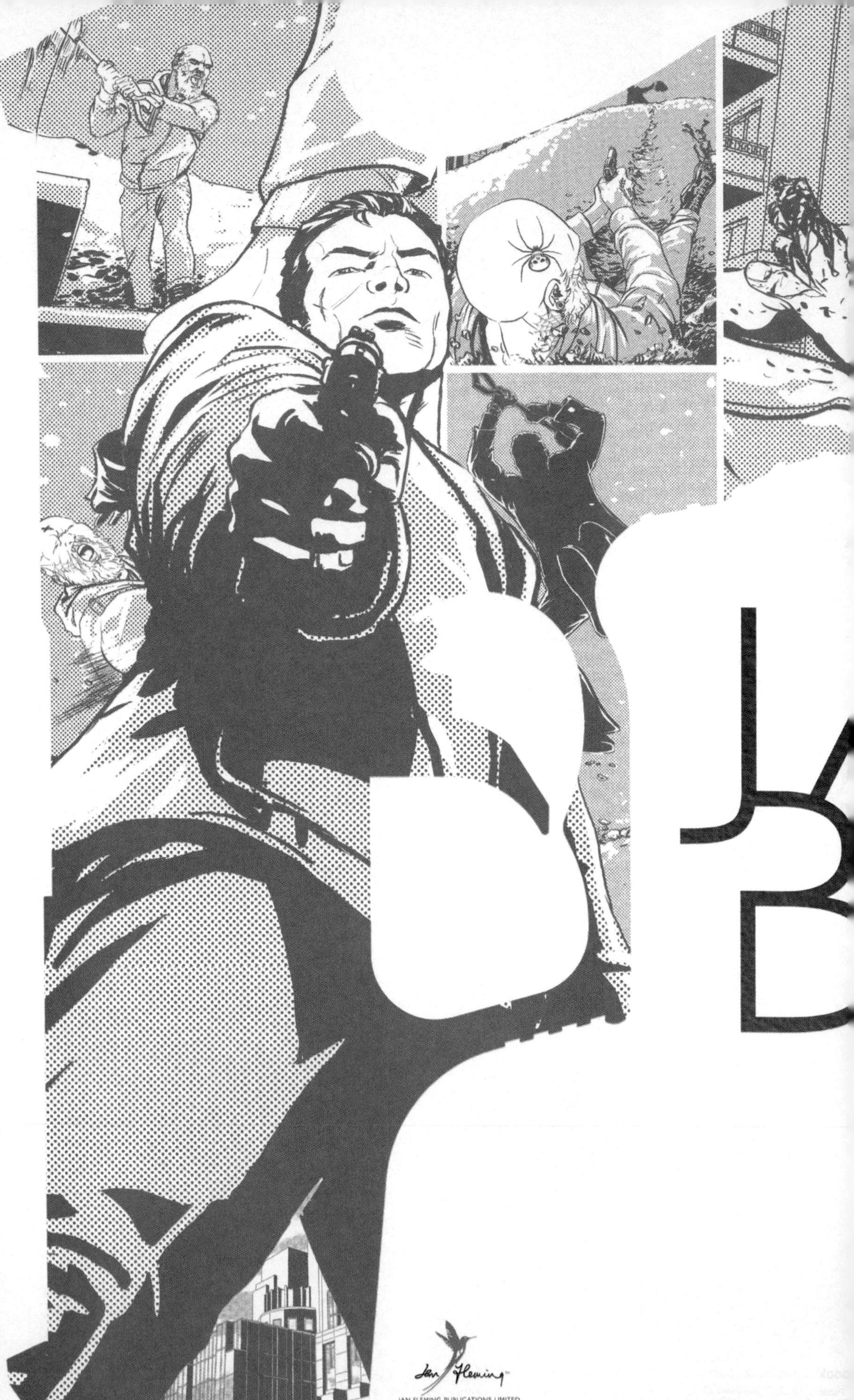

IAN FLEMING PUBLICATIONS LIMITED

N FLEMING'S

MES
OND
07™

VARGR

written by WARREN ELLIS
art by JASON MASTERS

hardcover in stores June 2016

learn more about **VARGR** online at **www.DYNAMITE.com** Twitter @dynamitecomics
book **/Dynamitecomics** YouTube **/Dynamitecomics** Tumblr **dynamitecomics.tumblr.com**

Publications, Ltd. James Bond and 007 are trademarks of Danjaq, LLC, used under license by Ian Fleming Publications Ltd. The Ian Fleming logo ™ and Ian Fleming signature ® are both
The Ian Fleming Estate and used under licence by Ian Fleming Publications Ltd. All Rights Reserved. Dynamite, Dynamite Entertainment, and its logo are ® & © 2016. All Rights Reserved.

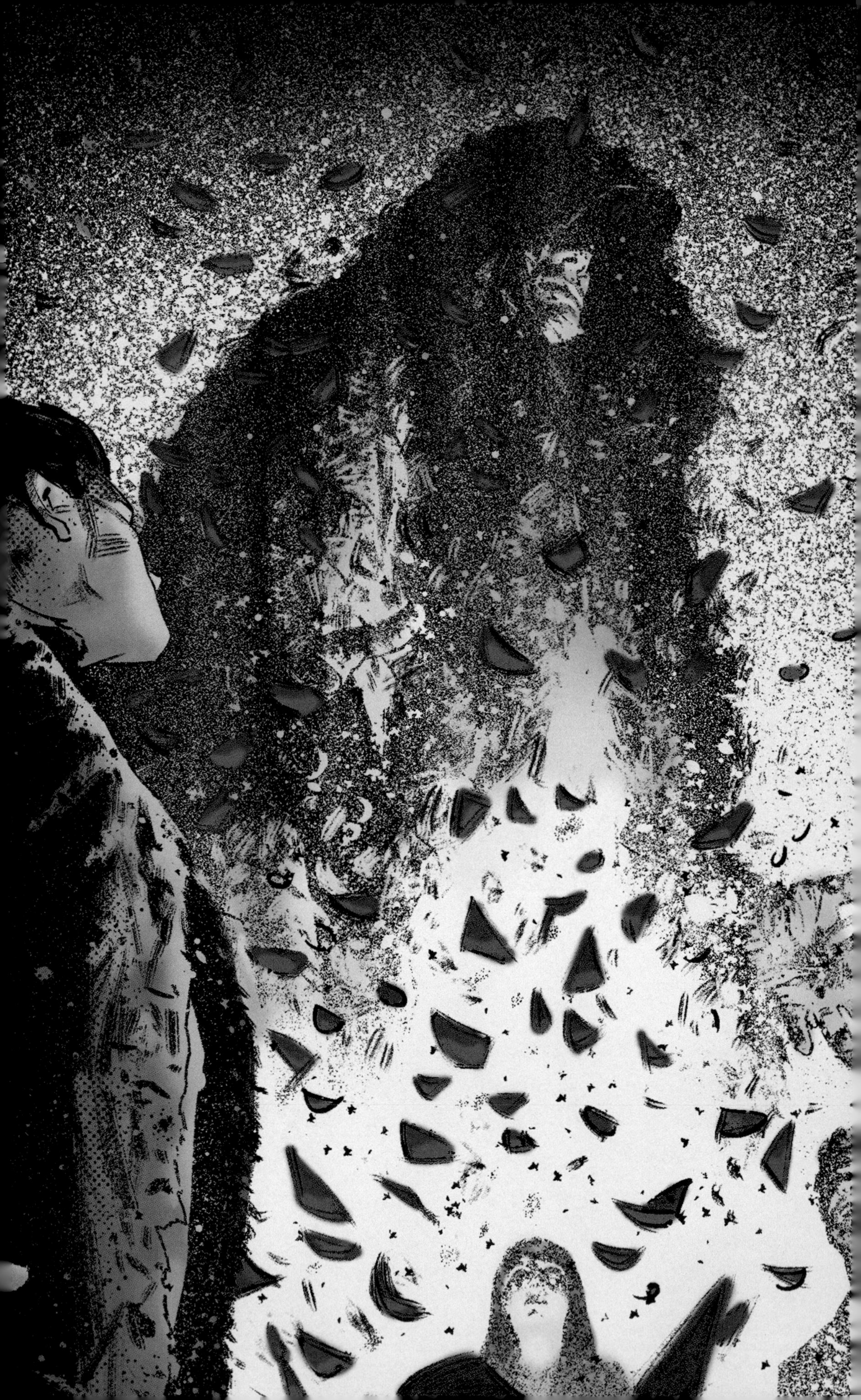